Structural Injustice and the Law

Structural Injustice and the Law

Edited by

Virginia Mantouvalou and Jonathan Wolff

UCLPRESS

First published in 2024 by
UCL Press
University College London
Gower Street
London WC1E 6BT

Available to download free: www.uclpress.co.uk

A CIP catalogue record for this book is available from The British Library.

ISBN: 978-1-80008-734-7 (Hbk.)
ISBN: 978-1-80008-737-8 (Pbk.)
ISBN: 978-1-80008-739-2 (PDF)
ISBN: 978-1-80008-738-5 (epub)
DOI: https://doi.org/10.14324/111.9781800087392

Contents

List of contributors

Editors

Virginia Mantouvalou is Professor of Human Rights and Labour Law, UCL, Faculty of Laws.

Jonathan Wolff is Alfred Landecker Professor of Values and Public Policy, Blavatnik School of Government, University of Oxford.

Chapter authors

Alan Bogg is Professor of Labour Law, University of Bristol.

Jude Browne is Jessica and Peter Frankopan Director of the University of Cambridge Centre for Gender Studies/Head of Department of Politics and International Studies, University of Cambridge.

Hugh Collins is Cassel Professor of Commercial Law, LSE; Emeritus Vinerian Professor English Law, All Souls College, University of Oxford.

Nicola Lacey is School Professor of Law, Gender and Social Policy, LSE.

George Letsas is Professor of the Philosophy of Law, UCL.

Maeve McKeown is Assistant Professor in Political Theory, University of Groningen.

Lynne McMordie is Research Associate, Heriot-Watt University.

Guy Mundlak is Professor in the Faculty of Law and Chair of the Department of Labour Studies, Tel Aviv University.

Vanessa E. Munro is Professor of Law, University of Warwick.

Colm Ó Cinnéide is Professor of Constitutional and Human Rights Law, UCL.

Beth Watts-Cobbe is Senior Research Fellow, Heriot-Watt University.

Lea Ypi is Professor in Political Theory, LSE.

Preface and acknowledgements

The origin of this volume was a conference on ‘Structural Injustice and the Law’ in May 2022, held at the UCL Faculty of Laws. The motivation for the conference was the recognition that, while in philosophy and political science, the concept of structural injustice had been widely discussed in the wake of Iris Marion Young’s landmark book *Responsibility for Justice*, published in 2011, there had been much less attention to this work from legal scholars. Our view is that not only could legal theory benefit from serious engagement with the concept, but also that a legal perspective on structural injustice will be of great benefit to all scholars, whatever their discipline, as the law can both create, and possibly mitigate, at least some structural injustices. Accordingly, we decided to invite scholars from a wide range of areas to reflect on how they might (or might not) usefully deploy the concept of structural injustice in relation to law.

We had high hopes for the conference, and are delighted to say that it even exceeded our expectations. We thought that the contributions were of such high quality that they should be collected into an edited volume, and this is the result. We are grateful to the UCL Faculty of Laws for generously funding our conference and to Cat Balogun for providing excellent administrative support at the UCL Faculty of Laws. We are deeply thankful to all participants who contributed to this book, to Sally Haslanger and Iyiola Solanke who also presented papers at the workshop, to Lizzie Barmes, Alison Diduck, Marija Jovanovic, Saladin Meckled-Garcia and Mary Rawlinson for chairing workshop panels, and to all participants for thoughtful and engaging discussions. We would not have been able to plan this workshop without the support of a British Academy Mid-Career Fellowship for Virginia Mantouvalou’s project ‘Structural Injustice and Workers’ Rights’. We are also enormously grateful to Danielle Worden for outstanding editorial assistance and the University of Oxford Alfred Landecker Programme for financial support in these final steps. Finally, many thanks are due to Pat Gordon-Smith, Chris Penfold, Laura Glover and Jaimee Biggins, of UCL Press, Lucy Hyde of Juicy Editing Limited and two anonymous reviewers for their encouragement and critical engagement with this project. We also want to acknowledge the immense benefit of UCL Press's policy of making this work, alongside all of the work they publish, Open Access, and therefore available without charge to scholars and students throughout the world.

Introduction

Jonathan Wolff and Virginia Mantouvalou

Structural injustice

The concept of 'structural injustice' has attracted significant attention in political philosophy; especially since the publication of Iris Marion Young's posthumous volume *Responsibility for Justice*, in 2011. The idea that people's lives can be unjustly affected by the social structures in which they live has been a commonplace of politics and sociology since Karl Marx, or before, but it is Young's work that brought the phenomenon to clear focus in the philosophical literature. In a much-cited passage, indeed a passage that will be cited in several papers in this volume, Young sets out her understanding in the following terms, stating that structural injustice:

> [E]xists when social processes put large groups of persons under systematic threat of domination or deprivation of the means to develop and exercise their capacities, at the same time that these processes enable others to dominate or to have a wide range of opportunities for developing and exercising capacities available to them. Structural injustice is a kind of moral wrong distinct from the wrongful action of an individual agent or the repressive policies of a state. Structural injustice occurs as a consequence of many individuals and institutions acting to pursue their particular goals and interests, for the most part within the limits of accepted rules and norms.[1]

1 Iris Marion Young, *Responsibility for Justice* (Oxford University Press 2011), 58.

Structural injustice, therefore, is distinguished both from individual wrong and state repression. Typically, cases of structural injustice will have a number of common features. Most notably, first, there is the issue of scale. Young begins her account of structural injustice by mentioning 'large groups of persons under systematic threat of domination or deprivation of the means to develop and exercise their capacities'. Implicit in this statement is the idea that many different people will face the same, or at least, similar threats, and that the threat is best understood as some sort of mass, or at least, large-scale phenomenon. As Young puts it, people suffer from structural injustice because of the position they are in, and not because of the details of their particular life story. A second feature follows closely from the first; secure remedies for structural injustice will also need to be systematic, in some sense, if they are to be effective. For example, in response to complaints of rising unemployment in the UK, in 1981, Government Minister Norman Tebbit famously advised unemployed people to follow the example of his father who 'got on his bike' to search for a job. But Tebbit does not explain how individuals intensifying their job search can create new jobs, rather than displace some potential workers with others. In other words, Tebbit may have had a solution for one person's unemployment (though arguably not even that) but had no solution to unemployment as a general – indeed structural – phenomenon.

The example of mass unemployment raises a third, perhaps more controversial, element. Young suggests that structural injustice involves both a harm, or threat, to one group of people while 'at the same time ... these processes enable others to dominate or to have a wide range of opportunities for developing and exercising capacities available to them'. She suggests, then, that some gain from the loss of others. But is this always the case? Although it could be argued that some employers, for example, gain from mass unemployment, as it drives down wages, need this be the case for unemployment to be regarded as a structural injustice? Can there be structural injustices from which no one gains? We leave this as an open question.

Further features of structural injustice refer not to scale, harm and benefit, but to the typical features of the types of social structures implicated in the idea of structural injustice. A fourth feature is that structures are, very often, self-reinforcing, in that 'normal' behaviour can make the structure more pervasive. For example, expected norms of personal appearance are often followed even by people who strongly object to narrow conceptions of acceptable appearance, thereby making the norms more pervasive still. But why should those who object to a norm follow it? Often those who rebel suffer a form of social punishment. If for an interview for an office job in a business with a formal dress-code, a woman does not wear make-up, or a man does not wear a tie, they are less likely to be appointed, and so they will conform, thereby inadvertently contributing to a pattern that will continue to make life difficult for non-conformists. Similarly, if in an economy there are norms of low wages, an employer who attempts to raise wages unilaterally may find it much harder to remain competitive in a harsh market and will face the dilemma of reducing wages or going out of business, thereby, once more, consolidating the norm of low wages. Structures can, therefore, be informally self-reinforcing by, in effect, punishing those who do not conform.

A fifth feature is that the causes of structural injustice are very often hard to trace.[2] They tend to be the unintended consequences of many different people acting together, for their own purposes, themselves subject to many structural forces in ways we just noted, incentivising them in numerous ways to act as they do. This, indeed, is how Young illustrates the idea of structural injustice with her focal example of Sandy, a fictional, though highly recognisable and evocative example. Sandy is a single mother of two and by a web of the type of everyday circumstances associated with a market economy and changing patterns of property use and development, finds herself facing the prospect of homelessness. Sandy suffers an injustice, according to Young, as no-one should be in a position of deep insecurity of housing; particularly in an affluent society in which others benefit from the practices that led to Sandy's predicament. Yet, according to Young, multiple factors come together to cause the situation, and no individual or company or law can be singled out as the key factor. Whether Young's example really does fit her analysis of structural injustice is discussed in a number of chapters in this volume, including those of George Letsas, Maeve McKeown, and Beth Watts-Cobbe and Lynne McMordie, but the example is intended to illustrate the idea of complexity and lack of traceability. On Young's analysis, this feature of structural injustice suggests that there is no backward-looking responsibility by identifiable agents for the injustice, which seems to be self-perpetuating.

A final factor is a natural consequence of the combination of all the previous elements, which is the difficulty of finding a remedy. How do we overcome pernicious, self-reinforcing social norms, which affect people at scale, and have causes that are very hard to trace? How can we find secure, affordable, convenient, accommodation for people in Sandy's

2 See Jude Browne, this volume.

precarious position? Young hopes to find the solution to social injustice in many people coming together in social movements to bring about change. She develops the idea of a 'social connection model', according to which anyone with a connection to an injustice has a forward-looking political responsibility to address it.[3]

However, even if social movements are key to social change, activism is not in itself social change. Ultimately, changes to government laws and policies will very often be needed, in addition to cultural, attitudinal and behavioural change. Hence to come to a full account of how structural injustice operates, and how it could be overcome, it is essential to explore the role of the law. And that is the purpose of this volume.

None of our authors claim that the law alone will be sufficient to overcome any particular structural injustice. Yet the picture that appears from the book is that the law, alongside other social forces, can be complicit in the creation and persistence of structural injustice; that it has a potential to remove at least some aspects of particular structural injustices; but also that this potential has not been fully grasped by law-makers and in many cases, there is much distance still to go.

The law and structural injustice

Rules of private law, including contract law and property law, are grounded on a particular conception of private property and contractual freedom. They constitute market relations and regulate interpersonal transactions. These rules may not protect individuals against social injustices. Instead, people who are advantaged because of their wealth and education can continue to gain further advantages from these rules, whereas the least advantaged cannot easily escape patterns of disadvantage.[4] In other words, these rules may set up the conditions for structural injustice. However, such private law rules do not have to be this way. Moreover, areas of law such as labour law and social security law may intervene to protect people from market powers and reduce their disadvantage.

The story that Young presents about Sandy as an instance of structural injustice is fictional, so we cannot examine more closely the role that concrete laws played in her predicament. Young's primary focus

3 Young (n 1), Chapter 4.
4 See Katharina Pistor, *The Code of Capital – How the Law Creates Wealth and Inequality* (Princeton University Press 2019); Virginia Mantouvalou, *Structural Injustice and Workers' Rights* (Oxford University Press 2023).

was not on the role of the law in any case as she was not interested in backward-looking responsibility. However, if we were to analyse the situation more closely, we might be able to identify concrete laws that are directly responsible (or a 'major cause' to use Young's words) for Sandy's situation, including rules of housing law and social welfare law.

In this volume, our purpose is to examine how legal rules may, first of all, create or exacerbate, structural injustice. In addition, our aim is to consider how legal reform can help address or mitigate injustices that can be described as structural. By paying closer attention to the law, we do not mean to argue that the concept of structural injustice, as developed by Young, is not useful and important. Quite to the contrary, part of our motivation is the belief that structural injustice is a complex and pressing social and political problem. However, our purpose is to focus on the role of the law because legal rules may drive injustice and affect large numbers of people, while a change in legal rules can help address aspects of this injustice and improve the position of many, as we explain further below.

It would be wrong to suggest that the role of law has been entirely ignored in accounts of structural injustice. Young herself, for example, when discussing Sandy suggests that '[s]ome laws, such as municipal zoning laws, and some policies, such as private investment policies, contribute to the structural processes that cause Sandy's plight, but none can be singled out as the major cause'.[5] It is interesting that Young considers the role of the law in creating structural injustice, though here she claims that it is just one factor among many others, which surely must be right in this example. However, subsequent analysis has highlighted the law's role both in contributing to structural injustice and to potentially finding remedies. For example, it has been argued that some laws with an appearance of legitimacy have consequences of increasing the vulnerability of some groups to exploitation.[6] Work permits, which typically tie migrant workers to particular employers, or visas restricting the types of employment people can take up, reduce the exit options. In turn, they reduce the bargaining strength, of the workers affected, and thereby create the threat, if not always the reality, of exploitation.[7] On an even wider scale, it has been argued that social security law in the UK, especially around Universal Credit, has created very widespread vulnerability; penalising behaviour, which under normal circumstances is socially encouraged, such as sharing your home with your partner, or

5 Young (n 1), 47.
6 Mantouvalou (n 4).
7 ibid, Chapter 3.

undertaking charitable work. In these cases, reporting such 'life changes' to the authorities can reduce benefits, thereby amounting to a cash penalty while not reporting can be a criminal offence, even leading to prison sentences in the worst cases.[8]

Yet law also has the potential to mitigate, or even remove, such risks. Labour laws allowing and facilitating collective bargaining and strike action or creating a mandatory floor of workers' rights, for example, greatly strengthen the position of workers and reduce some vulnerabilities.[9] Property laws around security of housing tenure improve the position of tenants,[10] even though such laws, it is sometimes argued, can have unintended consequences of their own, such as reducing housing supply. Social security laws that promote training opportunities for work can support welfare claimants, rather than forcing them to accept unsuitable jobs by sanctioning them. Reform in criminal justice can help advance aims of social justice instead of perpetuating structural injustice.[11] Discrimination law can help identify and address structural injustices, such as disadvantage on the basis of race.[12] Human rights law can help focus attention on the legal responsibility of the state in creating vulnerability to exploitation, and can require legal reform.[13] Although many of the examples discussed in this volume are taken from UK law, they typically have wider application through analogous legislation in other jurisdictions, and several papers also draw on EU and international law.

Of course, by this we do not mean that legal change can address all instances of structural injustice, which is a complex problem. Structural injustice is due to several factors, as Young's account illustrated, and social change is also a complex process. A variety of actors need to be mobilised to bring about and implement social change, including state agents and civil society groups. However, it is important to appreciate that the state is a powerful actor, and the law is a powerful institution.[14] Other powerful agents may use and manipulate legal rules to promote their interests, as can be seen in the example of multinational corporations implicated in

8 Simon Duffy and Jonathan Wolff, 'No More Benefit Cheats' (2022) 91 Royal Institute of Philosophy Supplement 103.
9 See Alan Bogg, this volume; Hugh Collins, this volume.
10 Beth Watts-Cobbe and Lynne McMordie, this volume.
11 Nicola Lacey, this volume.
12 Collins, this volume. See also Shreya Atrey, 'Structural Racism and Race Discrimination' (2021) 74 Current Legal Problems 1.
13 Mantouvalou, this volume; Bogg, this volume.
14 Sally Haslanger, *Resisting Reality – Social Construction and Social Critique* (Oxford University Press 2012), 318.

sweatshop labour.[15] By identifying powerful agents that are responsible for unjust structures, and particularly by focusing on the role of the state as an especially powerful actor, we are better placed to trigger structural reform. For this reform, the contribution of social movements would also be crucial.[16] Imaginative use of law, including strategic litigation to challenge unjust laws, can be a major contribution to the reduction of structural injustice.

It should also be noted that some legal rules already address different types of injustice, such as discrimination, exploitation and domination. Each of these kinds of injustice are often examined in existing scholarship, and tackled in law, frequently as interpersonal injustice where one person treats another in an unjust way. In these instances, legal rules provide for remedies that are typically individual remedies for the victims of the injustice. Rules of criminal law, for instance, may hold an individual to account for exploiting another; discrimination law may require payment of compensation to a victim of discriminatory treatment. However, to the extent that we are faced with structural injustice – structural discrimination, structural exploitation, structural domination – it is important to move beyond individual wrongdoing and remedies. The views developed in this volume press us to consider further the broader and more systematic processes in which the law affects large numbers of people. They also press us to assess more closely whether legal change has the potential to address some of the injustices in question.

The examples discussed above are enough to suggest that exploring the connection between law and structural injustice is potentially very fertile ground. The law's role in creating structural injustice, and its potential for removing it, needs much more detailed examination over a wide range of cases. Yet at the same time, such investigations may challenge aspects of Young's analysis of structural injustice, especially around traceability and difficulty at least of conceiving of remedies, though the reality of achieving meaningful, lasting, change may be another matter. The nuances of different forms of structural injustice have been explored in detail elsewhere[17] and such questions reappear here with their connection to law being given special emphasis.

---

15 Maeve McKeown, this volume. See also Pistor (n 4).

16 Sally Haslanger, 'How to Change a Social Structure' (2021) <https://www.ucl.ac.uk/laws/sites/laws/files/haslanger_how_to_change_a_social_structure_ucl.pdf> accessed 18 October 2023.

17 Maeve McKeown, 'Structural Injustice' (2021) 16 Philosophy Compass 1; Madison Powers and Ruth Faden, *Structural Injustice: Power, Advantage, and Human Rights* (Oxford University Press 2019); Maeve McKeown and Jude Browne (eds), *What is Structural Injustice?* (Oxford University Press 2024).

While several of the authors point out the potential for the law to address or at least mitigate some forms of structural injustice, it is also noted several times that any potential the law has in this respect is far from fully realised in the jurisdictions under discussion. Labour laws, for example, historically have strengthened the position of workers and therefore protected them from some of the worst forms of exploitation, yet more recent laws have made collective action much more difficult, and, arguably, increased structural injustice in terms of wage stagnation in the face of increasing profits. In other areas, such as equality law, it can be argued that institutional culture will be a much more important factor in combatting discrimination, as laws can be ignored or complied with in letter only and not spirit, and remedies can be hard, demanding and costly to seek. The judicial process particularly may be viewed as unsuitable for identifying background injustice that affects those involved in court proceedings.[18] Moreover, people may be disadvantaged for several reasons, including poverty, race, gender, or disability, and the law cannot often address prejudice and the broader culture, and tackle in depth each of the reasons that place people in a position of disadvantage. Hence the power of law to address structural injustice may be highly variable, and sometimes the best that can be done is to campaign for the removal of laws, such as laws against begging, which intensify structural injustice sometimes to inhumane levels.

Summary of chapters

The first chapter, by Lea Ypi, helps set out some of the conceptual background to understanding structural injustice. Ypi draws attention to what is often a neglected aspect of the deepest structural injustices: that those complicit in injustice often do so reluctantly; not seeing any alternative in that opportunities to change the system are either impossible or come at huge cost to those attempting (usually unsuccessfully) to make changes. This is an important corrective to those who think that once a structural injustice is identified, the world will somehow adapt itself to bring about a correction. Instead, as Ypi points out, dominators can themselves be dominated and are unable to make changes even if they accept such changes are required by justice. This is as true for lawmakers as it is for other agents in a system and hence makes addressing structural injustice through law a highly complex process.

18 Guy Mundlak, this volume.

In the second chapter, Colm Ó Cinnéide makes another important scene-setting contribution by exploring in more detail some of the connections between structural injustice and law touched on in this introduction. Ó Cinnéide analyses how law, and in particular equality and human rights law, is used to attribute responsibility for structural injustices to particular legal subjects, including both public authorities and private actors. He points out that legal innovations to address structural injustice have tended to be limited and incremental owing to law's limited 'operative lexicon', especially limited to the notion of legal liability. Hence Ó Cinnéide remains relatively pessimistic about the law's transformational power to address structural injustice, as can be seen even in the title of his paper: 'Cruel Optimism: The Limits of Legal Liability as a Tool for Engaging with Structural Injustice'.

George Letsas, in the third chapter in this volume, sees more ground for genuine optimism. Letsas starts from the common claim by theorists of structural injustice, including Young herself, as well as Ó Cinnéide in the previous chapter, that law alone is very often insufficient to address central structural injustices. While accepting that this can be true, Letsas also points out that those making this claim have often operated with an insufficiently nuanced understanding of the many varieties of legal instruments available. In particular, Letsas points out that the structures of social interaction that Young identifies are all mediated by law in that legal institutions can back up coercively these structures or frustrate them. One way in which it can frustrate them is by creating 'legal statuses', which vest vulnerable people with a package of protective rights. Examples include the status of an employee, a refugee, a tenant, a bankrupt, or a consumer among many others, and such statuses, Letsas argues, typically impose restrictions on the freedom of others, even if those others are not personally responsible for the wrong that threatens the status-holder. Letsas argues that patterns of social interaction are inherently juridical, and the legal model of responsibility is collective in that collective institutions (courts and legislatures) apportion coercively enforced legal rights and duties across persons. Law reform constitutes a way in which we carry out our collective responsibility for social justice, and a potential site for making the world a more just place for people like Sandy in Young's important example.

The fourth chapter, by Maeve McKeown, builds on her highly influential distinctions between pure, avoidable and deliberate structural injustice, to explain how law can be instrumentalised to create deliberate structural injustice. McKeown argues that the idea that structural injustice is always the unintended outcome of cumulative social, economic and political processes is implausible. Powerful agents sometimes deliberately manipulate and perpetuate structural injustice because they benefit from it, and sometimes there are powerful agents with the capacity to alleviate the injustice but fail to do it. Studying the law provides insight into these cases. The case study of sweatshop labour, which Iris Marion Young has used as a central example of structural injustice, is put under scrutiny by McKeown. Looking at the case in far more empirical and legal detail than Young, McKeown demonstrates how international law has been deployed by powerful agents to deliberately perpetuate this injustice, and then outlines two positive uses of the law to benefit workers and poor countries: joint liability initiatives and an example of a positive bi-lateral trade agreement – the US-Cambodia Textile Agreement (1999–2005).

The focus of the contribution of Hugh Collins is segmented labour markets. He explains how employment law rules on non-standard work create a dual labour market where the available employment in advanced economies is typically divided into good jobs and bad jobs. Good jobs, in the primary labour market, are typically full-time and long-term, with opportunities for promotion and the development of skills, and are relatively well paid. Bad jobs in the secondary labour market take a number of forms, but are often poorly paid, with irregular hours, often at unsocial times, and can be of uncertain length. This is the realm of 'precarious work', which is growing in many advanced economies as employers seek to cut costs and have a more flexible labour force in terms of hiring and firing. Yet, once in precarious work, it is very difficult to make the transition out. Collins argues such a barrier is a structural injustice, both because it denies fair opportunities to everyone and also because it disproportionately adversely affects women, minorities, and other already disadvantaged social groups. Collins suggests that the law provides some ways of addressing aspects of this structural injustice by reducing the disadvantage suffered by those working in the secondary labour market, by reducing the barrier to entry into the primary labour market, but also, in some cases, by challenging the very existence of the division between good and bad jobs. He considers that discrimination law can challenge some aspects of structural injustice, but concludes that for broader change, there is a need for private law reform, such as the law of contract.

A further discussion of injustice and labour follows, with Alan Bogg's chapter on 'bad work'; focusing in particular on three case studies involving collective action by workers in the face of structural injustice: gig workers in the delivery sector, garment workers in Leicester and sacked seafarers at P&O Ferries. Bogg argues for a positive and active role for the state, so that public institutions work collaboratively with workers and unions to transform oppressive structures. Bogg points out the limits of UK trade union law, especially around the right to strike, and explores Article 11 of the European Convention on Human Rights as an (imperfect) means of forcing law reform.

Nicola Lacey highlights the complex interaction between criminal law and structural injustice. Structural injustice not only restricts opportunities but also can have psychological impacts both of which effects can drive poor people to criminalised behaviours. Furthermore, people on low incomes are commonly victims of crime. Exploring three forms of injustice – distributive, epistemic and injustices of standing – Lacey argues that recent trends towards ever-increasing marketisation of the economy, as well as growing inequalities, have exacerbated these effects, while at the same time creating a zone of criminal impunity for the super-rich and elite. She concludes by synthesising the upshot of these various analyses for criminal justice, its legitimacy and efficacy, today.

Vanessa Munro explores how the concept of structural injustice can help us to navigate some of the complexities that arise in preventing, or responding to, situations in which victims of domestic abuse take their own lives. She concentrates in particular on Domestic Homicide Reviews (DHRs) in England and Wales, which are a response to such events, to demonstrate both the potential and challenges to Young's forward-looking focus on task responsibility. Building on a study, conducted for the Home Office, based both on DHRs and semi-structured interviews, Munro details the interlocking layers of personal, situational and systemic injustice that generated the sense of hopelessness and isolation often linked to suicidality. Doing so both shows the complexities in thinking in terms of causation and blame, and also, potentially, points to ways in which safer environments can be created for those who otherwise may have been future victims.

The practice of begging is the central focus of Virginia Mantouvalou's contribution, exploring its association with homelessness and in many jurisdictions, its criminalisation. Mantouvalou sets out European and African human rights case law that has considered the criminalisation of begging and notes that the courts increasingly recognise that such criminalisation intensifies structural injustice and violates human rights, such as the right to private life and freedom of expression. Not only does such criminalisation compound disadvantage, but also it can leave some people, especially those without formal citizenship, with no legal options, in the sense of having no way of legally staying alive. The criminalisation of begging is, therefore, what she terms a 'state-mediated structural injustice' and while decriminalisation will not transform the lives of people who beg, it will at least relieve their situation to some degree.

Homelessness is taken up in more detail in Beth Watts-Cobbe and Lynn McMordie's chapter, which analyses the legal framework on homelessness in Great Britain. The authors argue that Young's implicit claim that homelessness is an archetypal case of structural injustice is only partially right and that, to the extent that homelessness is a structural injustice, it is a counterexample to her claim that the law is not centrally important in addressing such injustices. Importantly both laws and practices by private individuals and entities can often be identified as among the causes of homelessness, and similarly by imposing enforceable legal duties on public bodies to prevent or relieve people's homelessness states can use the law to address the structural injustice of homelessness, and in some jurisdictions we see such paths being followed.

The final two chapters move away from particular case studies to the more general question of how structural injustice can be addressed by state action, and specifically the promise and limitations of law and legal bodies. Jude Browne examines regulatory public bodies, which have often been regarded with great suspicion as unaccountable, technocratic bodies that may not serve the public interest. Browne, however, sees much more potential in regulatory public bodies and returns to the theme opened by Letsas of a more nuanced understanding of governance mechanisms, making suggestions for how they can be developed beyond narrow conceptions of liability through lay storytelling and speculation whereby the public can help expose and begin to mitigate forms of structural injustice.

In the final chapter, the theme of storytelling is then developed in much more detail by Guy Mundlak, who explores perhaps the most important form of storytelling in the contemporary world: film. In particular, he looks at how structural injustice is depicted in the films of Ken Loach, which he compares to how structural injustice is depicted in another area of great drama: courtrooms. Through this unusual comparison, Mundlak draws together the highly interdisciplinary nature of the topic of structural injustice and shows that, while law can seem an abstract, academic subject, ordinary lives are structured by the application and enforcement of laws. Hence, law is a powerful instrument for both creating and relieving structural injustice, which of course is the central topic of this volume.

Conclusion

Typically, structural injustice is thought to lie in a complex web of social processes, with no single factor being isolatable as the cause or potential remedy, whereas the law is typically focused on individual matters and separated into various fields of law. Hence at first sight there is a mismatch between structural injustice and law. Yet the scholarship in this book shows that this stark contrast is misleading. There are several forms of structural injustice, and the paradigm analysis introduced by Iris Marion Young, while a hugely stimulating and important springboard for analysis, does not cover all the cases, and as argued in several chapters here, may not even apply to the cases she took to illustrate her account (Sandy's homelessness and sweatshop labour). Rather there are cases of structural injustice – understood at least in terms of scale and need for a systematic remedy – that are caused or at least intensified by law, and these, and others can sometimes be remedied in whole or part by legal action. Accordingly, we hope that this collection shows both that legal analysis can help illuminate cases of structural injustice, and also that the concept of structural injustice should become part of the standard toolbox of the legal reformer.

1
On dominated dominators

Lea Ypi

A case of domination

Let me start with an example from fiction.[1] At the age of 17, Effi Briest consents to marrying the much older Baron Geert von Instetten, and moves with him to the provincial Baltic town of Kessin. A local administrator, Instetten is away for much of the time, and Effi must adapt to her new surroundings. She lives in a large house, which she believes is haunted by ghosts and feels afraid, bored and neglected. A few months after the marriage, she succumbs to the courtship of a married man, Major Crampas, with whom she has an affair. The affair comes to an end shortly after and Effi has a daughter. Her married life is restored. But Effi lives in fear of it being discovered. Eventually, her fears are borne out: many years later, while the couple has moved to Berlin, Instetten discovers the letters exchanged between Crampas and Effi. Even though a long time has passed, he feels that he ought to defend his honour by challenging Crampas to a duel and punishing his wife. He ends up killing Crampas and divorcing Effi who, disowned by her parents, lives in misery and isolation and ends up suffering from depression until her premature death.

The case of Effi Briest is hardly unique. Not just by comparison to the Emma Bovarys and Anna Kareninas and Nora Helmers of this world. And not just by the standards of nineteenth-century treatment of women. Her life, like that of many fellow women, before and after, is severely constrained. And when she rebels, she is punished. Clearly, Effi is in all relevant senses 'unfree'. For most of her life, she is the target of the morally problematic interference of others and when that interference

1 Theodor Fontane, *Effi Briest*, originally published in 1895 (Penguin Classics 2000), 526.

materialises, her life is ruined. But in this chapter, I am *not* interested in the question of what form of interference Effi suffers from. Instead, I want to make the case that there is a form of interference from which her perpetrators, and in particular Instetten, *also* suffer and I am interested in exploring what form of interference that is. I want to argue that the form of interference that her perpetrators suffer from is a morally problematic constraint on freedom that can be best qualified as impersonal domination or, as I shall put it, domination by a structure. As I understand it, domination by a structure is a narrower subset of structural injustice more generally and has a direct relation to agents' freedom. I further argue that the wrong of structural domination results in alienation (of both dominated and dominators) and that this wrong is irreducible to the domination by agents that structures *also* enable.

I begin by exploring what makes structural domination part of structural injustice, how it relates to laws, and what implications this has for agents' freedom. I suggest that structural domination, the domination from which dominators suffer (over and above the dominated) constitutes a particularly pernicious type of unjust interference which ought to worry us just as much (and sometimes more) than the agential and intersubjective forms of domination that we have been so far mostly concerned with. I argue that structural domination generates alienation (of both dominators and dominated). I try to show that alienation is a moral wrong of a distinctive kind and that its wrongness vindicates the distinctive wrong of structural domination. I conclude by discussing some objections and showing that if the most hideous instances of agential domination are in fact secondary wrongs, wrongs that inherit their wrongness from the primary wrong of domination by structures, this has important implications for resistance, in particular class-based analysis of resistance.

The dominated dominator

That dominators might themselves be the victims of domination will at first appear puzzling. Let me give an example by returning to Effi Briest. She is the textbook example of an unfree agent; the paradigmatic case of the modern slave: her will is constrained by the exercise of a discretionary power that she seems unable to control. She is dominated by her parents, when they introduce her to Instetten. She is dominated by her lover, the Major Crampas, when she falls for his flattery. And she is dominated by her husband who ends up ruining her life by punishing her infidelity.

Nothing of what I suggest in what follows is supposed to dispute any of that, or to suggest that dominators are just as unfree as the dominated, or that the domination of dominators matters more.

What I am interested in is the fact that when asked to justify their actions, many dominators will invoke the rules of a higher order to account for why they had to act the way they did. They will do this even if there is little fear of sanctions and in the absence of any ulterior constraints on their action, including when their reputation might remain intact, as the case I am interested in shows. Of course, we can assume that they are acting in bad faith for some other reason, that they are just making excuses for themselves when they say that they had no choice. But we can also be more charitable in our reading and see if there is indeed more to be said. At the end of Effi Briest, her parents wonder if they made a mistake in encouraging her to marry so young and inexperienced. Somewhat acknowledging their failures, they end up condoning themselves by suggesting that to worry about what else they could have done opens up 'too vast a subject'. Indeed, this is also the last sentence of the book.[2] The Major Crampas also recognises Effi's agency in terminating their relationship and while confessing his unhappiness also reveals that he is succumbing to higher pressure.[3]

But the most interesting case by far is that of Instetten himself. When he discovers the infidelity, Instetten's first reaction is to ask for advice from a friend. He admits explicitly that he does not *want* to punish Effi. When he is asked whether he feels compelled to act in revenge, he answers: 'I love my wife […] and terrible as I find everything that has happened […] I feel inclined, in my heart of hearts, to forgive her'.[4] Why all the fuss, then, his friend asks? Here is what Effi's dominator has to say in reply:

> Because there's no way round it. I've turned it all over in my mind. We're not just individuals, we're part of a larger whole and we must constantly have regard for that larger whole, we're dependent on it, beyond a doubt. If it were a matter of living in isolation I could let it go […] But wherever men live together, something has been established that's just there, and it's a code we've become accustomed to judging everything by, ourselves as well as others.

2 ibid 526.

3 'I am beside myself' he writes in his last letter, 'but we must bless the hand that has forced this parting on us': ibid 421.

4 ibid 425.

> And going against it is unacceptable; society despises you for it, and in the end you despise yourself, you can't bear it any longer and put a gun to your head. Forgive me for lecturing you like this, when all I'm saying is what we've all told ourselves a hundred times. But – well, who can actually say anything new! So there it is, it's not a question of hate or anything like that, I don't want blood on my hands for the sake of the happiness that's been taken from me; but that, let's call it that social something which tyrannizes us, takes no account of charm, or love, or time limits. I've no choice. I must.[5]

Instetten's position reveals an instance of domination that remains unaccounted for in many contemporary discussions of morally problematic interferences on freedom. It explains how the freedom of some agents can be constrained by the intervention of others who appear to us as both free and unfree: free to choose whether or not to inflict harm on a third party and yet apparently so constrained as not to be able to choose otherwise. The fact that Instetten *can* and *does* reflect on the issue, and that he *can* make a decision on whether or not to punish Effi, means that he is in some relevant respect free. Clearly it is within his reach to do otherwise or else there would be no scope for deliberation. And yet his freedom is also severely constrained and in his own words, once his dilemma has been confessed to his friend, once it becomes public, it is effectively nullified. When Instetten tries to identify the reasons behind his likely future decisions, he emphasises the pull of social norms: 'a social something' that has been 'established' and that is 'just there' which affects anyone who lives in a social setting and 'tyrannizes' them, leaving such agents with no choice but to comply. I label the 'certain something' to which Instetten refers to in explaining his reasons for action a 'social structure' and try to explain the domination of dominators in terms of the constraints on their actions that arise from compliance with prevailing social structural norms.

What is a structure?

A social structure can be understood as a set of rules and norms recursively implicated in generating and maintaining practices that reflect the

5 ibid 425–426.

point and purpose of given social and political institutions.[6] The rules and norms that shape such practices may be formalised through their entrenchment in a particular legal system (whether national, international or transnational) and the related set of sanctions and enforcement provisions. The law has an important role to play in shaping social behaviour: it structures the background rules that discipline or incentivise the behaviour of different agents and their relation to one other.[7] In the case of Effi, for example, the laws that structure marital separation or child custody are key to understanding her loss of status in society and successive ruin. But social norms may also be informally recognised and enforced through the adaptation of behaviour, the regulation of expectations and the formation of relevant attitudes that influence agents' performance in society. By social and political institutions, we typically mean things like a family, a company, a political party, a state, an international organisation and so on.[8] Different interpretations of what social and political institutions are about (i.e. their point and purpose) typically refer to what subjects they include and exclude, to the rules that structure the relations between them, to how such rules ought to be modified, and to the way they capture (or fail to capture) the concerns and commitments of the agents that endorse (or contest) them. Institutions are effective only if they are preserved over time. At any given point, there might be a plurality of interpretations available concerning their point and purpose. The emergence, preservation and contestation of such interpretations tend to reflect, not merely the voluntary efforts of

6 The analysis that follows is informed by Lea Ypi, *Global Justice and Avant-Garde Political Agency* (Oxford University Press 2011), Chapter 2. For influential definitions and discussions of social structure that inform a number of recent normative studies, see Anthony Giddens, *The Constitution of Society: Introduction of the Theory of Structuration* (University of California Press 1984), 64 and W H Sewell, 'A Theory of Structure – Duality, Agency, and Transformation' (1992) 98(1) American Journal of Sociology 1. For some of the most important discussions in political theory, see Iris Marion Young, 'Equality of Whom? Social Groups and Judgments of Injustice' (2001) 9(1) Journal of Political Philosophy 1 and Sally Haslanger, *Resisting Reality* (Oxford University Press 2012), esp. Chapters 7 and 11. My understanding is different from Young and Haslanger who focus on resources and schemas and closer to Forst who emphasises the cognitive aspects related to the endorsement of a particular social order understood as an order of justification, see Rainer Forst, *Normativity and Power* (Oxford University Press 2017).

7 See for a recent discussion of the law in relation to structural injustice, Virginia Mantouvalou, *Structural Injustice and Workers' Rights* (Oxford University Press 2023).

8 For a discussion of different definitions of institutions see Geoffrey M Hodgson 'What are Institutions?' (2006) 40(1) Journal of Economic Issues 1–25; Geoffrey M Hodgson 'Institutions and Individuals: Interaction and Evolution' (2003) 24(1) Organization Studies 1–21; David Gindis 'The Social Ontology of Institutional Facts: Collective Acceptance and the Symbolic Understanding' (2010) 44(1) Journal of Economic Issues 97–112 as well as Geoffrey M Hodgson, and David Gindis. 'From Typical Products to Social Institutions' (2007) 17(3) Journal of Evolutionary Economics 303–326.

agents embedded in them, people who comply with certain laws or take advantage of them or are subjected to them, but also the system of values, the social meanings, the classifying categories that they inherit from their predecessors as well as the awareness of spaces for their critique and contestation.

Focus on social structures is useful in explaining actions that are not reducible to what such and such individual did and thought, or to inter-subjective or reciprocal interactions between different agents (as in the cases of contracts, promises and so on) and where larger patterns that tend to transcend reciprocal agential interactions must also be taken into account. When the Baron Instetten in the passage of Effi Briest that I have cited claims that there is a 'social something' on which 'we depend' and 'in accordance with which' we judge our actions and those of others, he draws attention to the limitations of both individualistic and inter-subjective explanations for his behaviour.[9] He refers to a broader framework of social norms within which his (eventually) vengeful behaviour toward Effi ought to be analysed. Structural norms establish background social patterns against which the behaviour of a typical man like him makes a decision concerning a typical conflict like the one in which he finds himself to be. But it is emphatically not about Instetten as such, nor is it about Effi as such. It is not about what Instetten *does* feel and about what he *does* think. It is rather about what someone in his social position *ought* to think and *ought* to do. His judgements and actions are informed by implicit reliance on an opaque yet powerful system of self-scrutiny, a reliance on a kind of invisible moral authority that informs the anticipated approval or disapproval of his behaviour, as well as related rewards and punishment. It is precisely once Instetten has revealed his secret to his friend that he feels he can no longer ignore the course of events and must respond to the imperative to react.[10] 'Now that somebody else knows', he says, 'there's no way back for me'. Indeed, he goes even further and denounces not just the way in which a specific social structure influences his behaviour but the fact that it poses an (almost) insurmountable obstacle to it. Given the social structural constraints he faces, Instetten can only think of punishing Effi. The 'social something' that determines how people ought to behave given a situation like his, he emphasises, operates in a tyrannical way. It is an injustice determined

9 For the distinction between individualistic, intersubjective and structural explanations of actions see Sally Haslanger, 'Culture and Critique' (2016) The Aristotelian Society Supplementary Volume XCI.
10 Fontane, *Effi Briest*, cit. 426.

by our belonging to a social structure. His friend acknowledges this. 'The world is as it is, and things don't take the course we want, they take the course other people want',[11] he concludes. So let me now turn to this second aspect, the moral problem of domination by a structure.

Domination by a structure

Domination is often understood as a morally problematic constraint on freedom. It is also often understood as a constraint on freedom that is robust across counterfactuals. To specify further, domination captures a type of constraint on freedom that does not need to be actual to interfere with the pursuit of justified purposes. The constraint need not be actual; it can be possible. The mere threat of interference suffices to render an agent unfree in the relevant sense. For Effi to be considered dominated, the punishment of Instetten need not have materialised; the threat of punishment is enough. If we care about freedom, robustly understood, we should care about non-domination. Or so it is often said.

All this is familiar from many prominent accounts of non-domination. There are of course many objections and open questions: how to define the relevant set of counterfactuals, how exactly to understand the difference between potential and actual interference, how to specify what counts as a relevant constraint and how to show that a purpose (or set of purposes) is justified. But I shall leave these questions to one side. I shall assume that we know what the relevant moral baseline is such that some interferences are considered morally problematic. And I will assume that the difference between potential and actual interference is clear. Here, I will focus on another dimension of domination as commonly understood, namely domination as a type of constraint on freedom that results from the exercise of unjustified power *by one agent over another*.

One can understand this in two ways. The first is what we might call strict agential domination. Here, domination is the result of one agent choosing to impose their will upon another. Effi Briest's parents, husband and lover are all dominators in the strict sense. The second is what we can call secondary agential domination. In this case, dominators exercise their will as a result of the impact of structures on their agency. So, for example, when Instetten argues that he feels he ought to punish Effi out of pressure to comply with existing conventions and social norms, he draws attention to precisely such an instance.

11 Fontane, *Effi Briest*, cit. 426.

In the second case, it is enabled by laws or other social structures whose persistence is the result of unintended consequences of the actions of independent agents in which the moral failure at stake may be one of omission (failing to remedy) rather than contribution (directly or indirectly causing) another agents' reduction of freedom.

Strict domination occurs when a powerful agent directly undermines the freedom of another without justification. Secondary agential domination, on the other hand, involves indirect constraints on freedom. Such constraints stem from the compliance of dominating agents with prevailing social norms and practices. Here, the constraints are facilitated by laws or social structures which tend to persist because of the unintended consequences of the actions of many other people, be them related or unrelated to each other. In the case of secondary agential domination, the moral problem therefore is not the direct contribution to another agent's unfreedom but the internalised compliance with or the failure to act against generally upheld social norms.

Secondary agential domination should not be confused with what I will call structural domination proper. Yet it is a mistake many authors sensitive to the problem of domination by structures are prone to.[12] To understand what structural domination proper is, we need to be able to formulate the wrong of *domination by structures* independently from the contribution of agents within them, whether in the form of directly causing domination (strict agential domination) or in the form of upholding it or in the form of failing to remedy it (secondary agential domination). We need to ask ourselves whether structures *by themselves* can trigger a loss of freedom, regardless of whether they are also instrumental to other forms of domination. The case of dominated dominators is an instructive one. Consider again the position of Instetten. In emphasising the limits of his action, he draws attention to how the 'social something' upon which his attitudes depend, and acts in a tyrannical way. It represents a powerful interference on his freedom to do otherwise. If structural domination could be reduced to the instances of strict and secondary agential domination we have described above,

12 The confusion is obvious in a number of formulations ranging from the stronger assertion that structures merely 'vitiate' but do not 'hinder' freedom, see Philip Pettit, *Just Freedom* (W.W. Norton and Company 2014) 53 and 73, that they 'enable' domination, see Frank Lovett, *A General Theory of Domination and Justice* (Oxford University Press 2010), 49, to the weaker formulation that they 'serve as important background resources for the exercise of power', see Rainer Forst, 'Noumenal Power' (2015) 23(2) The Journal of Political Philosophy 111, that 'they produce predictable patterns of action', see Clarissa Hayward and Steven Lukes 'Nobody to Shoot? Power, Structure, and Agency: A Dialogue' (2008) 1 Journal of Power 5, 15.

Instetten's dilemma would not exist. He would, at most, be an accessory for the loss of freedom caused to Effi, but would have no grounds to lament his own unfreedom. Social structures exercise power in such a way that the mere threat of sanctions from non-compliance affects agents' self-perception to the point of making them adapt personal preferences in the direction required to comply with them. But the issue of who would apply sanctions or enable them to exist is irrelevant to the moral problem at hand. The divorce between what one feels and does and what one ought to feel and do creates a void that unsettles agents' commitments and shakes the perception of their standing as members of a social order that they believe they ought to embrace. The result is, as in the case of the dominated dominator, a profound inability to identify with one's social roles combined with the difficulty of resisting the demands of that role. It is the divorce between the choice of individual moral ends and the choice architecture that affects the selection of those ends. The symptom of structural domination is agential alienation.

Freedom and alienation

When structural domination is pervasive, alienation affects both dominators and dominated alike (though not in equal measure). Seeing how both the dominators and the dominated are alienated enables us to capture the moral wrong of structural domination proper, a wrong that can be detected even when we abstract from the contribution or complicity of agents responsible for secondary domination. Recall my analysis of a social structure as a set of practices that reflect particular interpretations of the point and purpose of political institutions, indicating the concerns and commitments of those subjected to such institutions at different points in time. The interpretations, as I have argued elsewhere, can be more or less adequate. But they are *entirely* inadequate (and ready to be transformed) when even those agents who are supposed to be responsible for enforcing and upholding the social rules that enable the preservation of a particular social structure are unable to perform their role and occupy the required social positions without questioning the meaningfulness and validity of these social norms. Alienation is characteristic of a condition in which there is scrutiny of the meaningfulness of the social position one occupies, without there necessarily being the freedom to make the rules paving an alternative course of action.[13] And as I argued above, it is symptomatic of a certain restriction of freedom where the mere threat of non-compliance with background laws and structural norms is sufficient to paralyse one's disposition to resist and change such norms.

To understand what is at stake here, let me switch from the example of the domination of patriarchal social structures, with which I began, to another familiar case, also eminently compatible with my analysis: that of alienation under capitalism. In a much-discussed passage of The Holy Family, Marx emphasises how '[T]he propertied class and the class of the proletariat present the same human self-alienation'.[14] To put this in the terms I have been using: both the dominators and the dominated are alienated. But how can that be the case? The answer is that where structural domination takes an impersonal form, both the dominated and the dominators are unable to see themselves as autonomous agents able to freely determine the social order they are part of. Marx expresses the difference between agential and structural domination by drawing attention to two French proverbs: *nulle terre sans seigneur* and *l'argent n'a pas de maître*.[15] While the first reflects the personal nature of domination by landowners under feudal conditions, the second characterises social relations in a capitalist structure where both the capitalist and the worker are dominated by capital.[16] As he puts it, in a bourgeois society 'all personal relationship between property owner and his property ... cease'. No-one is firmly connected with the particular property he owns and 'the medieval adage, *nulle terre sans seigneur*, is replaced by the new adage *l'argent n'a pas de maître*, which expresses the complete domination of living men by dead matter'.[17]

What matters is that capital (understood as a structure) dominates; not the specific capitalist. The domination by capitalists is a secondary derivation of a primary wrong, the domination by capital: the dead matter controlling the actions of a living man to return to Marx's vivid prose.[18]

13 For an influential recent discussion of alienation, see Rahel Jaeggi, *Alienation* (Columbia University Press 2014), which seeks however to depart from traditional accounts that presuppose a particular conception of the human. My account is closer to the classical versions.

14 See Karl Marx, *The Holy Family*, originally published in 1844, *Selected Writings* (Oxford University Press, 2000), 148.

15 See, for example, Karl Marx, *Capital: A Critique of Political Economy*, vol 1, originally published 1867 (Penguin Press 1990), Chapter 4, 247.

16 See G A Cohen, 'Bourgeois and Proletarians' (1968) 29(2) The Journal of the History of Ideas 211.

17 See Tom Bottomore (ed), *Karl Marx: Early Writings* (Watts Publishing 1963), 37.

18 See for more William Clare Roberts, *Marx's Inferno* (Princeton University Press 2016) and see also Nicholas Vrousalis, 'The Capitalist Cage: Structural Domination and Collective Agency in the Market' (2020) 38(1) Journal of Applied Philosophy 40.

As G A Cohen puts it, 'it would be a mistake to conceive the capitalist as a human being who forms the intention of controlling the worker and uses his capital to do so. On the contrary, it is capital, the machine which controls the worker, and the capitalist does so only derivatively and abstractly, as an extension of capital, not because of any personal aspirations or through any individual virtues'.[19]

But Marx goes even further. He claims that when capital dominates structurally, both capitalists and workers are alienated, and both lose their freedom. Structural domination can take legal forms, for example, when workers are prevented by existing juridical rules to negotiate their working hours or when capitalists are bound by international regulations that favour concentrations of big capital over small ones. Marx's analysis on the workers' struggle to reduce the working day is an example of the attempt to change structural rules understood as a body of legal norms. As he puts it, 'for "protection" against "the serpent of their agonies", the labourers must put their heads together and as a class, compel the passing of a law, an all-powerful social barrier that shall prevent the very workers from selling, by voluntary contract with capital, themselves and their families into slavery and death'.[20] But domination can also be driven by social patterns of behaviour and competitive dynamics that strictly escape the legal control of any particular jurisdiction and incentivise behaviour that results in loss of freedom.[21] Both types of domination, the one that works through legal norms and the one that works through social ones, produce alienation. Legal structural domination coerces into compliance. Social structural domination raises the cost of non-compliance. Both produce alienation.

The wrong of alienation consists in the divorce between an idealised condition of freedom that ought to characterise human beings in so far as they are autonomous producers of their life[22] and the reality of that agency burdened by structural constraints. But the question of *who* enables the exercise of structural power and *who* carries it out is here entirely irrelevant to understanding alienation. If there was anyone to blame, either through contribution or omission, one would not feel

19 Cohen (n 16) 225.

20 See Marx (n 15) 513.

21 For examples of this kind, see the analysis of the reproduction of capitalist elites in Ralph Miliband's excellent *The State in Capitalist Society* (Basic Books 1969).

22 For a discussion of the relation between freedom and end-setting in Marx, see Lea Ypi, 'From Revelation to Revolution: The Critique of Religion in Kant and Marx' (2017) 22(4) Kantian Review 661 and Rainer Forst, 'Noumenal Alienation: Rousseau, Kant and Marx on the Dialectics of Self-Determination' (2017) 22(4) Kantian Review 523.

alienated but enraged. Structures exercise power by being ordered (or structured) compatibly with certain interpretations of the point and purpose of social institutions from which agents' judgements depend and the perception of their social offices and position. The more pervasive the structure, the more dominant the upheld interpretation, the less space for agents to question those interpretations and contest them. The problem of the dominated dominator, as I have described it above, is the failure to recognise himself as the free agent he ought to be without being able to account for why. The dominated dominator is alienated because he feels the unease of occupying the social position he occupies, without the motivation to step outside the structural constraints of that position and take on a different role. An alienated dominator is one who succumbs to the pressure of social demands in such a way that he feels he ought to uphold his role in the specific social order in which he takes part while also noticing the gap between that form of socially constrained freedom and authentic ('human', Marx, would say) freedom.

Domination by structures produces alienation in agents. And alienation is all the more pervasive because it is symptomatic of the frustration of freedom in conditions where not agents but structural relations (the set of laws, rules, the symbols and the objects that embody them) are responsible for the unjustified interference experienced by both the dominators and dominated. An alienated agent is someone who lives all the symptoms of a disease of which he does not know the cause.

Structural domination tends to emerge as the result of the unintended consequences of the actions of independent agents in which the moral failure at stake is one of omission (failing to remedy) rather than contribution (directly causing) a reduction in freedom. To really account for structural domination as a kind of domination that is distinctive from agential domination, we have to be able to explain how the structural curtailment of people's freedom regardless of the beliefs, intentions or pro-attitudes of the agents that operate within such structures is a distinctive kind of moral failure from that occasioned by the uncontrolled exercise of the will of powerful agents. In the case of patriarchy (with which we started), the dominated dominator experiences a loss of freedom caused by the impersonal upholding of problematic social norms related to gender. In the case of capitalism, the dominated dominator experiences a loss of freedom related to the imposition on him of market norms. In both cases, structural relations are anonymous but they affect the dominated dominators' self-perception in relation to others. Alienation enables us to analyse how exactly that happens. It allows us to understand structural domination not only as a distinctive type of hindrance (as in vitiation, influence or constraint on agents)[23] but as a distinctive type of wrong, a wrong *independent from* and *irreducible to* both the strict and secondary agential domination I highlighted above.

Structural domination as a primary wrong

So far, I have argued that there is a distinctive kind of wrong, structural domination, which ought to worry us more than the agential domination we have been mostly concerned about. Structural domination is primary in two ways. Firstly, it is primary because domination by a structure gives rise to the instances of secondary domination we have been mostly concerned about. Structural rules determine the social positions that create agents that dominate: the dominated dominators. Secondly, structural domination is primary because the moral wrong it generates does not inherit its wrongness from agential domination, rather it produces its own constraint on freedom in the form of alienation. Indeed, structural domination is the kind of domination from which both the dominators and the dominated suffer. The symptom of their domination is alienation.

All this might at first seem puzzling. It may be simple enough to understand how workers lose their freedom, but what about the capitalist? Surely, one might object, the capitalist benefits from the domination of workers by capital. And surely if there were no capitalists, there would be no capital as such able to restrict anyone's freedom. So how can structural domination be primary? How can it be irreducible to the domination of agents?

To start answering this objection, notice first the shift from the contribution and discussion of the properties of capitalist agents to the contribution of capitalists as a class. True, if there was no capitalist class, we would not understand what domination by capital means. But the point I am making is that a social structure determines the roles and positions of agents involved in that social structure such that the classes necessary to uphold that structure are part of the definition of the structure that it is. If we emphasise that the structure would not be there if there were no agents with the intention of upholding that structure, we are merely insisting on a tautology whose contribution to the moral analysis of the question at hand is irrelevant. True, talk

23 These are all the features emphasised in authors who highlight the role of structures in enabling the domination by agents.

about capital would be meaningless if there was no capitalist class. But it would also be meaningless if there were no factories, banks and credit cards. The capitalist class, just like the banks and credit cards are all essential components to understanding capitalism as the structure that it is. The fact that specific capitalists perform the social roles that allow the capitalist structure to be replicated is no more relevant to the moral analysis (to understanding the domination by a structure) than the fact that there are specific algorithms that enable financial activities and specific buildings that house banks. Elon Musk is no more relevant to our moral analysis than is the existence of the HSBC branch down the road. If Elon Musk was not there, and if there was no HSBC near Holborn Station, there would be another capitalist and another bank performing the same roles. So long as the social rules that organise productive activity in a way that complies with the imperatives of capital (for example, with a certain division of labour and a certain distribution of social roles) are in place, the wrong of structural domination is primary and irreducible to secondary agential domination.

But now consider the following critique. A capitalist is a moral agent, and a moral agent is (or so one hopes) different from a building. Being a moral agent who can make moral decisions, the capitalist could, if he wanted, withdraw his support to the structure and if all capitalists did this, the structure would no longer be there. This is true of course, but in a very trivial way. It is trivial because merely highlighting that there would be no capital without capitalists adds little to the moral analysis of structural domination as a primary wrong.

To see the point, consider the following (harmless) analogy. A university is a structure that performs a certain function, say producing specialised knowledge leading to a degree in higher education. It performs that function through a division of social roles such that there is a class of teachers (who have the authority to say what counts as a degree), a class of students (who pursue formal training so as to obtain the degree) and a class of administrators (who help run the whole thing so that teachers can teach and students can take degrees). It also performs its function through a set of rules and resources required to enable the people who occupy these offices to discharge the roles that go with their office, e.g. grading schemes, lectures, the assignment of degrees.

Now consider the case of the disaffected teacher. A disaffected teacher is someone who discovers that she no longer believes in knowledge imparted in the way universities impart it. Suppose she decides to switch careers and becomes an outdoor sports instructor. Her choice does nothing to undermine the overall structure of higher education.

Suppose there are 10, 100 or 1,000 disaffected teachers. Their exit from the university structure does nothing to undermine the fact that the structure works in a certain way. The university structure will continue to be the same so long as there are enough teachers left to teach and enough students interested in taking degrees. But having enough teachers left to teach and enough people taking degrees is guaranteed by the way universities discharge their functions, and the way they generate and reproduce knowledge. The class of teachers is reproduced by university structures continuing to discharge their function by simply following the rules that make them the structures that they are. So, just like a university reproduces a teaching class merely by being in place as the structure that it is, so a capitalist structure continuously reproduces the capitalist class by creating social roles in conformity with the rules about production and distribution characteristic of a capitalist system. There can of course be disaffected teachers, just as there are not-for-profit capitalists. But a disaffected teacher can really only stop being disaffected by no longer being a teacher, and the same reasoning applies to the capitalist. Once a capitalist claims to be not-for-profit, he is no longer really a capitalist. And just like for every disaffected teacher, the university structure will generate hundreds of others willing to perform that role, the same will be the case for the allocation of roles that leads to the alienated capitalist. The structure is replicated through the perpetuation of the social classes required to apply the system of rules that the structure entrenches and upholds. And replication need not always take the form of coercion or legal undermining of alternatives but also of co-optation; raising the costs of non-compliance.

Of course, social classes are made of individual agents. It is trivial to say that structural rules require individual agents to be upheld. But there is an important difference when it comes to how structures and agents constrain freedom. Structures constrain freedom by creating the social roles that allow the replication of structural rules. If domination is to be understood as a morally problematic constraint on freedom, then the fault is primarily with the morally problematic nature of the distribution of social roles. It is only as a secondary matter problematic because of the intentions and motives of the contingent agents that happen to perform these roles. The structure does not merely influence or enable these agents, it creates them. While domination by agents is a case of directing one's ends in a certain way, such as in a way that uses discretionary power to constrain other agents' freedom, in the case of structures, power is not discretionary but rather written in the way the social rules that make up the structure allocate social positions.

I also suggested that structural domination is a distinctive type of domination in that it produces a distinctive constraint on freedom. I called this distinctive constraint on freedom alienation by a structure. To see how this is the case, consider again the problems with which I started. Capitalism dominates through the system of rules that is responsible for the distribution of social roles between the class of holders of capital and the class of sellers of labour. And it alienates both capitalists and workers (though not in equal ways). Patriarchy dominates through the system of rules that is responsible for the distribution of social roles between men and women. And it alienates both men and women (though not in equal ways). To say that there are agents that apply the rules and therefore fill in the social roles that the structure requires in order to be replicated adds nothing relevant to our moral analysis of the wrong of alienation. This wrong is irreducible to the other wrongs that structural domination might also enable (for example, secondary agential domination).

Structural domination and resistance

I now want to go back to the proposition that I suggested earlier, which is that structures dominate by producing their own special kind of constraints on freedom, a form of constraint that I called alienation. And I argued that since structural domination affects both dominators and dominated, the dominated can be alienated too. I also explained the alienation of the dominated in terms of a divide or estrangement of the self; a kind of moral schizophrenia, between acknowledging the force of the demands of the social role one is required to perform (as a member of the social class that is typically required to perform that role) and the moral imperatives that question the significance of those demands when one steps out of that role. Now, in the light of all this, let me go back to my initial question. If structures create the social classes required to uphold them, when do they begin to crack?

I have suggested that an important symptom of the domination by structures is the alienation they generate in both the dominated (simpliciter or merely dominated) and those who are supposed to help upholding structural rules as in the case of what I have called dominated dominators. When existing dominant interpretations of the point and purpose of political institutions are no longer able to capture the concerns and commitments of the agents that uphold them, then there is a crisis that requires an intervention to change the system and open the space for new interpretations. Elsewhere, I have discussed how it may be possible to distinguish between new interpretations that are progressive from those that are not.[24] Here I will simply assume that we know when domination is morally problematic and try to explain what it means to be dominated by a structure. To be dominated by a structure means to be subject to the power of social norms that fail (or have ceased to serve) the concerns and commitments of those whose lives are constrained by the system of social rules that the structure embodies. These rules will not be arbitrary (at least not in the sense of arbitrary that theorists of domination tend to emphasise when discussing agential instances of domination), but they will fall short of enabling the pursuit of moral ends by a plurality of agents sharing a social world (however we decide on what the plausible threshold for such pursuit is).

Of course, dominated dominators will not be able to articulate their disaffection from structural rules in the same way as those who are merely dominated. Despite the great disadvantages (and suffering) of being merely dominated, the epistemic insights that those who are merely dominated gain when it comes to resistance is an important advantage. But, while the dominated dominators will be unable to find resources for articulating their resistance in the same ways as the agents they in turn dominate, their alienation still opens some space for interrogating their position and encouraging criticism of the system.

This, in turn, is an important element to take into account when dealing with a crucial objection one might pose to my alternative focus on structural domination and its implications for both the dominators and the dominated. That objection suggests that focusing on domination by structures is misleading since it blurs the lines of responsibility ascription between dominators and dominated. If we want to be aware of the differences that agents make to outcomes, so the critic might claim, then it is important not to let dominators 'off the hook' by allowing them to 'blame the system'.[25]

Notice, however, that this critique misses the mark of the distinction between agential and structural domination, including my emphasis on secondary agential domination. As emphasised above, nothing of what I have argued denies that there are essential differences in the positions of dominators and dominated, and that the wrong inflicted on the latter is morally much more significant. I also did not deny that structural features have important implications for the way they enable secondary

---

24 See my *Global Justice and Avant-Garde Political Agency*, Chapters 2 and 7.
25 Hayward and Lukes (n 12), 12.

agential domination. But that is not the whole story. It is important to insist that there is more to domination by structures than the secondary agential domination that they enable. The alienation of dominators is part of it. Rather than letting dominators off the hook, the structural approach suggests a different critique; one that shifts the focus away from the individual interventions of secondary agential dominators to an analysis of social classes as generated and reproduced through structural domination. The change required involves both fundamental change in the body of legal norms accounting for domination by the structure, and an awareness about the informal rules, class culture or patterns of behaviour that facilitate individual compliance or raise the cost of non-compliance.[26]

Therefore, rather than absolving dominators, my analysis of structural domination facilitates a different kind of critique, one that emphasises the contribution of classes rather than individuals and that redirects the target of critique and resistance along class lines. This vindicates a central insight of traditional structural critiques of society that have been relatively neglected in recent literature. It also provides a new perspective from which to contribute to existing normative discourses centred on the loss of agents' freedom through the arbitrary intervention of another agent. Alienation, understood as the moral unease provoked by the divorce between the standpoint of the moral agent on the one hand and the occupier of a particular social position, on the other, is only intelligible once we understand the wrong of structural constraints on freedom as a distinctive kind of moral wrong from that of the secondary domination by agents. Rather than paralysing social struggle, an alternative focus on the domination by structures, including the domination of dominators, enables it to reach surprising sites.

26 See, for a discussion of this point, Tamara Jugov and Lea Ypi, 'Structural Injustice, Epistemic Opacity, and the Responsibilities of the Oppressed' (2019) 50(1) Journal of Social Philosophy 7.

2
'Cruel optimism': the limits of legal liability as a tool for engaging with structural injustice

Colm Ó Cinnéide

Introduction

This is a chapter about how law engages with structural injustice.[1] More precisely, it examines whether law can deliver on its aspiration to do justice and play a meaningful role in tackling some of the harms generated by socially embedded forms of structural disadvantage and exclusion. In particular, it asks whether legal liability – a mode of attributing individual responsibility for specific acts of wrongdoing – can get to grips with the often complex, opaque and collective causal factors that give rise to such harms.[2] And if not, what implications does this have for our capacity as a society to address structural injustice?

This chapter begins with an analysis of why law is widely assumed to be a fairly useless tool for tackling structural injustice. Firstly, it outlines how political philosophers such as Iris Marion Young and

1 I use the term 'structural injustice' here to refer to social processes that condition in negative ways the life prospects of persons situated in particular social contexts, which are not directly attributable or 'traceable' to isolated and specific acts of wrongdoing by identifiable individual actors: see in general Iris Marion Young, *Responsibility for Justice* (Oxford University Press 2011). In contrast, see the wider definition of this concept adopted in Madison Powers and Ruth Faden, *Structural Injustice: Power, Advantage and Human Rights* (Oxford University Press 2019).

2 This line of analysis should be distinguished from research into how existing aspects of the law may magnify the impact of structural injustice, such as the examination of 'state-mediated structural injustices' undertaken by Virginia Mantouvalou in Chapters 3–6 of Virginia Mantouvalou, *Structural Injustice and Workers' Rights* (Oxford University Press 2023). This chapter is focused on attempts to turn law into an instrument for attributing legal responsibility for complicity in perpetuating structural injustice, rather than on how particular aspects of the legal system can play a role in amplifying the impact of such unjust social practices.

Catherine Lu have argued that legal liability is intrinsically incapable of addressing structural harms, on account of its reductive focus on establishing the existence or otherwise of individual responsibility for specific acts of alleged wrongdoing. Secondly, it argues that this critique resonates with similar analysis of the limits of the law put forward by Roberto Unger and other critical legal scholars over the years – but also with much orthodox opinion about the appropriate scope and focus of legal liability. Indeed, the constricted focus that Young identifies as characteristic of legal liability is built into law's 'operative lexicon', i.e. the standard way in which it frames and allocates responsibility for breaches of social norms.[3]

However, as argued later, there are alternative ways of framing legal liability, which adopt a more flexible approach to defining fault and responsibility by recognising that injustice can be generated by a failure to act – as distinct from the more deliberate and direct forms of wrongdoing, which are the normal target of legal regulation. This relatively new strand to legal thinking reflects shifts in popular understanding of what the demands of justice entail in contemporary society. It also reflects a wider appreciation of the corrosive impact of structural injustice, and the role played by inaction and inertia in allowing such injustice to persist. As such, this shift has the potential to make law more responsive to the harms generated by such injustice, as argued by Mantouvalou and others.[4]

Various attempts have been made to translate this potential into legal reality, as discussed in detail below.[5] These attempts to use law to tackle structural injustice have mainly been channelled through equality and human rights law, and involve the use of innovative legal mechanisms such as positive obligations, positive equality duties and the prohibition on indirect discrimination. All of these mechanisms depart in significant ways from law's standard operating lexicon, in particular by how they impose binding duties on public and private actors not to amplify the impact of structural injustice – even if these actors have not directly caused the harms in question. They are the product of creative legal engineering, designed to make legal liability more responsive to the harm generated

3 For the conception of the legal 'operative lexicon', plus an associated incisive critique of its grip over the legal imagination, see Justin Desautels-Stein and Abkar Rasulov, 'Deep Cuts: Four Critiques of Legal Ideology' (2021) 31(2) Yale Journal of Law & the Humanities 435.
4 Mantouvalou (n 2).
5 The legal material discussed here is primarily selected from UK and European law. It is intended to be illustrative rather than comprehensive. The reader is invited to consider for themselves whether the arguments made here hold good for legal systems in democratic states more generally.

by structural injustice. However, as analysed below, the impact of this creative engineering has been relatively limited. Conventional thinking about the appropriate scope and reach of legal regulation is still shaped by law's standard operative lexicon, and this has stunted the development of these putative new approaches.

This relatively discouraging track record sheds some light on the inherent limits of law as a 'technology' for bringing about social change – not to mention the ingrained conservatism of our collective moral and political imagination as a society. It begs the question, discussed in the conclusion to this chapter, of whether trying to use law to tackle structural injustice risks generating a situation of 'cruel optimism', to borrow a concept from Lauren Berlant writing in the context of the critical humanities.[6] Is it time to abandon the 'hollow hope' that law can be of real use in combatting structural injustice?[7]

This chapter suggests not, as long as there is no indulgence in excessive optimism about the redemptive potential of legal remedies. Law can be useful in combatting some specific types of structural harms, even if only in bounded and incremental ways – as shown by, for example, the track record of legislative prohibitions on indirect discrimination.[8]

Moreover, the innovative attempts to push the envelope of the standard form of legal liability mentioned above, such as the development of positive obligations doctrine, perform a useful signalling function. By requiring individuals and corporate bodies to take action to alleviate harm generated by structural inequalities, they loosen the grip of conventional assumptions about the limited nature of personal responsibility for such 'remote' harms. And this can help to provoke new thinking about our collective responsibility as a society, and the need for systemic political action to redress persisting patterns of social disadvantage and exclusion. In other words, the real impact of attempts to tackle structural injustice through law may play out in wider moral and political debate about what we owe each other as individuals embedded in a common social framework.

6 Laurent Berlant, *Cruel Optimism* (Duke University Press 2011).

7 Gerald Rosenberg, *The Hollow Hope: Can Courts Bring About Social Change?* (2nd edn, University of Chicago Press 2008).

8 See 'The gravitational pull of law's operating lexicon' below.

The limits of the 'liability model'

Before examining how law has been deployed to tackle structural justice, it is worth noting at the outset that many would consider such an endeavour to be a fool's errand. The limits of law as a tool for achieving social justice are well-known. Critical scholars writing from a range of different perspectives – Marxist, feminist, Foucauldian, anti-racist and so on – have emphasised how law's formalism, inherent conservatism and detachment from lived experience made it a relatively feeble instrument for challenging the status quo.[9] Legal academics spend plenty of time dutifully telling their students not to assume that law can provide solutions to all of society's ills, while practising lawyers are only too familiar with the limited capacity of legal action to achieve positive outcomes for their clients. Access to justice is highly dependent on access to money: legal aid and other forms of support for less privileged litigants often amounts to little more than sticking plaster.[10] And there is a consensus, well-established across more or less the full spectrum of legal and political opinion in democratic societies, that law cannot and should not displace politics when it comes to determining how societies should engage with questions of distributive justice – which courts are fond of endorsing.[11]

More specifically, it is widely acknowledged that law, almost by definition, can have little 'bite' when it comes to tackling structural injustice. Thus, for example, in her highly influential account of the nature and impact of structural injustice, Iris Marion Young emphasises its general impermeability to legal forms of redress:

> Structural injustice is a kind of moral wrong distinct from the wrongful action of an individual agent or the repressive policies of a state. Structural injustice occurs as a consequence of many individuals and institutions acting to pursue their particular goals and interests, *for the most part within the limits of accepted rules and norms.*[12] (Author's italics.)

---

9 For a few samples from a vast literature, see, for example, Hugh Collins, *Marxism and the Law* (Oxford University Press 1984), Richard Delgado, 'Critical Race Theory: An Annotated Bibliography' (1993) 79(2) Virginia Law Review 461; Nicola Lacey, *Unspeakable Subjects: Feminist Essays in Legal and Social Theory* (Hart 1998); Carol Smart, *Feminism and the Power of Law* (Routledge 1989).

10 Adrian Zuckerman, 'The Law's Disgrace' (27 Feb 2017) U.K. Const. L. Blog <https://ukconstitutionallaw.org/> accessed 18 October 2023.

11 See, for example, Lord Reed's remarks in *R (SC) v Secretary of State for Work and Pensions* [2021] UKSC 26.

12 Young (n 1), 52.

In particular, Young argues that 'liability-based' approaches to injustice, such as those deployed by legal systems, are not capable of getting to grips with the complex causal factors that generate structural injustice:

> A concept of responsibility as guilt, blame or liability is indispensable for a legal system and for a sense of moral right that respects agents as individuals and expects them to behave in respectful ways towards others. When applying this model of responsibility, there should be clear rules of evidence, not only for demonstrating the causal connection between this agent and a harm, but also for evaluating the intentions, motives, and consequences of the actions. But the liability model of responsibility, I suggest, is inappropriate for assigning responsibility in relation to structural injustice.[13]

In Young's view, this 'inappropriateness' stems from how the harm done by structural injustice tends to be (i) cumulative in nature, being caused by the interaction of multiple different agents working within the established rules of the status quo, and (ii) 'untraceable' in the sense that a direct line of causation cannot be drawn back to specific and quantifiable acts of individual wrongdoing performed by individuals which have predictable negative consequences.[14]

As such, Young is essentially claiming that there is a fundamental mismatch between the forms of injustice that the liability model (and by extension legal analysis) is capable of addressing, and the forms of injustice that she classifies as structural. Indeed, she argues that attempting to engage with structural injustice through a liability lens may have negative consequences. Not alone will it be ineffective. It also risks 'isolating' responsibility, i.e. focusing attention on the specific acts of alleged individual wrongdoers, rather than addressing the background structural dynamics at issue and the wider collective obligation that exists to alleviate or remedy their consequences.[15] As a consequence, Young advocates the adoption of a new 'social connection' model of responsibility to address the harms generated by structural injustice – which would be collectivist and forward-looking, avoid reliance on concepts of fault and past wrongdoing, and be strictly *political* in character. For her, law and

13 ibid, 98.
14 ibid, 52.
15 ibid, 100–106.

other associated approaches based around the liability model have little or any meaningful role to play to tackling structural justice – even if it may be useful in addressing other forms of injustice.[16]

Lu has made similar arguments, which supplement Young's analysis in interesting ways.[17] For her, the 'liability model' assumes that responsibility for injustice arises from the interactions that take place between different individual entities, who are deemed to 'cause and control' the consequences of their actions[18] – with any wrongful actions in this respect being treated as aberrations from an established 'baseline' of normal conduct that is assumed to be moral and just.[19] In general, no wider proactive obligations are imposed to act in a way that advances social justice. Instead, this model focuses on identifying specific acts of past wrongdoing and correcting them in ways that restore the status quo.[20]

As a result, Lu in tandem with Young argues that the liability model cannot adequately engage with the collective and embedded nature of structural injustice, and the way individuals can unintentionally contribute to the generation and perpetuation of such injustice 'through their ordinary day-to-day actions'.[21] In particular, it fails to recognise the need to transform the current 'morally defective baseline' that the interactional model treats as its normative benchmark – in contrast to Young's 'social connections' model of responsibility, with its commitment to reshaping and overcoming structurally unjust social norms through future-facing collective political engagement.

This extended critique has a long genealogy, with Young explicitly drawing on Arendt's distinction between moral/legal and political

16 For a very useful close analysis of the implications of Young's arguments in this regard, see Jude Browne, 'The Political Implication of the "Untraceability" of Structural Injustice' (2024) 23 Contemporary Political Theory 43.

17 Catherine Lu, *Justice and Reconciliation in World Politics* (Cambridge University Press 2017).

18 Clarissa Hayward, 'Responsibility and Ignorance: On Dismantling Structural Injustice' (2017) 79(2) Journal of Politics 396.

19 See the concise summary of Lu and Young's views in this respect in Swati Srivastava and Lauren Muscott, 'How to Hold Unjust Structures Responsible in International Relations' (2021) 65(3) International Studies Quarterly 573.

20 As Satkunanandan puts it, such interactional responsibility can be conceptualised in terms of 'a series of debts that can be identified in advance, reckoned up, negotiated, balanced out, and discharged': Swati Satkunanandan, *Extraordinary Responsibility: Politics Beyond the Moral Calculus* (Cambridge University Press 2015).

21 Catherine Lu, 'Responsibility, Structural Injustice, and Structural Transformation' (2018) 11(1) Ethics & Global Politics 42.

responsibility.[22] It is not confined to law. Instead, it potentially applies to all modes of framing responsibility – moral and political, as well as legal – in terms of individual wrongdoing, direct harm causation and observance of established social norms of good behaviour. However, both Young and Lu assume that the legal approach to framing responsibility is a paradigm case of the 'liability model' in action. And their critique has obvious and particular relevance for law: it provides a compelling explanation as to why legal systems often have little to say about structural injustice, as distinct from the 'interactional' harms which tend to be their meat and drink.

The constraints of law's 'operative lexicon'

What is perhaps particularly valuable about this critique is that it focuses on how personal responsibility is conceptualised and coded in the regulatory vocabulary of legal systems, i.e. law's 'operative lexicon'.[23] This lexicon is inevitably shaped by what law already regulates and the way it goes about such regulation. In turn, this shapes expectations as to what types of injustice law is expected to engage with, and how it performs this task. The grammatical structure of this operative lexicon – the form legal liability usually takes – thus inevitably exerts significant influence over how law frames responsibility for injustice. Types of framing that fit its existing form tend to be viewed as natural and appropriate: alternative modes of framing, not so much.

Young and Lu's 'liability model' picks out the key features of this operating lexicon, even if they paint with a broad brush. Some form of (i) willful misbehaviour, such as the deliberate infliction of harm or the negligent performance of a task, which (ii) fails to conform to established social and moral norms as to how a 'reasonable' person should act and (iii) directly leads on to the infliction of harm will

22 For an interesting critical take on Young's use of Arendt, see Valentin Beck, 'Two Forms of Responsibility: Reassessing Young on Structural Injustice' (2023) 26(6) Critical Review of International Social and Political Philosophy 918. For wider intellectual resonances, structured in terms of a dichotomy between 'moralism' and 'extraordinary responsibility', see Satkunanandan (n 20). An analogy could also be drawn with the much-discussed distinction between corrective and distributive justice, although caution is needed here: the blurred nature of that particular dichotomy as it applies to legal liability needs to be borne in mind. See the useful discussion in Adam Slavny, 'Corrective and Distributive Justice', in *Wrongs, Harms, and Compensation: Paying for our Mistakes* (Oxford University Press 2023), 153–175.

23 Desautels-Stein and Rasulov suggest this operative lexicon is an 'operative grammar-code' whose content imposes limits 'on the sorts of personal politics and agendas one could successfully bring into law': (n 3), 489.

normally be required before something is classified as a legal wrong.[24] Islands of full or quasi-strict liability do exist, where persons may be held liable for harm suffered by others even when they have not been actively at fault themselves. However, such 'no fault' liability can be controversial, being generally viewed as a blunt instrument. As such, these areas of deviation from the limited liability model tend to be deployed with caution and kept limited in scope: they occupy a suspect place within the extended lexicon of law.[25]

This focus on individual wrongdoing is natural, and perhaps inevitable. Law has always played an important role in regulating and guiding interpersonal conduct in ways that accord with established social norms. However, this orientation has certain consequences. It shapes the broad contours of legal liability, generates certain expectations about the appropriate scope and substance of sanctions, and can potentially restrict the regulatory reach of legal systems. As Lu notes, inaction in the form of a failure to prevent a particular state of affairs from coming into being, or to take adequate steps to limit its spread, will generally not attract legal liability.[26] Nor will questionable conduct, which cannot be shown to have directly caused or contributed to the harm at issue or which does not clearly fall short of established social expectations.

Similarly, a focus on active wrongdoing inevitably places the conduct of individual persons or organisations at the heart of legal analysis. Legal standards are mainly framed in terms of the behaviour of individual legal actors, both public and private, while a direct causal relationship has to be established between any alleged wrongful action and the harm at issue before individual responsibility is engaged. As a result, collective problems in society tend to become disaggregated within legal analysis, and conceptualised in artificial and atomised terms – the 'isolation' problem identified by Young.[27]

In addition, this focus on active wrongdoing also encourages an emphasis on framing legal liability in terms of clear rules and fixed

24 Note, for example, the role of the 'reasonable person' test (formerly the proverbial 'man on the Clapham omnibus') in establishing when a breach of a duty of care has taken place in negligence cases, and also the role played by irrationality and reasonableness analysis in public law.

25 John Gardner, 'Some Rule-of-Law Anxieties about Strict Liability in Private Law', in *Torts and Other Wrongs* (Oxford University Press 2019), 173–195.

26 Lu (n 17).

27 See, for example, the problem of persistently high levels of sexual violence in society, which often ends up becoming a discussion wholly focused round issues of individual legal liability. Attempts to reframe the debate by extending the reach of relevant personal responsibility, by, for example, creating new legal sanctions relating to the distribution of violent pornography that depart from the individual fault template, have received short shrift.

standards of behaviour.[28] The aim of much legal regulation is to specify when individuals will have crossed a line, which entails attempts to draw bright-line distinctions between 'right' and 'wrong' conduct. This reflects traditional liberal rule of law assumptions about the desirability of rule-based norms, legal certainty and the ability of rational actors to align their conduct with such norms. However, this appetite for bright-line standards can also limit the 'bite' of legal regulation – especially when combined with the default liberal presumption that no liability should attach to individuals, unless a claim is clearly made out in line with the appropriate burden of proof.[29]

This means, for example, that forms of harm that cannot be attributed directly to particular instances of wrongful behaviour will usually be left without a remedy, and that the onus will usually lie with often disadvantaged claimants to demonstrate that defendants have clearly broken a rule.[30] Furthermore, this desire to maximise rule-based regulation tends to encourage a perception that more flexible legal standards are inherently problematic. This can call into question the development of approaches such as proportionality or intersectional analysis, which sacrifice the precision of hard and fast rule-based distinctions for more holistic and contextual modes of attributing legal responsibility.[31] This inevitably constricts law's capacity to engage with harms generated by structural injustice, as discussed further below.

The way wrongdoing tends to be defined by reference to the existing 'baseline' of prevailing social expectations – either through legislation, or the way courts and tribunals interpret and apply legal concepts such as negligence or reasonableness – can also be a limiting factor. Law, of course, derives much of its legitimacy from being aligned with conventional morality. However, tensions can arise between evolving popular understanding of the requirements of justice and existing legal norms, or when law is used to drive forward an agenda of positive social

---

28 Desautels-Stein and Rasulov (n 3), 489.

29 Note the emphasis that dominant strands of liberal thought place on the importance of maximising individual freedom within the limits of the 'harm principle', as variously defined.

30 For example, challenges to embedded pay discrimination in particular sectors of the labour market regularly flounder on the need to demonstrate that a particular 'single source' employer is at fault: see, for example, Judgment of 13 January 2004, *Allonby v Accrington and Rossendale College*, C-256/01 EU:C:2004:18, [2004] ECR I-00873.

31 See, for example, the interesting critique of proportionality analysis set out in Grégoire Webber, 'Proportionality, Balancing, and the Cult of Constitutional Rights Scholarship' (2010) 23(1) Canadian Journal of Law & Jurisprudence 179. For the importance of contextual analysis to intersectional approaches in law, see Sherya Atrey, *Intersectional Discrimination* (Oxford University Press 2019).

change. In such situations, a presumption that the existing status quo is sound can blunt the edge of progressive legislation, limit the development of the law and encourage judges to be cautious and unduly deferential to existing practices. It can also absolve public and private actors from any obligation to go beyond the status quo.[32]

There is therefore plenty to be said for Young and Lu's incisive critique of law's lack of capacity to address harms generated by structural injustice. Not every element of its operative lexicon conforms to the template of the liability model: indeed, as discussed below, there are significant aspects of equality and human rights law that depart from it. However, as a general picture, it is broadly accurate.

Indeed, this critique echoes similar views about law's incapacity to get to grips with structural injustice, which can be found in critical race, gender and disability theory;[33] in the writings of Roberto Unger and other Critical Legal Studies (CLS) theorists;[34] and in Marxist and Marxist-adjacent commentary on the limits of legal progressivism.[35] In particular, Young and Lu's critique has interesting echoes of Unger's analysis of the inability of law to change embedded power structures within contemporary capitalist society. He shares their criticisms of its individual focus – while also emphasising the tunnel vision endangered by the faux-neutral 'formalism' and 'objectivity' of how law frames responsibility, and the way this can obscure the embedded social inequalities that underpin the specific isolated injustices law targets for redress.[36] Young and Lu also echo some of the most incisive radical feminist critiques of legal form; especially when they highlight its focus on individual wrongdoing and assumption of the inherent soundness of established social practices.[37]

But, perhaps ironically, Young and Lu's critique also chimes with much more conventional takes on the nature and function of law. Its formalism and acceptance of existing baselines are widely viewed as virtues, especially by theorists writing from a conservative perspective.[38] Similarly, liberal perspectives on law often welcome its self-restraint, modesty of ambition and constricted focus on interactional wrongs: this chimes with conventional rule of law thinking on the desirability of

32 Lu (n 17).
33 See, for example, Delgado (n 9).
34 Roberto Unger, *The Critical Legal Studies Movement* (Harvard University Press 1986).
35 Collins (n 9).
36 Roberto Unger, *What Should Legal Analysis Become?* (Verso 1996).
37 Lacey and Smart (n 9); also Catherine MacKinnon, *Towards a Feminist Theory of the State* (Harvard University Press 1989).
38 See, for example, John Finnis, 'On The 'Critical Legal Studies Movement' (1985) 30 Am. J. Juris. 21.

clear legal standards and limited interference with individual freedom.[39] Indeed, for many legal theorists, the virtue of law lies precisely in its adherence to the liability/interactional model, and its avoidance of less choate concepts of responsibility. In their eyes, broad projects of social reform should be left to the arena of democratic politics.

Tilting at structural injustice: stretching the envelope of the liability model

However, this is not the end of the story. Young and Lu's critique, and the associated views of both 'crits' and orthodox theorists, is generally on point. However, law's approach to allocating responsibility for harm does not always march in lockstep with the 'liability model'. Over the last few decades, legal mechanisms have been established which can impose liability for a failure to engage with harm generated by structural injustice, even in the absence of deliberate wrongdoing.

To understand how these mechanisms deviate to some extent from law's standard operative lexicon, it is helpful to go back to the binary distinction that Young draws between her 'liability' and 'social connection' models. As discussed, law is associated with the circumscribed scope of the former and thus assumed to have no real capacity of 'biting' on structural injustice – as distinct from interactional wrongs. However, this arguably undersells the flexibility of concepts of fault and wrongdoing as they apply in the context of structural injustice, and by extension, the potential reach of legal liability.

Indeed, a wave of recent literature has challenged this binary distinction.[40] Powers and Faden have argued that the complex causes of structural injustice cannot be sorted into such 'neat analytic categories'.[41] Barry and MacDonald have suggested that the type of behaviour caught by the liability model is significantly wider in scope than Young suggests, arguing for example that she overstates the strictness of its approach to

39 For a critical analysis of the limits of this view of what the rule of law requires, see Jeff King, 'The Rule of Law', in Richard Bellamy and Jeff King (eds), *The Cambridge Handbook of Constitutional Theory* (Cambridge University Press 2024), forthcoming.

40 Zheng interestingly reconfigures this distinction in terms of 'attributability' and 'accountability' respectively: Robin Zheng, 'What Kind of Responsibility Do We Have for Fighting Injustice? A Moral-Theoretic Perspective on the Social Connections Model' (2019) 20(2) Critical Horizons 109.

41 Madison Powers and Ruth Faden, *Structural Injustice: Power, Advantage and Human Rights* (Oxford University Press 2019). They also highlight how deliberate acts of individual wrongdoing, which clearly come within the scope of the liability/interactional model, are often a major contributor to the generation and perpetuation of such injustice – offering up examples such as police misconduct or human trafficking.

causation.[42] Similarly, Abdel-Nour in an incisive response to Lu suggests that there is no sharp qualitative difference between the liability/interactional and social connections models, and that there is 'continuity in the conceptual tools available for thinking about responsibility for both interactional and structural injustice'.[43]

Related points have been made by Sangiovanni, who has argued that individuals who behave in ways that help to reproduce structural injustice should be regarded as *prima facie* liable for any ensuing harm on the basis that a general obligation exists to avoid being implicated in causing or perpetuating such harm.[44] Nussbaum has similarly suggested that individuals who participate in some way in creating the background conditions for structural injustice and fail to take timely remedial action should be morally liable for any harm generated.[45] McKeown has set out an agency-based account of structural injustice, which makes room for a comparatively expansive account of when individuals may be at fault for acting in ways that perpetuate embedded social inequalities and the like – based on the assumption that we are all subject to a responsibility not to behave in ways that maintain or amplify harm-generating social structures, over which we exercise a degree of agency or influence.[46]

These criticisms have a point. The binary established by Young and Lu is too rigid. In many concrete situations, a breakdown of the relevant factors that contribute to the generation and perpetuation of structural injustice will make it possible to attribute responsibility to specific individuals and/or organisations – especially if it is accepted that individuals are subject to positive moral and political obligations not to act in ways that amplify harms caused by embedded inequalities and the like.

Furthermore, as knowledge and awareness of the nature of structural injustice expands, often as a result of socially disadvantaged groups challenging the complacencies of the mainstream 'baseline', conventional assumptions about fault, causation and responsibility can also shift in response.[47] Structural injustice often appears to be inevitable and

42 Christian Barry and Kate Macdonald, 'How Should We Conceive of Individual Consumer Responsibility to Address Labour Injustices?', in Yossi Dahan, Hanna Lerner and Faina Milman-Sivan (eds.) *Global Justice and International Labour* (Cambridge University Press 2016), 92–118.
43 Farid Abdel-Nour, 'Responsibility for Structural Injustice' (2018) 11(1) Ethics & Global Politics 13.
44 Andrea Sangiovanni, 'Structural Injustice and Individual Responsibility' (2018) 49(3) Journal of Social Philosophy 461.
45 Martha Nussbaum, 'Foreword', in Young (n 1), ix–xxv.
46 Maeve McKeown, 'Pure, Avoidable, and Deliberate Structural Injustice', in Jude Browne and Maeve McKeown (eds) *What is Structural Injustice?* (Oxford University Press 2023).
47 ibid.

unavoidable. In particular, it is often framed as a 'natural' phenomenon, and shielded by a protective cladding of justificatory assumptions that serve to deny the existence of any form of meaningful responsibility for its propagation. However, these justificatory assumptions often rest on the exclusion or disregard of the views of those most exposed to the consequences of structural justice.[48] And when this 'epistemological unknowing' eventually comes under serious attack, then the role of individual and organisational inertia in propping up such embedded inequalities often becomes more apparent.[49]

As Browne puts it, our 'perspective on the consequences of our connections to structural injustice may, in time, be met with new forms of knowledge that render a transition of structural actions into moral or legal actions which are captured by the realm of liability' – even if, as Browne also convincingly argues, this may leave a residue of 'untraceable' harms for which no link to individual misconduct can be established.[50]

It is precisely this kind of epistemic shift that has underpinned the development of new forms of legal liability over the last few decades or so, which operate so as to impose sanctions in certain circumstances to individual legal actors who act (or fail to act) in ways that perpetuate or amplify harms caused by structural injustice. These new legal mechanisms are the product of shifts in popular understanding of what the demands of justice entail in contemporary society. They also, in effect, recognise that the existing social 'baseline' may require adjustment in the light of new perspectives relating to the impact of structural justice on marginalised groups. Furthermore, as already mentioned, they also deviate in some respects from how fault is usually conceptualised within law's operative lexicon. Instead of individual responsibility being assigned on the basis of active wrongdoing and a direct causal link to the harm in question, liability is imposed on the basis of a failure to act in ways that avoid amplifying specific forms of fallout from embedded structural inequalities.[51]

---

48 Elizabeth Anderson, 'The Epistemology of Injustice' (2020) 58(1) The Southern Journal of Philosophy 6.
49 ibid.
50 Browne (n 16).
51 It is striking how closely these legal developments track the dynamic process underpinning the extension of liability frameworks to cover more harms generated by structural injustice that has been mapped out by McKeown and Browne, *op cit*.

Targeting structural injustice: positive obligations, indirect discrimination and positive equality duties

These developments have primarily been channelled through the field of equality and human rights law, which is made up of distinct if mutually influencing layers of anti-discrimination legislation, national constitutional rights law and international human rights treaty standards.[52] This framework itself is the product of very fundamental shifts of opinion as to the baseline of norms that legal systems should reflect and embody. Prior to 1945, law was generally not in the business of protecting individuals against discrimination on grounds such as race, sex and so on, except at a highly abstract level. Similarly, it tended to provide very little *direct* protection for human rights: the existing state of the law was assumed to provide just and sufficient indirect protection for such rights, insofar as their fundamental character was recognised at all, and allegations of a breach of such rights did not generally constitute grounds for a legal cause of action. However, all this came under sustained challenge after the Second World War. In the wake of the Holocaust and the other atrocities of that era, a reaction set against the rights-impoverished lexicon of legal systems. A new consensus emerged that the imperative force of human rights claims should be reflected in law, and that legal systems lacking a rights protective dimension were falling short in terms of their commitment to justice.[53]

International legal standards for the protection of human rights were thus established, such as the European Convention on Human Rights (ECHR). National law in liberal democracies slowly but surely followed suit. Rights guarantees were written into domestic law and made enforceable through the court, as expectations grew that legal systems should not alone respect individual rights but also provide effective mechanisms against violations of such rights – whether by public authorities or private actors. This process was further amplified with the emergence of the civil rights, feminist, gay liberation and disability rights movements of the 1960s, with their demands for effective protection against discrimination to be enshrined in the law.[54] And this expectation for effective treatment came hand-in-hand with a recognition that

---

52 For example, in UK law, the provisions of the Equality Act 2010, retained EU law, the Human Rights Act 1998 and the European Convention on Human Rights can all be relevant in a particular case, and exert a mutually overlapping influence: see, for example, the judgment of the UK Supreme Court in *Lee v Ashers Baking Co.* [2018] UKSC 49.
53 Charles Epp, *The Rights Revolution* (University of Chicago Press 1998).
54 ibid.

concrete manifestations of discrimination in everyday life were invariably bound up with (i) epistemic injustices in how legal systems conceptualised fault, harm and responsibility more generally and (ii) the persistence of deeply embedded structural inequalities which had become normalised and accepted within the established social 'baseline'.

Given this background, it is not surprising that new forms of legal liability emerged out of this 'rights crucible', to coin a phrase – and that they depart in significant aspects from many of the established features of law's operative lexicon. Three particular such developments can be singled out: the emergence of the positive obligations doctrine in domestic and international human rights law, the prohibition of indirect discrimination within national law, and the imposition of positive duties on public and private actors to promote compliance with equality and rights standards.[55]

Originally, constitutional and human rights legal guarantees were interpreted so as to only prohibit negative violations of individual rights, i.e. state action, which actively infringed upon basic rights and liberties in ways which were clearly unreasonable or otherwise unjustified. However, over time, international human rights courts began to interpret such rights guarantees as also imposing 'positive obligations' upon state actors, i.e. requirements to take positive measures to ensure individuals were able to effectively enjoy their rights.[56] Such positive obligations arise in situations where state authorities were aware or should have been aware of third-party action or other impediments which impact the enjoyment of individual rights and require these authorities to take reasonable steps to alleviate or remedy the effect of this interference.[57] National courts have taken up this jurisprudence and applied it in domestic law, and gradually the scope of positive obligations doctrine has widened over time in response to the gradual evolution of case-law.[58]

---

55 It is possible to point to other elements of the contemporary legal landscape which also could be said to track this line of development: for example, see the emergence of modern health and safety law as set out in legislation such as the UK Health and Safety at Work Act 1974.

56 See, for example, *X and Y v Netherlands*, Judgment (Merits and Just Satisfaction), Case No 16/1983/72/110, App No 8978/80 (A/91), (1986) 8 EHRR 235 (European Court of Human Rights); Judgment of 29 July 1988, *Velásquez-Rodríguez v Honduras* (Inter-American Court of Human Rights).

57 See in general Vladislava Stoyanova, *Positive Obligations Under the European Convention on Human Rights* (Oxford University Press 2023); L Lavrysen, 'Positive Obligations in the Jurisprudence of the Inter-American Court of Human Rights' (2014) Inter-American and European Human Rights Journal 94.

58 See Mantouvalou (n 2) for a comprehensive analysis of the scope of existing positive obligations doctrine as it relates in particular to labour law issues.

It is clear that positive obligations represent a departure from the general character of law's operative lexicon. Liability is not attributed on the basis of active wrongdoing, or by virtue of direct and foreseeable causation of harm. Instead, public authorities may be sanctioned for a failure to take action to ameliorate or redress the impact of structural harm, if the latter amounts to a tangible interference with fundamental individual rights. Furthermore, both the national and international jurisprudence recognises that public authorities cannot justify inertia by citing established practice: departures from the normal baseline of public sector conduct may in fact be mandated if public authorities knew or should have known that individuals or groups were particularly vulnerable to having their rights eroded.[59] Also, what constitutes reasonable steps by a public authority to discharge their positive obligations will be assessed on a holistic and contextual basis, taking into account the particular situation of affected individuals and groups and the background structural factors that may make them particularly at risk of having their basic dignity eroded or denied.[60]

Given how positive obligations doctrine thus appears to slip free of the constraints of the liability model as described by Young and Lu, it is not surprising that commentators have been quick to highlight its potential as a tool to combat at least some of the harms generated by structural injustice. Mantouvalou has in particular outlined how positive obligations can frame legal responsibility in ways that make it possible to target structural harms which impinge on the enjoyment of core rights.[61] And it is notable that attempts by civil society activists to use the law to tackle embedded structural inequalities now regularly invoke the doctrine of positive obligations – as highlighted, for example, by the extensive litigation relating to Roma rights in Central and Eastern Europe that has played out over the last decade or so before European human rights adjudicatory bodies.[62]

Within the specific sphere of anti-discrimination law, a similar dynamic has been in play in respect of the prohibition of discrimination on the basis of protected characteristics such as disability, gender, race,

59 Lourdes Peroni and Alexandra Timmer, 'Vulnerable Groups: The Promise of an Emerging Concept in European Human Rights Convention Law' (2013) 11(4) International Journal of Constitutional Law 1056.

60 ibid. For an example of this contextual approach in action, see Application no. 47159/08, *B.S. v Spain*, Judgment of 24 July 2012.

61 Mantouvalou (n 2).

62 See, for example, *D.H. v Czech Republic* (2008) 47 EHRR 3 (ECHR), Complaint46/2007, *European Roma Rights Centre v Bulgaria*, Decision of 3 December 2008 (European Social Charter).

sexual orientation and so on. When anti-discrimination legislation was first introduced in the 1960s, only direct discrimination was initially prohibited, i.e. treating someone less favourably on the grounds of their sex, race, or possession of some other protected characteristic. This fitted well within law's operative lexicon, as a decision to discriminate on this basis could generally be viewed as an act of active wrongdoing – absent the existence of a relevant defence. Furthermore, the prohibition was understood to reflect a new social consensus as to the importance of tackling racism, sexism and other outmoded beliefs. However, the desire to ensure effective protection against discrimination and the growing recognition of how much discrimination was the product of embedded structural inequalities, soon lead to the legal framework being extended.[63]

To start with, the evolving case-law on direct discrimination established that liability could be imposed even in the clear absence of an active intent to discriminate.[64] This ensured that direct discrimination cases did not get bogged down into messy debates about motive and the state of mind of alleged discriminators. But it also in effect changed how fault was conceptualised for the purposes of this area of the law: the focus shifted from sanctioning 'bad intent' to prohibiting behaviour that contributed to wider patterns of group stigmatisation and subordination, even if not improperly motivated.[65] By itself, this did not deviate substantially from law's standard operating lexicon: active wrongdoing was still required in the form of direct reliance upon a protected characteristic to differentiate between individuals. However, it is notable that wider patterns of structural injustice were taken into account for the purposes of defining liability, with existing law interpreted so as to enhance its capacity to break down embedded inequalities.

An even more consequential development has been legal recognition of the concept of indirect discrimination. As fleshed out by legislation and judicial interpretation, this supplements the ban on direct discrimination by imposing liability in situations where the application of apparently neutral rules or practices has the effect of placing persons sharing a protected characteristic at a particular disadvantage compared to other persons, when the use of such rules or practices cannot be shown to be objectively justified.[66] The extension of liability to cover this type of

63 See the discussion in Anthony Lester and Geoffrey Bindman, *Race and the Law* (Penguin 1972).
64 See, for example, *James v Eastleigh Borough Council* [1990] 2 AC 751.
65 Iyiola Solanke, *Discrimination as Stigma: A Theory of Anti-Discrimination Law* (Hart 2017).
66 See, for example, Case C-83/14, *CHEZ Razpredelenie Bulgaria AD v Komisia za zashtita ot diskriminatsia*, Judgment of 16 July 2015 (European Court of Justice).

situation is designed to enhance the effectiveness of anti-discrimination law – as explained by Burger C.J. in the US case of *Griggs v Duke Power* by reference to the ancient fable of the offer of milk to the stork and the fox.[67] It also departs from law's standard operative lexicon in significant ways. As Khaitan and Steel argue, active wrongdoing ('culpability') is not required to ground liability for this form of discrimination, which is essentially strict in nature – although it can be relevant at the remedy stage, when damages are being assessed.[68] Liability under indirect discrimination can be established even in the absence of any knowledge of how disparate impact might be generated, or how it might impact a particular group.[69] In essence, for this cause of action, individual responsibility has been framed in terms of a requirement to take reasonable steps to avoid amplifying the impact of background structural inequalities – or, as Deborah Hellman has put it, it imposes a 'duty to avoid compounding injustice'.[70]

In other words, indirect discrimination is another example of the liability model being stretched in order to frame responsibility in wider terms than is usual within law's operating lexicon. This has been expressly done for the purpose of enhancing the capacity of anti-discrimination law to engage with the consequences of structural injustice. It also represents an acknowledgement that the existing baseline is often tilted against disadvantaged groups: marginalised groups have repeatedly challenged the assumed 'neutrality' of rules and practices that effectively serve to reinforce their subordination.[71] Furthermore, once again, contextual factors may be taken into account in establishing the existence of disparate impact, or an absence of reasonable justification – thus opening the way for courts to engage with how embedded structural inequalities impact the lives of individual claimants and the groups defined by reference to their possession of particular protected characteristics with which they are affiliated.[72]

Like the development of positive obligations doctrine, indirect discrimination law has opened up important new avenues for law to be deployed against manifestations of structural injustice. Litigants

67 401 U.S. 424 (1971), 430–434.
68 Tarunabh Khaitan and Sandy Steel, 'Wrongs, Group Disadvantage, and the Legitimacy of Indirect Discrimination Law', in Hugh Collins and Tarunabh Khaitan (eds.), *Foundations of Indirect Discrimination Law* (Hart 2018), 197–221.
69 See, for example, *Essop v Home Office* [2017] UKSC 27.
70 Deborah Hellman, 'Indirect Discrimination and the Duty to Avoid Compounding Injustice', in Collins and Khaitan (n 68), 105–122.
71 Tarunabh Khaitan, *A Theory of Discrimination Law* (Oxford University Press 2015).
72 See, for example, the discussion of the particular impact of drug sentencing laws on indigenous communities in the Canadian case of *R v Sharma* [2022] SCC 39.

have used it to achieve significant legal victories against both public and private bodies, by for example, challenging rules and practices that amplify the gendered nature of pay and pension policies,[73] the negative impact of many social welfare arrangements on carers and persons with disabilities,[74] or the exclusionary impact of educational or employment policy on particular racial and ethnic groups.[75]

The prohibition on indirect discrimination has also helped to raise public awareness of the nature and extent of structural inequalities, and incentivised public and private bodies to take proactive measures to lessen their impact – if only to minimise their possible exposure to legal action. Indeed, it could be argued that the legal 'activation' of indirect discrimination has helped to focus political attention on structural injustice as a distinct category of social wrong, and reinforced the sense that persons are under a moral obligation not to amplify its negative effects. (In this respect, it is striking that legal debates about the nature and justification of indirect discrimination have tended to predate sustained philosophical reflection on the existence of structural inequalities by a few decades.[76]) And as with positive obligations, the potential reach of indirect discrimination law is considerable: there is an academic consensus that the existing case-law has only begun to explore its possible application to a range of different social contexts.[77]

A third category of legal measure designed to engage with the consequences of structural injustice, namely positive equality duties, can be seen as sharing common roots with both positive obligations doctrine and indirect discrimination law. This is a general category, covering several different types of legal requirement. In the UK, these range from the general equality duty to eliminate unlawful discrimination and promote equality of opportunity imposed on British public authorities by s. 149

---

73 Case 170/84, *Bilka Kaufhaus* [1986] ECR 1607 and also the fascinating Canadian case of *Fraser v Canada (Attorney General)* [2020] 3 SCR 113.

74 See, for example, *RF v Secretary of State for Work and Pensions* [2017] EWHC 3375 (Admin) (21 December 2017).

75 See, for example, *D.H. v Czech Republic*, n. 61 above; also *London Underground v Edwards (No 2)* [1997] IRLR 157, a particularly striking example of the potential range and effectiveness of indirect discrimination law.

76 Iris Marion Young's 2011 book, *Responsibility for Justice*, cited throughout this chapter, is often treated as the Urtext for philosophical analysis of structural injustice. In contrast, legal papers have been analysing the manner in which the prohibition on indirect discrimination can have a redistributive impact in response to structural inequalities since the late 1980s if not before: see, for example, John Gardner, 'Liberals and Indirect Discrimination' (1989) 9(1) Oxford Journal of Legal Studies 1.

77 See in general Collins and Khaitan (n 68).

of the Equality Act 2010;[78] to the employment equity duties imposed on public and private employers in Northern Ireland by the Fair Employment and Treatment (Northern Ireland) Act 1998; to the specific public sector duties regarding socio-economic equality set out by s. 1 of the 2010 Act, which have as yet not yet been brought into force in England;[79] and to the pay audit requirements imposed on larger employers by the Equality Act 2010 (Equal Pay Audits) Regulations 2014. Similar duties exist in a range of other states, including Sweden, Australia, the USA and Canada.[80] In essence, such duties require targeted bodies to monitor the contextual impact of their policies on structurally disadvantaged groups, and to take steps to alleviate any identified negative impact. The duties are future-facing and are imposed irrespective of any past wrongdoing: their aim is to require the public and private bodies subject to their requirements to take proactive measures to address the fallout of structural injustice, and to take on board the perspectives of disadvantaged groups in implementing the requirements of the duty.[81]

Such duties thus represent another attempt to stretch the envelope of the liability model, and to allocate responsibility on the basis of capacity to alleviate structural harm rather than on the basis of any active wrongdoing as such. The duties are relatively weak legal mechanisms. They can be enforced via judicial review proceedings in the case of public authorities, or by enforcement action initiated by equality commissions in the case of private bodies. However, both public and private bodies subject to their requirements will in general only need to show that they took account of the duty as a matter of procedure, rather than having to demonstrate they also fully engaged with their substance.[82] They nevertheless provide a point of leverage for both internal staff and external stakeholders to push for action, and help establish the redress of structural injustice as a legitimate organisational objective – which can be particularly important for public

78 See also the duty established by s. 75 of the Northern Ireland Act 1998.
79 Note, however, that this duty has been brought into force in relation to the performance of devolved functions by specified Scottish and Welsh public authorities: see The Equality Act 2010 (Authorities Subject to the Socio-economic Inequality Duty) (Scotland) Regulations 2018; Equality Act (Authorities Subject to the Socio-economic Inequality Duty) (Wales) Regulations 2021.
80 For a comprehensive overview, see Alysia Blackham, 'Positive Equality Duties: The Future of Equality and Transparency?' (2021) 37(2) Law in Context 98.
81 ibid.
82 Aileen McColgan, 'Litigating the Public Sector Equality Duty: The Story So Far' (2015) 35(3) Oxford Journal of Legal Studies 453–485.

bodies, that need to ground their activities on a clear legal basis.[83] The duties also perform a useful symbolic role, by signalling the importance of assuming responsibility for tackling the consequences of structural injustice.[84]

Taken all these legal innovations together, they represent a sustained attempt to reconfigure the liability model and to supplement its focus on individual wrongdoing with wider requirements to act in a manner that alleviates the impact of structural injustice. The strictly 'interactional' approach to responsibility that Young and Lu treat as a defining characteristic of this model has been complemented by what Mantouvalou describes (while referring to positive obligations) as a 'legal responsibility to change some of these state-mediated structures of injustice'[85] – with indirect discrimination and certain of the positive equality duties extending that positive, proactive responsibility into the private sector. These innovations have had some real incremental impact, as already outlined. Many commentators also consider that their potential has yet to be fully realised.[86] For example, discrimination on the basis of poverty, class or associated forms of socio-economic status is generally not covered by discrimination law or the scope of positive equality duties[87] – and it is rare for domestic human rights law to make positive obligations relating to the enjoyment of core socio-economic rights enforceable in law.[88] These gaps are widely viewed as impeding law's capacity to tackle structural injustice, and have prompted plenty of academic and civil society commentary arguing that they should be closed. Indeed, Fredman has argued that the positive duty/obligation framework could provide a coherent underpinning framework for human rights law taken as a whole.[89]

However, while these innovations have added a new dimension to law's operating lexicon, they still remain overshadowed by the standard norms, expectations and assumptions that shape its daily functioning. This has limited the impact of these legal innovations and constrained

83 Colm O'Cinneide, 'Positive Duties and Gender Equality' (2005) 8(1–2) International Journal of Discrimination and the Law 91; Blackham (n 80).
84 ibid.
85 Mantouvalou (n 2), in particular Chapter 7.
86 ibid. See also Sandra Fredman, *Discrimination Law*, 3rd edn (Oxford University Press 2022), Ch 8.
87 Note, however, the socio-economic equality duty set out in s. 1 of the Equality Act 2010, as mentioned above.
88 See in general Ingrid Leitjen, *Core Socio-Economic Rights and the European Court of Human Rights* (Cambridge University Press, 2017).
89 Sandra Fredman, *Human Rights Transformed: Positive Rights and Positive Duties* (Oxford University Press 2008).

law's capacity to respond to structural injustice. And in assessing law's capacity to tackle structural injustice, the legal and political impact of this 'drag factor' needs to be taken into account.

The gravitational pull of law's operating lexicon

The legal innovations discussed previously all represent add-ons to the standard rules of law's operating lexicon. They define responsibility by reference to the need to avoid amplifying the impact of structural injustice, instead of focusing on past individual wrongdoing. They also adopt a holistic and contextual approach to determining liability, which recognises that it may be necessary to depart from existing 'business as usual' according to the structural dynamics of a particular factual situation – instead of framing individual responsibility in terms of adherence to clear rules of behaviour, as defined by an established baseline of normal conduct.[90]

However, these deviations from the norm are ultimately limited in scope. For the most part, they only take effect in relation to structural harms which (i) impact the enjoyment of fundamental rights, in the case of positive obligations, or (ii) have a disparate impact on persons belonging to groups that can be defined by reference to the small set of protected non-discrimination characteristics, in the case of indirect discrimination and positive equality duties. Attempts to extend their substantive scope of application tend to attract resistance at both the legal and political level – often justified on the basis that these innovations threaten to corrode important and valuable elements of law's operative lexicon.

Thus, for example, civil society advocacy has sought for decades greater legal protection for socio-economic rights, by (as discussed above) amplifying the range and scope of positive obligations enforceable in domestic law and/or extending the reach of anti-discrimination law and positive duties to cover poverty.[91] However, such advocacy has by and large run into a stone wall. The difficulty in framing individual responsibility in relation to such rights, and defining what would be the scope of the associated positive obligations and non-discrimination duties, has been repeatedly cited as a reason for not extending legal

90 Fredman, ibid.

91 See, for example, the campaigning work of the NGO Just Fair, at <https://justfair.org.uk/> accessed 18 October 2023.

protection in this way.[92] So too has the concern that this would give too much power and discretion to judges, and stretch the legitimacy claims of legal discourse to breaking point. Attempts to ensure greater legal protection against intersectional discrimination have run into similar problems, while calls to impose extensive equality duties to all large-scale private sector employers have not attracted political support.[93] The desire to maintain law's standard operating model has trumped attempts to enhance its capacity to engage with structural injustice. The legal innovations discussed in this chapter remain confined in scope and limited in application.

Furthermore, courts applying these new legal innovations have often been reluctant to give them real bite. The case-law on positive obligations is full of uncertain judgments,[94] lines of precedent that start strongly and then trail away into semi-incoherence,[95] and strong deference being given to state actors – especially in situations where a clear line of causation cannot be shown to exist between a particular structural harm and a tangible, clear-cut act of neglect on the part of the state.[96] Similar tendencies can be seen for decades now when it comes to the indirect discrimination case-law, in particular when it comes to the application of the objective justification test – where the standard operating lexicon's preference for clear causative responsibility and bright-line rules has repeatedly surfaced, even though the underpinning logic of indirect discrimination law would arguably point in another direction.[97] Courts have also been very slow to give any substantive definition to legal obligations arising under the

---

92 See Mary Dowell-Jones, 'The Economics of the Austerity Crisis: Unpicking Some Human Rights Arguments' (2015) 15(2) Human Rights Law Review 193.

93 Note that s. 14 of the Equality Act 2010, which prohibited 'combined discrimination' based on the intersection of two protected characteristics, has never been brought into force by the required ministerial order. As previously noted, the same is also the case in England (but not in Scotland and Wales) for the positive duty imposed by s. 1 of the same Act on public authorities to consider the socio-economic consequences of their policies. Attempts to include wide-ranging positive equality duties within the scope of the 2010 Act did not meet with government favour: see Bob Hepple, 'Enforcing Equality Law: Two Steps Forward and Two Steps Backwards for Reflexive Regulation' (2011) 40(4) Industrial Law Journal 315.

94 See Stoyanova (n 57) for somewhat critical commentary on much of the relevant ECHR case-law.

95 See, for example, the line of ECHR precedent relating to the scope of Article 8 right to privacy positive obligations and their potential application to the accommodation of Traveller housing needs in the UK, which started strongly with *Connors v UK* [2004] 40 EHRR 9 but has become more dilute over the years.

96 See, for example, Applications nos. 24816/14 and 25140/14, *Hudorovič v Slovenia*, Judgment of 10 March 2020.

97 See, for example, Barbara Havelková's critique of the ECHR indirect discrimination jurisprudence, which perfectly illustrates the trend discussed here: Barbara Havelková, 'Judicial Scepticism of Discrimination at the ECtHR', in Collins and Khaitan (n 68).

positive equality duties, for similar reasons.[98] More generally, they have also been slow to depart radically from the baseline of established norms – in part due to concerns about the legitimacy of their judicial role, and deference to the conventions of the standard operative lexicon.[99]

Finally, it should also be noted that these innovative legal mechanisms have attracted a considerable degree of backlash, both within legal and political discourse – precisely because of how their concern with structural injustice cuts across the inherent conservativism of law's standard operating lexicon. Thus positive obligations in general have been subject to considerable criticism on the basis that they are too woolly and lacking in bright-line definition; that they give unelected judges too much leeway to attribute responsibility in respect of complex issues of structural injustice; and that they lack the precision and narrow focus of the standard operating lexicon. Indeed, they have never taken real root in US law[100] – while the UK government, in its 2021 Bill of Rights consultation paper, questioned their legal integrity.[101] Similar criticisms have been directed at indirect discrimination law, with conservative judges on the US Supreme Court repeatedly calling its integrity as a legal test into question.[102] The positive equality duties only escape similar criticism on account of their weak enforcement mechanism. However, they remain politically controversial, and have periodically been watered down by government intervention.[103]

In general, taking all the foregoing into account, it is striking how much resistance these innovative legal mechanisms have attracted. They deviate from how law's operative lexicon normally frames responsibility, and as a consequence are often viewed as potentially problematic and interpreted in a narrow and restrictive manner. This has not prevented these innovations taking root within various legal systems, with indirect discrimination in particular proving to be a relatively robust transplant. However, they sit uneasily alongside the standard legal rubric, are out of alignment with conventional expectations as to how law should attribute fault, and thus continue to be regarded as aberrations or deviations from a settled norm.

---

98 McColgan (n 82).
99 See, for example, *R (SC) v Secretary of State for Work and Pensions* [2021] UKSC 26.
100 *DeShaney v. Winnebago County Department of Social Services* 489 U.S. 189 (1989), 195.
101 UK Ministry of Justice, *Human Rights Act Reform: A Modern Bill of Rights* (December 2021) CP 588, [151]–[170].
102 See, for example, Scalia J.'s comments in *Ricci v. DeStefano*, 557 U.S. 557 (2009).
103 UK House of Lords, Select Committee on the Equality Act 2010 and Disability, *The Equality Act 2010: The Impact on Disabled People* (24 March 2016, HL Paper 117) Ch. 8.

Now, there are interesting arguments to be had about how far such legal innovations can and should be stretched so as to tackle the harms generated by structural injustice. The old orthodoxy that law is a poor tool for such a purpose is certainly open to challenge but cannot be readily dismissed out of hand.[104] However, for the purposes of this chapter, the key point to register is that law's standard operative lexicon exerts a very strong gravitational pull – and this has limited attempts to stretch the envelope of the liability model, and frame individual responsibility in wider terms.

This would seem to impose real limits on the extent to which law can be deployed to combat structural justice: its operative lexicon seems to be naturally resistant to attempts to define fault in terms of individual or organisational failure to act in ways that avoid amplifying the toll of such injustice. At first glance, this would appear to confirm Young and Lu's views about the limits of the liability model. However, digging a little deeper, the problem may not be the inherent nature of legal liability as such – which after all has been reframed in innovative ways to accommodate wider concepts of responsibility. Instead, the key constraining factor would appear to be the persistent grip of law's standard operating lexicon over the legal imagination, and how this limits the reach and scope of innovative new ways of defining fault. More generally, this may tell us something significant about the embedded limitations of our collective moral and political imagination as a society. Just as law seems to be more comfortable clinging to the comfort blanket of its standard operative lexicon rather than embracing new ways of framing individual responsibility, the same can perhaps be said for other modes of social discourse. It is striking how often moral and political debates about social justice in general continue to be framed in terms of liability and fault, as Young has noted. It is also striking how such debates continue to be heavily influenced by law's conventional emphasis on framing responsibility in terms of individual wrongdoing, active causation and bright-line delineations of liability – as can be seen in particular in the context of recent pushback against the equality claims tabled by the Black Lives Matter and MeToo movements, and disclaimers of responsibility for both the legacy of colonialism and ongoing environmental degradation.[105]

104 See Dowell-Jones (n 92).

105 See, for example, how the Commission on Race and Ethnic Disparities established by the UK Government in 2020 queried many of the existing 'progressive' narratives relating to responsibility for existing inequalities affecting ethnic minorities in Britain in areas such as employment and access to social goods more generally: see *Report of the Commission on Race and Ethnic Disparities* (the 'Sewell Report'), April 2021, available at <https://www.gov.uk/government/publications/the-report-of-the-commission-on-race-and-ethnic-disparities> accessed 18 October 2023.

There is much to be said for attempts to re-conceptualise responsibility for structural injustice in terms of agency liability, as for example, McKeown does. However, such reconceptualisation may have to grapple with the current limits of our collective social imagination and the way law's standard operative lexicon may be playing an important role in stunting the development of new ways of framing liability for structural harms.

Conclusion

Turning back to issues of legal liability more specifically, this somewhat pessimistic analysis of law's readiness to tackle structural liability raises the question of whether attempting to innovate around the status quo might squander time and energy that might be better spent in other ways – by, for example, engaging in the hard political graft necessary to develop the 'social connections' model of shared, future-facing responsibility, which for Young, represents the best way forward in this context. Similar questions have haunted the development of equality and human rights law over the last few decades.[106] But Lauren Berlant's concept of 'cruel optimism' referred to in the introduction to this chapter, which she defines as a situation when an attachment to an intrinsically desirable thing actually gets in the way of the reasons why you became attached to that thing in the first place, has particular resonance here.[107] Does investing too much hope in the potential of, for example, positive obligations to tackle structural injustice risk investing too much faith in law and the usefulness of framing responsibility for structural injustice in terms of individual liability more generally? Does it risk holding out false hope and providing ideological reassurance of law's capacity to deliver justice, which is fundamentally misleading?

I would suggest not, even if a degree of 'cruel optimism' does seem to come with this territory. Law does some useful work in combatting some of the harms generated by structural injustice, even if only in bounded and incremental ways: while the reach of innovations like positive obligations, indirect discrimination law and positive duties may be limited, they still have had real impact. However, there is another angle also in play here. These attempts that have been made to push the envelope of the standard form of legal liability also have a useful signalling function, which extends beyond their circumscribed legal utility into wider areas of moral and

106 See Rosenberg, *Hollow Hope* (n 7).
107 Berlant (n 6).

political debate. By affirming that individuals have a responsibility to act in ways that avoid amplifying harm generated by embedded structural inequalities, these innovations arguably help to challenge and destabilise conventional thinking about fault and individual responsibility – and thus help to counteract the stunting impact that orthodox liability thinking otherwise exerts on wider moral and political debates. Browne is right to emphasise that there is often an 'untraceable' dimension to structural injustice, which cannot be adequately captured by any form of liability framing.[108] But the process of generating the sense of political connectivity necessary to tackle this aspect of structural injustice may gain momentum from liability innovation within the law, and the way this can help to liberate our common sense of responsibility from the shackles of law's standard operative lexicon.

108 Browne (n 16).

3

Structural injustice and the law: a philosophical framework

George Letsas[1]

Introduction

As mentioned in previous chapters, Iris Marion Young uses the fictional story of Sandy to illustrate a distinct kind of wrong, which she calls structural injustice.[2] Sandy, a low-income single mother with two kids, ends up homeless following an eviction, lack of affordable housing and limited employment opportunities where she lives. It is constitutive of this type of wrong, Young claims, that it is not interactional: all the persons with whom Sandy interacts (the landlords, the employers, the estate agents) act within their rights, and no specific individual is blameworthy for the injustice that is inflicted on her. But it is also the case, she claims, that the wrong is not attributable to a specifically unjust state policy, such as laws regarding housing or employment. Instead, she argues, the wrong relates to the social position Sandy occupies: her social circumstances make her – along with several others – vulnerable to homelessness through no fault of her own. The limited options and constraining background conditions with which she is faced are the result of multiple, complex and wide-ranging patterns of social behaviour, none of which is the single cause of the injustice. They are, moreover, patterns of conduct in which all of us engage and for which we are therefore collectively responsible.

1 I am very grateful to the editors, Virginia Mantouvalou and Jonathan Wolff, for their invaluable comments on a draft of this chapter. Many thanks also to all the participants in the UCL conference on Law and Structural Injustice for their comments and suggestions.

2 Iris Marion Young, *Responsibility for Justice* (Oxford University Press 2011).

The contrast between individual wrongdoing and unjust policies, on the one hand, and structural injustice on the other, informs Young's restrictive approach to law. She gives at least three reasons why law has a very limited role to play in matters of structural injustice. The first is that the law, just like interpersonal morality, employs what she calls a *liability model of responsibility*. The model works by pinning liability for a harm on a particular individual, or group of individuals, based primarily on elements of causation and fault. No single individual, however, is responsible for Sandy's homelessness according to Young – that is the core of the idea of structural injustice. Instead, Young argues, responsibility for structural injustice is collectively shared by all of us, in virtue of the fact that we participate in the patterns of social behaviour that make Sandy vulnerable to homelessness.

The second reason Young gives is that specific legal rules (such as legislation regarding housing and property) are not, on their face, unjust. The individuals who interact with Sandy, she argues, act within their legal rights to property or contract. It is not clear whether Young means that the landlord's legal right to evict, or the employer's right to dismiss, are *just*, or whether she simply means that they are not *grossly*, or *manifestly* unjust. She may be assuming that the justice of legal rules is a matter of degree and that the threshold for what counts as an unjust legal rule has not been crossed in Sandy's case. Examples of manifestly or grossly unjust laws would be the historical rules of allowing chattel slavery, or prohibiting women from having the legal right to own property (tutelage). Clearly, the right to evict a tenant, or dismiss an employee, are not unjust in the same sense as these atrocious laws and these rights are still common in many countries. But that is not to say that they are *fully* or *perfectly* just. It is possible that Young wants to leave open the possibility that better, more restrictive, legal rules could be *more* just, compatible with saying that the legal rules that apply to Sandy are not *unjust*. I think this interpretation is more charitable and that is the one I will attribute to her.

Finally, Young adds a third, related, reason for why law is of little significance to matters of structural injustice. She claims that legal rules are in any case only a fraction of the social causes that make Sandy vulnerable to homelessness. This is because she understands Sandy's vulnerability to result from a multitude of patterns of social interaction in which we all participate. And she takes the exercise of people's legal rights to be only one such pattern, and a small one at that. A landlord may invoke the right to evict a tenant who is behind in their rent. But other causes, such as how many affordable properties are available close to Sandy's employment, are not the result of the exercise of legal rights. It could be, for instance, that businesses likely to employ Sandy have suddenly moved away from residential areas because office space in remote locations is cheaper. This third reason for not taking law to be important for matters of structural injustice is connected to the second one because, even if better legal rules were put in place, they would not prevent all the patterns of behaviour that render Sandy's position vulnerable.

We can summarise Young's view about the relation between law and structural injustice as follows: law is only part of the problem and by its very nature, it cannot be the solution. It is only part of the problem because there are many causal factors contributing to Sandy's vulnerability and the legislative framework is only a small part. And it cannot be part of the solution because it works on the model of individual responsibility. But no single individual is responsible for structural injustices; all of us are.

In this chapter, I aim to challenge Young's reductive approach to law. There have been strong arguments that law can do more to change the patterns of social behaviour that create vulnerability of the kind illustrated by the example of Sandy, say through legal reform or human rights adjudication.[3] Indeed, other jurisdictions arguably do a better job than the US legal system in mitigating vulnerability and I will later offer several examples of how different legal rules can achieve this. But my critique of Young's position aims to cut much deeper than that. Perhaps the most distinctive element of the idea of structural injustice is that the relevant responsibility is collective, not individual. This, however, is in my view even more reason to take law to be central to the problem of structural injustice. This is because the structures that Young identifies are all *legal* or *juridical* relations for which, I will argue, we are all collectively responsible. Sandy's homelessness is not a purely factual condition, brought about by the cumulative effect of individual patterns of behaviour. We should view it as primarily a legal condition, created by the way in which legal rights (say over property or contract) are allocated across classes of person.

In what follows, I shall sketch an account that places collective responsibility for social justice at the heart of law. My sense is that most political philosophers employ a rather positivistic picture of law, treating it as only one of the many domains that might be relevant for matters of

3 See Virginia Mantouvalou, 'Structures of Injustice, Workers' Rights and Human Rights' (2020) 73(1) Current Legal Problems 59.

social justice. By contrast, legal theorists (particularly those theorising about specific areas of law), perhaps unsurprisingly, view law in a more expansive way: as the main battleground of social justice. It is not my aim here to defend this more expansive approach to law, but mainly to illustrate how Young's insights into the problem of structural injustice take a radically different shape under that approach. Not only is law relevant to the notion of structural injustice, but also it is central to it. The claim that Sandy is the victim of structural injustice entails a claim about the injustice of the scheme of legal rights that are collectively enforced. The patterns of social interaction which Young takes as crucial are inherently juridical and so is any injustice that they produce.

Having said that, I want to leave open the possibility that the notion of structural injustice can be applied in settings that are not governed by legal institutions, or where legal institutions are malfunctioning. Perhaps, for example, there were structural injustices in early hunter-gatherer societies or in war-torn communities with an ineffective judiciary and executive. Or perhaps there are structural injustices within practices that law – for good reason – leaves unregulated, such as personal or intimate relationships.[4] In that sense, the wrong of structural injustice is not necessarily tied to law. But I want to focus here on Sandy's case, as Young describes it, which is situated within an advanced legal system with well-functioning branches of government and a healthy respect for the rule of law, and which relates to a particular vulnerability, that of homelessness. It is in this context that the role of law seems to me salient. The approach I will put forward aims to retain from Young's account the emphasis on collective responsibility, while rejecting her claim that law's model of responsibility is individualistic and peripheral to the problem of structural injustice.

The juridical nature of social structures

Young's treatment of law is largely restricted to the *retail* level of a court finding an individual liable for a given harm. She is right to point out that this is too narrow a focus to help us deal with the problem of

4 I hasten to add that, even with intimate relations, the law effectively regulates them, by taking a binary view about which actions are permitted and which are prohibited within them. What I mean is that it might be possible, within the class of legally permitted actions, for the wrong of structural injustice to occur. Perhaps, for example, it can be said that those who remain single after a certain age become vulnerable to loneliness and social exclusion, by losing friends that have a family and by facing difficulty to make new ones. I am sceptical that this case qualifies as an injustice but, even if it does, it seems to me different in kind to Sandy's case.

structural injustice, since no single individual is responsible for Sandy's homelessness. Yet there is also the *wholesale* level of how legal rights and duties are allocated across classes of persons; particularly against the background knowledge that people like Sandy are very likely to end up vulnerable. Here, there are several features of law that engage our collective responsibility directly, in a non-contingent way. The most significant one, though easy to miss, is that the patterns of social interaction in which we all engage are in a crucial sense enabled and protected by law. For, if we are in any way inhibited from engaging in these patterns by third parties, we can go to court and avail ourselves of its coercive apparatus (such as bailiffs or the police) to force them to stop. For example, if Sandy were to oppose her eviction, turn up for work at a business where she is no longer employed, or send her kids to day-care without paying the fees, then she will be physically forced to stop by state officials, pursuant to a court order. These state officials, however, belong to political institutions (such as courts and the police) who act in the name of the community. And they could equally direct that very force they command towards frustrating or terminating these patterns. They could, for instance, issue an injunction to stay Sandy's eviction, compel her employer not to dismiss her or to reinstate her, or order her local authority to provide affordable housing. In other words, the patterns of social interaction that render Sandy vulnerable do not just simply occur, like a natural event does. They are normatively salient in that they are marked out by the possibility of using collective force to shield them from interference, as a matter of an institutional right.

Of course, when people engage in these patterns, they do not necessarily take themselves to be exercising legal rights, let alone rights that can be backed up with collective force. This is why this aspect of legal practice is easy to miss. A business owner will simply move location, make redundancies or fail to renew someone's contract. A landlord will simply choose the highest bidder as a tenant or sell the property to make a profit. When engaged in these activities, people need not have the law in their minds, and they may even be ignorant of what their legal position is. It is mainly when they are obstructed by a third party, or threatened with a lawsuit, that people might call the police or consult a lawyer. A company might, for example, seek a court injunction against climate activists interfering with mundane actions, such as its employees crossing the street to enter the business premises. Few would think of the act of crossing the street as an exercise of a legal right, let alone one that might require protection by police officers.

Nevertheless, the point here is that for any conceivable action (and *a fortiori* for existing patterns of social interaction), it is the case either that the law permits it, or that it prohibits it. This assertion is, of course, contentious territory in general jurisprudence. Legal positivists deny it[5] and so do many ordinary people who consult legal materials seeking to understand what their legal rights are. Non-positivists, by contrast, emphasise the distinction between uncertainty and indeterminacy.[6] They argue that the linguistic vagueness of legal materials, or gaps in legislation, do not entail indeterminacy about whether the law prohibits or allows an action. This is a well-known theoretical dispute, which I will bracket here, assuming a non-positivist account. But this is mainly because the dispute does not affect the main point here, which is that, for any dispute, the court will inevitably have to side with one of the litigant parties, and against the other. In either case, the use of collective force is available, on demand, to protect or prevent conduct and more generally, patterns of behaviour. In that sense, law is, so to speak, *ubiquitous* in social structures.

It might sound exaggerated to claim that the possibility of collective force (as mediated through judicial enforcement) enables and solidifies whatever patterns of social interaction are in place. But the point is not descriptive or causal. Since the use of collective force can be deployed vis-à-vis any action, existing patterns of social interaction necessarily have – in so far as they are lawful – the seal of approval of the political community. Courts and the police are public institutions whose aim is to act in the name of all citizens. At first instance, therefore, these institutions are directly responsible for which actions or patterns may attract the powerful protection of licensed collective force. To put it crudely, in so far as businesses are at liberty to move offices and choose their employees, and landlords are at liberty to evict tenants, this is because courts and the police allow them to do so by being ready to issue injunctions and orders against anyone who tries to interfere. The liberty in question is not merely the physical ability to engage in those actions. After all, people will always have – to varying degrees – the physical ability to act criminally; for example, to commit murder, theft or assault. Crime rates fluctuate depending, among other things, on how successful

5 Legal positivists hold that it may be indeterminate whether some action is permitted or not because the legal meaning of relevant valid rules might be indeterminate. See H L A Hart, *The Concept of Law* (3rd edn, Oxford University Press 2012).
6 See Ronald Dworkin, 'No Right Answer?' (1978) 53 New York University Law Review 1; Nicos Stavropoulos, 'Hart's Semantics' in Coleman (ed), *Hart's Postscript: Essays on the Postscript to 'The Concept of Law'* (Oxford University Press 2001) 59–98.

various forms of deterrence and police enforcement are. The liberty to engage in patterns of social interaction is very much unlike the liberty to commit a crime, since it is normatively salient: it is the liberty to engage in conduct while having the right to use the state's enforcement machinery in one's favour if need be.

If this picture of legal practice is correct, then it raises doubts about Young's reductive approach to law. Young takes patterns of social interaction to be a constitutive element of the wrong of structural injustice, but these patterns are all protected institutionally by law. In that sense, law is not merely a fraction of the structures that generate injustice, as Young claims, but permeates these structures. I do not mean that the law plays a dominant *causal* role with respect to these structures, since it is hard to make sense of a purely causal relation between collective patterns of behaviour and individual vulnerability. Indeed, we should note here that in her discussion, Young singles out specific groups of actors (such as employers, landlords and estate agents), whose actions contribute to structural injustice, and ignores others (such as parents), whose actions or omissions also causally affect where Sandy ends up. This suggests that some patterns of social interaction matter morally more than others, even if their causal link to vulnerability is equally strong. For example, I do not think we should count among the patterns that contributed to Sandy's vulnerability the fact that her parents could have put pressure on her to earn higher job qualifications or have instilled in her a career ambition yet did not. The liberty of landlords to evict tenants does not seem on a par with the liberty of parents to raise their children as they see fit.[7]

In any case, what I have in mind is a normative, rather than a causal relation between law and structural injustice: law makes a normative difference as to what *counts* as structural injustice. Consider all the actors that Young singles out with respect to Sandy's vulnerability. If their conduct was illegal, and they nevertheless engaged in it, then that would no doubt be a serious problem, but it would not be a problem of structural injustice. Suppose that Sandy had a legal right not to be evicted, a legal right to affordable housing and a legal right not to be dismissed. Yet all the relevant agents behaved in the way Young describes, resulting in Sandy's homelessness. We would not, in that case, describe her as a victim

7 I am not sure if Young would exclude from the relevant structures the behaviour of parents, not only Sandy's but the parents of all the people against whom she competes in the labour market. She might not, treating parental practices as part of the structures that contribute to vulnerability. The point is that some patterns of behaviour are clearly less relevant, even if they are causally efficacious, because of a prior judgement that we are not collectively responsible for changing these patterns.

of structural injustice, but rather as a victim of several legal wrongs for which she would be entitled to remedies. She would be able to go to court and get a court order against all the legal wrongdoers, forcing them to act accordingly. And if Sandy were to choose not to exercise her legal rights, even though she was aware of them and could have done so,[8] then she would hardly qualify as a victim of structural injustice, even if she were to end up homeless.

One may object here, following Young's line of thought, that the wrong of structural injustice is not just the result of the actions of specific individuals who interacted with Sandy, such as her employer or her landlord, but all the people who own houses, or who work in the area. For instance, if it had not been the case that lots of people moved into her area, pushing prices and job competition up, then Sandy would not be struggling to find affordable housing or decent employment. But she cannot file a lawsuit against the thousands of people whose individual decisions had the cumulative effect of making her vulnerable to homelessness, through changing the ratio of demand and supply. Moreover, there seems to be nothing wrong with people moving to different areas and seeking housing and employment there. On the contrary, there would be something amiss if freedom of movement within a country was not legally guaranteed.

All that the objection reveals, however, is the interconnectedness between the legal position of Sandy and that of all these other actors. The legal right to own real estate, and to rent it out to make a profit in the property market, is what makes possible the legal position of a tenant as well as the legal position of a homeless person. We would not normally call homeless someone who owns property yet chooses to sleep rough or, like George Orwell,[9] lives in destitution to collect materials for one's book.[10] Homelessness, in its central case, involves lack of ownership, or

8 I set aside some important complications here, such as whether people like Sandy would be aware of their legal rights and could afford a lawyer, or whether courts would hear her claim in due course and award remedies, without any discrimination. Such problems are structural in a different sense, relating to institutional inadequacies with respect to the value of rule of law. Any injustice with respect to that value would be directly committed by the relevant institution (for example, the court) and would not be the result of *citizens'* patterns of behaviour. It is not clear that phenomena such as institutional racism count as structural injustices. For a view that it would be wrong to identify structural injustice with institutional injustice see Sally Haslanger, 'Systemic and Structural Injustice: Is There a Difference?' (2022) 98(1) Philosophy 1. See also Lea Ypi's contribution to this volume.

9 See George Orwell's memoir, *Down and Out in Paris and London* (Penguin Classics 2013). Thank you to Jonathan Wolff for the reference.

10 We might though use the term in case of a natural disaster when people are temporarily unable to occupy the house that they own or rent. But it seems to me clear that the homelessness of communities struck by natural disasters is not the same kind of injustice that Young finds in Sandy's case.

other legal rights over real estate, such as tenancy. It is the flipside of being a homeowner or a tenant.[11] It is not a purely factual notion. Sandy's position as a person vulnerable to homelessness is in part constituted, normatively and not just descriptively, by the legal rights of thousands of other people who have and exercise legal rights over real property. And those rights exist in virtue of the decisions of public institutions regarding which property rights should be given protection through collective force. Homelessness, in other words, is a *legal* or *juridical* condition.[12]

In discussing the case of Sandy, Young assumes that background policies around employment and housing are not unjust. But we can now see that this might be too quick. If Sandy's homelessness is in part constituted by there being background legal rights to real property, then the statement that her homelessness is unjust presupposes the injustice of these rights. These background legal rights could be specified or qualified in different ways so as to mitigate or extinguish the known risk of homelessness on the part of those who are not homeowners. For example, the legal right to real property could be limited to residential use and exclude commercial exploitation (so called 'buy-to-lets'). Likewise, the state could implement a scheme of universal public housing, like that used in Sweden, where public housing companies own a very large stock of good-quality housing, which they make available for rent to the public at a low rental cost for as long as they wish. Universal housing schemes reduce incentives to buy and own property and by so doing, reduce the size of a residential property market, thus preventing fluctuations in supply and demand from affecting housing affordability.[13] Less drastic qualifications to legal rights would include the right not to be evicted or the right against disproportionate or arbitrary rent increases (rent control), which are used in many states. The point here is not merely that law could marginally improve on the justice scale by qualifying property rights in these ways. Rather, it is that granting unqualified legal rights

11 This point is emphasised by Marxist theories of law, which treat law as a means through which the underlying structure of economic relations is sustained. But we do not need to assume an instrumental approach, as Marxist theories of law do, in order to hold that economic relations cannot be understood independently of legal relations.
12 See also the discussion in Jeremy Waldron, 'Homelessness and the Issue of Freedom' in Jeremy Waldron, *Liberal Rights* (Cambridge University Press 1993).
13 For a critical account of Sweden's universal housing scheme, see Martin Grander, 'New Public Housing: A Selective Model Disguised as Universal? Implications of the Market Adaptation of Swedish Public Housing' (2017) 17(3) International Journal of Housing Policy 335. Similarly, states can reduce incentives to buy private health insurance, by having a public healthcare system that is free (or affordable) and provides good quality care.

over real property, given the known risk that this poses to people like Sandy, *itself* constitutes the injustice of the resulting vulnerability.

The preceding remarks point to another important dimension of the relation between law and structural injustice. The very judgement that Sandy is the victim of structural injustice necessarily implies that large parts of the law (such as property law, employment law, corporate law, bankruptcy law and tax law) are problematic from the point of view of justice. This is because the legal rights of landlords and employers are in turn dependent on further rights found in other areas of law. For example, most employers are corporations, whose financial viability depends on favourable legal rules around taxation, investment and bankruptcy. The bargaining power they have over employers is partly constituted by having these rights. What I think Young's account overlooks is that we cannot claim that Sandy is the victim of structural injustice without presupposing a claim about the injustice of the background scheme of legal rights. A claim that someone is the victim of structural injustice necessarily implies both an interpretation and a critique of existing law.[14]

This further raises the question of whether (and if so, how) the existing scheme of legal rights and duties can be rearranged so as to remove the injustice that Sandy suffers without at the same time inflicting injustice on others. I suggested earlier that granting tenants and employees a protected legal status is one way in which the law can improve the legal relation between Sandy and other actors. But granting tenants unqualified protection from eviction might negatively affect a poor landlord for whom the modest rent they charge is the only source of income. Similarly, granting employees protection from dismissal might negatively affect a struggling family-run business with little bargaining power. Any rearrangement of legal rights and duties must take into account new risks that this might create. The issue then becomes one about the fairness of the scheme of legal rights as a whole: is it fair to shift risks from Sandy to these other individuals? Are there other rights in law whose effect is to mitigate the vulnerability of these other individuals? Will a shifting of the risk to others impact people like Sandy in ways that are even worse than the risk of homelessness?

We can see immediately, that on this new emerging picture, the focus shifts from the plight of Sandy to the broader question of whether law

14 For how the application of particular legal rules results in structural injustices against workers, see Virginia Mantouvalou, *Structural Injustice and Workers Rights* (Oxford University Press 2023). For a general argument that law systematically creates patterns of inequality, albeit in a rather different sense to mine, see Katharina Pistor, *The Code of Capital* (Princeton University Press 2019).

allocates risks across different persons *fairly or justly*. And this question is different from asking what policies would be ideally just starting from scratch. Suppose, for instance, that ideal justice requires a scheme of public housing, similar to the Swedish one, which eradicates a market for residential housing. That would not make it fair for the governments of countries that lack this scheme to expropriate overnight the real property of everyone without compensation. People would have made choices (for example, work hard to make savings, or undertake certain risks) in their lives under the reasonable expectation that the law guarantees property rights over real estate. What is needed, therefore, is not an isolated judgement about Sandy's position but a more general judgement about the comparative fairness of one scheme of legal rights over another, given the history of a given legal system. It may be, for instance, that the fairest reconfiguration is to make Sandy's legal right not to be evicted conditional upon several factors, such as whether the use of the property is purely residential, whether the landlord is a corporate entity, whether she faces an imminent risk of homelessness and many others. Lawyers are well aware of the need to tailor the justificatory rationale for granting a legal right to the circumstances of each case and urge caution about unqualified statements about what legal rights people have. For instance, there is no unqualified legal right to decent living conditions, but asylum seekers do have a legal right to not be left in conditions of destitution while their application for asylum is pending.[15]

The resulting picture is one where law, understood as a complex scheme of interdependent rights backed up by collective force, is itself a social structure and very significant one at that. Political philosophers might be surprised by this assertion. Ever since John Rawls's claim that principles of justice regulate the basic structure of society,[16] political philosophers have been concerned with the question of which institutions and practices fall within the basic structure and which do not. Rawls himself included in the basic structure a number of social and political institutions (such as the family) alongside legal ones (such as a 'political constitution with an independent judiciary')[17] while at the same excluding certain areas of law (such as contract law)[18] from the basic structure. Although he used the term 'structure' in a different sense to Young, both

15 See *MSS v Belgium and Greece*, App No 30696/09, Grand Chamber Judgment of 21 January 2011.
16 John Rawls, *A Theory of Justice* (Harvard University Press 1971) 54.
17 John Rawls, *Justice as Fairness: A Restatement* (Harvard University Press 2001) 53.
18 John Rawls, *Political Liberalism* (Columbia University Press 1993) 269 ff.

treat law in a positivistic way, as one institutional entity amongst many, and one that is not entirely governed by principles of social justice. The approach I propose, instead, takes law more seriously, treating it as the baseline against which judgements about structural injustice must be evaluated.[19]

Nevertheless, the juridical nature of social structures, as I have presented it, retains one of Young's main insights, which is that we are collectively responsible for any injustice they generate. I think this is so in two related ways. The first is that collective force is ultimately licensed by public officials (mainly courts) who decide, following a lawsuit or a prosecution, which patterns to protect and which to frustrate. These public officials act in the name of the law and have the responsibility of exercising their power in a way that respects everyone's standing as a free and equal person. The second, equally important way, is that every legal subject will inevitably avail themselves of the protection of the law in one way or another. They might report criminal conduct to the police, from nuisance by a neighbour to a mugging; they might sue for damages following a tort or a breach of contract, or they might simply threaten to do so; most commonly, they will engage in mundane tasks (such as entering their house and closing the door) safe in the knowledge that it will be illegal for others to interfere with them. Since all of us, in different ways and to varying degrees, receive the benefit of legal enforcement, we are collectively responsible for the scheme of rights that it protects. At a minimum this supports the familiar political obligation to take political action (for example, through voting in elections) to reform, or abolish unjust laws. But it also supports a duty to conceive of one's *own* legal rights in a way that makes the community's overall scheme of legal rights as just and fair as possible across persons. As is widely known, one's legal position on any given interaction is routinely a matter of interpretation, even if there is relevant legislation. As an intentional action, legislation is by nature sporadic, covering only certain types of actions and envisaging only certain types of risks and consequences associated with these actions. We might assume, for instance, that no legislator ever contemplated that Sandy should become homeless as a result of all the factors that Young highlights. The citizen, just like the court, must exercise an evaluative judgement about which interpretation makes the scheme of enforceable

19 Lawrence Sager has argued that certain structural injustices, such as institutional racism, though unconstitutional, exceed the bounds of judicial enforcement and bind institutions and individuals more broadly. See Lawrence Sager, 'Imperfect Duties and Structural Injustice' (on file with author).

rights as just as possible.[20] For instance, if the best interpretation of the existing scheme of property rights over real estate is that tenants who are likely to be left homeless have a right not to be evicted, then landlords have a duty (both moral and legal) not to evict. They have this duty even before the court decides the matter in favour of tenants (as it must do) and even if tenants never go to court.

A closer look at law's model of liability

Young's first assumption is that law employs an individualist model of responsibility, which fails to engage our collective responsibility for matters of social justice. There is an implicit contrast here between private and criminal law on the one hand, which focuses on wrongs committed between two individual parties, and social justice, which focuses on how burdens and benefits are distributed across persons. This, however, seems to me a distorted account of how legal responsibility works, and I want to highlight ways in which this assumption has been challenged in general jurisprudence. As I argued already, assigning legal liability to an agent for a given harm, or risk of harm, should itself be seen as a collective exercise, for which all citizens bear responsibility. For example, a legal system can hold individuals accountable for a given wrong, such as marital rape, forcing them to suffer sanctions, or pay damages, in the name of the community; or it can license them to engage in that wrong, as English law did in respect of marital rape until 1991,[21] forcing the rest of us to abstain from interfering with the activity. Whichever way the law does things, it has genuine normative implications for all of us and therefore, we are all responsible for which claims law backs up with its coercive apparatus. Admittedly, there is little each one of us can do individually to change the legal structure and the primary burden falls on government officials, particularly the legislature and the courts. But officials act in the name of the community, that is, in the name of us all. And at least in democratic regimes, citizens are directly responsible for how officials exercise their power to enforce a scheme of legal rights.

My point here is that the collective dimension of the responsibility for structural injustice, which Young emphasises, pertains to the scheme

20 I here follow Ronald Dworkin's view that the practice of law is governed by the value of integrity, which is a dimension of the value of justice. See Ronald Dworkin, *Law's Empire* (reprint edn, Belknap Press 1988).
21 See the judgment of *R v R* [1991] UKHL 12, in which the House of Lords overturned centuries of case-law and held that there is no marital rape exemption in English law.

of legal rights that is institutionally enforced, rather than the action of each one of us taken together. I take this point to be perfectly in line with the spirit of Young's account and one that she would have little reason to resist. My proposal is to try to understand the role of law in a way that reinforces her insights.

It is important to point out further that an account of collective responsibility for justice is often necessary in order to figure *what it is* in the first place that the law allows, or prohibits given the inherent uncertainty of legal materials (be they statute or precedent). It is not clear, for example, whether the abstract legal right to property includes the right to extend one's house, the right to prevent others from blocking one's view, or the right not to have it expropriated by a government that wants to demolish it to build affordable housing. Principles of social justice appear necessary to decide how far the right to property extends. This is typically done, for instance, through the judicial interpretation of the test of reasonableness.[22]

Young is certainly right that the legal model of responsibility results in some individual(s) being held legally responsible for some harm. It is individualist in its *output*. But that does not entail that the normative principles that justify why a particular individual should be held liable must necessarily be principles governing episodic interactions and the responsibilities of the individuals involved. They can also be principles of social justice, whose subject-matter is not the interaction between two given individuals, but a fair allocation of burdens and benefits across persons. Hence, the legal model of responsibility need not be individualist in its *input*. If the property right to my house, for example, does not extend to the right to prevent the government from expropriating it to build affordable housing, then this must be because this is the fair, or egalitarian way to allocate property rights collectively.

Young attributes to law what she calls a liability model of responsibility, according to which a person is responsible when they are blameworthy for an act or an outcome. She includes in that model cases of strict liability, where no fault is required, such as the case of employer's liability. What she thinks is distinctive about the legal model of responsibility is that law seeks to identify a liable agent whose position (say an employer) or actions/omissions (say a tortfeasor) bear a causal connection to a cognisable harm. The idea of structural injustice, by contrast, concerns wrongs which are not caused by any single individual

22 See on this Dworkin (n 20), Chapter 8.

or group of individuals, but are instead the result of complex patterns of social interaction. It is this claim about causation that sets Young on a path to shift the emphasis away from law and onto collective responsibility. The former, she argues, is backward-looking, whereas the latter is forward-looking. More specifically, Young makes the following assumption: since law holds some determinate agent(s) as causally responsible for some harm, then the law's model of responsibility is individual and backward-looking. Responsibility for structural injustice, by contrast, is collective and forward-looking.

Young's assumption, however, has been widely contested in jurisprudence. The best example is the law and economics movement.[23] The economic analysis of law holds that the question of who caused a cognisable harm turns on the more fundamental question of who, as a matter of a utilitarian theory of social justice, should bear the cost of that harm. It holds, for instance, that people should conduct themselves in ways that impose the least financial cost on the community and that we collectively, through courts, should assign legal liability with a view to encouraging that conduct prospectively. The economic analysis of legal liability is both collective and forward-looking. It claims moreover, not only that this is how law should do things from a normative point of view, but also – crucially – that this is the most accurate description of legal doctrine as it exists *already*. Decades of law and economics literature have sought to show that the way law assigns liability tracks the value of efficiency and has nothing to do with rights-based arguments about individual responsibility.

It is possible, of course, to deny that legal liability should ever turn on principles of social justice, be they utilitarian or otherwise. There is a long-standing debate within private law theory about whether tortious and contractual liability are grounded on principles of corrective justice or whether, instead, they are grounded on distributive justice.[24] Much of that debate assumes that it is either one or the other, but the more plausible view is that the determinants of legal liability contain both

23 See, for example, Richard Posner, *Economic Analysis of Law* (Little Brown, 1973); Richard Posner, 'The Ethical And Political Basis of the Efficiency Norm in Common Law Adjudication' (1980) 8 Hofstra Law Review 487–598; Louis Kaplow and Steven Shavell, 'Fairness versus Welfare' (2001) 114 Harvard Law Review 961–1388.

24 See, for example, Stephen Perry, 'On the Relationship between Corrective Justice and Distributive Justice' in Horder (ed), *Oxford Essays in Jurisprudence* (Oxford University Press 2000) 237; William Lucy, *Philosophy of Private Law* (Oxford University Press 2006); Jules Coleman, *Risks and Wrongs* (Oxford University Press 2002); Samuel Scheffler, 'Distributive Justice, the Basic Structure and the Place of Private Law'(2015) 35(2) Oxford Journal of Legal Studies 213.

elements. The law of contract cannot adequately be explained without presupposing that promising creates *pro tanto* obligations and that the breach of those obligations is sometimes sufficient for the law to hold the promisor liable. But promissory principles on their own cannot account for vast areas of contract law such as the doctrines of consideration, intention to create legal relations, expectation damages and mitigation.[25]

For example, it is not clear how principles of interpersonal morality can explain why the law does not usually force promisors who breach their contract to perform but instead, requires them to pay expectation damages.[26] In order to explain this feature of contract law, we have to make a number of normative assumptions: that a market economy is in principle justifiable, that most of us rely on the market to buy and sell goods and services, that markets provide easily accessible substitutes for most goods and services, that it is in the interests of most of us to pay damages rather than having to perform broken promises, that it is unfair to force promisors to perform when promisees can easily get an equivalent substitute from the market and so on.[27] These assumptions relate to the question of how we should collectively allocate the burdens and benefits of market-based exchanges in a fair or egalitarian way, rather than how to regulate episodic interactions between a promisor and a promisee. This is even more evident in specific categories of contracts, such as consumer contracts. The economic power of manufacturers within a market economy makes the position of consumers vulnerable in several ways. Consumer law allocates contractual liabilities with a view to balance this asymmetry in social positions and make consumer transactions more fair.

The problem therefore with the economic analysis of law, in so far as there is one, is not that it allows principles of social justice to determine legal liability, but of a different kind altogether. One objection, for instance, is that the economic analysis allows the wrong moral principles, such as efficiency, to determine legal liability and that other, non-utilitarian, conceptions of distributive equality are required to do the normative work. Another objection is that any theory of distributive justice must also make some space for a permissive attitude on the part

25 See George Letsas and Prince Saprai, 'Contract Law without Foundations' (2018) SSRN <https://papers.ssrn.com/sol3/papers.cfm?abstract_id=3211283> accessed 13 October 2023.

26 This has triggered a debate about whether contract law diverges from promissory morality and whether that is a good or a bad thing. See Charles Fried, 'The Convergence of Contract and Promise' (2007) 120 Harv. L. Rev 708 and Seana Valentine Shiffrin, 'The Divergence of Contract and Promise' (2007) 120 Harv. L. Rev 708.

27 This is the position followed by Anglo-American contract law. Other legal systems might strike a different balance between the principle of fairness and other competing considerations.

of individuals, where they have a right to pursue their own projects, free from the demands of others. A utilitarian account of legal liability does not recognise the intrinsic importance of individual autonomy and rights. It forces wrongdoers to compensate right-holders only if efficiency requires it to do so. These are familiar objections to utilitarian accounts of law, but they are retail, rather than wholesale. They draw our attention to the fact that attribution of legal liability, much like a complete theory of justice, contains elements of both distributive justice and individual autonomy. Any normative assessment of the shape of our laws must look at how any given legal system balances concerns about individuals' personal autonomy (for example, their right to pursue their own projects, which must include a degree of contractual and proprietary freedoms) and concerns about the equal or fair distribution of the resources that we command collectively. Hence, when a landlord has a legal right to evict a tenant, it is not simply an exercise of interpersonal rights. Government officials back the landlord's eviction by giving landlords the power to go to court, get an eviction order and get bailiffs physically to evict the tenant, should she refuse to do so. Whether, morally speaking, eviction laws are justified is a matter of whether the currently enforced scheme of property rights respects both the value of distributive equality and the value of personal autonomy.

Once again, all this shows that we must not be too quick to assume, as Young's account appears to, that US law on property and employment is generally fair and just. It is true that some degree of proprietary freedom, particularly over personal belongings and movable objects, is necessary in order to allow people to pursue autonomously their own projects and plans of life. But should that be extended to developers and other landlords who seek to make a profit from a commodified property market? It is not obvious that this should be the case. In many European countries, there is a long tradition of regulating rental properties with a view to strengthening the position of tenants. This includes not just rent control, but also long statutory lengths of tenancy agreements that only the tenant can break, and prohibition of eviction except where the landlord is moving into the property as their primary residence. This is because, in heavily commodified property markets, tenants become severely disadvantaged in ways that are clearly incompatible with an egalitarian theory of distributive justice. The legal right to property is therefore an umbrella term, whose precise scope is governed by a mix of principles of personal autonomy and distributive justice.

Any theory of distributive justice must accommodate a sphere of liberty to pursue one's projects, which includes the right to own personal property, such as one's books and clothes. Arguably, it should accommodate the right to own one's home, at least in the sense of the right of secured tenancy. But it is not obvious why it should allow landlords' business interests in rental property to prevail over tenants' interest in having a home. Landlords' interests are not grounded on rights-based considerations of personal autonomy, and they are in tension with the demands of egalitarian theories of social justice. This is particularly the case in countries where there is no welfare state providing adequate social housing to everyone who needs it.

Similar observations apply to childcare and employment. Sandy is a single mother, with two kids, who cannot afford to live near her job and must drive a long distance. The law could impose on employers a duty to share part of the employees' childcare costs, in the same way it does with healthcare (the rest of it being subsidised by the government). This would not only keep the costs of childcare low but also enable employees to take up new employment and work standard office hours, without the uncertainty that childcare arrangements cause.

Would Sandy be equally vulnerable to homelessness if she had a legal right not to be evicted, a legal right to rent control and a legal right to have her employer cover part of her childcare costs? I do not think she would. I do not mean this as a prediction or a hypothesis about how social facts would play out if legal facts were different. Whether any single measure, such as rent control laws, reduces the risk of homelessness is an empirical question that might be difficult to answer.[28] Moreover, rent control laws may have unintended consequences, such as reducing the number of affordable properties available, and law would have to tackle these too, once they become known. My point is that we know full well that tenants, single parents and employees occupy social positions that make them vulnerable to outcomes that are incompatible with an egalitarian theory of distributive justice. Taken this social fact as a given, it is unjust to enforce collectively a scheme of legal rights that completely ignores it and lets the vulnerability lie where it falls.[29] We can make sense of this injustice even if, say through sheer fortune, Sandy does not end up homeless. Contrariwise, I doubt that our sense of injustice would be the same if Sandy had all these legal rights but ended up homeless due to contingent factors, such as a breakdown in her relationship that triggered

28 See Paul W Grimes and George A Chressanthis, 'Assessing the Effect of Rent Control on Homelessness' (1997) 41 Journal of Urban Economics 23.

29 For the many ways in which legal institutions are responsible for homelessness, see Beth Watts-Cobbe and Lynne McMordie, 'Structural Injustice, Homelessness and the Law', in this volume.

mental health issues. What scheme of rights the law enforces is, in my view, relevant to the question of which vulnerabilities count as matters of structural injustice. A legal system that acknowledges the vulnerable position of tenants, single parents and employees and seeks to mitigate it, is more just to Sandy, even if we do not know how effective the mitigation will be in her case. This legally mediated notion of vulnerability, I want to suggest, is the one that primarily matters to judgements of collective responsibility for structural injustice.

If this is correct, then it is wrong to suggest that law has a small part to play in all of this. One could describe the relevant legal framework as a neutral baseline that lets everyone exercise their rights, the exercise of which results in structural injustice for Sandy. But this is a very misleading description. By allowing landlords, estate agents and employers to exercise their legal rights against Sandy, we collectively make her vulnerable to homelessness. And by restricting the contractual freedom of employers, landlords or manufacturers, we collectively can distribute resources in a fairer and more egalitarian way.

It might be objected at this stage that I am making a utopian argument about how the law should be. But this is far from the case. These issues arise also when we ask what the law *already* is. Law commonly uses abstract tests for assigning legal liability, such as reasonableness, fairness, arbitrariness, due care, proportionality and so on. Courts decide who is liable by constructing, implicitly or explicitly, general theories of liability. A human rights court, for instance, may be called upon to decide the legal question of whether eviction legislation violates the tenant's human right to a home under the European Convention on Human Rights. It might rule that the state has the positive obligation, under law, to take legislative action that frustrates patterns of behaviour that have rendered the claimant vulnerable to an injustice.[30] In doing so, courts rely inevitably on normative assumptions about what is a fair or egalitarian allocation of burdens and benefits within the community.

This is also reflected in how the test of causation works in law. Causation is not just 'in-fact' causation, seeking to determine in a morally neutral manner which agents acted in a way that empirically brought about a harm. Causation in law is a moralised test. Law infuses the test of causation with normative assumption about which agents *ought* to bear the cost of a given harm. The legal doctrines of strict liability, vicarious

30 See, for example, the European Court of Human Rights judgment of *Siliadin v France*, App No. 73316/01, Judgment of 26 July 2005.

liability, market-share liability, liability for omissions – all pin liability on an actor in part because this is a fair or just way to distribute collectively burdens and benefits. It is wrong to think of causation as a neutral condition for liability, which necessarily ties responsibility to individual agents. The point here is not that some agents may be held legally liable even though they may not have caused a harm. The point is stronger: the question of whether an agent has *caused* a harm cannot be divorced from the question of what is, collectively, a fair way to assign legal liability. Sometimes, as in the case of negligent driving, it is by holding an individual liable under principles of interpersonal morality alone. Other times, as in the case of employer or manufacturer liability, it is by applying principles of social justice, or a mix of both.

Methodologically, Young's account of legal liability seems lopsided. It begins by focusing on a given harmful outcome (Sandy's homelessness) and works backwards, trying to identify responsible individuals who have caused the harm and should be blamed for it. As US law (and most jurisdictions) does not hold anyone liable for Sandy's homelessness ('everyone acted within their rights'), then law is inadequate to capture the relevant wrong because *all* of us have caused it. But this is the wrong place to start. Our normative assessment should start much earlier, before any harm occurs, and look at the way we collectively, through the legislative framework, allocate risk. Does the legal baseline allocate burdens and benefits around employment and housing in a fair way? Or does it let, for example, landlords, employers and estate agents act in ways that are unjustified from the point of view of social justice? If the latter, then landlords and employers are not off the moral hook. It may turn out that, interpretively, they have actually not acted within their legal rights.[31] Or maybe that they have acted within their legal rights (assuming that interpretively this is the case), but that the existing scheme of property rights requires radical reform. In neither case are they off the moral hook. They are morally responsible for Sandy's vulnerability. But at the same time, we would also be collectively responsible for the fact that there is this discrepancy between the legal and the moral baseline.

That a normative assessment of structural injustice should not be outcome-oriented is clear I think from Young's own account. It is not the fact of homelessness itself that constitutes a structural injustice, but *how* it comes about. Let us suppose that a wealthy and well-educated business

31 Lawyers may advise Sandy that she has no case under American law, but law is full of cases, such as *R v R* [1991] UKHL 12, where a court finds that the standard interpretation of an area of law is incompatible with its underlying values.

owner, Randy, goes bankrupt because of reckless risks taken and a lavish lifestyle. He is a particularly mean and unpleasant character and nobody in his social circle or family is willing to offer him a helping hand. He gets addicted to expensive drugs, and being unwilling to take up mundane employment, ends up homeless. Randy's case is rare, but nevertheless serves as a significant contrast to Sandy's. Young's notion of structural injustice does not apply to Randy, because he does not occupy a social position that makes its occupiers *unfairly* vulnerable to homelessness. In fact, it is not even clear whether Randy's case qualifies as an injustice in the first place. But even if it is, it is surely not a case of *structural* injustice. Arguably we collectively have a duty to make it the case that everyone – including Randy – has a roof over their head, irrespective of how they ended up homeless. But this duty is different to the duty we owe Sandy. Sandy is rendered vulnerable to homelessness because of the social position she occupies, and that social position is the product of an unjust distribution of legal rights over real estate.

The picture that emerges from the preceding discussion is one that retains many of the insights of Young's account: we are indeed collectively responsible for Sandy's homelessness. But we are responsible not in a causal sense (because we all acted in ways that brought about a harm) but because we are collectively responsible for how law allocates risks and benefits, through its coercive apparatus. And the claim that Sandy has suffered a structural injustice is an implicit claim that the legal baseline allocates risks in a way that is unjustified from the standpoint of a theory of social justice, a standpoint that includes both distributive and non-distributive elements. Law, therefore, is not simply part of the causal mechanism that results in Sandy's homelessness. It is the baseline against which to judge whether we collectively have inflicted an injustice on Sandy.

I am aware that the view that social relations are inherently juridical may come across as a self-aggrandising claim on behalf of law, and one to which lawyers are particularly likely to be attracted. But I should like to point out that it follows an important Kantian tradition in moral and political philosophy, which begins with the assumption that the state's organised force is both necessary and justified and asks when the use of that force against one another is legitimate.[32] According to this tradition, we can only understand notions such as rights and wrongs within

32 This tradition is nowadays best expressed and defended in the work of Arthur Ripstein. See Arthur Ripstein, *Force and Freedom* (Harvard University Press 2009). As Ripstein emphasises, this tradition holds that the state's claim to authority is inseparable from the rationale for coercion.

the context of coercive institutions with the power to use force. Much contemporary political philosophy, by contrast, treats the issue of state coercion as secondary, concerning when it is permissible to force people to do what – coercion aside – it is right for them to do. For those who reject this approach however, and are attracted to the Kantian view, the claim that Sandy has suffered an injustice cannot be divorced from the juridical question of how coercion is used to distribute rights and duties to citizens.

What can law do for Sandy? The example of legal status

I want to conclude with a brief illustration of how law can have a more prominent role to play in helping us to think about the problem of structural injustice. Much of the pessimism about whether law can address structural injustice stems from an outcome-oriented focus on liability for an occurred harm. We must shift this focus. Law does not only impose liabilities for a harm. It often imposes prophylactic duties and rights, when no harm has yet occurred. The duty not to evict tenants, the duty not to dismiss employees unfairly, or the duty of non-refoulement of refugees are not about trying to pin liability for a given harm on someone. Their point is to create a scheme of enforceable legal rights that allocates risks fairly.

One distinctive way in which the law does this is by recognising legal statuses (such as the status of an employee, a tenant, a refugee, or an insolvent person) for social positions that, as a matter of wide public knowledge, are arbitrarily vulnerable.[33] The point of legal status is to bundle together a set of rights and duties whose aim is to make asymmetrical social interactions fair and equal, under a background theory of social justice. Law has always recognised that certain social positions systematically and arbitrarily disadvantage their occupiers and that the legal baseline can either *reinforce*, *ignore* or *mitigate* this disadvantage.[34] In ancient times, legal status was used to reinforce

33 I have developed this account of status in greater detail in George Letsas, 'Offences Against Status' (2023) 43(2) Oxford Journal of Legal Studies 322–349.

34 Jeremy Bentham is perhaps the first philosopher to point out that the law can either exacerbate the inequality of a social interaction or mitigate it. He argued that when law does the former, the vulnerable party is called a 'servant' and the powerful party is called a 'master'. But when law does the latter, the vulnerable party is called a 'ward' and the powerful party is called a 'guardian'. See Jeremy Bentham, *The Collected Works of Jeremy Bentham: An Introduction to the Principles of Morals and Legislation* (Clarendon Press 1996), 238.

asymmetrical social relations (such as between landowners and workers), through the legal statuses of slaves and masters. But law can instead balance the asymmetry found in many social interactions through the status of an employee, a tenant, a parent, a bankrupt, and so on. When law ignores social positions that cause arbitrary vulnerability, the solution is not to shift the emphasis away from law, but to create more and better protected legal statuses.

Legal status, as a normative device employed by law, vests the occupiers of such social positions with a set of institutional rights and entitlements, whose aim is to mitigate the relevant vulnerabilities. It addresses the problem of structural injustice, not by holding someone liable for when harm occurs, but prophylactically, by imposing heightened duties of care on others and by shifting the relevant risks. When law does so successfully, it creates a moral baseline against which we can assess whether pernicious social structures amount to an injustice. If US law properly recognised and protected the statuses of an employee, of a tenant and of a parent, as many countries in Europe do for example, Sandy would not face the vulnerabilities that Young identifies. That is not to say of course that she might not end up homeless. But having these legal statuses would have made a massive difference to Sandy. First, she would be able to seek remedies through courts and reduce the likelihood of homelessness. Second, having these legal statuses would have an expressive function, communicating publicly that she occupies – unfairly – a vulnerable social position. This, in turn, would put relevant classes of actors (such as estate agents, job agencies and employers) on notice that they must interpret their own legal rights in light of Sandy's vulnerability, and act accordingly. Finally, Sandy and others in her social position would be able to campaign politically for strengthening legislatively the existing legal statuses. This is likely to be way more effective than campaigning to tackle homelessness when the risks to the relevant social positions that people like Sandy occupy have already materialised.

The notion of legal status crystallises the point made earlier; that homelessness and joblessness are legal and not just social conditions. If the scheme of rights that we collectively enforce recognises and protects the rights of landlords/homeowners and employers, it should also recognise rights for tenants and employees, rights which fairly allocate the relevant risks and vulnerabilities in the relevant social interaction. Sandy is not someone who suffered an injustice because of an indeterminate number of permissible actions taken by an indeterminate number of persons. She suffered an injustice because her status as a tenant, as an employee and as a single parent was not properly recognised and protected by law.

4

The law's contribution to deliberate structural injustice: the case of the global garment industry

Maeve McKeown

Introduction

The idea that structural injustice is always the unintended outcome of cumulative social, economic and political processes is implausible. Powerful agents sometimes deliberately manipulate and perpetuate structural injustice because they benefit from it, and sometimes there are powerful agents with the capacity to alleviate the injustice but fail to do it. Studying the law provides insight into these cases. In this chapter, I focus on the deliberate structural injustice of sweatshop labour. Powerful players in this field – predominantly the USA, the EU, Japan and their corporations – have manipulated and used legal mechanisms in order to entrench their dominance and further their own interests to the detriment of sweatshop workers and garment-exporting countries. If the law is the 'code of capital,' these agents are experts in manipulating the code.[1]

In the first section, I will briefly outline the three types of structural injustice – pure, avoidable and deliberate. Then I will explain the law's contribution to these forms of structural injustice and explain why sweatshop labour is a structural injustice. Next, I will demonstrate how international law has been deployed by powerful agents to deliberately perpetuate this injustice. I will then outline two positive uses of the law to benefit workers and poor countries: joint liability initiatives and an

1 Katharina Pistor, *The Code of Capital: How the Law Creates Wealth and Inequality* (Princeton University Press 2019).

example of a positive bi-lateral trade agreement – the US-Cambodia Textile Agreement (1999–2005). Throughout this chapter, I will demonstrate that the law is a background condition of the global garment industry and that it can be changed. By the end of this chapter, there should be no doubt remaining that structural injustice can be deliberately maintained for the purposes of furthering the interests of powerful agents.

Pure, avoidable, deliberate structural injustice

The now classic definition of structural injustice was developed by Iris Marion Young in response to the pervasive domestic and transnational structural injustices that characterised the early twenty-first century.[2] She describes the structural injustice of housing deprivation as follows:

> … the all-too-common social position of being housing-deprived arises from the combination of actions and interactions of a large number of public and private individual and institutional actors, with different amounts of control over their circumstances and with varying ranges of options available to them. Most of these actors have their own perceived interests in view. While some do things that are individually wrong, such as break the law or deceive, or behave in ruthless ways towards others, many others try to be *law-abiding* and decent even as they try to pursue their own interests. The process nevertheless should be described as producing structural injustice, because in it some people's options are unfairly constrained and they are threatened with deprivation, while others derive significant benefits.[3]

I argue that what Young is describing here is 'pure structural injustice', meaning the injustice is, properly speaking, the result of the cumulative outcomes of lots of agents (for the most part) blamelessly pursuing their own interests. But housing deprivation does not quite meet that criterion. In the case of housing deprivation, there are actors who could do much

---

2 This section is a summary of another paper, 'Pure, Avoidable, and Deliberate Structural Injustice' in Jude Browne and Maeve McKeown (eds), *What is Structural Injustice?* (Oxford University Press 2024). In that chapter, and also in my monograph, *With Power Comes Responsibility: The Politics of Structural Injustice* (Bloomsbury Academic 2024), I explain the underlying cause for the issues with Young's conception of structural injustice, which is a confused social ontology that draws on two conflicting social ontologies – critical realism and structurationism. I show how critical realism provides insight into the role of power within structures.

3 Iris Marion Young, *Responsibility for Justice* (Oxford University Press 2011), 52 (my emphasis).

more to alleviate the injustice. The power of landlords to charge too-high rents that price working-class people out of the market is backed up by a social alignment including the government, courts and police. Young describes the behaviour of actors in property markets as 'law-abiding', when, in fact, the law is implicated in reproducing this injustice. Changes in housing policy or property law could significantly improve the relational position of tenants in housing markets.[4] Also, some landlords are in a position to choose to ignore market prices, but the vast majority choose to cash in.[5]

For these reasons, I consider housing deprivation to be an 'avoidable structural injustice'. In these cases, there are agents in positions of power that could change the unjust structures and fail to do so. In the case of housing deprivation, these agents are landlords and the government. The category of 'avoidable structural injustice' also calls into question the idea that structural injustice is an unintended consequence of social-structural processes. The outcomes may be unintended, but they are foreseeable and avoidable. The case of housing deprivation is well-documented and thoroughly researched, and there are available solutions. What is lacking is political will.

There is a third category of structural injustice – 'deliberate structural injustice'. In these cases, powerful agents recognise that there are groups who are disadvantaged by social structures, take advantage of that situation, deliberately reproduce the injustice and reap benefits by exploiting the disadvantaged. In cases of deliberate structural injustice, all agents are constrained, but powerful agents have enough room to manoeuvre to be able to change the situation. What distinguishes avoidable from deliberate structural injustice, however, is that not only do powerful agents have the capacity to change the situation, but they actively maintain it. So the consequences are not unintentional; they are intentional.

The role of law

What interests us here is Young's thought that the agents acting within social structures are trying to be 'law-abiding'. But what if the problem is the law itself? The law determines what agents can and cannot do, but it is also changeable. The role of the law, therefore, is crucial when

4 Matthew Desmond, *Evicted: Poverty and Profit in the American City* (Penguin Books 2016). See also Beth Watts-Cobbe and Lynne McMordie, 'Structural Injustice, Homelessness and the Law' (this volume).
5 Suzanne Bearne, '"We're Not All Terrible": The Landlords Who Keep Rents Low' *The Guardian* (London, 2022).

considering whether or not structural injustices are pure, avoidable or deliberate, and also in considering how they could be addressed (see 'Using the law for good' below). Young did not consider the possibility that the law has been created, maintained or manipulated to serve the interests of powerful actors within any particular social structure.

The call to examine law at state level seems fairly straightforward. For instance, legislation obviously plays a role in setting the rules of property ownership, buying and selling property, and laws that protect (or fail to protect) tenants. Young's claim that agents within these structures are 'law-abiding' begs questions about whether those laws are themselves just, whose interests they are serving, and what the state could do to change them.

But the same cannot be said at the global level when analysing a structural injustice like sweatshop labour, which crosses multiple legal jurisdictions and involves non-state actors, including actors to which international laws do not apply. Ordinarily it is assumed that the shape of global supply chains, or global value chains (GVCs), is the result of market processes. However, increasingly, this view is coming under scrutiny. As the Institute for Global Law and Policy and Global Production Working Group argues:

> ... placing law at the centre of the analysis of what have historically been treated as primarily 'economic structures' will not only enrich our understanding of the shape, nature and dynamic of GVCs, but will also help to illuminate the complex inter-relationship between law and global political economy more broadly.[6]

In fact, this group argues that one of the reasons why the law is often neglected in discussion of GVCs, is that 'it is generally treated as exogenous rather than an endogenous factor – an institutional backdrop against which the economic and inter-organisational dynamics driving the globalisation of production play out'.[7]

However, the point of Young's theory of structural injustice, and responsibility for it, was precisely to reveal the role of background conditions that are structurally unjust. If the law is one such background condition, then it is not sufficient to claim that background conditions are a mere outcome of cumulative processes that are beyond the control

6 The IGLP Law and Global Production Working Group, 'The Role of Law in Global Value Chains: A Research Manifesto' (2016) 4 London Review of International Law 57, 58.
7 ibid 60.

of any agents. Laws are created and shaped by agents, usually by a combination of more powerful and less powerful agents, with the more powerful shaping the laws in their interests. If this is true, then we can see that there is agency in the shaping of background conditions – the agency of the powerful. An examination, then, of any kind of structural injustice, be it deliberate, avoidable or pure, necessitates an understanding of the role of law in the creation and maintenance of the injustice. In cases of deliberate and avoidable structural injustice, the law may be an important factor in explaining why that structural injustice is avoidable or is being deliberately perpetuated, and thus what needs to change. The laws I will examine here in the global garment industry – international trade agreements – have been created by and for the powerful in their interests, and it is to that extent that I believe that sweatshop labour is a deliberate structural injustice. Now I will show why sweatshop labour qualifies as a structural injustice and in 'The law's contribution to sweatshop labour', I discuss how the law has been deployed to maintain it in the interests of powerful actors.

Sweatshop labour as structural injustice

In 1849, Charles Kingsley used the term 'sweatshop' to refer to labour outsourced to small shops or workers' homes where they were 'sweated' by a jobber (more on jobbers later).[8] Sweatshops hit international attention after a fire in the Triangle Shirtwaist Factory, New York, in 1911 in which 146 people (mostly young, women immigrants) died. Although 'sweatshop' has no fixed definition, sweatshops today are associated with poverty wages, poor working conditions, arbitrary discipline and restrictions on collective organising.

Sweatshops are also associated with the Global South. This is due to a profound shift in the capitalist economy in the 1960s–1970s, the period of decolonisation and the rise of globalisation and a new international division of labour. Industrial manufacturing almost exclusively took place in Western Europe, the USA and Japan until the 1970s; at this point, production relocated to Third World countries for at least four reasons.[9] First, with the dissolution of European empires, a huge reservoir of labour emerged that was under-educated, unskilled, poor and willing to work for very low wages under poor conditions. Second, the processes

8 Ashok Kumar, *Monopsony Capitalism: Power and Production in the Twilight of the Sweatshop Age* (Cambridge University Press 2020), 4.

9 Folker Fröbel, Jürgen Heinrichs and Otto Kreye, *The New International Division of Labour* (Cambridge University Press 1980) 13.

of production fragmented, so that the most basic processes require little skill; for instance, the lowest rung of the garment production chain is 'Cut Make and Trim' (CMT), where cutting involves cutting material to pre-designed patterns and trimming is adding trimmings like buttons or zips. Third, the development of transport and communications facilitated the globalisation of production processes, including the 'subcontracting' of deskilled labour across various locations. Fourth, there is a greater intensity of work among Third World workers because of few labour protections.

Globalisation saw Third World women, in particular, enter the labour market as a cheap, flexible and for the most part, un-unionised labour force. For instance, in 2006, there were Export Processing Zones (EPZs) in 130 countries, employing 66 million people, 70–80 per cent of whom were women.[10] Some of the reasons why women are employed in industrial manufacturing in sweatshops is because they learn sewing skills at home, so they do not need to be trained;[11] women are deemed to require lower wages because they are not the breadwinners;[12] and because employers prefer to hire women as they are seen as more docile and disciplined.[13]

As well as being associated with extremely low pay, poor working conditions, arbitrary discipline and restrictions on collective organising, sweatshops are also widely associated with human rights violations and child labour. Almost everyone can agree that human rights violations (such as physical and sexual abuse) and child labour are wrong. But not everyone agrees that sweatshops minus these egregious harms are wrong. Libertarians argue that sweatshops provide jobs to people who would otherwise not have them. On this view, sweatshop labour might be exploitative – because the surplus created from the labour of sweatshop workers is unfairly divided between corporations and the workers – but it is not *wrongfully* exploitative. The exploitation is mutually beneficial

10 Hye-Ryoung Kang, 'Transnational Women's Collectivities and Global Justice' in Alison M Jaggar (ed), *Gender and Global Justice* (Polity Press 2014) 43.

11 Diane Elson and Ruth Pearson, 'The Subordination of Women and the Internationalization of Factory Production' in Nalini Visvanathan, Lynn Duggan and Laurie Nisonoff (eds), *The Women, Gender and Development Reader* (2nd edn, Zed Books 2011); Maria Fernandez-Kelly, 'Maquiladoras: The View from the Inside' in Nalini Visvanathan and others (eds), *The Women, Gender and Development Reader* (Zed Books 2011).

12 Elson and Pearson (n 11) 96.

13 Lourdes Benería and Martha Roldán, *The Crossroads of Class and Gender: Industrial Homework, Subcontracting, and Household Dynamics in Mexico City* (University of Chicago Press 1987); Deepita Chakravarty, 'Docile Oriental Women's and Organised Labour: A Case Study of the Indian Garment Manufacturing Industry' (2007) 14 Indian Journal of Gender Studies 439.

and is not morally wrong. For instance, as Matt Zwolinski argues, 'How ... can it be permissible to *neglect* workers in the developing world, but impermissible to *exploit* them, when exploitation is better for both parties ... ?'[14]

As I have argued elsewhere, such a view fails to account for the background structural conditions that force certain social groups into these jobs; namely poor, racialised women.[15] These social groups are placed in the position of having very limited options for employment, such as subsistence farming, domestic labour, scavenging, sex work or a sweatshop job.[16] The individual worker's decision to work in a sweatshop appears to be a free choice, but taken as a group or class we see that these workers have few meaningful options. These groups are positioned in global social structures as socially inferior and their productive powers are transferred to the advantage of groups positioned as socially superior – Northern consumers and corporations. This is an injustice because the self-development of workers is inhibited through the long hours of tedious intensive labour, as well as the associated health risks, low pay, harassment and repression of collective organising.[17]

One of the features of structural injustice is that all connected agents are constrained. In competitive global markets, corporations are forced to play by the rules of the game in order to stay competitive and to continue competing for business. If corporations refuse to do this, they will go bust, which is bad both for them and the workers. Arguably, corporations in the global garment industry face 'the structural imperative of "exploit or fail"'.[18] Corporations are constrained by the rules of the capitalist game. Also, poor countries need the foreign direct investment of the garment industry, so create favourable conditions for multi-national corporations (MNCs).

Another feature of structural injustice is that it is not the fault of any one agent. Sweatshop labour is not some masterplan. Instead, it has emerged from the confluence of a history of colonialism, global economic restructuring in the postcolonial and globalised neoliberal eras, endemic

14 Matt Zwolinski, 'Structural Exploitation' (2012) 29 Social Philosophy and Policy 154, 162.
15 Maeve McKeown, 'Sweatshop Labor as Global Structural Exploitation' in Monique Deveaux and Vida Panitch (eds), *Exploitation: From Practice to Theory* (Rowman and Littlefield Publishers 2017).
16 These are some of the alternatives available to sweatshop workers in Bangladesh and Mexico, see Jeremy Seabrook, *The Song of the Shirt: The High Price of Cheap Garments, From Blackburn to Bangladesh* (C Hurst & Co Publishers 2015); Fernandez-Kelly (n 11).
17 Maeve McKeown, 'Global Structural Exploitation: Towards an Intersectional Definition' (2016) 9 Global Justice: Theory Practice Rhetoric 155.
18 Robert Mayer, 'Sweatshops, Exploitation and Moral Responsibility' (2007) 38 Journal of Social Philosophy 605, 611.

poverty, gender stereotyping and rampant consumer culture in the Global North, as well as countless other factors. As Iris Young argues:

> Structural injustice is a kind of moral wrong distinct from the wrongful action of an individual agent or the repressive policies of a state. Structural injustice occurs as a consequence of many individuals and institutions acting to pursue their particular goals and interests, for the most part acting within the limits of accepted rules and norms.[19]

However, large garment corporations and the states that host them (the USA, EU and Japan) have acted in various ways to enhance their positions and power within these structures. The 'deliberate' aspect of this structural injustice is, therefore, not the creation of the injustice in the first place, but rather the deliberate *maintenance* of the injustice in order to continue extracting benefits. One of the ways powerful agents have done that is to use the law to enhance and maintain their dominant position in the industry. Understanding how they have done this necessitates opening the black box of the global garment industry to reveal the machinations of the most powerful players.

The law's contribution to sweatshop labour

Conditions in the global garment industry are the cumulative, unintended effect of economic processes, but that is only part of the story. To stop there is to misunderstand this industry. It would be naïve and simply inaccurate to think of the structure of the global garment industry as the result of unfettered market processes, because ever since John F. Kennedy's international trade agreement on US cotton in 1961, 'apparel production has been among the most protected manufacturing activities in the global economy'.[20] Not only that but, as Jennifer Bair puts it, the global apparel industry is 'a single organizational field in which the experiences and trajectories of individual firms, countries and regions are tied to the dynamics of international trade and production networks'.[21]

19 Young (n 3) 52.
20 Jennifer Bair, 'Surveying the Post-MFA Landscape: What Prospects for the Global South Post-Quota?' (2008) 12 Competition & Change 3, 3.
21 ibid 4.

The global garment industry has increased 128-fold from the 1970s to the early 2000s.[22] Today it is worth $2.4 trillion, making it the world's seventh largest economy.[23] The EU, USA and Japan accounted for 75 per cent of garment imports in 2008.[24] The powerful players in this industry are the garment-importing countries – the EU, USA and Japan – as well as their retail corporations. Understanding why these players are so powerful comes down to two things: the structure of the global garment supply chain and the ways in which this concentration of power has been enabled by trade agreements imposed by the Global North.

The structure of the global garment supply chain

Gary Gereffi's 1994 analysis of global supply chains remains influential. He argues that there are two types of structure in contemporary global supply chains.[25] *Producer-driven* commodity chains are characteristic of capital- and technology-intensive industries like cars, aircrafts and electrical machinery. In these chains, large integrated industrial enterprises control the production system. *Buyer-driven* commodity chains are characteristic of consumer goods industries like clothing, footwear, toys and homeware. Retailers at the top of the chain provide designs and specifications and outsource production to contractors. The retailers do not own production facilities. Their role is to design, brand and advertise the goods, oversee and integrate the production process and to distribute goods. Their profits derive from 'unique combinations of high-value research, design, sales, marketing, and financial services'.[26] Their profits also derive from keeping production costs as low as possible, which is enabled by the new international division of labour.

The global garment industry has become the most salient example of buyer-driven supply chains. It is difficult for newer or smaller businesses to become buyers and break into the retail sector because of the high

22 Jennifer Hurley and Doug Miller, 'The Changing Face of the Global Garment Industry' in Angela Hale and Jane Wills (eds), *Threads of Labour: Garment Industry Supply Chains from the Workers' Perspective* (Blackwell Publishers Ltd 2005) 17.
23 Imran Amed and others, 'The State of Fashion 2017' (2016) <https://www.mckinsey.com/industries/retail/our-insights/the-state-of-fashion> accessed 24 August 2023.
24 Gary Gereffi and Stacey Frederick, 'The Global Apparel Value Chain, Trade and the Crisis: Challenges and Opportunities for Developing Countries' (The World Bank Development Research Group 2010) Policy Research Working Paper 5281.
25 Gary Gereffi, 'The Organization of Buyer-Driven Global Commodity Chains: How US Retailers Shape Overseas Production Networks' in Gary Gereffi and Miguel Korzeniewicz (eds), *Commodity Chains and Global Capitalism* (Praeger 1994) 97.
26 ibid 99.

investment costs in product development, advertising and retailing.[27] By contrast, there are low entry costs to manufacturing garments, which requires only basic equipment, and in countries where labour protections are weak, wages can be low, and health and safety standards bypassed. Thus, over time there has been a consolidation of buying power in the top retailers and a proliferation of manufacturers.[28]

In the USA, power is concentrated in the hands of an increasingly small number of retailers. In the 1980s–1990s, the US retail landscape was changing. Smaller retailers and obsolete retailers, such as the department stores that were popular in the 1950s and 1960s, were going bankrupt or being bought out. The 'big buyers' experienced 'spectacular growth strategies' and were engaging in mergers and acquisitions; making them larger and reducing competition.[29] This increased pressure down the supply chain, as the large retailers' monopoly meant they could command lower prices and expect faster production.[30] This pressure was felt by manufacturers in developing countries.

As Gereffi explains:

> This combination of concentrated buying power in the retail/wholesale sector and excess capacity in overseas factories has permitted the big buyers in GCCs [Global Commodity Chains] to simultaneously lower the prices they are paying for goods and dictate more stringent performance standards for their vendors (e.g., more buying seasons, faster delivery times and better quality) in order to increase their profits.[31]
>
> The two sourcing trends in the global apparel industry since the 1990s have been a 'price squeeze' and a 'lead time squeeze': buyers dictate prices and they dictate how quickly goods need to be produced, both of which put pressure on workers at the bottom of the chain.[32]

Further insight into the dominant position of retailers can be gained by understanding subcontracting. It is not simply that Northern

27 ibid 103.
28 ibid 115–116.
29 ibid 115.
30 ibid 103.
31 ibid 116.
32 Mark Anner, 'Binding Power: The Sourcing Squeeze, Workers' Rights, and Building Safety in Bangladeah Since Rana Plaza' (Penn State Centre for Global Workers' Rights 2018) 22 March Research Report 4.

retailers outsource work to Southern manufacturers. Rather, there is a complicated supply chain at the point of production, most of which is hidden from view. As Hurley and Miller argue:

> … the structure is best characterized not as a pyramid but an iceberg … The dense and complex webs at the bottom end of the chain are invisible not just to outsiders such as government monitors, but also to the retailers that issued the order and sometimes even to the manufacturers that subcontracted the order.[33]

Hurley and Miller identify five tiers of workers. The Tier 1 manufacturers are closest to the retailers and are often large MNCs themselves, backed by foreign direct investment (FDI). They provide a range of services including 'full package' production. They often dominate the industry at the national level; for example, in the Philippines, five firms out of 1,500 control 20 per cent of the industry. These manufacturers are powerful at the national level and influence policy-making.[34] The conditions in these factories are often good, because they are used as showcases for inspectors and buyers. Jobs are more secure and union organising easier, if it is allowed. Tier 1 manufacturers are more prevalent in emerging markets, who can also tap into a growing domestic demand for garments – China, India and Turkey.[35]

Tier 2 manufacturers are also large but lack the connections and international reach of Tier 1. They either receive direct orders from international or domestic buyers or are subsidiaries of Tier 1. They focus on 'Cut Make and Trim' (CMT) services. Tiers 3 and 4 are a mixture of small factories, workshops and groups of people working out of someone's house. These units are funded by local capital and are relatively powerless in the supply chain. Workers' rights, health and safety are seriously compromised at this level. Tier 5 refers to homeworkers, who were found in each of the nine countries in Hurley and Miller's study. Homeworking tends to be seasonal. The products are either passed to an agent or contractor, or sold directly at local markets. In the supply chain, homeworkers provide 'stop-gap production' when manufacturers are under time pressure to finish orders. Their

33 Hurley and Miller (n 22) 23.

34 Jennifer Hurley, 'Unravelling the Web: Supply Chains and Workers' Lives in the Garment Industry' in Angela Hale and Jane Wills (eds), *Threads of Labour: Garment Industry Supply Chains from the Workers' Perspective* (Blackwell Publishers Ltd 2005) 97.

35 Gereffi and Frederick (n 24) 8.

connection is with Tiers 4 and 3; not higher up the chain. They have to meet their own equipment and overhead costs. They are powerless in the supply chain and organising is extremely difficult.

Subcontracting increases the power of the retailers at the top of the chain because it creates competition for their business. It benefits them by keeping costs low and turnaround times quick. It distances retailers from the poor working conditions that they can blame on companies further down the supply chain and it creates division among workers.[36] Criticism of subcontracting in garment supply chains peaked in the 1990s. Campaign groups sprung up in Western countries demanding brands take responsibility for the exploitative and unsafe working conditions in the Global South. Brands responded by stepping up their efforts in corporate social responsibility (CSR). This started with the jeans specialist Levi-Strauss, but soon codes of conduct became the norm in the garment industry. While codes of conduct have led to improvements in some cases, it is questionable whether these improvements filter down throughout the supply chain, or only reach Tier 1 and at best, Tier 2 manufacturers. Moreover, codes of conduct are written by the retailers themselves with no input from the workers.[37]

Subcontracting is in constant flux. The current trend is for retailers to streamline their sourcing processes and to downsize the number of manufacturers they work with.[38] This makes supply chains shorter and coordination and management easier. Large manufacturers in the Global South are moving towards a 'full-package' service, where they coordinate the whole manufacturing process, including sourcing raw materials, dealing with intermediary roles (pattern making, laying and cutting, assembly, quality control and finish), as well as delivery and distribution.[39] This move towards Tier 1 suppliers and full-package services is an interesting development because it could increase the power of workers against MNCs.[40]

---

36 Hurley (n 34) 96.

37 Angela Hale, 'Organising and Networking in Support of Garment Workers: Why We Researched Subcontracting Chains', *Threads of Labour: Garment Industry Supply Chains from the Workers' Perspective* (Blackwell Publishers Ltd 2005) 62.

38 Hurley and Miller (n 22) 23.

39 ibid.

40 Richard P Appelbaum, 'Giant Transnational Contractors in East Asia: Emergent Trends in Global Supply Chains' (2008) 12 Competition & Change 69.

Despite the shifting sands of the garment industry, wealth and power continues to concentrate in the hands of a few top players. As the Business of Fashion and McKinsey report 'The State of Fashion 2019' states:

> Polarization continues to be a stark reality in fashion: fully 97 percent of economic profits for the whole industry are earned by just 20 companies, most of them in the luxury segment. Notably, the top 20 group of companies has remained stable over time. Twelve of the top 20 have been a member of the group for the last decade. Long-term leaders include, among others, Inditex, LVMH, and Nike, which have more than doubled their economic profit over the past ten years ... According to our estimates, each racked up more than $2 billion in economic profit in 2017.[41]

Ninety-seven per cent of profits might seem surprising given that there is a lot of competition on the high street and in high fashion. But the largest MNCs give the illusion of competition and choice. Many of them own multiple brands.[42]

The role of international law

So far, it appears that the concentration of power in the hands of Global North MNCs is the unintended result of social-structural processes. But this impression is misleading. The law has been used to create and maintain the conditions that entrench the power of these actors and reduce the conditions of workers. As we saw above, the garment industry is one of the most protected industries in the global economy.

In the early 1970s, manufacturers in the Global North were concerned about the sudden groundswell of cheap labour that became available in the Third World. In 1974, the Multi-Fibre Agreement (MFA) implemented a global quota system for textile and clothing exports. The aim was to protect the Global North's textile and garment manufacturing industries from being decimated by cheap imports from overseas. Countries had to sign bi-lateral agreements for garment exports with Global North countries. The MFA implemented different quotas for

---

41 Imran Amed and others, 'The State of Fashion 2019: A Year of Awakening' (2018) <https://www.mckinsey.com/industries/retail/our-insights/the-state-of-fashion-2019-a-year-of-awakening> accessed 24 August 2023.

42 For example, VF Corporation, which has stayed in the top 20 global retailers since 2008, owns Dickies, Horace Small, Jansport, Kipling, Lee, Riders of Lee, Napapijri, Red Kap, The North Face, Timberland, Vans and Wrangler.

different countries depending on their comparative advantage in global markets. The effects of the MFA were multifaceted. On the one hand, many countries were able to manufacture garments for export, because retailers had to find supplies from multiple countries in order to bypass the quota system.[43] Thus, manufacturing jobs were spread across developing countries. On the other hand, the MFA concentrated power into the hands of US, EU and Japanese retailers. These countries determined how much each exporting country could export on a case-by-case basis with a view to protecting their domestic industries and furthering the interests of MNCs. The MFA shaped the global garment industry at a time of exponential growth. The industry was shaped in such a way as to protect the interests of Global North industries.

With the replacement of the GATT by the WTO in 1995, this uneven protectionist approach was unsustainable in the context of a new free trade agenda.[44] There was pressure to liberalise the highly protected garment industry. The end of quotas was seen as a good thing by developing countries and was in fact used as a bargaining chip in the 1986 Uruguay Round to encourage Global South countries to sign up to the new WTO framework.[45] With the establishment of the WTO in 1995, the MFA was replaced by the Agreement on Textiles and Clothing (ATC), which aimed to phase out quotas by 2005. This process was supposed to benefit Global South countries; however, it has been managed by importing countries who were able to choose which products would be integrated. The USA decided to 'end-load' the process so that only non-significant products were liberalised at first, such as parachutes and seatbelts, with 80 per cent of the products remaining under quotas by 2003.[46] In addition, the USA and EU lobbied hard to include articles that would hinder the end of quotas. This included an article on transitional safeguard measures to prevent the sudden rise of imports from any particular country; a reciprocal market access clause demanding access to developing countries' markets in return for the end of quotas; and a false origins rule, so that developing countries have to prove the origins of products (a costly and time-consuming process).[47]

43 Gereffi (n 25) 101.
44 Angela Hale and Maggie Burns, 'The Phase-Out of the Multi-Fibre Arrangement from the Perspective of Workers' in Angela Hale and Jane Wills (eds), *Threads of Labour: Garment Industry Supply Chains from the Workers' Perspective* (Blackwell Publishers Ltd 2005) 211.
45 ibid.
46 ibid.
47 ibid 213.

The phase-out of quotas threatened the diversity of garment-exporting countries as manufacturing concentrated in low-cost countries.[48] Smaller countries were no longer guaranteed access to Northern markets. These fears have panned out to some extent. China has been the main beneficiary of the end of quotas, more than doubling its share of apparel exports between 1995–2008.[49] A new division of labour emerged with the most labour-intensive aspects of production occurring in poorer countries, such as Cambodia, Vietnam, Bangladesh and Indonesia. The capital-intensive production – producing man-made fibres, machinery manufacturing – is occurring in richer countries like China, India and Turkey:[50]

> Since the removal of quotas, the global apparel industry is faced with overcapacity that is creating intense competition in low-cost countries. Quotas created too many factories in too many countries, and now these factories are competing for fewer orders. In the short term, this has significantly raised the bar to be a global competitor; manufacturers must be more creative and comprehensive in the development of their products and services ... Buyers place stricter demands on manufacturers and are asking for better products (quality), more services, and faster turnaround times, all for lower costs. Suppliers must meet buyer demands to keep orders, increase volume, and reduce costs ... When this is coupled with the ongoing consolidation in the retail sector, the result is more power in the hands of the global buyers (i.e. retailers, global brands, and large manufacturers that have outsourced their production).[51]

The shape of the garment industry was created by the MFA in the first place. Under this regime, power and wealth were concentrated into the hands of Northern retailers. Also, to some extent, to first-tier manufacturers in countries like Hong Kong and Korea who circumvented quotas by outsourcing themselves to neighbouring countries. As Hale and Burns put it:

> ... these global players, whether buyers or manufacturers, can now reap the profits from the industry without any need of government

48 Gereffi and Frederick (n 24) 13.
49 ibid 7.
50 ibid 13–14.
51 ibid 22.

protection. In fact they do not want complicated quota restrictions since these may prevent them from sourcing from the most profitable locations.[52]

Not all Northern businesses benefitted, however; many textile manufacturers and smaller retailers were unable to adapt. It is large branded-retail MNCs who were the winners.

After the phase-out of the MFA and ATC, a further crisis for garment-exporting countries was the 2008 financial crash. Lower demand from the USA, EU and Japan meant that a lot of the smaller, more vulnerable manufacturers went out of business.[53] It also meant that retailers were demanding lower-cost production.[54] Thus, the financial crisis also benefitted the big Northern retailers and large Southern manufacturers but not the smaller firms who lacked the resources and knowledge to adapt to the changes, or garment workers.[55]

Once the ATC expired in 2005, the USA and EU sought other strategies for preserving their advantages in the global garment industry. They have secured their position through bi-lateral and regional trade agreements.[56] They have been enabled in this by the failure of the World Trade Organisation's Cancun round, after which the USA declared it would be creating its own free trade agreements.[57] The Generalised System of Preferences (GSP) is a scheme dating from the 1970s designed to promote imports from developing countries into industrialised countries under a number of conditions. However, textiles and apparel are excluded from the GSP schemes of both the EU and US.[58] The EU and the USA argue that developing countries already have competitive advantages in these industries so do not need GSPs. Instead, the USA and EU have brought local, regional states into their orbit through trade agreements. Through the North Atlantic Free Trade Agreement (NAFTA), the USA has secured favourable terms for apparel production in Mexico, Central America and the Caribbean Basin. With the Europe Agreements adopted in the 1990s with Eastern and Central European states seeking to join the EU, as well as the Mediterranean Basin, the EU has secured

52 Hale and Burns (n 44) 215.
53 Gereffi and Frederick (n 24) 19–20.
54 ibid 21.
55 Hale and Burns (n 44) 216.
56 ibid 217.
57 ibid.
58 Bernard Herz and Marco Wagner, 'The Dark Side of the Generalized System of Preferences' (2011) 19 Review of International Economics 763, 764. Some agricultural goods are also excluded.

preferential terms for manufacturing. In a process known as Outward Processing Trade (OPT), the USA and EU allow tariff-free imports of apparel from these regions provided they use US and EU produced materials. The EU's OPT regime was written into trade rules in the 1980s and 1990s, but has been phased out as an official trade regime with the end of quotas. However, it continues as a form of production process and has increased since liberalisation.[59] As Hale and Burns put it 'Bilateral and regional trade agreements are being used by the USA and EU to bypass the WTO and establish their own rules which institutionalise their control of the industry. Although many of these agreements give preferential market access for poorer countries, even this is being used to ensure protection of US and EU business interests, notably the still profitable textile industries'.[60]

Using the law for good

So far, I have stressed the negative impacts of international law on the global garment industry, insofar as it is manipulated to serve the interests of powerful states and their corporations to the detriment of poor states and workers. However, power is 'Janus-faced' (two-faced) and it can also be mobilised for good.[61] The law too can be used for good. There are at least two examples of this in the global garment industry – initiatives to promote 'joint liability' and the bi-lateral US-Cambodia Textile Agreement. These examples demonstrate that the law, while it has mostly been deployed to benefit the powerful, can also be a fruitful site of political contestation by subordinate agents in power structures.

Joint liability in the garment industry

As mentioned above, the sweatshop system began in the USA. But it was also eliminated (at least for a time) in the USA. How? The answer is 'jobbers agreements'.[62] The system in the USA in the late nineteenth and early to mid-twentieth century was similar to the current global system.

59 Bob Begg, John Pickles and Adrian Smith, 'Cutting It: European Integration, Trade Regimes, and the Reconfiguration of East-Central European Apparel Production' (2003) 35 Environment and Planning 2191.
60 Hale and Burns (n 44) 217.
61 Amy Allen, Rainer Forst and Mark Haugaard, 'Power and Reason, Justice and Domination : A Conversation' (2014) 7 Journal of Political Power 7.
62 Mark Anner, Jennifer Bair and Jeremy Blasi, 'Toward Joint Liability in Global Supply Chains: Addressing the Root Causes of Labor Violations in International Subcontracting Networks' (2013) 35 Comparative Labor Law & Policy Journal 1, 4.

Initially, factories designed and produced their own clothes, but over time this model was supplanted by the 'outside model' whereby the majority of the industry was made up of 'jobbers' – companies that designed clothes and outsourced production to smaller factories. This system, as it does now, put downward pressure on wages and working conditions. Following the Triangle Shirtwaist factory fire in 1911, the governor of New York investigated the industry. It was found that the main problem in the industry was the jobber system and recommendations were made to regulate it.

It took time and persistence on the part of the International Ladies Garment Workers Union (ILGWU) to get implementation of these recommendations, but eventually the 'jobbers agreements' were signed into law. These were collective bargaining agreements between the union, the factory and the buyer (the jobber). These were difficult to enforce because they were done on a case-by-case basis, but eventually in 1933, they were established in federal law in the National Industrial Recovery Act (NIRA) as 'Codes of Fair Competition'. While the NIRA was rescinded in 1935, the New Deal era resulted in further consolidation of the jobbers agreements in the National Labor Relations (Wagner) Act (1935) and the Fair Labor Standards Act (1938). As Anner, Bair and Blasio put it, 'Within a decade, jobbers agreements had become the lynchpin of an industrial relations model described as triangular collective bargaining – so named because the goal was to regulate, via a set of paired contractors' and jobbers agreements, relations between the three sides of the production triangle: the workers as represented by the union, and the jobbers and contractors, each represented by their own employers' associations'.[63]

The impact of this legislation was transformative. Between 1947–1990, the annual average wage of garment workers never fell below 146 per cent of the national minimum wage, they achieved benefits like retirement pay and medical insurance, and working hours were the shortest of any group in the manufacturing sector.[64] These gains were achieved because the jobbers agreements institutionalised buyer liability into law in three crucial ways: jobbers were obligated to ensure minimum wages and hours of work; jobbers had to regulate factories, ensuring they were unionised, they had to declare which factories they were working with and that work was evenly distributed, generating stability; and jobbers had to guarantee payments to workers if factories went bust.[65]

---

63 ibid 17.
64 ibid 18–19.
65 ibid 21–25.

Given that all of this occurred within one domestic legal jurisdiction, it might seem to have little relevance to today's globalised, hyper-dispersed garment industry. But the underlying principle is the principle of joint liability of buyers and the application of this principle is being explored in the contemporary global garment industry with some signs of success. The most prominent is the Bangladesh Fire and Building Safety Accord, which was implemented after the catastrophic Rana Plaza factory collapse in 2013, which killed 1,132 people and injured more than 2,500 others.[66] The Accord was signed by more than 100 brands and retailers, as well as two global union federations, IndustriALL and UNIGLOBAL.[67] The Accord reflects jobbers agreements in four ways: it regulates the buying practices of brands who are required to pay for factory repairs; it includes workers' representatives as equal participants; it is legally binding; and it covers a large section of the industry in Bangladesh.[68] The Accord only applies to fire and building safety, not wages and other working conditions, and it is limited in scope to Bangladesh. Moreover, while it was successful in remediating fire and building safety issues in over 90 per cent of factories in Bangladesh, it has now expired and the independent regulation has been taken over by the Bangladesh government with fears that corruption will lead to diminishing standards in the industry.[69] Nevertheless, this exercise in joint liability was a 'breakthrough' event in the global garment industry.[70]

And there have been other successful joint liability initiatives in the arena of university-licensed sportswear, a $4 billion a year industry in the USA. Fruit of the Loom and its subsidiary Russell Corporation were the subjects of a legal dispute with the *Central General de Trabajadores* (CGT) in Honduras. In 2008, it closed a factory, making 1,200 workers redundant

---

66 ILO statistics quoted in Anne Trebilcock, 'The Rana Plaza Disaster Seven Years on: Transnational Experiments and Perhaps a New Treaty?' (2020) 159 International Labour Review 545–546.

67 It should be noted that some MNCs, notably Wal-Mart and GAP refused to sign the Accord and created an alternative, watered-down (because it is not legally binding) Alliance for Bangladesh Worker Safety.

68 Anner, Bair and Blasi (n 62), 27–31.

69 Elizabeth Paton, 'Fears for Bangladesh Accord' *The New York Times* (New York, 28 May 2021) <https://www.nytimes.com/2021/05/28/business/bangladesh-worker-safety-accord.html> accessed 24 August 2023; Trebilcock (n 66) 549–550. From 2018–2021, there was the 2018 Transition Accord. That has now expired, but the Accord office remains in Amsterdam and a new International Accord has been established. This project aims to replicate the successes of the Bangladesh Accord internationally but it is in the early stages – <https://internationalaccord.org/about-us/> accessed 24 August 2023.

70 Anner, Bair and Blasi (n 62) 42. It is worth noting here that post-Rana Plaza there were two other initiatives: the Arrangement, which provided compensation to families of the deceased and to the injured, and the Rana Plaza Trust Fund, which received third-party donations for victims. However, both were funded by charitable contributions, which 'essentially perpetuated a denial of firms' responsibility for the potential costs of doing business' Trebilcock (n 66), 555.

and an investigation found that this was done to suppress union activities. A coordinated campaign by the CGT, workers and student activists led to further support from retailers like Sports Authority and Dick's Sporting Goods who put pressure on Russell to resolve the dispute. Fruit of the Loom conceded, and more than that, it opened a new factory, rehired all the employees, paid them nine months backpay, gave them a 27 per cent pay raise, agreed to allow union organising, and provided the CGT access to all its Honduran factories.[71]

Brands have also been held responsible as guarantors of wages.[72] In 2010, Nike paid $1.54 million to workers after closures of two of their contractors' factories in Honduras, and in 2011, $1 million to workers in Indonesia, and Adidas paid $1.8 million to workers in Indonesia in 2012 after the closure of the PT Kizone factory.[73] Adidas has also been the target of a campaign to secure a 'buyer responsibility agreement' by a coalition of garment unions in Latin America and Asia called the International Union League for Brand Responsibility. These tactics have been replicated during the Covid-19 pandemic, when garment workers experienced massive layoffs as demand for clothing shrank and orders were cancelled. The Asia Floor Wage Alliance (AFWA) took out suits in India against H&M, and in Sri Lanka against Levi-Strauss, Columbia Sporting Company, Asics, DKNY and Tommy Hilfiger.[74] They claim that cancellations of billions of dollars' worth of orders had severe humanitarian consequences. Ashim Roy of the AFWA put it like this:

> We are confident that in some countries there is a very strong case law for joint liability, but it has never been tested for a brand and a supplier. Our core argument is that the reality of the fashion supply chains is that brands do not just buy garments. They determine and control every step in the production process of that garment being made and so they should not be able to continue to argue that the workers who make their clothes do not work for them.[75]

This is what the ILGWU argued way back in 1923 – that the garment supply chain is 'an integrated process of production' so that jobbers were

71 Anner, Bair and Blasi (n 62), 33–34.
72 ibid 35–37.
73 Ashok Kumar and Jack Mahoney, 'Stitching Together: How Workers Are Hemming Down Transnational Capital in the Hyper-Global Apparel Industry' (2014) 17 Working USA 187.
74 Annie Kelly, 'Top Fashion Brands Face Legal Challenge over Garment Workers' Rights in Asia' *The Guardian* (London, 9 July 2021).
75 ibid.

jointly liable for wages and working conditions, and this was eventually recognised in US law.[76] While there is obviously no state at the global level, Anner, Bair and Blasio point to transnational activist alliances of unions, students, NGOs and coalitions of unions who 'have used consolidation at the top of the apparel industry to their advantage by targeting brands, institutional buyers (universities) and retail chains to bring about major agreements with powerful corporations including Nike, Fruit of the Loom/Russell, and Adidas'.[77] An Open-ended Intergovernmental Working Group (OEIGWG) at the UN Human Rights Council is working on a draft 'Legally binding instrument to regulate, in international humans rights law, the activities of transnational corporations and other business enterprises'.[78] The proposed instrument would require businesses to prevent human rights abuses and provide evidence of due diligence, as well as assuming legal liability for such abuses and providing redress to victims.[79] This instrument has yet to be adopted, but demonstrates that joint liability is now on the table at the level of global governance.

The US-Cambodia Textile Agreement

Achieving laws of joint liability might seem like a Sisyphean task, even if it has had intermittent success. But another route is to use the prevalence of bi-lateral trade deals in the industry to the benefit of workers. One such example is the US-Cambodia Textile Agreement. Apparel exports from Cambodia grew from virtually nothing to half a billion dollars between 1994–1998.[80] This was because Cambodia was not part of the GATT/WTO, so was not part of the quota system. Manufacturers from Hong Kong, Korea, Singapore and Malaysia took advantage of this situation and set up factories there.[81]

American textile unions were worried about the exploitative working conditions and the threat to American textiles. They wanted to bring Cambodia into America's textile quota system. There were major scandals involving child labour in Cambodian factories that led to the withdrawal of Nike and Disney in the late 1990s. Following the 1997 Asian financial

76 Anner, Bair and Blasi (n 62) 16.
77 ibid 42.
78 The OEIGWG quoted in Trebilcock (n 66) 558.
79 ibid 559–560. See also <https://www.ohchr.org/en/hr-bodies/hrc/wg-trans-corp/igwg-on-tnc> accessed 24 August 2023.
80 David Vogel, 'Taming Globalization? Civil Regulation and Corporate Capitalism', *The Oxford Handbook of Business and Government* (Oxford Scholarship Online 2010) 482–483.
81 Don Wells, '"Best Practice" in the Regulation of International Labor Standards: Lessons of the US-Cambodia Textile Agreement' (2006) 27 Comparative Labor Law & Policy Journal 357.

crisis, conditions in factories worsened, forced labour and child labour were rampant. In response, a growing labour movement led to strikes and unrest. The USA agreed to a bi-lateral trade deal with Cambodia in 1999 on the condition that it improved conditions in factories. Cambodia did not have the capacity to do this, so the USA worked with the International Labour Organisation (ILO) to establish a monitoring system. The USA also provided funds for this, along with Western MNCs and the Cambodian government. This is immensely different to the rest of the industry, where enforcement of standards of corporate social responsibility is voluntary and rarely enforced; the involvement of the US state and the ILO was unprecedented. The USA provided a carrot rather than a stick approach, by increasing quotas with increased compliance with labour laws.[82]

The ILO Garment Sector Working Conditions Improvement Project was funded by the US government and had the following objectives: to develop an independent monitoring system; to draft laws to improve labour conditions; to increase worker and employer awareness of international and national labour standards; and to increase capacities of workers, employers and government to improve labour standards.[83] The impacts were not all positive. As Wells puts it, and as I have been emphasising throughout this chapter, there was an inherent and massive power imbalance: 'Given the asymmetrical power relation between the United States as garment importer and Cambodia as garment exporter, the United States was able to set most of the terms of the agreement.'[84] Moreover, the Agreement was part of an overarching initiative to bring Cambodia into the WTO and to liberalise its economy. The ILO could point out labour rights violations but could do little to enforce them. Cambodia became completely dependent on the garment industry, which grew to account for 80 per cent of its exports, and the USA accounts for 71 per cent of its imports. Cambodia is also reliant on investors from neighbouring countries who own the factories and technology; so Cambodia is exposed to future shocks in the industry.

Despite these drawbacks, the Agreement led to significant gains for garment workers in Cambodia, including increased employment, higher wages and improvements in labour standards.[85] Garment workers are 'the best-paid group of workers in the country',[86] they account for two-thirds of the industrial workforce, and 85–90 per cent of them are

82 ibid.
83 ibid 364.
84 ibid 365.
85 ibid 367.
86 ibid 368.

women, contributing to improvements in gender equality. By 2004, there were 14 national labour unions and 499 factory unions.[87] Improvements in working conditions led to the return of Nike and Disney. In fact, Cambodia's reputation for high labour standards enabled it to weather the storm of the end of the quota system. The Cambodia Minister of Commerce stated at the time of the end of quotas:

> We are extending our labor standards beyond the end of the quotas because we know that is why we continue to have buyers. If we didn't respect the unions and the labor standards, we would be killing the goose that lays the golden egg.[88]

As one trade unionist put it, 'The US trade agreement with Cambodia was more beneficial to workers than any anti-sweatshop campaign.'[89]

Conclusion

In this chapter, I have argued that sweatshop labour is a form of deliberate structural injustice. While it is the result of economic processes, these processes have been shaped by powerful and rich states in the interests of their domestic industries and corporations. In fact, there probably isn't a better example of an industry that has been shaped by the Global North in its own interests than the global garment industry. So, while I am not claiming that the structural injustice of sweatshop labour has been created by particular powerful agents, I am claiming that it has been shaped and deliberately perpetuated by powerful agents in order to further their own interests. In that sense, it is a deliberate structural injustice.

Examining the role of international trade agreements demonstrates how the background conditions of the global garment industry have been shaped and manipulated by the powerful. I also demonstrated that there are instances where the law has been used to serve the interests of workers and poor countries. I would suggest that these successes are rare; they are the exception that prove the rule that the law is used to serve the interests of the powerful. However, they show that political contestation of the legal framework is possible and that this is a fruitful area for subordinate agents in these power structures to push for change.

87 ibid 369.
88 ibid 375.
89 ibid 357.

5

Segmented labour markets, structural injustice and legal remedies

Hugh Collins

Segmented labour markets

In developed economies, particularly those transitioning from an industrial to a service economy, labour markets appear to be segmented.[1] To put the matter crudely, there are good jobs and bad jobs. The good jobs are typically full-time, long-term, offer opportunities for promotion and the development of skills, create possibilities for personal fulfilment, and provide salaries that are typically significantly above any national minimum wage and include additional benefits such as contributions to pensions. The bad jobs have some or all of the opposite features: their hours vary but are frequently less than full-time; the jobs will often be precarious in the sense that they may be casual as required by the employer, temporary, or fixed-term, or seasonal; the job will offer no opportunities for advancement to higher grades with better remuneration; and the wages will usually be at best the national minimum wage. Of course, there have always been wide disparities between employees in respect of earnings and terms of employment. Labour market statistics reveal, however, clustering around the two poles of good jobs and bad jobs, with rather fewer workers occupying a middle ground.[2] Insofar as there is a middle ground, it may be constituted by 'dead-end jobs', which, though full-time and secure, are

1 Patrick Emmenegger, Silja Hausermann, Brunol Palier, Martin Seleib-Kaiser (eds) *The Age of Dualization: The Changing Face of Inequality in Deindustrializing Societies* (Oxford University Press 2012).

2 Maarten Goos, Alan Manning and Anna Salomons 'Explaining Job Polarization: Routine-Biased Technological Change and Offshoring' (2014) 104(8) American Economic Review 2509.

nevertheless paid at the minimum wage and offer no opportunities for advancement.[3] Another group in the middle are at present in good jobs, but expect in the near future to be ejected into the secondary labour market as a result of business restructuring.[4]

Before the 1980s, the size of the pool of bad jobs or the scope of the secondary labour market was relatively small. Large and medium-sized firms and the public sector offered jobs that complied with the model of good jobs. Those standards were maintained in part because they helped employers to recruit and retain staff, but also in part because trade unions could organise these groups of workers effectively and bargain for the maintenance of favourable terms of employment. Unions could protect job security and bargain for a good package of benefits. The secondary labour market of insecure and badly paid jobs was occupied by those who were unable to obtain access to the internal labour markets of large firms.[5]

From the 1980s onwards, however, the relative size of the secondary labour market and number of bad jobs has been growing. According to the theory of segmented labour markets, this expansion of the secondary labour market has been primarily driven by managerial strategies designed to reduce labour costs by excluding jobs from the relatively high rate of pay offered by the internal labour market of large firms and organisations.[6] Under the strategy of outsourcing or vertical disintegration,[7] private businesses and the public sector have exploited the possibility of exporting part of the workforce to external contractors, who then provide a service to the core business. An example might be the use of external contractors to provide cleaning or catering. The principal advantage of this managerial strategy to the core firm is that it saves on labour costs. The external contractors typically operate in the secondary labour market where they avoid trade union organisation and collective bargaining, so they can offer the minimum wage, with no fringe benefits such as pensions. In some cases, the strategy of outsourcing goes further

3 Hyojin Seo, '"Dual" Labour Market? Patterns of Segmentation in European Labour Markets and the Varieties of Precariousness' (2021) Transfer 1, 10.

4 ibid.

5 Peter B Doeringer and Michael J Piore *Internal Labor Markets and Manpower Analysis* (Heath Lexington Books 1971); Michael Reich, David M Gordon and Richard C Edwards, 'A Theory of Labor Market Segmentation' (1973) 63 American Economic Review Papers and Proceedings 359.

6 Arne L Kalleberg, Barbara F Reskin, Ken Hudson, 'Bad Jobs in America: Standard and Non-standard Employment Relations and Job Quality in the United States' (2000) 65 American Sociological Review 256.

7 Hugh Collins, 'Independent Contractors and the Challenge of Vertical Disintegration to Employment Protection Laws' (1990) 10 Oxford Journal of Legal Studies 353.

by treating these workers as independent contractors, with a view to avoiding even minimum labour standards such as the minimum wage and the right to be a member of a trade union. Outsourcing led to the core and periphery model of the organisation in which only key staff with firm-specific skills would be retained in the core workforce of the firm and most other jobs would be outsourced.[8] Another managerial strategy is to divide the employed staff more rigorously into those who participate in a career structure with training opportunities and those who have dead-end jobs in the sense that there are no opportunities for career advancement or training for more complex and responsible jobs. Perhaps the most important managerial strategy is the pursuit of flexibility in order to match exactly the supply and need for labour. Casual work on demand, zero hours contracts, and the use of temporary agency workers enable employers to minimise labour costs by avoiding any payment of wages when work is not required. For example, the number of workers on temporary contracts in the European Union (EU) grew by 15–20 per cent annually in the 1980s and 1990s.[9] The polarisation of the labour market into good and bad jobs has increased inequalities in income and job quality.[10]

This drive to reduce labour costs by transferring jobs into the secondary labour market is often assisted by legislation that grants employment law rights to those in the primary labour market but excludes those in the secondary labour market. Exclusion from employment rights is achieved by various techniques such as:

- limiting employment rights to employees and excluding those classified by private law as self-employed even though they are economically dependent contractors
- requiring qualifying periods of months or years before employment rights are acquired, thereby excluding most precarious jobs from coverage
- not holding core firms responsible for working conditions of employees of contractors and agencies.

---

8 Jill Rubery and Frank Wilkinson, 'Introduction' in Jill Rubery and Frank Wilkinson (eds), *Employer Strategy and the Labour Market* (Oxford University Press 1994) 1, 4.

9 Guy Standing, 'Labor Regulation in an Era of Fragmented Flexibility,' in Christoph F Buechtemann (ed), *Employment Security and Labor Market Behaviour*, (ILR Press 1993) 425, 433.

10 Duncan Gallie, 'Inequality in Job Quality: Class, Gender and Contract Type' in Chris Warhurst, Chris Mathieu, Rachel Dwyer (eds) *The Oxford Handbook of Job Quality* (Oxford University Press 2022) 318.

These restrictions on the scope of employment rights reduce compliance costs for employers in the secondary market, which provides a further incentive for employers in the primary labour market to try to export as many jobs as possible to the secondary segment of the labour market.[11]

While few would deny that there is a clustering around the poles of good jobs and bad jobs in developed economies, the theory of segmented labour markets makes one further controversial claim. This is the contention that most workers in the secondary labour market of bad jobs find it very hard to move into the better jobs in the primary labour market. Workers in the secondary market find themselves trapped in a cycle of moving from one bad job to another, always blocked from the opportunity of a permanent career with good prospects. Neo-classical economic theory would normally explain such a barrier between the segmented and non-competing labour markets by reference to either educational attainment or to search costs, but the theory of segmented labour markets doubts the adequacy of such explanations.

If it is true that the better jobs typically require at least school leaver qualifications and most will require some kind of further education, the barrier to entry to the primary labour market could be explained simply by differences between individual education or 'human capital'.[12] But segmented labour market theories insist that educational attainment cannot explain the barriers to entry into the primary labour market, because the differences in attainment on average are not sufficiently great to explain the enormous divergence of terms of employment in the labour market.[13] Furthermore, certain groups such as women are disproportionately represented in the secondary labour market, as evidenced by persistent gender pay gaps, even though their levels of education are broadly similar to men's attainment.

Another economic explanation of the existence of a barrier between the segments of the labour market is the availability of limited resources to conduct a job search. Workers in the primary labour market who lose their jobs are likely to have the resources and savings to remain

---

11 Hugh Collins, 'Independent Contractors and the Challenge of Vertical Disintegration to Employment Protection Laws' (1990) 10 Oxford Journal of Legal Studies 353; Einat Albin and Jeremias Prassl, 'Fragmenting Work, Fragmented Regulation: The Contract of Employment as a Driver of Social Exclusion', in Mark Freedland (ed), *The Contract of Employment* (Oxford University Press 2016) 209.

12 Glen G Cain, 'The Challenge of Dual and Radical Theories of the Labor Market to Orthodox Theory' (1975) 65(2) American Economic Review, Papers and Proceedings of the Eighty-seventh Annual Meeting of the American Economic Association (May 1975) 16.

13 Michael Wachter, 'The Primary and Secondary Market Mechanism: A Critique of the Dual Approach' (1974) 74(3) Brookings Paper on Economic Activity 637.

unemployed for several months to try to obtain another job in the primary labour market. In contrast, workers in the secondary labour market need to find another job quickly because they lack a cushion to fall back on and will be subject to stringent provisions of welfare conditionality.[14] Looking urgently for a job, they are likely to take the first they find, even if it is badly paid and precarious. Although this explanation of patterns of job search partly explains some of the difficulty experienced by workers in transferring into the primary labour market, again it does not seem to be sufficient to account for the full exclusionary force of the barrier. The conclusion drawn by theories of segmented labour markets is that there must also be institutional and social causes of the barrier to entry into the primary labour market.[15]

The idea that the division between primary and secondary labour markets is caused by managerial strategies is also contested by supply-side aspects of neo-classical economic theory. It is argued that, to the extent that there is bunching in the labour market between good jobs and bad jobs, this is an equilibrium produced by the fact that many workers are looking for jobs that are part-time, casual, intermittent, or seasonal. The large and growing number of non-standard jobs is explained by this theory, which is frequently repeated in official policy documents, as a response by employers to these supply-side constraints.[16] For example, in the official UK report *Good Work: The Taylor Review of Modern Working Practices*, it is said that in our diverse labour force, people are looking for work 'that suits their individual lifestyle and preferences'.[17] On this view, it is the workers who are looking for flexible work arrangements in order to suit their roles as carers, parents, students, older workers seeking less demanding jobs, and so forth. In order to obtain the necessary labour, employers have to offer part-time or flexible work arrangements. The growth of the secondary labour market, on this account, is largely the product of changing rates of participation in the labour market, particularly the greater participation of women, who often seek non-standard employment to manage their caring responsibilities.

---

14 Virginia Mantouvalou, *Structural Injustice and Workers' Rights* (Oxford University Press 2023), Chapter 5.

15 Duncan Gallie and Michael White, 'Employer Policies and Employee Contracts' in Jill Rubery and Frank Wilkinson (eds), *Employer Strategy and the Labour Market* (Oxford University Press 1994) 69, 91.

16 Deirdre McCann, *Regulating Flexible Work* (Oxford University Press 2008), 174–177.

17 *Good Work: The Taylor Review of Modern Working Practices* (Department for Business, Energy and Industrial Strategy 2017) 26.

This kind of claim that the existence of the secondary labour market is a lifestyle choice by workers rather than an efficiency-driven gradual degradation of the terms on which work is offered by employers has been severely criticised.[18] It is true that some people such as students and carers of young children look for part-time work. But this is normally a heavily constrained choice or adapted preference: students without grants facing large bills try to pay for their studies and basic living expenses through a part-time job during term-time; because child care is unaffordable, parents try to manage to make ends meet by reducing their hours of work.[19] Furthermore, there is scant evidence that those who do seek non-standard work such as part-time work also want the job to have no fixed hours, to be temporary or of uncertain duration, to have few employment rights, and to be badly paid.[20]

An additional reason for scepticism about the story that workers' preferences cause the expansion of the secondary labour market is based on the different representation of groups in the non-standard jobs.[21] Women are the great majority of the 26 per cent of the workforce in part-time jobs, and they are also over-represented in casual work and temporary agency work. Jobs largely populated by women are often located in secondary labour markets; not because they do not require skills or commitment from employees, but because it is easy for employers to recruit women at low pay to do these jobs.[22] Young workers are also over-represented in casual work and agency work. Workers in their 50s or 60s are twice as likely to be self-employed as other groups. Black and minority ethnic workers are disproportionately represented in most types of work in the secondary labour market. These patterns

---

18 Sian Moore, Stephanie Tailby, Bethania Antunes and Kirsty Newsome, '"Fits and fancies": The Taylor Review, the Construction of Preference and Labour Market Segmentation' (2018) 49(5–6), Industrial Relations Journal 403.

19 V Gash, 'Preference or Constraint? Part-time Workers' Transitions in Denmark, France and the United Kingdom' (2008) 22 Work, Employment and Society 655.

20 Moore et al (n 18), 416.

21 Proportions vary between different countries, but the same groups such as women, ethnic minorities, migrants and young workers are always overrepresented in the secondary labour market: Silja Häusermann, Hanna Schwanderin, 'Varieties Of Dualization? Labor Market Segmentation and Insider-Outsider Divides Across Regimes' in Patrick Emmenegger, Silja Hausermann, Brunol Palier, Martin Seleib-Kaiser (eds) *The Age of Dualization: The Changing Face of Inequality in Deindustrializing Societies* (Oxford University Press 2012), 27.

22 Damian Grimshaw, Colette Fagan, Gail Hebson and Isabel Tavora, 'A New Labour Market Segmentation Approach for Analysing Inequalities: Introduction and Overview' in Damian Grimshaw, Colette Fagan, Gail Hebson and Isabel Tavora (eds), *Making Work More Equal* (Manchester UP 2017) 1, 13; Jill Rubery, 'Developing Segmentation Theory: A Thirty Year Perspective' (2007) 28:6 Économies et Sociétés 941 quoted in Grimshaw et al at 1, 3 and 12–15; Christine Craig, Elizabeth Garnsey and Jill Rubery 'Labour Market Segmentation and Women's Employment: A Case Study from the United Kingdom' (2007) 124(3) International Labour Review 267.

cast doubt on the claim that employers create bad jobs to match the preferences of workers. The groups who are disproportionately represented in the secondary labour market are the groups that usually find it harder to obtain a job at all. Workers in these groups are therefore disproportionately likely to accept precarious and badly paid employment because of the absence of alternatives.[23] The existence of a secondary labour market depends therefore to some extent on the background social structures that construct disadvantaged groups in society and at the same time this segmented market structure tends to entrench those divisions and encourage stigma to be attached to those who are locked into the secondary labour market.[24]

What this brief survey of the theory of labour market segmentation establishes is that this equilibrium of dualism in the labour market is not achieved by matching the preferences and skills of workers to the jobs that need to be done. On the contrary, the segmentation is produced to a significant extent by employers' strategies for minimising labour costs. Employers can use their bargaining power, which is relatively strong when dealing with already socially and economically disadvantaged groups, to insist on terms of employment that impose the risk of absence of work on workers, to avoid any supplementary payments for overtime or unsocial hours, and to use the continuous threat of dismissal (or simply not providing further work to casual workers) to reinforce structures of subordination, to discourage resistance to these poor terms of employment and to encourage cooperation on the part of the workforce without any significant reciprocity in helping employees to manage their work-life balance. It is much harder for employers to make such demands on workers in the primary labour market because these workers have stronger bargaining power, are often unionised and enjoy employment rights and a full social security safety net based on contributory benefits that enables them to resist attempts to worsen their terms of employment. The segmentation of the labour market represents an invisible structure that places a significant barrier for workers in the secondary labour market (the outsiders) to obtain the better jobs and a higher standard of living of the insiders in the primary labour market.[25] Nevertheless, the risk of falling into the secondary

---

23 Jill Rubery, 'Internal and External Labour Markets: Towards an Integrated Analysis' in Jill Rubery and Frank Wilkinson (eds), *Employer Strategy and the Labour Market* (Oxford University Press 1994) 37, 56–57.

24 Moore (n 18), 417.

25 Thomas Biegert, 'On the Outside Looking In? Transitions out of Non-employment in the United Kingdom and Germany' (2014) 24 Journal of European Social Policy 3.

labour market grows all the time as employers try to reduce labour costs in response to competitive pressures of automation and globalisation by making more of their workforce hold precarious positions.[26] The white men who have in the past tended to be the main beneficiaries of the segmented labour market are waking up to the danger that they might lose their privileged position. Their response to this predicament may account for greater support for populist leaders and nationalist politics.[27]

Injustice

Does this structure of segmented labour markets cause injustice? There are several grounds on which the segmentation of the labour market can be criticised for leading to injustice. I will briefly consider three: equality, autonomy or self-realisation, and fair opportunity.

Equality

The first ground for describing labour market segmentation as unjust is the claim that that it leads to greater inequality in society. Segmentation into good jobs and bad jobs certainly corresponds to inequalities in income and therefore in the material conditions in which people live. Divergence in material conditions is likely to be correlated with inequalities in wellbeing or human flourishing. Unless one believes that all inequalities in income from wages are unjust, however, disparities in wages are not automatically unjust. The criticism of the injustice of segmented labour markets may therefore be better stated as the unjust degree of differentiation in pay between those in the good jobs and those in the secondary labour market. On this view, some differences in pay might be justified as merited on the ground that it is right to reward those with better skills and education more highly to the extent that they are likely to be more productive than others. Yet this justification of wage differences by reference to human capital is inadequate, according to segmented labour market theory, as we have seen, because the differences in pay are too great to be accounted for by those factors such as skills and education, especially for women and minority groups. The construction of the secondary labour market and precarious jobs by employers has apparently permitted them to isolate and hire predominately from groups that have weak bargaining power

26 Goos, Manning, Salomons (n 2).
27 Arlie Russell Hochschild, *Strangers in their Own Land* (The New Press 2016).

(though not necessarily poor education and skills), thereby creating greater inequalities than before and greater inequalities than might be justified by reference to their demand for particular skills.

Although it might be accepted that the wage differentials between primary and secondary labour markets are excessive, it may be responded that this is an unfortunate necessity in order to help disadvantaged groups. It can be argued that the secondary labour market, though constructing and sustaining greater inequality in incomes, has the merit that it can absorb very quickly large numbers of workers, so that unemployment rates are likely to be lower. High levels of employment are likely to favour those who find it hardest to obtain jobs. The higher levels of employment can, it might be argued, offset the greater inequalities in income in a segmented labour market by avoiding the poverty associated with unemployment. In short, without secondary labour markets, workers would be even worse off by being more likely to be unemployed and forced to rely on meagre social welfare benefits from the state.

A different kind of equality argument approaches the issue dynamically. On this approach, a just society is one that seeks to achieve a progressive equalisation of resources and material wealth for all citizens.[28] A society that permits employers to establish institutional structures that enable them to take steps such as outsourcing and casualisation in order to reduce the pay of their workers is unjust. On this view, it is not the absolute or relative amounts of income that are of concern, but rather the direction of movement in wages. The gradual impoverishment of workers in the secondary labour market in comparison with those in the primary labour market, or the growth in relative deprivation, is what amounts to injustice. This examination of justice in terms of the direction of movement looks at whether the changes improve or damage justice. This approach does not try to develop abstract principles of justice that should guide the basic institutions of society, but rather asks of each institution or decision whether it improves justice in society. This kind of 'realisation-focused' approach to justice is articulated in the work of Sen,[29] and is at the heart of the political catch-phrase 'levelling-up'.

---

28 This idea of progressive equality appears to lie at the core of the assessment of segmentation in Grimshaw et al (n 22).

29 Amartya Sen, *The Idea of Justice* (Penguin 2009), 8–10.

Self-realisation

Another ground for criticising the justice of segmented labour markets is their interference with the possibility of participants in the secondary labour market of pursuing their own life plans. To understand this point, it is necessary to appreciate the lived experience of work for many employed in the secondary labour market, particularly those in precarious jobs in which it is uncertain whether there will be work to be done and when it may be available. Workers in such jobs have a feeling of insecurity about their job and livelihood, a feeling of profound uncertainty about what even the near future may hold, and are conscious of an underlying risk to their personal life and its structures such as possessions and membership of a community.[30] This situation effectively undermines their freedom to develop and pursue their own life plan, which in turn is likely to harm wellbeing and provoke mental stress.[31] This kind of positive freedom to develop and pursue one's own life plan is described in political theories using a variety of terminology such as the value of 'autonomy',[32] self-development, self-determination,[33] or self-realisation.

Opportunity

A third ground for regarding segmented labour markets as unjust focuses on the distribution of opportunities to obtain good jobs. The claim is that the current distribution of opportunities is unjust because of the barrier facing those working in the secondary labour market. Even those with the talents and skills to perform the higher paying and more rewarding jobs in the primary labour market are in practice frequently excluded. In Rawls' theory of justice, his revised second principle of justice for the basic institutions of society was that social and economic inequalities are to be attached to offices and positions open to all under conditions of fair equality of opportunity.[34] Although it is arguable whether or not the labour market and its segmentation is part of the 'basic structure' in the sense intended by Rawls,[35] it is clear that Rawls believed that the rules

---

30 Arne L Kalleberg and Steven P Vallas, 'Probing Precarious Work' in Arne L Kalleberg and Steven P Vallas (eds) *Research in the Sociology of Work* (vol 31 Emerald Publishing 2017) 1, 4.
31 ibid, 17–18.
32 Joseph Raz, *The Morality of Freedom* (Oxford University Press 1986).
33 Iris Marion Young. *Justice and the Politics of Difference* (Princeton University Press 1990), 37.
34 John Rawls, *Justice as Fairness: A Restatement* (ed E Kelly) (Harvard University Press 2001), 42
35 Samuel Scheffler, 'Is the Basic Structure Basic?' in Christine Sypnowich (ed), *The Egalitarian Conscience: Essays in Honour of GA Cohen* (Oxford University Press 2006); Samuel Scheffler, 'Distributive Justice, the Basic Structure and the Place of Private Law' (2015) 35 Oxford Journal of Legal Studies 213.

of the basic institutions should prevent the wealthy and powerful from using their resources to distort background conditions of procedural justice, such as the condition of fair equality of opportunity with regard to political office and jobs.

It is also possible to analyse the denial of opportunity to workers in the secondary labour market in Sen's language of capabilities.[36] His focus is on the extent to which a person has the capability to do things he or she has reason to value. Although there are other requirements of justice to be taken into consideration, an important general aim of justice, according to Sen, is to augment people's advantages in terms of their capabilities. Segmentation theory argues that some disadvantaged groups in society are effectively blocked from obtaining one kind of thing that they are likely to have reason to value: a well-paid, secure job. These groups have less real opportunity in practice than most people, even though some of their members may be lucky and obtain a good job. Having a good job is not the only capability that people have reason to value of course: many may value a different work-life balance than may be available in full-time permanent jobs. It follows that a person being in the secondary labour market is not necessarily a diminution of their capability. Even so, for most people, the barrier to better jobs is likely to frustrate their aspirations and ambitions. On Sen's approach, therefore, subject to the point previously made about levels of unemployment for disadvantaged groups, justice could arguably be improved by trying to dismantle the barriers to access of good jobs.

Structural or instrumental injustice?

For at least these three reasons concerning equality, self-realisation and fair opportunity, there is ample reason to think that segmented labour markets lead to injustice. But is this injustice the result of some individuals committing wrongs against others or is it simply a product of the structures of a market economy? If the latter, it is the kind of injustice that Iris Marion Young called 'structural injustice'.[37] It is the kind of injustice that is not deliberately or at least recklessly inflicted by anyone, but is rather the product of everyone acting in accordance with the

36 Amartya Sen, *Development as Freedom* (Oxford University Press 1999); Amartya Sen, *The Idea of Justice* (Penguin 2009); Brian Langille (ed), *The Capability Approach to Labor Law* (Oxford University Press 2019).
37 See the excellent account in Maeve McKeown, 'Structural Injustice' (2021) 16 Philosophy Compass, e12757.

normal rules of a market society, those rules that lawyers might call the rules of private law such as contract law and property law. Theories of the segmentation of labour markets provide evidence for differing answers to the question of how this injustice comes about. The theories can be divided broadly into structural accounts and instrumental accounts.

Structural accounts tend to stress that patterns in labour markets are simply the product of a vector of forces of supply and demand resulting from economic actors all pursuing their rational self-interest in lawful ways. The outcome of these market forces is that there are good jobs and bad jobs. Nevertheless, this labour market segmentation does produce a kind of structural injustice, because (and this is the crucial point) the existence of the bad jobs helps to sustain the existence of the good jobs. In this model of the equilibrium between primary and secondary labour markets, it is the savings in labour costs by paying wages matching the secondary labour market rates that enables the employer to pay the much higher wages for permanent staff in the primary labour market. Furthermore, outsourcing enables employers both to offer secure permanent jobs to employees in the primary sector while at the same time achieving numerical flexibility efficiently for when there is a decline in demand by simply terminating the contracts of contractors, agency workers and casual workers. There is a labour market equilibrium that gradually increases the disparities of pay and job security between the primary and secondary labour markets as employers drive hard bargains with those with weak bargaining power in order to pay for the rapidly growing salaries and job security of their managerial and professional employees.

This outcome of the interdependence of good and bad jobs producing structural injustice fits Young's much cited proposed definition of structural injustice closely:

> Structural injustice, then, exists when social processes put large groups of persons under systematic threat of domination or deprivation of the means to develop and exercise their capacities, at the same time that these processes enable others to dominate or to have a wide range of opportunities for developing and exercising capacities available to them.[38]

38 Iris Marion Young, *Responsibility for Justice* (Oxford University Press 2011), 52.

On this structural account of labour market segmentation, it is the workers in the primary sector who end up 'dominating' those in the secondary sector, because the quality of the jobs of the insiders depends on the exploitation of the outsiders.

This account of who are the 'dominators' in the structure of injustice in the labour market tends to be rejected by theorists of labour market segmentation. They prefer to present capital and the managers running business organisations as dominators and wrongdoers. These instrumental accounts stress the important role of employers in constructing a divided labour market. It is claimed that employers are the 'architects' of institutions in the labour market,[39] of which segmented labour markets is one institution that has come to predominate and cause injustice. Often governments are also held to be complicit by not intervening to prevent labour market segmentation and bypassing laws that support and promote outsourcing and various kinds of flexibility.

Are there wrongdoers? Or is labour market segmentation and its associated injustices simply the result of everyone going about their lawful business? Are the dominators those who hold good jobs or are they the employers and supportive governments who use their bargaining power to impose these unjust structures? The choice between these rival accounts of the source of injustice in segmented labour markets seems to me to require a quite nuanced account. An example may help us to see the complexity of this issue.

Consider the case of Mandy, the CEO of a hospital trust in the NHS that is facing a shortfall of funds running to several millions of pounds. Under the legal rules of public accounting, savings must be made. One way to cut costs is to reduce the service to the public by, for instance, delaying non-urgent operations and thereby lengthening waiting lists. Other kinds of changes to the services might also be made. An alternative that has been proposed is to outsource the catering services for the hospital to an independent contractor. After a competitive tendering for the service, an external contractor is likely to produce the necessary savings in the costs of catering to keep all the hospital services running as normal. Mandy is concerned about the fate of the existing kitchen staff, but she is informed (correctly) that all of them will be offered jobs by the contractor. Mandy decides to outsource catering services and thereby avoid lengthening the waiting lists and damaging public health.

39 Rubery (n 22).

The external contractor which can provide catering services more cheaply may be able to take advantage of economies of scale and make savings in various administrative and logistical ways. But the bulk of the savings in the long run will come from a reduction in labour costs. In the medium term, the contractor will try to reduce staff numbers, remove fringe benefits and reduce wages. The contractor will deny recognition to any trade union and not observe the terms set in other collective agreements governing similar jobs. It will also put downward pressure on wages by hiring new people at lower rates of pay than incumbents.

In deciding to outsource the catering work, was Mandy a wrongdoer or merely a cog in the machine of the state and the economy who acted in what she reasonably understood to be in the public interest after balancing the interests of patients against those of the catering staff? Could she be a wrongdoer if what she did was arguably just?

Although these are difficult questions to answer, it seems to me that any injustice resulting to the catering staff is mostly the product of structure rather than wrongdoing. Employers act under structural constraints. Managers will lose their jobs unless they make hard decisions about efficiency savings. The option that Mandy does not consider is to impose a pay cut on all the existing staff or the better paid staff in the hospital. That option is probably not practicable because those groups are unionised, benefit from collective agreements and have the bargaining power to close the hospital or quit and get better jobs elsewhere. From that point of view, Mandy cannot challenge the 'dominators' in the primary labour market, such as the doctors, nurses and highly paid managers. Her only option is to exclude a weaker group of staff from the scope of the primary labour market by contracting out the service. Mandy is trapped by the structure of the segmented labour market like everyone else. However, it seems to me that there are two grounds on which a charge of wrongdoing might be levelled against Mandy.

First, as Mandy will be aware, the strategy of outsourcing work to contractors does inevitably take employees outside the organisation. They are excluded from the social and ethical norms of the employing organisation, which in this case will be infused with the moral aspirations of the NHS. Not only will outsourced workers therefore lose a connection with the relevant standards of just and fair working conditions within the organisation and all the opportunities for career development that such an organisation might offer, but also they will be excluded from an ethos of a public health service that may cause a significant setback to their experience of self-determination.

Second, Mandy may possibly be aware that the cleaning contractor is likely to take much greater advantage of its superior bargaining power over various kinds of disadvantaged groups in the labour market; especially women, migrants and members of racial and ethnic minorities, all of whom find it difficult in practice to obtain good jobs. I am less confident that Mandy is aware of this point, but she must have some kind of view about how the contractor can provide the catering service at lower cost than the in-house operation, and it is hard to escape the conclusion that she must appreciate that savings will be achieved by paying staff less and that people who are prepared to accept low wages tend to be disproportionately drawn from disadvantaged groups.[40] Mandy is therefore condoning the market practices that tend to relegate minorities and women to poverty wages in the secondary labour market.

The conclusion that I draw from this analysis of the hypothetical example of Mandy's decision to outsource the catering services is that it is in general true that segmented labour markets illustrate Young's concept of structural injustice. Yet like many other examples of structural injustice, there are possible grounds for holding people responsible to some degree for the negative consequences for those people who are involuntarily stuck in the secondary labour market.

Legal remedies

To what extent does the current law challenge the structural injustice of segmented labour markets?[41] It is important to recall that this structural injustice is largely the product of people using the ordinary rules of private law, such as contract and property law. The whole point of private law is to permit individuals and organisations to make their own plans, forge their own transactions and pursue their interests. The starting point of the law is therefore deference to whatever is done by businesses under the ordinary rules of private law. However, employment law and related branches of the law have always placed some constraints on those business activities by regulating contracts of employment and

40 Some may object that it is not Mandy but the contractor who is the wrongdoer in my example. It may be true that the contractor is a wrongdoer in exploiting the vulnerable, but my enquiry is about the segmentation of the labour market. It is Mandy who makes the decision to segment the labour market in this case – she is the architect – and the question is whether that decision amounts to wrongdoing.

41 The following discussion concerns the law in the United Kingdom. Much of this law is based on the law of the European Union (EU), so it applies in roughly the same way throughout the EU. The law in other jurisdictions such as the USA may differ considerably.

granting workers mandatory rights. What we need to consider here is what employment laws, if any, place constraints on the functioning of segmented labour markets in ways that relieve structural injustice.

The following discussion considers three tasks performed by the current law in the United Kingdom. First, the law can reduce the disadvantage experienced by workers in the secondary labour market. Second, the law can challenge the validity of the barriers experienced by workers when seeking to obtain jobs in the primary labour market. Third, the law can also sometimes challenge the construction of secondary labour market institutions by employers. This last purpose of legal regulation is of particular interest because in principle it would permit a challenge to the decision by Mandy to outsource work in my hypothetical example. In other words, the third type of legal regulation purports to identify a possible wrong that might be committed by Mandy or other employer architects of a fractured labour force.

Reducing the disadvantage for workers in the secondary labour market

Most of these laws are designed to place a mandatory floor on terms of employment. For instance, minimum wage laws and working time regulations establish a floor on the level of disadvantage for those confined to jobs in the secondary market.[42] Gaps in the statute's coverage are sometimes exploited by employers, as in the attempts, often unsuccessful, to present workers as independent contractors to whom minimum wage laws and working time regulations are inapplicable. But with careful drafting of legislation and purposive interpretation by the courts,[43] the law can be written in a comprehensive manner to include everyone who engages in paid labour except those who are genuinely self-employed running their own business.

The Transfer of Undertakings Regulations place some constraints on using outsourcing to move jobs from the primary labour market to the secondary labour market.[44] The Regulations require the contractor to which work is outsourced to take on the same employees on the same

42 National Minimum Wage Act 1998; Working Time Regulations 1998 SI 1833; Paul Marx, Peter Starke, 'Dualization as Destiny? The Political Economy of the German Minimum Wage Reform' (2017) 45(4) Politics and Society 559.

43 For example, *Uber BV v Aslam* [2021] UKSC 5 [2021] ICR 657, [2021] IRLR 407; Guy Davidov, *A Purposive Approach to Labour Law* (Oxford University Press 2016); Michael Ford and Alan Bogg, 'Between Statute and Contract: Who is a Worker?' (2019) 135 LQR 347.

44 Transfer of Undertakings (Protection of Employment) Regulations 2006, SI 2006 No 246, based on the Acquired Rights Directive 2001/23, formerly Directive 77/187.

terms and conditions as they enjoyed when previously employed by the core employer. The contractor is also bound to observe the terms and conditions of any applicable collective agreement that the core employer had entered with a recognised trade union. These legal requirements remove the possibility of transferring the workers onto the lower levels of remuneration in the secondary labour market immediately. However, after a time, the contractor is entitled to reorganise its business, reject any relevant collective agreement, and offer new terms and conditions, provided such measures are not regarded as connected to the original transfer or outsourcing.[45] Furthermore, a contractor can always reduce the size of the labour force for redundancy or similar kinds of financial reasons.

Under the influence of the law of the European Union, there are also limited protections against unfair treatment of workers who work under non-standard contracts. For part-time workers, there is a requirement that they should be paid pro rata in comparison to full-time employees of the same employers.[46] The effect of this rule is to protect part-time jobs in the business from relatively disadvantageous treatment. The employer cannot simply erect a barrier between these two groups of employees and insist that the part-time group receives lower rates of pay per hour. However, the legislation contains a potentially broad exception. The employer can present a defence that there are objective grounds that justify the difference in treatment of part-time workers. Although the legislation does not specify what might constitute objective grounds, a saving on labour costs by paying part-timers less or granting them fewer fringe benefits such as pensions is not in itself an objective ground for different treatment.[47] However, in all challenges to discriminatory treatment, disadvantaged part-time workers must demonstrate that they work under the same kind of contract as the comparator full-time workers. The comparison will not be possible, for instance, if the full-time workers have permanent jobs with fixed hours, whereas the part-timers are casual workers, employed as when required with no fixed hours of work.[48]

45 *Wilson v St Helens Borough Council* [1998] ICR 1141 (HL); *Alemo-Herron v Parkwood Leisure Ltd* Case C 426/11 [2013] ICR 1116 (CJEU).

46 Part-time Workers (Prevention of Less Favourable Treatment) regulations 2000, regulation 5, based on Council Directive 97/81/EC concerning the framework agreement on part-time work concluded by UNICE, CEEP and the ETUC.

47 *Ministry of Justice v O'Brien* [2013] UKSC 6, [2013] ICR 499.

48 *Wippel v Peek and Cloppenburg GmbH & Co KG Case* C-313/02 [2005] ECR I-9483, [2005] ICR 1604.

Another common feature of jobs in the secondary labour market is that they are often temporary, fixed-term jobs. In such instances, the employer seeks to achieve numerical flexibility by putting staff on short-term contracts such as a year or six months. At the expiration of that term of employment, the contract comes to an end under the terms of the agreement. The law in the UK deems such an expiration of a fixed term to count as a 'dismissal' for the purposes of bringing a claim for unfair dismissal or a redundancy payment. Unfortunately, since these rights have a qualifying period of two years, fixed-term workers are unlikely to be protected. An additional regulation requires, however, that once an employee has worked for an employer in a succession of fixed-term contracts for four years, their contract is automatically converted into a permanent contract.[49] In effect, the employee is possibly converted from the secondary labour market into the primary labour market by operation of law. This mechanism is easily avoided by the employer stopping issuing fixed-term contracts as the four years deadline approaches. There is also an exception where the employer can present an 'objective justification' for not converting the contract into a permanent arrangement. This justification has been interpreted broadly to include any kind of business reason for offering fixed-term contracts, provided the employer is not using a succession of fixed-term contracts as a device to disguise permanent employment.[50]

There is a similar easy avoidance device for temporary agency workers. The regulations require temporary agency workers to receive the same pay and basic conditions as those enjoyed by comparable employees of the client for whom they are working on assignment once they have worked for that client for more than 12 weeks. Clients who use agency workers as a source of cheap precarious labour therefore are likely to terminate the agency workers' assignments after 12 weeks. This regulation seems unlikely to provide significant protection for agency workers against poor working conditions in the secondary labour market and may indeed provide employers with an incentive to make jobs even more precarious than they had originally envisaged at the time of hiring.

In short, the legal measures currently taken to protect workers in the secondary labour market against exploitative labour conditions are flawed in many respects. Even the effectiveness of the legislation

---

49 The Fixed-term Employees (Prevention of Less Favourable Treatment) Regulations 2002, based on Directive 99/70/EC concerning the framework agreement on fixed-term work concluded by ETUC, UNICE and CEEP.

50 *Secretary of State for Children, Schools and Families v Fletcher* [2011] UKSC 14, [2011] ICR 495.

on the statutory minimum wage can be questioned because it seems likely to cause some employers to devise ways to minimise wage costs by introducing zero hours and casual work contracts. To reduce that incentive to create precarious jobs, it would be necessary to require employers to offer jobs with minimum hours of work, or more invasively, to make 'zero hours' or 'on demand' contracts unlawful.

Challenging the validity of the barriers to access to the primary labour market

The law of discrimination provides the only broad legal basis on which hiring decisions of employers can be challenged. The claims are limited to members of the groups that are protected under the Equality Act 2010 such as women, racial minorities and the disabled. Trade union members also receive protection against discrimination in hiring decisions on the ground of their membership and activities for the union.[51] The question here is whether discrimination law can help to challenge the invisible barriers to primary sector jobs.

As we have noted already, women and racial minorities are disproportionately represented in the secondary labour market. The law of discrimination initially tackles this problem for women and minorities by manipulating the standards of proof of wrongdoing.[52] An employer may deny that any kind of intentional discrimination is exercised when hiring for positions in a primary labour market job. Indeed, discrimination on the basis of stereotypes may be due to wholly unconscious bias. However, the law is prepared to infer direct discrimination from a statistical pattern. If women and minorities apply for these jobs, but few or none are appointed, a pattern emerges from these hiring decisions from which a court may be prepared to infer the presence of discrimination. Proof of intention to discriminate is not required. However, gathering the necessary statistical evidence is often time-consuming and expensive, putting this legal remedy beyond the reach of most workers in the labour market. Moreover, an employer can rebut this inference of discrimination by demonstrating that the selection of staff has been done in accordance with objective criteria that are untainted by gender or racial bias. These objective requirements

51 This protection is based on domestic legislation (Trade Union and Labour Relations (Consolidation) Act 1992 s.137(1)) and Article 11 European Convention on Human Rights.
52 Equality Act 2010, s.136(2): 'If there are facts from which the court could decide, in the absence of any other explanation, that a person (A) contravened the provision concerned, the court must hold that the contravention occurred.'

might be educational and skills requirements, or an examination or test, or some other formal and recognised way to try to measure a potential employee's aptitude for a job.

If an employer can demonstrate that the hiring decisions were based upon such objective criteria, it will succeed in rebutting the inference of direct discrimination. However, the employer then opens itself up to a potential claim that it has committed indirect discrimination in its hiring decisions. The law of indirect discrimination tackles rules and practices which, though neutral in appearance, in practice have a disproportionate adverse impact on a disadvantaged group such as women and minorities.[53] The employer can justify those rules and practices, however, if they are a proportionate means of achieving a legitimate aim. The employer has the burden of demonstrating a legitimate aim, such as hiring people who are competent to perform the job, and (what is much harder) that other means for ascertaining competence would not avoid that disadvantageous impact on the protected group.

Challenging the use of the secondary labour market

As I have noted, in general, the law is unlikely to seek to interfere with managers of a business or public sector organisation who are trying to reduce costs by outsourcing some jobs to the secondary labour market. Typically, Parliament and judges defer to managerial decisions about efficiency. Yet the law of indirect discrimination may sometimes provide a way of challenging outsourcing. If the outsourced jobs are disproportionately occupied by women, racial minorities, or some other protected group, it may be possible to argue that the decision to outsource work, and therefore for the jobs to be paid less than in-house workers, has an adverse effect on the protected group that is disproportionately represented in the outsourced jobs.

A claim of this kind was made in *Boohene and others v The Royal Parks Agency*.[54] The employer is responsible for the Royal Parks in London, including keeping them clean and tidy. The Agency decided to outsource the work involving the cleaning of toilets and buildings. The successful bidder offered the Agency two prices, one where the workers would be paid the statutory National Minimum Wage and the other where they would receive, like the other employees of the Agency, the substantially higher, but not legally required, London Living Wage. The Agency opted

53 Equality Act 2010, s.19.
54 ET Cases 2202211/2020, 2204440/2020 and 2205570/2020.

for National Minimum Wage to keep the cost to a minimum. The evidence demonstrated that nearly all the workers for the contractor were black and migrants. The consequence of the Agency's decision was that the largely white in-house employees of the Agency were paid the London Living Wage (in accordance with public sector practice) and the mostly black, migrant workers for the contractor were on the National Minimum Wage.

The workers employed by the contractor went on strike and succeeded in gaining the London Living Wage. The question before the employment tribunal was whether there had been indirect discrimination prior to the successful strike. The Agency had clearly applied a criterion that in-house workers would be paid at or above the London Living Wage and that some outsourced workers would only receive the national minimum wage. That decision put the outsourced workers at a particular disadvantage. It had a discriminatory effect, given the racial composition of the two groups of workers. The Agency failed to put forward any relevant justification. The mere fact that acceptance of a bid entailing the London Living Wage would cost more was not in itself an adequate justification. Therefore, the tribunal concluded that there had been indirect discrimination, though on appeal the decision was overturned on the technical ground that there was insufficient evidence put forward to support the conclusion.[55]

This challenge to the employer's practice of outsourcing to take advantage of segmented labour markets does not, of course, address all aspects of the operation of the secondary labour market. Furthermore, this case is unusual because it could use a special provision in the Equality Act 2010, which holds the main employer liable for the terms and conditions of workers employed by a contractor.[56] Outside of this provision, it is normally not possible to hold one employer responsible for the practices and conduct of another. If an outsourced contractor or an employment agency pays very low wages or refuses to recognise a trade union for the purposes of collective bargaining, it is of no concern to the core business.

Yet the *Boohene* case does provide a glimpse into the possibility of sometimes finding the employer, as architect of the institutional structure, guilty of wrongdoing. This is not an intentional harm, but it may be thought to be negligent or careless not to consider the adverse

55 *The Royal Parks Ltd v Boohene & Ors* [2023] EAT 69 (05 May 2023).
56 Equality Act 2010, s.41.

consequences for already disadvantaged groups.[57] The disadvantage to the workers from a racial minority may have been what Young calls 'unintended consequence',[58] but it seems to me to be a foreseeable consequence of many employers' decisions to try various mechanisms such as outsourcing and temporary agency workers in order to be able to exploit the lower labour costs in the secondary labour market. The law of indirect discrimination demonstrates, contrary to Young's assumption, that the law can sometimes label employers wrongdoers for unintended consequences. On this basis, Mandy in my hypothetical example above, would be at a small risk of a claim for compensation for indirect discrimination.

Conclusions and future possibilities

Segmented labour markets in advanced post-industrial economies illustrate features that can be described as structural injustice. The analysis is supported by two features of labour market segmentation. The first is provided by the almost invisible barriers between the primary and secondary labour markets that effectively prevent transition to the better jobs for those stuck in the secondary labour market. The second is that the existence of the better conditions in the primary labour market depends to a considerable extent on employers being able to obtain the efficiencies of exploiting labour in the secondary labour market to reduce labour costs. Although these features of segmented labour markets tally closely with the theory of structural injustice, there is evidence that to some extent employers are deliberate architects of labour market segmentation, especially in instances of outsourcing and vertical disintegration.

Employment law in the United Kingdom places some constraints on how far employers can exploit the use of segmented labour markets such as the imposition of mandatory minimum standards and prevention of discrimination in hiring practices. For the most part, the legal framework gives employers a free hand in devising strategies that can take advantage of and extend the depth of the divide between the primary and secondary labour markets. Current *laissez-faire* government policy seems to be influenced by overstated and misleading claims that workers in the secondary labour market choose those jobs because of the flexibility they

57 Sophia Moreau, 'The Moral Seriousness of Indirect Discrimination' in Hugh Collins and Tarunabh Khaitan (eds), *Foundations of Indirect Discrimination Law* (Hart Publishing 2018) 123.
58 Young (n 38), 52–64.

accord. In so far as the use of secondary labour markets can be presented as a deliberate managerial choice, as in the case of outsourcing and other techniques of flexibilisation, occasionally it may be possible to use the law of discrimination to demonstrate that the practice is unlawful because it amounts to indirect discrimination.

The source of the structural injustice presented by labour market segmentation is not for the most part particular pieces of legislation, though sometimes legislation may make the situation even worse. In those latter cases, it may be possible to challenge the validity of the legislation by reference to fundamental rights.[59] However, most labour market segmentation is constructed and regulated by ordinary private law. An organisation can decide to outsource some of its work by entering a commercial contract with a supplier or employment agency. That decision is regulated by the ordinary law of contract, which in general favours freedom of contract. Similarly, an employer can decide to employ workers directly, but to obtain flexibility and savings in labour costs by offering the workers only casual work, temporary work, part-time work, or fixed-term contracts. Usually there is no legal restriction on such a choice.

To tackle the origins of the structural injustice presented by segmented labour markets therefore requires a reconsideration of the rules of private law. Limitations on freedom of contract may be required. Such limitation might include mandatory rules that guarantee casual workers a minimum number of hours of work and the opportunity to convert their jobs into permanent contracts. Similarly, there could be a mandatory legal framework for agency workers that ensured that they benefit from all employment law rights that are enforceable against both the agency and the client of the agency for whom they work. Alternatively, businesses may have to be held accountable for the decisions of other businesses to which they outsource work in their supply chains. Legislation might compel core employers to be responsible to some extent for what happens to workers employed by their contractors and in their supply chains. At present, responsibility of one company for the employment practices of another is limited to some occasions where the contractor is a wholly owned subsidiary or a company with the same parent company.[60]

59 Mantouvalou (n 14), Chapters 7 and 8.

60 Hugh Collins, 'Ascription of Legal Responsibility to Groups in Complex Economic Organisations' (1990) 53 MLR 731.

In the absence of such mandatory legislation to combat the worst effects of labour market segmentation, it may be possible for judges to develop the common law in directions that may assist in the reduction of disadvantage. For instance, the common law has traditionally been reluctant to imply contracts unless they seem strictly necessary to explain the business relations. It might be argued, however, that such implied contracts might be appropriate for casual workers, gig workers and agency workers. Casual workers or zero hours workers, though having a contract of employment when they perform work, appear to lack any binding contract at all between jobs, which has the effect that they also have no employment law rights (whether mandatory or not). It may be possible to draw on the emerging theory of relational contracts in employment to justify a finding of a permanent contract based upon reasonable expectations rather than explicit commitments, in which case casual workers might benefit from employment law rights.[61] Similarly, where the division of labour relies upon a series of closely connected and interdependent contracts, as in the case of agency workers and some gig workers such as Uber drivers,[62] it may be possible to draw on the emerging theory of networks of contracts to justify the implication of contract between parties who lack a formal contract but are nevertheless functioning as if it were an integrated organisation.[63]

---

61 Hugh Collins, 'Employment as a Relational Contract' (2021) 137 LQR 426.
62 *Uber BV* (n 43).
63 Hugh Collins, 'Networks as a Legal Concept: Mythical Beast No More?' in Sinead Agnew and Sir Marcus Smith (eds), *Law at the Cutting Edge* (Hart Publishing 2024).

6

Freedom of association and structural injustice

Alan Bogg[1]

Introduction

Iris Marion Young's *Responsibility for Justice* provides a powerful manifesto for rethinking the nature of political responsibility. The lawyer's reflex is to consider justice as a bi-lateral corrective relation. This correlativity paradigm has been particularly influential in private law theory.[2] There is a right-holder and there is a duty-bearer. When the right-holder suffers a wrong, we look for the party who has wronged her. We are ordinarily concerned with identifying a causal connection between the wrongdoer and the injury to the victim, voluntary conduct by the wrongdoer, and a measure of blameworthiness and culpability. This might result in public accountability in a court. We also expect contrition from the wrongdoer who has breached the duty. The wrong may trigger further duties of reparation so that the wrongs are ameliorated and the situation of the victim is restored as far as possible to its original state. Young calls this the 'liability model' of responsibility and it is integral to legal responsibility for harms.[3]

By contrast, Young develops a 'social connection model' of responsibility that may be better situated in politics rather than law.[4] Political responsibility is not based on the individualised attribution of blame for past wrongs. Instead, it is shared within a political

1 I am extremely grateful to the editors and Danielle Worden for very helpful comments on an earlier draft. All errors remain my own responsibility.
2 Ernest J Weinrib, *The Idea of Private Law* (Oxford University Press 2013).
3 Iris Marion Young, *Responsibility for Justice* (Oxford University Press 2013), 97.
4 ibid Chapter 4.

community. We all must shoulder the responsibility for addressing the structural determinants of injustice. Structural injustice describes the situation where:

> … social processes put large groups of persons under systematic threat of domination or deprivation of the means to develop and exercise their capacities, at the same time that these processes enable others to dominate or have a wide range of opportunities for developing and exercising capacities available to them.[5]

The legal framework is often deeply implicated in the generation of these systematic threats. These legal structures might include migration status, the laws regulating tenancies and access to housing, welfare and social security systems, and labour laws. Whereas the 'liability model' operates within the bi-lateral legal relationships created by these structures, the 'social connection model' looks to the transformation of the structures themselves.

One of the more controversial aspects of Young's account is that those most affected by structural injustice share a responsibility to challenge those oppressive structures and to contribute to their eradication. My initial reaction was that there is something jarring about this. Legal responsibility usually places the reparative burden on the blameworthy wrongdoer rather than the innocent party. And there is something intuitively appealing about this 'liability model', at least in situations where an individual's rights have been violated by a culpable party. True enough, even on the 'liability model', the burden rests upon the injured party to hold the wrongdoer to account in a court. Yet the task of *collective* transformation may be far more burdensome. Is it not compounding the structural injustice to expect those who are marginalised and oppressed to share in the responsibility of collective transformation? And would it not be fairer to impose that burden on the beneficiaries of structural injustice; particularly in circumstances where powerful actors have deliberately capitalised on those structures at the expense of oppressed groups? This is an important challenge to structural injustice theory and it has been described as the 'victim blaming' objection by Maeve McKeown.[6]

5 ibid 52.
6 Maeve McKeown, 'Structural Injustice' (2021) Philosophy Compass 6.

Young is surely correct in her claim that structural emancipation is a political task. As a political task, it depends upon collective action. Structural change is often not the sole product of feats of individual heroism. To be transformative, these heroic feats must usually galvanise collective action. Ultimately, this depends upon collective organisation, solidarity and the patient collaborative work of collective transformation. Only through politics is it possible to reshape legal and social structures through coordinated action. There is a place for the 'liability model', of course. The oppressed and marginalised still have their rights, and whenever they are wronged, it is imperative that those wrongs are redressed. That is usually the province of law and courts. Yet Young's account of the 'social connection model' reminds us that politics is never conducted in solitude. It is an intensely practical and solidaristic activity whereby conflicting values and interests are conciliated in real political communities.[7]

We can detect strong echoes of these debates about responsibility within labour law. Within the domain of individual legal rights for workers, the 'liability model' is the dominant framework for our ideas about responsibility. This 'liability model' perspective on individual rights has always been complemented by a 'social connection model' perspective. This emphasises solidarity, self-organisation and collective action. Broadly speaking, this has corresponded to the basic division between (individual) employment law and (collective) labour law. Enduring industrial freedom for workers has always been achieved through the organisational efforts of workers themselves. Through trade unions and collective bargaining, workers have defended their own interests in order to lead dignified working lives. The history of labour law teaches us that it is only through collective action that organised workers have resisted the depredations of capitalism and political hostility. In this respect, the 'social connection model' in labour law reflects the brute reality of emancipation in labour markets and it credits the victims of capitalism, the workers, with agency, dignity and self-respect.

Yet there is a trap hidden away in some accounts of this 'social connection model' in labour law. It is based in a kind of 'victim blaming' and we must be scrupulous in rejecting it. It is rooted in the idea that trade unions and collective action arose spontaneously out of the voluntary efforts of workers themselves. Workers helped themselves without the assistance of law or state support. Conversely, where this spontaneous

7 Bernard Crick, *In Defence of Politics* (London and New York, Continuum, 2000) 5th edn.

self-organisation did not occur, workers themselves must be to blame for their fate. This mythology of self-help was encouraged by the descriptive labels sometimes used to describe the historical development of British labour law, such as 'voluntarism' or even 'collective laissez-faire'.[8] Later accounts have emphasised that strong state support has been critical to the growth and stability of collective bargaining.[9]

This chapter may be read as an intervention in these debates about the virtues and limits of the 'social connection model' in labour law. It is focused on freedom of association, a fundamental labour right that provides the legal foundation for trade union activities in the labour market. The second section examines three case studies involving collective action by workers in the face of structural injustice. These case studies are focused on specific examples involving gig workers in the delivery sector, garment workers in Leicester, and sacked seafarers at P&O Ferries. This case study method has epistemic advantages in locating discrete worker struggles within a broader structural context. It enables us to see the structural dimensions of injustice, such as migration laws or the legal prohibition of certain forms of strike action, that might otherwise be obscured by a 'liability model' of responsibility for wrongs.[10] It is only by understanding the shape of this structural context that we can identify how freedom of association might provide the effective support for collective action. The remainder of the chapter examines the current state of legal protection of freedom of association under Article 11 of the European Convention on Human Rights (ECHR). It identifies some important priorities for legal reform based on this structural injustice perspective.

Drawing on the case studies and the legal analysis, the chapter will develop three main arguments. First, trade unions are indispensable to effective collective action for the most marginalised and precarious workers. Trade unions have significant pooled resources, a permanent union bureaucracy with expertise, and the ability to coordinate collective action and deploy power strategically in labour markets and

8 For the historical development of these terms, see Alan Bogg, *The Democratic Aspects of Trade Union Recognition* (Hart 2009), Chapter 1.
9 K D Ewing, 'The State and Industrial Relations: "Collective laissez-faire" Revisited' (1998) 5 Historical Studies in Industrial Relations 1.
10 For a discussion of 'contextualism' over 'formalism' in examining the obstacles to human freedom, see Martha C Nussbaum, 'Foreword: Constitutions and Capabilities: "Perception" Against Lofty Formalism' (2007) 121 Harvard Law Review 4.

politics.[11] It is important that the law on freedom of association reflects the special importance of groups such as trade unions in empowering the most disadvantaged and providing them with a more audible voice. Secondly, states are under a positive duty to support these groups in organising the marginalised and oppressed. The legal structures that are constitutive of oppression and disempowerment are maintained with the active connivance or indifference of governments. There is no 'neutral' stance for the state in structural injustice: inaction or acquiescence compounds the disadvantage of those who are already structurally oppressed. The state must also ensure that associations have the rights and resources needed to respond effectively to these structural elements, and this empowerment will usually require active state support. Finally, freedom of association must be reformulated to underwrite a more positive and active role for the state, so that public institutions work collaboratively with workers and unions to transform oppressive structures. In this way, the vital importance of workers' agency is affirmed. At the same time, state responsibility to support the marginalised (and their associations) responds to the 'victim blaming' critique of structural injustice theories.

Structural injustice in employment: three case studies

In *Responsibility for Justice*, the story of 'Sandy' is central to Young's development of the distinctive idea of structural injustice. Sandy is struggling to make ends meet. She experiences multiple disadvantages in relation to her job situation, access to affordable and secure housing and educational opportunities for her children. These disadvantages interact cumulatively. They also tend to cascade, with precariousness in one domain (say, housing) rippling out into other domains (say, access to a bank account or a steady job). Her access to relevant goods and opportunities is not obviously curtailed by culpable employers or landlords acting to violate her legal rights. The constraints are structural. They concern the distribution of affordable housing, the law on leases and rental protection, access to public schools, social welfare eligibility, city planning, and safe and cheap public transportation within the urban environment. The narrative of Sandy's story is highly

11 Michael Ford QC and Tonia Novitz, 'There is Power in a Union? Revisiting Trade Union Functions in 2019', in Alan Bogg, Jacob Rowbottom and Alison Young (eds), *The Constitution of Social Democracy* (Hart 2020), 263.

contextualised. It means that we can understand the real nature of her disadvantages; the ways in which those disadvantages interact and reinforce each other. We can also trace the sheer multiplicity of different agents (many of them acting innocently within existing legal structures) who contribute almost invisibly to her disadvantaged life situation.

This rich narrative method of the case study, of which Sandy's story is an example, counters some reductive tendencies in the 'liability model' of justice. The 'liability model' is focused on identifying the culpable agent who has wronged Sandy and must be held accountable for the wrong. It is typical of the lawyer's view of the world. It is reflected in a tendency to decontextualise wrongdoing, focusing on a narrow time frame encompassing the essential juridical matter between the right-holder and the duty-bearer.[12] This is obviously deficient if there is no culpable wrongdoer implicated in the injustice. It also unduly limits our moral gaze on the bi-lateral corrective justice relation, blinkering us to the broader structural context. The case study method allows us to explore the real nature of the disadvantage. This is a prelude to addressing it effectively. In this section, we will examine three case studies of structural injustice in labour markets. We will also examine the role of freedom of association within each case study, its potential to emancipate and its limitations.

Delivery riders: structural injustice in the gig economy

Delivery work in many UK cities is often mediated through app-based platforms operated by well-known companies such as Deliveroo or CitySprint. Platform companies provide a mechanism for 'digital work intermediation',[13] with platform software connecting work-providers with customers or service-users. Many of those working in platform-based delivery work are migrant workers.[14] Such workers can experience broader patterns of exclusion and disadvantage linked to their migration status, including limited language skills, exclusion from social security safety nets and limited labour mobility resulting from visa restrictions. In some cases, platform work provides economic opportunities for undocumented migrants where platform companies

12 See Guy Mundlak 'Free or unfree? Depicting structural injustice in courtrooms and in film', this volume.
13 Jeremias Prassl, *Humans as a Service* (Oxford, OUP, 2018) 14.
14 Peter Timko and Rianne van Melik, 'Being a Deliveroo Rider: Practices of Platform Labour in Nijmegen and Berlin' (2021) 50 Journal of Contemporary Ethnography 497.

recruit using 'remote' techniques requiring minimal documentation.[15] Many migrant workers in the platform economy have little financial resilience. They may be paying high rents to landlords with limited security of tenure and exposed to high levels of personal indebtedness in order to satisfy basic needs.[16]

Health and safety risks in delivery work are shaped by the urban environment and provision for safe cycling in cities. They are also shaped by the opaque algorithms that allocate work opportunities and which may incentivise dangerous risk-taking, for example, in accepting tasks during inclement weather. During the Covid-19 pandemic, the public health context to delivery work attracted significant political attention. These workers were unable to work from home during lockdown periods and their labour was critical to the smooth functioning of health and social care, and supply chains for food and other essential items. As a result of their occupational position in the frontline of the Covid-19 response, many delivery riders were exposed to higher risks of infection, serious illness, and death from Covid-19. Yet their self-employed status meant that they did not have access to the same levels of social protection as employees under the social security system. It also meant that some delivery workers were not provided with 'personal protective equipment' by their employers, and they did not have the statutory right to refuse dangerous and unsafe work.[17] The economic precariousness in the broader life circumstances of many platform workers meant that paid work was necessary for subsistence.

According to van Doorn, this platform-based delivery work 'is marked by unstable pay, job insecurity, minimal worker control, risk-offloading, and/or a lack of labour protections and rights'.[18] In legal terms, contractual arrangements in the platform economy are often designed to present the delivery rider operating as an independent and self-employed business undertaking. This can correspond with significant temporal flexibility for the worker over the timing and duration of work

15 Niels van Doorn, 'Liminal Precarity and Compromised Agency: Migrant experiences of gig work in Amsterdam, Berlin, and New York City' in Immanuel Ness (ed), *The Routledge Handbook of the Gig Economy* (Routledge 2023), 158.
16 On the relations between personal debt and collective action, see Giorgos Gouzoulis, 'What do Indebted Employees Do? Financialisation and the Decline of Industrial Action' (2023) 54 Industrial Relations Journal 71.
17 These health and safety risks in the context of Covid-19 were considered by the High Court in *R (on the application of The Independent Workers' Union of Great Britain) v The Secretary of State for Work and Pensions and the Secretary of State for Business, Energy and Industrial Strategy* [2020] EWHC 3050 (Admin).
18 van Doorn, n 15, 160.

assignments. However, it also entails the legal exclusion of delivery riders from basic statutory protections relating to working time and wages, which are based upon the existence of an employment contract. Many academic studies have criticised this 'dark side' of platform work in terms of its precarity, exploitation, income and employment insecurity, and low pay.[19] This normative critique generally reflects what Iris Marion Young has described as the 'harms of individual interaction'.[20] The platform company is a culpable wrongdoer that deliberately leverages its economic power to exploit precarious workers. This is a specific relational injustice perpetrated by the company against its workers. The platform company also uses its economic power to extract political concessions to maintain the lightly regulated labour markets, which enable its exploitative practices.[21]

Yet some ethnographic studies of migrant delivery riders have identified platform work as a 'scene of ambivalence'.[22] This 'ambivalence' perspective supports a structural injustice framing of gig employment. Many migrant workers value the sense of autonomy that attaches to self-employment status, and they find creative strategies to manage the exigencies of social and economic life under algorithmic management systems.[23] It also provides an economic lifeline for many undocumented migrant workers. While misclassification of worker status by platform companies may sometimes be akin to fraud,[24] many legal systems confer contractual freedom on the parties to negotiate work contracts. In these circumstances, it may be permissible for the parties to opt for genuine self-employment. The employment contract is a contractual option, not a mandatory legal form.[25] Platform companies also operate in circumstances of intense market competition. They must grow their market share aggressively to secure the advantages of network effects

---

19 Prassl n 13, 26–28.

20 Young n 3, 46.

21 Kari Paul, 'Prop 22: Why Uber's Victory in California could Harm Gig Workers Nationwide' (*The Guardian,* 11 November 2020) <https://www.theguardian.com/us-news/2020/nov/11/california-proposition-22-uber-lyft-doordash-labor-laws> accessed 25 August 2023.

22 Van Doorn n 15.

23 ibid.

24 Ewan McGaughey, 'Uber, the Taylor Review, Mutuality and the Duty not to Misrepresent Employment Status' (2019) 48 Industrial Law Journal 180.

25 In the recent Supreme Court judgment of *Uber BV and others v Aslam and others* [2021] UKSC 5, Lord Leggatt applied a 'purposive and realistic' approach to determining employment status. The point of this legal test is to prevent employers from manipulating contractual documentation with the object of avoiding statutory protections. Nevertheless, this purposive enquiry is still embedded in a contractual paradigm, and consequently it is liable to instability as a result of freedom of contract.

against competitors. In some cases, this has been financed by venture capital with investors sustaining astronomical losses, at least in the short term. This has also witnessed some large players exiting national markets, such as Deliveroo quitting Germany.[26]

The virtue of the structural injustice perspective is the recognition that serious injustices may exist even where the parties are simply exercising market freedoms and respecting legal rules. It is sensitive to the multiple and intersecting vulnerabilities experienced by platform workers both within *and beyond* their employment situation: in urban transport design, social security, migration law, landlord and tenant and laws protecting debtors from creditors.[27] It is also attuned to the ways in which these vulnerabilities are, in van Doorn's words, types of 'institutionalised vulnerability that form structural obstacles' to flourishing.[28] These ethnographic perspectives on the lived experiences of delivery drivers should engender humility in the selection of remedial strategies. Fundamentally, the selection of these strategies must be sensitive to the voices and perspectives of workers themselves, supported by their trade unions. That is why prioritising the collective agency of representative associations, such as trade unions, should be at the centre of any agenda for reform. This is because those who experience the disadvantage have 'a unique understanding of the nature of the problems and the likely effects of policies and action proposed by others situated in more powerful and privileged positions'.[29] It is also important to recognise that the disadvantaged group itself is likely to encompass a range of views and interests.

Sometimes the incorporation of worker perspectives may militate against policy proposals that appear to be academically defensible, such as the restriction of flexible employment in the gig economy. For example, the potential loss of flexibility, autonomy and employment opportunities resulting from legal reclassification of delivery workers as employees may not be regarded as beneficial by some disadvantaged workers targeted by the reforms.[30] Some workers may prefer a narrower suite of basic statutory rights while retaining more temporal flexibility than a traditional employee, opting for an intermediate category of

26 Tobias Buck and Tim Bradshaw, 'UK's Deliveroo Quits Germany Amid Fierce Competition' (*Financial Times,* 12 August 2019) <https://www.ft.com/content/a11802ca-bd17-11e9-b350-db00d509634e> accessed 25 August 2023.
27 van Doorn n 15.
28 ibid 175.
29 Young n 3, 113.
30 Van Doorn n 15, 175.

employment status. Also, many delivery riders work through multiple apps simultaneously to maximise their earning capacity. Of course, these economic choices may themselves be constrained by structures of injustice, such as exclusion from welfare support or strict laws on migration status. In these circumstances, a robust floor of statutory rights enforceable across all platform employers might be more beneficial than a firm-specific collective agreement. The basic point is that we should be wary of withdrawing remedial options in advance from democratic consideration for the workers' own good. We would do better to empower workers' voices in the democratic process.

This necessitates state support for new institutions of labour market governance, ensuring the full plurality of worker voices is heard before regulatory solutions are adopted. This may require the proportional representation of different trade unions, reflecting membership levels rather than allowing an employer the power to accord unilateral recognition to a single bargaining representative. These solutions may be implemented through collective agreements or enacted through legislation. The legislative route, backed by state coercion, could provide a more effective way of prompting the necessary structural changes. There may also be a need for city-based institutions of governance, enabling unions and employers to engage with local authorities on issues of housing and transport.

Garment workers: structural injustice in the Leicester garment factories

In May 2018, a leading investigative journalist at the Financial Times, Sarah O' Connor, published an important article on labour exploitation in Leicester garment factories.[31] It exposed an appalling context of widespread and systematic exploitation of workers who were paid at rates significantly below the national minimum wage. As the report acknowledged, these problems were longstanding, systemic and widely known about, even attracting the attention of the Joint Committee on Human Rights in 2017.[32] Leicester is the largest hub for the UK garment industry. It is composed mainly of very small factory units

31 Sarah O'Connor, 'Dark Factories: Labour Exploitation in Britain's Garment Industry' (*Financial Times*, 17 May 2018) <https://www.ft.com/content/e427327e-5892-11e8-b8b2-d6ceb45fa9d0> accessed 25 August 2023.

32 Ashley Armstrong, 'Fresh Powers to Shut Down UK's Clothing Sweatshops' (*The Telegraph*, 4 May 2017) <https://www.telegraph.co.uk/business/2017/03/04/fresh-powers-shut-uks-clothing-sweatshops/> accessed 25 August 2023.

usually employing fewer than 10 workers, and there may be anything between 1,000–1,500 such units operating at any one time.[33] There is considerable fluidity, with factories disappearing and then others quickly reappearing under new names. Many of these garment workers are migrant workers, and some of those migrants have undocumented status and may be victims of trafficking.[34] For this reason, factories that have lax approaches to documentation are more attractive to undocumented workers. Such workers are more likely to be paid wages significantly below the legal rate. As a result of their precarious migration status, they are also less likely to complain to the public authorities. Given the extreme poverty of the lowest paid migrant workers in Leicester, O'Connor reported housing arrangements where three or four families shared a single three-bedroom house. In this way, liminal migration status, exploitative working conditions and poor living conditions compounded the vulnerabilities of many Leicester garment workers. In 2020, Leicester suffered from a spike in high levels of Covid-19 infection. This resulted in a prolonged local lockdown with the infection spike likely to have been precipitated by appalling working conditions in cramped factories.[35]

The Leicester workers being paid £4 per hour are victims of serious injustice. Most obviously, this injustice consisted in clear violations of the national minimum wage legislation. This was usually orchestrated by the underreporting of working hours in order to inflate the recorded hourly wage rate. These violations are more difficult to detect through inspecting the employer's records. Understandably, workers in economic desperation rarely challenged these illegal practices and were sometimes actively complicit in them. In terms of a narrow 'harms of individual interaction' perspective, the culpable wrongdoers are the garment factory owners violating the law. The injustice consists in the failure to pay what is legally due to the workers. It would seem to follow from this that the appropriate legal response would be to enforce the relevant laws more vigorously against those direct employers. This would ensure that the duty-bearers (the direct employers) comply with the duties owed to the right-holders (the workers in the garment factories).

33 *Labour Behind the Label* 'UK Garment Industry' <https://labourbehindthelabel.org/uk-garment-industry/> accessed 25 August 2023.
34 ibid.
35 Sarah O'Connor, 'Leicester's Dark Factories Show up a Diseased System' (*Financial Times*, 2 July 2020) <https://www.ft.com/content/0b26ee5d-4f4f-4d57-a700-ef49038de18c> accessed 25 August 2023.

As with the delivery riders in the gig economy, a structural injustice framing reveals some limitations of this 'harms of individual interaction' approach.[36] This emerges out of O'Connor's contextual reporting of the systematic exploitation in the Leicester factories. One of the main drivers for systemic non-compliance with minimum wage laws was the role of large fashion retailers like Boohoo and Missguided. These companies supplied low-cost fashion items in an agile way to consumers who were eager for low prices and extensive choice. The negotiation of commercial contracts between these large well-resourced retailers and the smaller garment factories in a highly competitive geographical market reflected significant inequalities of bargaining power. As the retailers pressed for lower prices in these contracts, garment suppliers were forced into 'losing contracts' where the only way of operating at a profit was to pay workers below the legal minimum wage rate.[37] The retailers themselves were faced with significant competitive pressures as rival retailers might reduce costs using new suppliers in countries with lower wage costs. In Leicester itself, factories that complied with the legal rules were at a significant competitive disadvantage compared with the majority of firms that continued to break the law with impunity. For workers with undocumented migration status, there were evident attractions in seeking employment with factories that operated on the fringes of legality. Meanwhile, local officials were deterred from pursuing a zealous approach to law enforcement because of fears that lead companies in supply chains might withdraw entirely from Leicester. This withdrawal could precipitate the total collapse of the garment industry in the region. The resulting economic deprivation would have significant negative social and health consequences for the local population.

It is apparent that the serious injustices in the Leicester garment industry cannot be explained reductively through a 'blame' narrative of culpably exploitative employers in a local labour market. The moral complexion was multipolar. It involved interactions between many different actors and across different scales: lead companies operating in competitive consumer markets; consumers desirous of cheap fashion products; workers in low-wage countries competing in a global market

---

36 Young gives sweatshop labour as an example of global structural injustice. See Young n 3, 125–134.

37 For discussion of the phenomenon of 'losing contracts' within the context of national minimum wage compliance, see Alan Bogg and Paul Davies, 'Accessory Liability for National Minimum Wage Violations in the Fissured Economy', in Alan Bogg, Jennifer Collins, Mark Freedland, and Jonathan Herring (eds), *Criminality at Work* (Oxford University Press 2020), Chapter 22.

with Leicester workers; local workers afraid of unemployment; and local authorities sensitive to the disastrous economic and social consequences of retailers withdrawing business from the Leicester region. The work of the Trades Union Congress (TUC) in the aftermath of the public scandal was astute to this moral complexity.[38] It focused on building partnerships between retailers, the local authority and trade unions to develop a culture of compliance in the Leicester garment industry.

Rather than traditional collective bargaining methods, unions engaged in a quasi-public role of promoting compliance with statutory standards. They did so in cooperation with retail companies and public enforcement agencies, using the economic leverage of the supply chain to improve compliance outcomes in the garment factories. This partnership strategy also involved building links with community organisations in Leicester, recognising the intersections between employment precarity and precarity in other dimensions of workers' lives. This was presented as a way of securing economic prosperity by keeping decent jobs in Leicester, which required the continued commitment of lead retailers to the region. While exploitative practices have not been eliminated in Leicester garment factories,[39] the partnership approach has led to improvements in terms of minimum wage compliance. The responsibility of lead companies has been critical to that improvement. The involvement of trade unions has also been instrumental in achieving this outcome. However, the traditional forms of collective action, such as strikes and collective bargaining, were not promising responses to structural injustice. It would have been futile to strike against the direct employers. They would likely have disappeared overnight, with hundreds of other factories waiting to take on the work and employ the workers. Instead, unions have worked collaboratively with lead companies and public agencies to improve enforcement outcomes for basic statutory standards. The 'stick' for enforcement in the garment factories was the economic leverage of the lead retailers and the potential withdrawal of commercial opportunities, rather than the withdrawal of labour by workers.

---

38 TUC, *Fixing Leicester's Garment Industry One Year On – Building Partnerships, Ending Exploitation* (TUC, 2021).

39 Sarah Butler, 'Poor Working Conditions Persist in Leicester Garment Factories, Finds Survey' (*The Guardian*, 12 June 2023) <https://www.theguardian.com/uk-news/2022/jun/13/poor-working-conditions-persist-in-leicester-garment-factories-finds-survey> accessed 25 August 2023.

Seafarers: structural injustice and the seafarers at P&O Ferries

On 17 March 2022, P&O Ferries implemented the redundancies of nearly 800 seafarers with immediate effect. This was a unionised workforce with workers represented by the RMT; and RMT had a recognition agreement with P&O Ferries. Most of the affected seafarers sailed out of Dover and they worked under contracts that were subject to UK employment protection laws. P&O Ferries was owned by Dubai-based DP World, a significant global player in shipping and maritime services.

Under UK law, collective redundancies must be preceded by a specified period of consultation with the recognised trade union. The importance of this consultative duty is reflected in the remedial framework, which provides for a 'protective award'. This is a monetary award which is not merely compensatory but includes a penal element. It is, however, capped at 90 days' pay.[40] The P&O dismissals were unlawful and constituted a clear breach of the statutory rules on collective consultation. The company executed a deliberate plan to implement the dismissals without advance notice. This element of surprise would circumvent the resistance likely to be mobilised by the union and a workforce faced with mass redundancies. The company calculated the likely costs of the tribunal claims it would face – made more predictable by capped financial awards – and it offered financial settlement packages exceeding those costs.

Within a short space of time, the vast majority of seafarers (bar one) had accepted the financial settlements. The work was switched almost immediately to crews provided by agencies in order to maintain continuity of ferry services. This new workforce was employed on employment contracts that were outside the territorial scope of UK minimum wage laws. It was reported that some of those Indian and Filipino agency workers were employed at less than £2 per hour, working on ships that were registered in Cyprus.[41] Overnight, P&O Ferries had effectively switched from a unionised to a non-unionised workforce. Within P&O itself, the seafarers who were subject to UK employment laws were specifically targeted for redundancy whereas seafarers subject to French and Dutch law were not. It was suspected that this was because those other legal systems provided for more robust enforcement and penalties

40 For a full discussion of the relevant law on collective redundancies, see John McMullen, *Redundancy: Law and Practice* (4th edn Oxford University Press 2021), Chapter 11.

41 BBC, 'New P&O Crew on Less Than £2 an Hour, Union Claims' (22 March 2022) <https://www.bbc.co.uk/news/business-60821266> accessed 25 August 2023.

than UK laws. There was thus a race to the bottom *within* P&O's corporate organisation, as well as in its outsourcing in favour of cheaper agency workers beyond the territorial scope of UK laws.

In the immediate aftermath of the mass sackings, there was palpable shock and political outrage. Following an appearance before a joint session of the Transport and Business Select Committees a week later on 24 March 2022, the CEO Peter Hebblethwaite expressed his regret at the company's deliberate violation of the law. He nevertheless justified the actions as necessary to secure the financial survival of P&O Ferries, with its business impacted by the Covid-19 pandemic. According to DP World, the business decision was taken independently by P&O Ferries, but DP World gave its full public backing to Mr Hebblethwaite.[42] In the company's view, it was a regrettable measure that sacrificed some jobs so that the company could survive and provide employment to the remaining employees. The reduction of wage costs by using extraterritorial agency contracts generated competitive pressures on other ferry companies operating out of UK ports. More broadly, the brazen visibility of a household corporate name simply choosing to disregard the law and buy itself out of legal compliance contributed to a wider culture of impunity for large corporations. Nor was it fanciful to speculate that this might damage the more general sense of respect for the rule of law in the labour market.

In important respects, the P&O scandal is a paradigm case of the 'harms of individual interaction' scenario. There is a culpable and calculative wrongdoer, P&O Ferries, and it engaged in a planned and purposive violation of the law. This decision was based on a rational economic assessment of the costs and benefits of legal compliance. It did not involve a scenario where innocent actors are implicated in injustice by respecting legal rules. The immediate political response reflected this narrow legal model of responsibility, with the Insolvency Service considering the possibilities for criminal liability and/or director disqualification for those involved most closely in the corporate decision-making to break the law. At the current time, there have been no prosecutions or director disqualifications arising out of the scandal. In terms of more general law reform, much of this discussion was focused

42 Chris Giles, 'Dubai Owner of P&O Ferries Hails Management's "Amazing Job" Over Sacking' (*Financial Times*, 29 May 2022) <https://www.ft.com/content/be0734b3-35a7-4930-a21f-a631d664e862> accessed 25 August 2023.

on stronger remedies to deter deliberate wrongdoing.[43] Once again, this discourse was framed around modifying the costs and benefits of legal compliance to deter culpable wrongdoing. It was also concerned to hold corporate wrongdoing to public account in the courts, by curtailing the scope for wrongdoers to effectively 'contract out' of judicial accountability.

In cases like P&O Ferries, the 'harms of individual interaction' framing of injustice is entirely appropriate given the deliberate nature of the wrongdoing. The focal injustice is the blameworthy wrong perpetrated by the company against its workforce by violating their legal rights. But even here, with deliberate wrongdoing, the broader consideration of structures is useful and important in providing a complete account of the relevant responsibilities. The fixation on blameworthy actors can sometimes be used cynically for political purposes. This is because a discourse of 'villains' can obscure broader structures of injustice from political scrutiny and critique. In this case, while ministers heaped scorn on Hebblethwaite, this avoided any detailed consideration of DP World's role in decision-making or the ethics of professional advisers such as lawyers in assisting corporations with formulating plans to break the law. Most importantly, it shielded the Government from political accountability for maintaining the weak enforcement regime that enabled the culture of impunity to take root in the first place. This evasive aspect was a strong feature of the public discourse surrounding P&O Ferries. While the focus remained on Peter Hebblethwaite and his personal role, the discussion was steered away from critical scrutiny of governmental acquiescence in the broader non- or under-enforcement of labour standards.

In what ways does structural injustice advance the analysis of P&O Ferries and the appropriate political and legal responses? This case study is a powerful example of Young's concern with 'responsibility across borders'.[44] The corporate restructuring was driven by the search for cheaper labour by exploiting the territorial limits of UK employment protection statutes. The Seafarers' Wages Act 2023 was enacted in response to the P&O scandal. It extends the coverage of the UK national minimum wage to employment on some vessels travelling from UK ports. If the new law is properly enforced, it does at least limit the scope for the hourly wages of £3 per hour for agency seafarers reported in the early days of the mass sackings. Even if this legislation had been in force at the time of the mass sackings, however, it is unlikely to have avoided

---

43 Alan Bogg, 'Labour Constitutionalism: Effective Judicial Protection as a Constitutional Principle in United Kingdom Labour Law' (2022) 43 Comparative Labor Law and Policy Journal 45.
44 Young n 3, Chapter 5.

the dismissals. The wage costs of a strongly unionised workforce with collective bargaining would still exceed national minimum wage rates by a significant margin.

This 'responsibility across borders' perspective also identifies the importance of 'solidarity' in the responses of social actors to P&O Ferries. For Young, 'solidarity' describes 'a relationship among separate and dissimilar actors who decide to stand together, for one another... solidarity must always be *forged* and *reforged*. It looks to the future because it must constantly be renewed'.[45] This forging of solidarity across borders was critical in the aftermath of the sackings. For example, Dutch and French port workers indicated that they would refuse to dock P&O ships at their ports.[46] Interestingly, the rhetoric around the replacement agency workers also avoided hostile nativism. This reflected a recognition that these workers were themselves victims of exploitation in a global labour market in the maritime sector. Furthermore, French and UK unions recognised the importance of transnational collective bargaining as the most effective way to regulate a form of employment that was inherently cross-border and transnational in its very contractual performance.[47]

The fallout at P&O Ferries also exposed the serious legal constraints on collective action for trade unions in UK law. Within weeks of the sackings, almost the entire workforce had accepted the settlement packages. There was no longer a unionised workforce operating on the affected P&O routes. In fact, the corporate strategy could be understood as an extreme de-unionisation strategy. It was an attack on freedom of association, despite its presentation as a necessary cost-cutting exercise to avoid the closure of the company. Under UK law, 'solidarity' or 'secondary' action is unlawful. It was therefore impossible to place industrial pressure on P&O Ferries by organising strikes against its direct suppliers or customers. Given the importance of 'solidarity' to structural injustice, the prohibition of secondary industrial action is difficult to justify. By restricting lawful strike action to the primary employer, this reflects the 'harms of individual interaction' paradigm. It is focused entirely on the dispute between the employer and its own workforce, marginalising the broader web of

45 ibid 120.

46 Alexandra Wood, 'P&O Ferries: French and Dutch Dockers Issue "Scab" Warning over P&O Agency Crews' (*The Yorkshire Post,* 20 March 2022) <https://www.yorkshirepost.co.uk/news/people/po-ferries-french-and-dutch-dockers-issue-scab-warning-over-po-agency-crews-3619078?> accessed 25 August 2023.

47 Nautilus International, 'French Unions Back Nautilus in P&O Ferries Battle' (27 April 2022) <https://www.nautilusint.org/en/news-insight/news/french-unions-back-nautilus-in-po-ferries-battle> accessed 25 August 2023.

connections and responsibilities in our shared social world. This provides an example where maintaining the restrictive rules on lawful strike action represents a deliberate political choice by the state. It is implicated in the structural injustice because it is responsible for the legal rules that obstruct an effective solidaristic response. Since it has the power to rectify those structures, it also has a political responsibility to do so.[48]

In the law on collective action for unions, there is a final dimension of solidarity to be considered in the P&O dispute. The company deliberately broke the law. In so doing, it effectively insulated itself from collective action by the trade union because of the extensive legal restrictions that apply to lawful strike action. This includes the prohibition of secondary action. In shedding its unionised workforce overnight, the only way that the company could be subjected to industrial pressure was through secondary action leveraged through customers and suppliers with commercial links to the company. This was prohibited by strict UK strike laws, which allow no scope for secondary action of this kind. The new replacement workers were very likely non-unionised and employed through agencies, and not in a position to undertake primary strike action.

Young's 'social connection' model draws attention to the political value of reciprocity. Reciprocity demands that the benefits and burdens of living in a community governed by the rule of law should be distributed fairly among its members.[49] Just as we benefit from the legal compliance of others who forbear from pressing advantages derived from lawlessness, we should comply with the law ourselves and limit our own freedom of action. Legal violations such as P&O's conduct do not simply involve wrongs against those whose rights are directly violated. It also undermined the systemic effectiveness of labour laws. The rule of law is a public good rather than merely a private benefit or advantage, and it is damaged by visible disregard of the law's demands by powerful actors where state institutions acquiesce in that disregard. Reliable enforcement of legal duties supports the expectations of citizens. In turn, this provides the basis for civic respect and cooperation in a shared social world. When this social fabric is eroded, the background structural conditions for fair social cooperation (which includes the rule of law) are degraded.

48 See further Virginia Mantouvalou, *Structural Injustice and Workers' Rights* (Oxford University Press 2023), 8–9.
49 HLA Hart, 'Are There Any Natural Rights?' (1955) 64 Philosophical Review 175.

This invites the question whether 'enforcement' strike action, responding to deliberate breaches of the law by the employer, should be subject to a different legal framework. There is an unfairness in holding the union to burdensome legal standards, such as the ban on secondary action, while the employer enjoys effective impunity in virtue of its superior financial resources and buying off litigation. The starkness of this asymmetry is reflected in the availability of legal remedies. Whereas it was almost impossible for the union to seek relief through an injunction to restrain mass dismissals in these circumstances, it would be comparatively easy for an employer to gain an interlocutory injunction where strike action is arguably unlawful. By introducing a more permissive framework for 'enforcement' strike action, in circumstances where an employer is capitalising on its own wrongdoing, this would ensure reciprocity in the enforcement of labour laws. 'Enforcement' strike action would allow the union to organise secondary strike action, and perhaps for it to be exempted from the strict general requirements on notice and balloting. This adjustment in the legal rules restores reciprocity between the parties. In the circumstances of P&O, it is unfair to expect unions to ameliorate structural injustice while forcing them to operate within lopsided legal rules that perversely favour the wrongdoer. 'Enforcement' strike action removes that unfair legal advantage from the employer.

Structural injustice in the case studies: some general themes and lessons for freedom of association

Some general themes emerge from these case studies of structural injustice. Most obviously, the role of trade unions is critical in ensuring an effective voice for workers. Freedom of association must be central to any effective strategy for challenging structural injustice, and trade unions must occupy a focal position within the legal architecture of freedom of association. Young's work has emphasised that political responsibility for contesting structural injustice is shared. The victims of that injustice themselves have a responsibility to organise and challenge those structures of oppression. This includes challenging the powerful actors that benefit from unjust background conditions, holding them to public account, and agitating for broader regulatory changes to those background conditions.[50] Each case study also reveals the variety of ways

50 Young n 3, 148–149.

in which legal rules and structures can either facilitate or obstruct the ability of unions and workers to mobilise and contest structural injustice through collective action. Distilling the lessons from these case studies, five 'structural injustice' themes are of particular relevance to worker empowerment and freedom of association.

The first theme is the critical role of background legal norms in creating and/or magnifying the vulnerabilities of workers. In this way, vulnerability is not merely a natural fact. It is often created by political choices reflected in regulatory frameworks. The importance of migration laws to labour market vulnerabilities is reflected in each of these case studies. In 'Delivery Riders' and 'Garment Workers', the precarious migration status of workers (including undocumented status) meant that they were especially vulnerable to labour market exploitation. The relative informality of recruitment processes, often through existing social networks of migrant workers, is an attractive feature of the work. The criminalisation of certain migration statuses in the employment context also means that such workers are less likely to challenge their employers' non-compliance. Undocumented workers will seek employment in illicit contexts with low levels of legal compliance, which was a particular problem in 'Garment Workers'. In extreme cases, this can involve trafficking and modern slavery. In 'Seafarers', outsourcing to foreign workers outside the territorial scope of minimum wage laws provided the context to the employer's deliberate flouting of the law. In the maritime sector, the transnational scope of labour markets is an important contextual factor in structural injustice.

Other regulatory frameworks may also be relevant to the construction of vulnerability. For example, during the Covid-19 pandemic, the exclusion of some self-employed workers from social safety nets and certain health and safety rights contributed to the vulnerability of those workers to worse health outcomes from Covid-19 infection. Such workers were already disadvantaged in public health terms because of intersections between race and poverty. This was a particular problem in 'Delivery Riders' and 'Garment Workers' for workers who, because of the material nature of their work, could not 'work from home' to protect themselves from the risk of infection. Even in 'Seafarers', the severe economic impact of Covid-19 provided the context to the competitive pressures faced by P&O Ferries despite it having received some government support during the pandemic.

The second theme is the multipolar nature of structural injustice, which often involves interactions between a broad range of different actors. These actors will usually have varying degrees of power and culpability in relation to the unjust background conditions that frame social interactions. Employment law tends to operate using a 'liability model' of legal justice. It is bi-lateral in structure. Injustice consists in the violation of a right-holder's right by a duty-bearer. In employment law, generally speaking, the right-holder is the worker and the direct employer is the duty-bearer. Legal justice is corrective in nature. In the case studies, this perspective is still important. The direct employers in each case study ought to bear a significant responsibility for the injustices experienced by their workers. They are blameworthy actors who derive significant economic benefits from deliberately exploiting a vulnerable workforce. However, there are also actors wielding significant social power other than direct employers. In 'Garment Workers', for example, fashion retailers as lead companies in supply chains exercise significant economic power indirectly over labour conditions in Leicester garment factories. The commercial prices fixed in supply contracts, which are effectively set by the lead companies given their market power, determine whether minimum wage payments are affordable for factory employers. This also reinforces the political power of these lead companies in local contexts, because the withdrawal of commercial investment could be catastrophic for local urban economies. In 'Seafarers', DP World denied it had influenced P&O Ferries' commercial decision-making. Yet there may be other similar contexts where commercial policies are effectively determined by non-employer corporate entities which exercise significant influence over direct employer policies. The web of responsibility can be extended further to local councils, enforcement agencies, and even the consumers who take advantage of cheap food deliveries and fashion clothing.

Young's account of responsibility provides an important corrective to this narrow 'liability model' of responsibility. Her own 'social connection model' account of political responsibility emphasises its character as forward-looking and not centred on the allocation of blame for past wrongs. It also involves shared responsibility to improve our shared social world, channelled through collective political action to reshape legal and social structures.[51] This has generated a lively debate among theorists who are broadly sympathetic to Young's work. For example, in Martha Nussbaum's introductory essay to *Responsibility for Justice*, she argues that blame and culpability are important elements in motivating actors to undertake broader political responsibilities to improve social and

51 Young n 3, 104–113.

legal structures.[52] When powerful actors do not shoulder the appropriate burden of political responsibility, *that* is an occasion for blame and holding to account. McKeown's illuminating account locates power at the centre of a nuanced taxonomy of types of structural injustice.[53] To this end, she distinguishes 'pure structural injustice' (where there is no culpable agent but the injustice arises cumulatively out of innocent actions that respect the rules); 'avoidable structural injustice' (where a powerful agent can use its power and resources to change an unjust structure but declines to do so); and 'deliberate structural injustice' (where a powerful agent deliberately perpetuates an unjust background structure for its own gain).

In terms of remedial strategies, this typology is helpful in prioritising the targeting of legal resources (which are inevitably scarce). In 'Garment Workers', for example, the lead companies represent a paradigm case of 'deliberate structural injustice'. They are culpably implicated in unjust background conditions, they derive significant economic benefits by exploiting those conditions, and their market power in commercial supply chains means that they are very well-positioned to bring about structural change.[54] Where social power, culpability and effective influence over structural processes coincide, the burdens of political responsibility ought to be regarded as especially strong and amenable to legal enforcement. In turn, there is a stronger case for using law to enforce political responsibilities against powerful social actors implicated in 'avoidable structural justice' than innocent social actors implicated in 'pure structural injustice'. While Young is surely right to suggest that everyone ought to reflect on their own responsibilities, even in 'pure structural injustice' scenarios, coercive legal enforcement will usually track culpable (including negligent) actions or failures to act. In fact, the use of legal coercion to enforce political responsibilities in 'pure' scenarios is troubling. There is an intrinsic value in maintaining some space for social interactions that are free from state coercion. This includes undertaking responsibilities willingly and in a self-directed way, rather than through legal compulsion. Given that everyone is potentially implicated in 'pure structural injustice', legal coercion may be indiscriminate, expansive and oppressive.

The third theme is the crucial role of the state in empowering marginalised groups to challenge structural injustice. A controversial aspect of Young's argument is the claim that victims of structural injustice

52 ibid xxii–xxv.
53 McKeown n 6, 4–5.
54 See also Young n 3, 144–145.

are subject to political responsibilities to challenge and ameliorate unjust structures. To be sure, the argument has some virtues. The history of progressive social change has been driven by the collective action of oppressed and marginalised groups. Powerful beneficiaries of structural injustice rarely cede their advantages willingly. In reality, social justice is the product of social struggle by organised groups rather than the outcome of a clever argument. There is also dignity in the ascription of agency rather than passivity to the victims of structural injustice. We respect them as agents capable of shaping their own lives and changing their situations. This is also the basis of self-respect. The transformation of structures will be more enduring and effective when those who are most affected have a voice in shaping alternatives. As Young argues:

> It is they who know the most about the harms they suffer, and thus it is up to them, though not them alone, to broadcast their situation and call it injustice. Unless the victims themselves are involved in ameliorative efforts, well-meaning outsiders may inadvertently harm them in a different way, or set reforms going in unproductive directions.[55]

We have already encountered the 'victim blaming' objection to Young's account of responsibility.[56] To some extent, this can be avoided by emphasising that political responsibility is not (on Young's approach) rooted in blame. The 'victim blaming' objection reflects the 'liability model': the wrongdoing agent owes duties of reparation to the wronged agent. The reparative onus here is on the wrongdoer. Nevertheless, we should proceed carefully when the most disadvantaged appear to be subject to the dual burden of the injustice itself *and* the responsibility to ameliorate the structures that gave rise to it.

In each of the case studies, the role of trade unions and other civil society groups has been vital in empowering workers to challenge structural injustice. Collective organisation is a form of empowerment. The coordinated actions of many, where those actions are facilitated by groups with expertise and resources, is far more effective and less burdensome than actions undertaken alone. In 'Delivery Riders', smaller

55 ibid 146.
56 McKeown n 6, 6, referring to C Gould, 'Varieties of Global Responsibility: Social Connection, Human Rights, and Transnational Solidarity' in A Ferguson and M Nagel (eds), *Dancing with Iris: The Philosophy of Iris Marion Young* (Oxford University Press 2009), 199.

unions such as the Independent Workers' Union of Great Britain (IWGB) have been instrumental in organising workers to protest exploitative working conditions. More informal networks, sometimes based on ethnic identities, have also provided opportunities for solidarity, mutual support and collective action.[57] In 'Garment Workers', the collaboration between trade unions, retailers in supply chains, local government and community groups have led to improvements in working conditions in the Leicester factories. The coordination between state actors and civil society groups was far more powerful than civil society activism alone, given the potential for state actors to use legal coercion to promote structural change. In 'Seafarers', while the recognised union was unable to reverse the mass dismissals, individual unions and the TUC have mobilised the public anger about P&O Ferries' actions to lobby for improvements to the general legal regime of enforcement and remedies. Transnational networks of solidarity between UK unions and unions in other European countries have also been important, given the transnational nature of employment in the maritime sector.

The 'Garment Workers' case study is a good example of effective collective action leading to positive improvements in workers' lives. An important factor was the presence of positive and active state support for civil society groups and trade unions. State institutions are often uniquely positioned to coordinate the actions of different groups. This coordination can make collective action more powerful and effective. Public institutions can also use coercive legal measures against recalcitrant companies or to underpin the agreements between companies and unions. This can be important in eliciting corporate engagement with remedial efforts. This was crucial in 'Garment Workers' particularly in relation to the retailers operating as lead companies in supply chains. In 'Delivery Riders' and 'Seafarers', by contrast, the state avoided an active role supporting the groups challenging structural injustice. Many smaller unions have been reliant on very limited resources, especially organising in gig economy contexts. Often, this organising has been undertaken in the face of both corporate resistance and governmental intransigence.

In situations where workers are organising against structural injustice, the state itself has a political responsibility to provide material support to workers' organisational activities. This positive duty of active support on governmental institutions would temper legitimate concerns about 'victim blaming' in Young's account of political responsibility. Since

57 Van Doorn n 15.

state institutions are inevitably implicated in structural injustice through the operation of the legal system, they bear a significant responsibility to empower those marginalised groups pressing for structural changes. The predictable effect of state neutrality is to entrench unjust background structures. This inevitably works to the advantage of the powerful groups that benefit from structural injustice and it compounds the disadvantage of marginalised groups seeking to change it. States must not be 'neutral' on issues of structural injustice.

The fourth theme concerns the sheer variety of collective actions undertaken by trade unions to challenge and ameliorate structural injustice. The core functions of trade unions are focused upon individual representation, collective bargaining and strike action.[58] While these activities continue to be central to strategies of collective action, structural injustice may require a broader range of approaches. In the gig economy, for example, trade unions have been using public law litigation to prompt necessary changes to regulatory frameworks. The advantage of these regulatory changes is that they cannot easily be circumvented by individual employers as they constitute a mandatory floor of legal norms. By contrast, a collective agreement with a single company may be less effective where gig workers often work for multiple employers through different apps. Public law techniques like judicial review can lead to systemic impacts by triggering structural changes that improve the welfare of large numbers of workers.

As an example, *R (Adiatu and another) v H M Treasury* was concerned with job support measures in response to the economic impact of the Covid-19 pandemic.[59] The legal challenge was focused on the 'Coronavirus Job Retention Scheme' (CJRS), which provided financial payments to employers in respect of employees who were 'furloughed' (temporarily laid off) as a result of Covid-19. The CJRS was restricted to employees who received their pay and whose income tax was collected through PAYE. This excluded many individuals in the wider 'limb (b) worker' category paid and taxed on a self-employed basis. While there was a parallel scheme for self-employed individuals, the qualification thresholds for the self-employed scheme meant that some workers would be left without a safety net. The IWGB challenged the exclusion of limb (b) workers from the CJRS, and the Government's decision not to raise the level of Statutory Sick Pay (SSP) or remove the lower earnings limit to

58 The classic modern account is still K D Ewing, 'The Function of Trade Unions' (2005) 34 Industrial Law Journal 1.

59 [2020] EWHC 1554 (Admin).

qualify for SSP. The legal challenge failed. The High Court emphasised the extraordinary political context of the decision-making, which required the rapid implementation of welfare policy in an emergency. On that basis, the exclusion of some self-employed workers from the CJRS was subject to a wide margin of appreciation and it could not be said to be 'manifestly without reasonable foundation'. While the litigation did not succeed, it did ensure the political visibility of precarious workers and the absence of a safety net for workers affected by the pandemic. It placed a spotlight on structural issues of insecurity and precariousness, particularly among essential frontline workers exposed to significant health risks.

Another example is *R (on the application of The Independent Workers' Union of Great Britain) v The Secretary of the State for Work and Pensions and the Secretary of State for Business, Energy and Industrial Strategy*.[60] This was a judicial review challenge to the restriction of certain European Union (EU)-based health and safety rights (most notably, the provision of personal protective equipment and the 'right to refuse' unsafe work) to 'employees'. According to Mr Justice Chamberlain, the relevant EU Directives should be construed as broadly and inclusively as possible, particularly in view of the fundamental nature of the health and safety rights guaranteed in the EU Charter of Fundamental Rights. The exclusion of limb (b) workers from the scope of statutory coverage, many of them working in circumstances of vulnerability during the pandemic, was not compatible with this broad and inclusive approach. This judgment led to the extension of health and safety statutory protections to the wider category of limb (b) workers.[61] The litigation triggered structural changes through statutory reform, with the litigation functioning as a form of political voice. In providing a safety net for all workers through legislation, rather than through an employer-specific collective agreement, it modified the background structural conditions in the labour market.

From a structural injustice perspective, collective action directed at structural changes (especially through law reform) may be more effective than the traditional focus on 'private' collective bargaining. This explains the importance of litigation as a form of collective action in the gig economy. It also extends to other forms of collective action. In the Leicester garment factories, for example, the involvement of unions in the effective enforcement of statutory labour standards is likely to be more beneficial than pursuing enterprise-based collective bargaining with individual

60 [2020] EWHC 3050 (Admin). I acted as an academic consultant to the legal team in this case.
61 The Employment Rights Act 1996 (Protection from Discrimination in Health and Safety Cases) (Amendment) Order 2021.

factory owners. And in the aftermath of P&O Ferries, once the scope for reversing the sackings had vanished, collective action shifted to politics and the need to address weaknesses in the legal framework that allowed the scandal to happen in the first place. The importance of these public regulatory functions also reinforces the case for positive state support for unions and civil society groups, perhaps through a 'structural injustice' fund which allocates legal aid grants to meritorious cases with potential for systemic impact.

The fifth theme concerns the reorientation of union strategies even within the core activities of collective bargaining and striking. In the UK, for example, collective bargaining mirrors the bi-lateral structure of the 'liability model' of justice. The trade union negotiates with an individual employer on behalf of a circumscribed group of workers within a 'bargaining unit' at the enterprise level. It seeks to negotiate a collective agreement with the individual employer, regulating terms and conditions of employment within the enterprise. At the collective level, this envisages a single bi-lateral relationship between the union and the direct employer. The contours of the right to strike are shaped by this bi-lateral model of collective bargaining. To be lawful, the strike must concern a primary 'trade dispute'. This is a dispute between workers and their employer about terms and conditions of employment.

In UK labour law, there is no legal scope for 'political' strikes and 'secondary' strikes. Political strikes are forms of protest against governmental policies. This category encompasses a range of possible scenarios. These include protests aimed at subverting a democratically elected government to protests at specific legislation to remove or downgrade employment protections. While most legal systems prohibit 'pure' political strikes, many legal systems do permit 'socio-political' strikes where workers' social and economic interests are directly affected by governmental policies. UK law is at the most restrictive end of the comparative spectrum in prohibiting all political strikes. From a structural injustice perspective, socio-political strikes are of vital importance. Given the importance of background structures to structural injustice, 'socio-political' strikes provide a tool for challenging laws that disempower or degrade the employment and living conditions of workers. Many of those workers, such as irregular migrants, may be formally disenfranchised in the political process. Even where workers are able to vote, legislators may ignore or override their interests to support groups with greater economic and political power.

In relation to 'secondary' strikes, these are strikes directed at other employers who are not in a primary dispute between a group of workers and their direct employer. It might include companies who are suppliers or customers of the employer in the primary dispute. We have already seen that Young's 'social connection model' of responsibility emphasises the importance of solidarity.[62] Effective responses to structural injustice often depend upon coordination and collective action. Secondary action provides a conduit for workers to stand in solidarity with oppressed groups. Where workers in a primary dispute do not have effective bargaining power, secondary strike action can bolster their bargaining position by allowing other workers to stand with them in solidarity. Most legal systems protect some forms of secondary action, and this is generally based upon shared occupational interests between workers and/or that the employers are 'allies'.[63] Once again, UK labour law is unusually restrictive in prohibiting nearly all forms of secondary strike action.

The case studies reveal the serious limitations of existing UK strike laws. While these limitations are well-documented in the legal literature, the structural injustice perspective provides us with a powerful moral language for critique. In 'Delivery Riders', it is unclear if some riders count as 'workers' under the relevant labour legislation. If they are not 'workers', organisers of strike action are not protected from civil liabilities under the legislative framework. This means that trade unions can be sued in tort for damages and they will be unable to use the statutory 'trade dispute' defence even in a primary dispute with a gig employer. In 'Garment Workers', strike action aimed at the primary employers, the factory owners, would have been utterly futile. These workers were unorganised and no doubt unable to afford the privations associated with loss of pay. Where a single factory was targeted with strike action, hundreds of other factory owners would simply take on the work. The key actors were the lead companies in the supply chain. The threat of secondary boycotts against retailers like Boohoo, for example, is far more likely to induce systemic changes than primary strike action against employers. In 'Seafarers', the dismissal of a unionised workforce meant that secondary strike action was the only effective way of exerting industrial pressure on P&O Ferries. This includes both national and transnational solidarity action. Given the political stalling and inaction in the aftermath of P&O Ferries, and the failure to address the weaknesses in the enforcement regime, a 'socio-political' strike could also have provided extra political leverage to the union in pressing for legal reform.

---

62 Young n 3, 120.

63 See further Alan Bogg, 'The Right to Strike, Minimum Service Levels, and European Values' (2023) SSRN <https://papers.ssrn.com/sol3/papers.cfm?abstract_id=4410323> accessed 25 August 2023.

Human rights and structural injustice: the case of freedom of association

Given these themes, to what extent does human rights (specifically freedom of association) provide a framework to support collective empowerment? This final section considers the case-law of the European Court of Human Rights (ECtHR) on the protection of trade union rights under Article 11 of the European Convention on Human Rights (ECHR or the Convention). While Article 11 provides an important legal support for trade union activities, the structural injustice perspective identifies some areas where a more radical approach is needed. In particular, there needs to be greater recognition of positive state obligations and stronger protections for a broader range of trade union activities such as 'secondary' strike action.

Human rights as a tool for challenging background conditions of structural injustice

'Delivery Riders' and 'Garment Workers' demonstrate the importance of background conditions such as migration rules in constituting vulnerability and precariousness. The law creates migration statuses which then creates vulnerabilities for those workers, particularly in situations of undocumented status. When considering the effective opportunities for workers to exercise freedom of association and act through trade unions, these background rules may be more important than the specific legal provisions in trade union law. From a narrow legal perspective, the migration regime may seem rather remote to the legal facilitation of freedom of association. From a structural injustice perspective, however, these background conditions may be determinative of effective associative freedom.

Litigation in human rights courts may have transformative potential because the court is prepared to assess the broader legal context to the human rights' claim. A leading example of this is *Rantsev v Cyprus and Russia*.[64] The case arose out of the suspicious death of a Russian woman who had been working as a dancer in Cyprus on a 'cabaret-artiste visa'. This visa regime imposed strict limitations on her employment, which was then linked to her migration status. It created a system where club owners could exercise significant levels of control over the dancers, underpinned by their role in enforcing the migration regime itself. These restrictions

64 [2010] ECHR 25965/04 (7 January 2010).

effectively curtailed the ability of dancers to exit an abusive employment situation by linking migration and employment status. This exposed the women to risks of trafficking and modern slavery, which engaged Article 4 of the ECHR. It also created a systemic problem because many young women travelled from Russia to Cyprus under the visa regime in arrangements that were widely understood to be exploitative and abusive.

The Court held that Cyprus had violated Article 4 because it had failed in its positive obligations to put in place an appropriate legal and administrative framework to combat trafficking effectively. The maintenance of the visa regime was one important way in which Cyprus had violated Article 4. The regime augmented the coercive powers of employers, and in so doing, it increased the risks of trafficking for migrant women travelling into Cyprus under the visa regime.[65] From a structural injustice perspective, this judgment is very important. Trafficking is a serious wrong perpetrated by traffickers against those who are trafficked. When we consider trafficking from the 'liability model' of injustice, the visa regime simply forms part of the context within which serious wrongs are perpetrated by culpable agents. *Rantsev* is such a powerful judgment because it uses the legal tool of positive obligations under Article 4 to engage states in the process of reforming the background legal rules that facilitate serious exploitation.

This approach is particularly well-developed under Article 4. Is this also reflected in Article 11? In *Association of Civil Servants and Union for Collective Bargaining and Others v Germany*, the ECtHR considered the fundamental principles under Article 11. According to the Court:

> The substance of the right to freedom of association under Article 11 is marked by two guiding principles: firstly, the Court takes into consideration the totality of the measures taken by the State concerned in order to secure trade union freedom, subject to its margin of appreciation; secondly, the Court does not accept restrictions that affect the essential elements of trade union freedom, without which that freedom would become devoid of substance.[66]

At the current time, the scope of this 'totality' is not entirely clear. Is it restricted to those measures that relate narrowly to the essential elements of trade union freedom, such as collective bargaining machinery and

65 ibid [291]–[292].
66 05.07.2022 (application no. 815/18 and 4 others), [56].

the right to strike? Or does it extend to other parts of the legal system that could also render trade union freedom 'devoid of substance'? The approach in *Rantsev*, examining the visa regime and its impact on freedom, would support this wider approach to 'totality'. Some of the existing jurisprudence under Article 11 may support the narrower approach to 'totality'.

This narrow approach is demonstrated by *Unite v United Kingdom*.[67] In 2013, the UK Government abolished the Agricultural Wages Board of England and Wales (AWB). The AWB was composed of employer and worker representatives and independent members, and it set minimum wages and conditions of employment in the agricultural sector. The union challenged the abolition of the AWB as a violation of Article 11 and the right to collective bargaining. The basis of its challenge was that the general labour laws were practically unavailable to agricultural workers. The union recognition procedure in the UK only covers employers employing at least 21 workers. Given the structure of employment in the agricultural sector, the vast majority of employers failed to meet this threshold. This meant that the general recognition procedure was practically unavailable to most agricultural workers. While it was theoretically possible for agricultural workers to engage in strike action to achieve union recognition, the highly dispersed and precarious nature of employment meant that this means of securing collective bargaining was unlikely to be effective. In a controversial judgment, the ECtHR rejected the union's claim as inadmissible. The formal access of agricultural workers to the general statutory framework was sufficient for Article 11. The court did not consider the real obstacles to union organising for agricultural workers. Such work is often undertaken by workers under temporary migration programmes, with all the structural vulnerabilities that this entails. The work is hard, dangerous and conducted under poor working and living conditions. Instead, the judgment in *Unite* was focused narrowly on the paper rights of agricultural workers rather than whether those rights were 'practical and effective'.[68] It did not contextualise those rights within the particular difficulties of agricultural work, and it seemed to take a narrow view of the 'totality' in its formalistic approach to Article 11.

67 *Unite the Union v United Kingdom* (2016) 63 EHRR SE7.
68 *Artico v Italy* (1981) 3 EHRR 1, [33].

Freedom of association and positive state support

The 'positive obligation' feature of Convention jurisprudence is particularly promising for challenging structural injustice. It may require positive state interventions to modify unjust background conditions, as in *Rantsev*. The position under Article 11 is somewhat mixed. The leading case on positive obligations and Article 11 is still *Wilson v UK* handed down on 2 July 2002.[69] It involved a legal challenge to UK law, which permitted employers to offer financial inducements to workers to induce them to forgo union representation. The ECtHR recognised that the case did not involve a direct state interference with Article 11 rights. Instead, it engaged the state's positive duty to protect the Article 11 rights of both workers and the trade union itself from interference by private sector employers using financial sweeteners to undermine the union.[70] The Court observed (emphasis added):

> ... it is of the essence of the right to join a trade union for the protection of their interests that *employees should be free to instruct or permit the union to make representations to their employer or to take action in support of their interests on their behalf.* If workers are prevented from so doing, their freedom to belong to a trade union, for the protection of their interests, becomes illusory. *It is the role of the State to ensure that trade union members are not prevented or restrained from using their union to represent them in attempts to regulate their relations with their employers.*[71]

UK law at the time of the complaints was such that it:

> ... permitted employers to treat less favourably employees who were not prepared to renounce a freedom that was an essential feature of union membership. Such conduct constituted a disincentive or restraint on the use by employees of union membership to protect their interests.[72]

Accordingly, the Court found a violation of Article 11. The Court did not go on to examine whether the interference under Article 11(1) was justified under Article 11(2). While this was not explained in the

---

69 *Wilson v UK* [2002] 35 EHRR 20.
70 ibid [41].
71 ibid [46].
72 ibid [47].

judgment, it may reflect the very narrow margin of appreciation in cases where individual trade unionists are subjected to discriminatory wrongs such as penalties and detriments. It did not seem to matter here that the employer was in the private rather than public sector.

Wilson was an important case in terms of subsequent jurisprudential development for trade union rights under Article 11. It enlivened the dynamic potential of the ECHR for trade unions and workers engaged in litigation, leading to an expansion in its strategic use. In *Demir and Baykara v Turkey*, the Grand Chamber finally recognised the fundamental right to bargain collectively as protected under Article 11.[73] *Demir* is widely regarded as a watershed moment for trade union rights under the Convention. In certain respects, however, *Wilson* still represents the high-water mark of Article 11 in positive obligation cases. In *Unite v UK*, for example, the ECtHR emphasised the extremity of the facts in *Demir* which involved the direct judicial annulment of the collective agreement. In this way, *Demir* involved a direct state interference with freedom of association which was 'a very far-reaching interference with freedom of association.'[74] This reinterpretation of *Demir* as a direct state interference case is designed to entrench a wide margin of appreciation in positive obligation cases under Article 11. Cases like *Unite v UK* may indicate that even the complete withdrawal of collective bargaining machinery, leaving a purely voluntary system, could be within the state's wide margin of appreciation. At the current time, the positive obligation extends to the state's duty to protect workers and trade unions from employer discrimination, as in *Wilson* itself. It does not appear to require the state to undertake positive measures to *promote* collective bargaining or to empower trade unions. The ECHR does not preclude states from giving more active support to trade unions and collective bargaining. It sets a floor rather than a ceiling. From a structural injustice perspective, it is vital that governments provide strong positive state support to trade unions. The case studies indicate the multiplicity of ways in which states could provide such support to empower workers. Given the margin of appreciation in positive obligation cases, the ECtHR is unlikely at the current time to develop legally enforceable positive duties to promote collective bargaining through human rights adjudication. The creative design of promotional strategies is perhaps better suited as a political demand to governments in national contexts.

---

73 *Demir and Baykara v Turkey* (2009) 48 EHRR 54.
74 *Unite the Union* n 67, [60].

Freedom of association and trade union rights

The case studies reveal some limitations of the more traditional forms of trade union action, focused on collective bargaining and primary strike action in a bi-lateral relationship between the direct employer and the trade union. Sometimes, 'socio-political' strikes and secondary strike action may be a more effective tool given the complex and multipolar aspects of structural injustice in the labour market. 'Garment Workers' and 'Seafarers' both provide powerful examples where these alternative forms of strike action would have been more effective than traditional strikes against the direct employer. To what extent does Article 11 protect these other forms of strike action, such as the 'socio-political' strike or the secondary strike?

In relation to the right to strike, the ECtHR has not yet recognised it as an essential element of trade union freedom under Article 11; nevertheless, it is 'clearly protected' as a form of trade union activity.[75] The prohibition of secondary strike action was considered in *RMT v United Kingdom*.[76] Most European countries permit some form of secondary strike action. The UK represents an extreme case in maintaining a longstanding statutory prohibition of secondary strikes. As an expression of solidarity, it was one of the main targets of the Thatcher governments in its incremental restriction of strike laws during the 1980s and 1990s. In *RMT*, the ECtHR accepted that there was an interference under Article 11(1) but concluded that it was justified under Article 11(2). In particular, the Court emphasised the broad margin of appreciation on the specific facts of the case. The union had in fact been able to mobilise some industrial pressure, albeit not to the degree that it would have wanted. As such, the interference with Article 11 rights was not maximally invasive. The law obstructed the social power of the union, but it did not negate it. The Court also drew a controversial distinction between 'core' and 'accessory' forms of collective action:

> If a legislative restriction strikes at the core of trade union activity, a lesser margin of appreciation is to be recognised to the national legislature and more is required to justify the proportionality of the resultant interference, in the general interest, with the exercise of

---

75 *Association of Civil Servants* n 66, [59].

76 *National Union of Rail, Maritime and Transport Workers v United Kingdom* (2015) 60 EHRR 10; see Alan Bogg and Keith Ewing, 'The Implications of the *RMT* Case' (2014) 43 Industrial Law Journal 221.

trade union freedom. Conversely, if it is not the core but a secondary or accessory aspect of trade union activity that is affected, the margin is wider and the interference is, by its nature, more likely to be proportionate as far as its consequences for the exercise of trade union freedom are concerned.[77]

The argument that primary strike action is 'core' whereas secondary strike action is 'accessory' reflects a normative valuation of their importance in the internal architecture of the right. In practical terms, it also means that restrictions on 'accessory' freedoms are more easily justified because of a wider margin of appreciation. Unfortunately, the evaluative basis of the distinction was simply asserted by the Court without any supporting argument. There is a certainly a distinction between 'primary' and 'secondary' employers though this is simply descriptive of the configuration of the parties in the industrial dispute. The distinction is factual, not normative. The case studies indicate that these alternative forms of action should sometimes have political primacy because they reflect our social connections and duties of solidarity. Furthermore, they may provide the only means of empowering the most disadvantaged workers who would otherwise be abandoned to circumstances of extreme exploitation.

The importance of trade unions' political role is reflected in other Article 11 judgments. *ASLEF v United Kingdom* concerned the right of a trade union to exclude those with antithetical far right views from its membership.[78] The ECtHR recognised the political nature of trade unions and this affected the balance struck between the associative freedoms of potential members and the trade union itself:

> Historically, trade unions in the United Kingdom, and elsewhere in Europe, were, and though perhaps to a lesser extent today are, commonly affiliated to political parties or movements, particularly those on the left. They are not bodies solely devoted to politically-neutral aspects of the well-being of their members, but are often ideological, with strongly held views on social and political issues. There was no hint in the domestic proceedings that the applicant erred in its conclusion that Mr Lee's political values and ideals clashed, fundamentally, with its own.[79]

77 ibid [87].
78 [2007] IRLR 361.
79 ibid [50].

This is an important recognition that trade unions have a political dimension, and they are entitled to maintain an ideological position. While *ASLEF* concerned the ability of unions to apply their own membership criteria to applicants for membership, it also recognises the importance of political activism as a core (rather than accessory) trade union activity.

Freedom of association and personal scope

In order to access most statutory protections for freedom of association, it is necessary to establish 'worker' status. This can sometimes be especially difficult for the most precarious workers where the contracts present the work as involving independent self-employment. Paradoxically, those most in need of the protective rights find it most difficult to access them. Under Article 11, the dominant approach of the ECtHR is to treat trade union rights as applying to those in an 'employment relationship' as set out in the ILO Recommendation 198 on Employment Relationship (2006). This received a strong endorsement in the Grand Chamber decision of *Sindicatul 'Pastoral Cel Bun v Romania* (*Pastoral Cel Bun*).[80] According to the Grand Chamber, the 'only question' relevant to whether the clergy in this case qualified for Article 11 protection was 'whether such duties, notwithstanding any special features they may entail, amount to an employment relationship rendering applicable the right to form a trade union within the meaning of Article 11'.[81] The Court based its assessment of the employment situation on relevant international instruments, in particular using the indicative criteria in ILO Recommendation No 198 on Employment Relationship.

The breadth of the criteria in the ILO Recommendation has sometimes provided a basis for broadening the domestic criteria for workers. The leading example of this is in relation to foster carers who were seeking to have their union 'listed' under the relevant statute. The foster carers faced a formidable obstacle in that they were treated as not working under 'contracts' under English law. In a significant judgment, Underhill LJ in the English Court of Appeal concluded that the non-listing of the National Union of Professional Foster Carers was an 'interference' with the trade union rights protected under Article 11 of the ECHR; and this 'interference' was not justified either by the non-contractual nature of their employment or by the special quasi-familial

80 *Sindicatul Păstorul cel Bun v Romania* (2013) 58 EHHR 10.
81 ibid [141].

character of fostering.[82] In a carefully reasoned decision, he examined whether the foster carers were in an 'employment relationship' for the purposes of Article 11, applying the indicative criteria in the ILO Recommendation on Employment Relationship. Since the work of foster caring was remunerated through fees and allowances (even if this was not akin to a typical wage), and it was subject to a degree of disciplinary oversight and control to ensure that the interests of the fostered child were safeguarded, Lord Justice Underhill concluded that this was an 'employment relationship' within the scope of Article 11.

The importance of this broader perspective is that it examines the facts of the employment situation and whether there is a substantive need for employment protection. In adopting this more purposive approach, it avoids the limitations of an employment status test that is focused excessively on the terms of the contract. This allows courts to consider the wider position of claimants within broader structures of disadvantage and injustice rather than abstracting the contractual analysis from its social and economic context. This purposive approach was also adopted in the landmark case of *Uber v Aslam,* which concerned the worker status of Uber drivers.[83] Legal criteria of employment status should be applied inclusively and realistically. This exercise is sensitive to those features of the work arrangement indicating that it should fall within the class of cases the legislator intended to be protected under the relevant statutory provision. Where the work arrangement in its practical operation displays features of exploitation-vulnerability, it is more likely to be treated as within the protective scope of the statute. This involves consideration of many factors: subordination and control, the ability to influence the terms in the written contract through negotiation, the degree of 'integration' into another's business or whether the worker is in business on her own account, whether the worker can market her services widely or is tied to a single purchaser of her labour power. It is certainly possible that the overall structural disadvantage of the worker, in the labour market and beyond, may be considered in this assessment of exploitation-vulnerability. Potentially, this could provide a powerful legal tool for addressing the structural injustice experienced by the precarious workers in labour markets.

82 *National Union of Professional Foster Carers v Certification Officer (Independent Workers Union of Great Britain and others intervening)* [2021] EWCA Civ 548; [2021] ICR 1397.
83 *Uber BV and Others v Aslam* [2021] ICR 657.

Conclusion

Structural injustice provides a powerful tool for identifying the structural parameters of disadvantage and precariousness in labour markets. It also provides rich insights into the most effective strategies for improving workers' lives. Human rights are central to that emancipatory political project. In turn, freedom of association should occupy a focal position in any human rights-based strategy. This is because workers themselves are not simply passive recipients of pity or beneficence on the part of governments and employers. Our public institutions must respect workers as agents with dignity and self-respect. The surest way to challenge structural injustice is by empowering workers to take charge of their own fates. Empowerment must be rooted in collective action. In turn, political responsibility depends upon effective organisation in civil society. Trade unions and other labour associations still represent the most powerful way in which Young's 'social connection model' of responsibility can be realised in the world of work. Freedom of association is the human right that most directly facilitates the collective action necessary to transform our social world.

This chapter has examined structural justice as both diagnostic and remedial tool based on three case studies. It then considered the potential of human rights' jurisprudence under the ECHR to support freedom of association as a response to structural injustice. Three underlying themes have been latent in the development of this argument and it is time to make them explicit.

The first theme is the salience of *injustice* as the political focus. It often feels more politically comfortable to reflect on the nature of justice in the polity and economy, the design of just institutions, the achievement of *good* work. By contrast, structural injustice would accord strategic and political priority to the eradication of *bad* work. Trade unions should also focus their organisational energies on bad work, with the support of governmental institutions. When bad work has been eradicated, there is a stronger case then to shift the public focus more decisively towards promoting good and meaningful work. While politicians have been happy to support 'good work' plans, I suggest that we need to prioritise public policies and enforcement efforts around a national 'bad work' plan. There is still plenty to be done in eradicating the most exploitative forms of work, and for now this should be the political and organisational priority.

The second theme is the importance of collective empowerment to freedom of association. For example, the Supreme Court of Canada has recently emphasised the special role of freedom of association in giving a voice to marginalised and oppressed groups. Under the Canadian Charter, some associative freedoms attract special constitutional protection such as 'the right to join with others to meet on more equal terms the power and strength of other groups or entities'.[84] There is no reason why this justificatory approach could not be adopted by the ECtHR, and it could support a stronger 'positive duty' jurisprudence under Article 11. By justifying freedom of association in this way, associations that empower the marginalised should be given stronger protections and more extensive legal support. Without this positive support, there is a danger that incipient collective action by disadvantaged workers will be stymied by the powerful actors that benefit from structural injustice. We may also lapse into the 'victim blaming' trap lurking in structural injustice accounts of political responsibility. We cannot insist that the victims of structural injustice undertake their political responsibilities without first providing them with the rights and resources necessary to do this.

The third theme is the need to rethink freedom of association rights using structural injustice and the empowerment model of freedom of association as an organising principle. This could justify stronger support for political and secondary strike action by trade unions. 'Enforcement' strike action, responding to legal violations by employers, should also attract a more permissive legal framework, perhaps with modified support thresholds in ballots and reduced notice requirements. It would also justify a more robust development of positive state duties to promote effective trade union activities. While the jurisprudence of the ECtHR contains some promising signs in this regard, much work remains to be done. Structural injustice helps us to understand the scale of that endeavour, and the most effective legal tools to improve the working lives of the disadvantaged. Ultimately, such transformation is more likely to be deep and enduring when workers themselves take charge of their own fates through collective organisation. In the lexicon of labour rights as human rights, this is the true meaning of freedom of association.

84 *Mounted Police Association of Ontario v Canada* 2015 SCC 1, 1 SCR 3, [66].

7

Criminal justice and social (in)justice

Nicola Lacey[1]

Introduction

A recognition of the obstacles to achieving criminal justice in a society marked by structural injustice has been a longstanding feature of philosophical, legal and criminological literatures.[2] Inequalities and injustices in social attitudes to certain groups and in the distribution of resources and opportunities in fields ranging from family life, education, health care, shelter and secure employment are perhaps the most obviously relevant features of a social order. Moreover, the experience of abuse, prejudice, violence or nutritional or emotional deprivation is now understood to affect not simply economic and life opportunities but psychological development.[3] The consequent threat to the legitimacy of punishment is particularly acute when the state itself bears substantial responsibility for either creating, or failing to alleviate, the relevant

1 I am grateful to Jacob Bronsther, Henrique Carvalho, Mark Dsouza, Katya Franko, Zelia Gallo, David Garland, Rocio Lorca Ferrecio, Hanna Pickard, Federico Picinali, Valeria Ruiz Perez, Inger-Johanne Sand, Alec Walen and Lucia Zedner for helpful comments on an earlier draft; to Valeria Ruiz Perez for exemplary research assistance; and to members of the Political Turns in Criminal Law seminar, the Oxford University Jurisprudence Discussion Group, and participants at seminars at King's College London, University College London, the University of Syddansk, and the University of Oslo for lively discussion and feedback.

2 See, for example, Jeffrie G Murphy, 'Marxism and Retribution' (1973) 2 Philosophy & Public Affairs 217; Richard Delgado, 'Rotten Social Background: Should the Criminal Law Recognize a Defense of Severe Environmental Deprivation?' (1985) 3 Law & Inequality 9; Jeffrey Reiman, *And the Poor Get Prison: Economic Bias in American Criminal Justice* (Blackwell 1966); Michelle Alexander, *The New Jim Crow: Mass Incarceration in the Age of Colorblindness* (New Press 2010).

3 Tim Newburn, *Criminology* (2nd edn, Routledge 2013), 13–256.

conditions.[4] Though the causal chains are complex,[5] it is no exaggeration – nor is it inconsistent with a recognition of the role of individual agency – to speak of many injustices as criminogenic.

Meeting the challenge of doing a measure of criminal justice in these circumstances remains important, however, not least because of a further consideration, and one that complicates the moral and political challenge. This is the fact that disproportionalities in the impact of criminalisation and punishment on groups disadvantaged by injustice are matched in many countries by comparable disproportionalities in criminal victimisation.[6]

Economically marginalised groups and those subject to racism and other forms of prejudice find themselves not only on the sharp end of the criminal justice system, but also disproportionately the victims of crime. They also, all too often, face poor provision of criminal justice services such as policing. It was of course this realisation that gave the impetus to the re-emergence of a left-of-centre version of criminological 'realism' in the 1980s;[7] and a recognition of its electoral implications underpinned Labour Party policy in Britain during the Blair era.

Over the last 30 years, however, this longstanding challenge has arguably been exacerbated by emerging features of political economy in the so-called advanced democracies: notably the growth and embedding of economic inequalities.[8] The deceleration or reversal of longer term redistributive trends and of post-Second World War welfarism has been accompanied by an increase in poverty and the emergence in many relatively wealthy countries of a polarised demographic featuring a substantial minority excluded from many of the benefits of economic growth, and even of political association.

---

4 R A Duff, *Punishment, Communication, and Community* (Oxford University Press 2001), 175–201.

5 Nicola Lacey and David Soskice, 'American Exceptionalism in Inequality and Poverty: A (Tentative) Historical Explanation' in Nicola Lacey and others (eds), *Tracing the Relationship between Crime, Punishment and Inequality: Space, Time, and Politics* (Oxford University Press 2020); John Hagan and Ruth Peterson, *Crime and Inequality* (Stanford University Press 1995); Christopher Muller and Christopher Wildeman, 'Punishment and Inequality' in Jonathan Simon and Richard Sparks (eds), *The Sage Handbook of Punishment and Society* (Sage 2013).

6 Robert J Sampson and William Julius Wilson, 'Toward a Theory of Race, Crime and Urban Inequality' in John Hagan and Ruth Peterson (eds), *Crime and Inequality* (Stanford University Press 1995); Ruth Peterson and Lauren J Krivo, *Divergent Social World. Neighborhood Crime and the Racial-Spatial Divide* (Russell Sage Foundation 2010).

7 Richard Kinsey, John Lea and Jock Young, *Losing the Fight against Crime* (Blackwell 1986).

8 Thomas Piketty, *Capital in the Twenty-First Century* (Harvard University Press 2013); Thomas Piketty, *Capital and Ideology* (Harvard University Press 2020); Anthony B Atkinson, *Inequality: What Can Be Done?* (Harvard University Press 2015); Mike Savage, *The Return of Inequality: Social Change and the Weight of the Past* (Harvard University Press 2021).

This has both complicated the political challenge facing democratic governments, and significantly aggravated injustices that had long been apparent. Conversely, the consolidation of a small, super-wealthy elite has arguably created a zone of impunity for certain crimes of the powerful, with corrosive implications for the legitimacy of the state's criminalising power. In this chapter, I analyse these developments, and consider their normative upshot and practical implications for criminal justice, and their role in the re-emergence of new forms of criminal justice abolitionism.

The chapter proceeds as follows. In the first section, I analyse the forms and implications for social justice arising from philosophical, legal and criminological literatures respectively. I set out a typology of three forms of injustice, distinguishing between material injustices, epistemic injustices and injustices of standing,[9] and trace their ramifications in different disciplinary and institutional contexts. I then move on, secondly, to consider how recent changes in political economy and society in wealthy democracies, such as the UK, have exacerbated both these injustices and the challenges which they pose for the effort to nonetheless realise some degree of criminal justice. And in the final section, I attempt to synthesise the upshot of these various analyses for criminal justice, including its legitimacy and efficacy, today.

Criminal justice and social (in)justice in philosophy, law and criminology

As I have already observed, a range of considerations about injustice and its upshot for criminal justice have featured in philosophical/justificatory, legal/classificatory and criminological/explanatory scholarly literatures. Of course, the boundaries between these literatures are porous: much criminal law theory deploys philosophical concepts; and since the latter part of the twentieth century, the primarily explanatory project of criminology in its more critical modes has often expanded into the terrain of political philosophy. Nonetheless, it is useful

9 Criminal law can, of course, itself perpetrate injustice, either directly – for example, in the case of proscriptions on homosexual conduct – or indirectly – for example, where laws forbidding begging or rough sleeping are in effect impossible for some people to comply with: Terry Skolnik 'Homelessness and the Impossibility to Obey the Law' Fordham Urban Law Journal 43/3 (2016) 741. Indeed, many debates about de/criminalisation have been framed explicitly in terms of the need to render the law more just. Important as such cases of unjust criminal laws are, my focus in this chapter is on the upshot for criminal justice of background injustices not directly expressed in or perpetrated by the law itself.

for our purposes to distinguish between the core contributions of each discipline, so as to tease out the various potential implications arising from their analyses for the legitimacy or possibility of criminal justice.

Philosophical perspectives: distinctive forms of injustice

It makes sense to begin with philosophy's contribution, not least because the concept of injustice itself has been a central object of philosophical analysis from philosophers of the ancient world such as Aristotle to the present day, and because the conceptions of justice elaborated in different philosophical traditions have informed, directly or indirectly, debates about criminal in/justice. In thinking about the bearing of social justice on criminal justice, perhaps the most obvious issues have to do with what we might call *material or distributive injustice*: the ways in which the unjust distribution of access to public goods, opportunities and material resources shapes potential offenders' substantive opportunity to conform their behaviour to the norms of criminal law, and places special barriers or difficulties in the path of their efforts to do. While some philosophers have been inclined to regard punishment in terms of retribution, and to ring-fence the concept of retributive justice so as to insulate it from the upshot of broader distributive justice,[10] most retributivists today would probably accept, following Murphy,[11] that background injustices in the distribution of resources and opportunities do potentially affect an individual's desert, for example, in influencing the proportionality of a given penalty, posing a conundrum for the very project of criminal justice in an unjust society. But to say this is, of course, to beg the question of what counts as distributive injustice. Are all inequalities of resources, or of welfare outcomes, of or opportunities, presumptively unjust? Are ostensibly uneven opportunities and outcomes unjust only when not shaped by other qualifications such as 'merit', talent or 'natural desert'?

The literature on justice is vast and even a brief overview is well beyond the scope of a single chapter. Instead of attempting such a survey, I will focus on one example – that of John Rawls' famous *A Theory of Justice*,[12] first published just over half a century ago. I do so not only because of the extraordinary influence that Rawls' theory of justice as

10 Michael S Moore, *Placing Blame: A Theory of the Criminal Law* (Oxford University Press 1997).
11 Murphy (n 2).
12 John Rawls, *A Theory of Justice* (Harvard University Press 1971).

fairness continues to exert across political philosophy, but also because it has recently been deployed to telling effect by philosopher Tommie Shelby in his searing work on the 'dark ghetto' in the United States.[13] The environment of the disadvantaged, segregated, disrespected ghetto produces, in Shelby's view, conditions which standardly undermine fair equality of opportunity in areas such as access to marketable skills, decent housing, adequate health care and other areas certain to affect the level of difficulty which ghetto residents face in confirming their behaviour to criminal law. These unfairnesses in the distribution of opportunity – along with inequalities far greater than those that Rawls would have seen as justifiable in terms of the difference principle[14] – reflect failures of justice in the basic structure of society. Indeed in some instances they even fall below the less demanding Rawlsian test of compliance with constitutional essentials. These systemic injustices in core social arrangements themselves amount to a form of 'extortion, even violence'[15] which undermine the consent and reciprocity on which political obligation is based. In the absence of real efforts by the state to reverse them, crime may be seen as a form of resistance, of civil disobedience: those systemically excluded from the benefits of political association cannot justly be held to their civic obligations.

Shelby's analysis of the 'dark ghetto' is a paradigm for the philosophical exploration of the upshot of distributive injustice for criminal justice. But I also mentioned his reference to the disrespect with which ghetto residents are not only treated, but viewed. And this brings us to a second form of injustice which also poses challenges to the project of criminal justice: what Miranda Fricker, in an influential book, has called *Epistemic Injustice*.[16] The argument is relatively simple, but its upshot is profound. The distribution of power in society shapes how claims to knowledge are received and validated, rendering the truth claims of disrespected and marginalised groups less 'valid', less audible – and to ever more severe degrees, the greater the disparities of power and respect involved. The upshot for criminal justice is obvious: where the state accuses an individual, the individual – even with legal representation – is inevitably in a less powerful position: and if that individual is, in addition,

---

13 Tommie Shelby, 'Justice, Deviance, and the Dark Ghetto' (2007) 35 Philosophy & Public Affairs 126; Tommie Shelby, *Dark Ghettos: Injustice, Dissent, and Reform* (Harvard University Press 2016).

14 Rawls' 'difference principle' specifies that inequalities can be justified only where they benefit the least advantaged over the longer term.

15 Shelby, 'Justice, Deviance, and the Dark Ghetto' (n 13) 126.

16 Miranda Fricker, *Epistemic Injustice: Power and the Ethics of Knowing* (Oxford University Press 2007).

a member of a culturally or materially marginalised group, direct and indirect mechanisms are liable to undermine the credibility of their words and even the audibility of their voices. Sometimes this epistemic injustice will be a product in part of material injustice – as, for example, where an indigent defendant cannot afford high-level legal representation and has to rely on poorly resourced public defence arrangements. But it may, more subtly, flow from factors such as implicit biases, for example, in how veracity or credibility are assessed.[17] And these biases likely affect groups marginalised in terms of a wide range of factors including age, gender, ethnicity, homelessness and insecure migration status.[18]

There is now a very substantial literature, in sociology and economics as well as philosophy and psychology, on the operation of such implicit biases, as well as on the impact of cultural – particularly gendered and racialised – stereotypes.[19] While perhaps less obvious than the upshot of material injustices, the implications of epistemic injustice for criminal justice are no less radical. The recent overturning of the convictions of dozens of postmasters for a 'fraud' which was in fact caused by a software failure is a case in point.[20] Probably the most extensive miscarriage of justice case in English/Welsh legal history, it is horrifyingly eloquent

---

17 I emphasise here the contemporary literature in psychology and philosophy; but historians, social theorists and critical race theorists too have tracked the longstanding impact of social status on the ability of individuals to have their truth claims affirmed, in areas as diverse as the natural sciences and commercial life as well as the criminal law. See for example, Margot C Finn, *The Character of Credit: Personal Debt in English Culture, 1740–1914* (Cambridge University Press 2003); Deidre Shauna Lynch, *The Economy of Character: Novels, Market Culture, and the Business of Inner Meaning* (University of Chicago Press 1998); Steven Shapin, *A Social History of Truth: Civility and Science in Seventeenth Century England* (Chicago University Press 1994); Patricia Hills Collins, *Black Feminist Thought: Knowledge, Consciousness and the Politics of Empowerment* (Routledge 1990).

18 Katja Franko, *The Crimmigrant Other: Migration and Penal Power* (Routledge 2019).

19 Nilanjana Dasgupta, 'Implicit Attitudes and Beliefs Adapt to Situations' (2013) 47 Advances in Experimental Social Psychology 233; Patricia Devine, 'Stereotypes and Prejudice: Their Automatic and Controlled Components' (1989) Attitudes and Social Cognition 1; Elizabeth Anderson, 'Epistemic Justice as a Virtue of Social Institutions' (2012) 26 Social Epistemology 163; Sally Haslanger, 'Social Structure, Narrative and Explanation' (2015) 45 Canadian Journal of Philosophy 1; Jules Holroyd, 'Responsibility for Implicit Bias' (2012) 43 Journal of Social Philosophy 274; Jules Holroyd and Federico Picinali, 'Implicit Bias, Self-Defence and the Reasonable Person' in Claes Lernestedt and Matt Matravers (eds), *Criminal Law's Person* (Oxford University Press 2017); Daniel Kelly and Erica Roedder, 'Racial Cognition and the Ethics of Implicit Bias' (2008) 3 Philosophy Compass 522; Kristin Lane, Jerry Kang and Mahzarin Banaji, 'Implicit Social Cognition and Law' (2007) 3 Annual Review of Law and Social Science 427; Brendan O'Flaherty and Rajiv Sethi, *Shadows of Doubt: Stereotypes, Crime, and the Pursuit of Justice* (Harvard University Press 2019); Elijah Anderson, *Black in White Space: The Enduring Impact of Color in Everyday Life* (University of Chicago Press 2022); Jennifer Lackey, 'False Confessions and Testimonial Injustice' (2020) 110 The Journal of Criminal Law & Criminology 43.

20 The Guardian, 'Appeal Court Quashes 12 More Convictions in Post Office IT Scandal' (19 July 2021) <https://www.theguardian.com/business/2021/jul/19/appeal-court-quashes-more-convictions-post-office-it-scandal> accessed 18 August 2022.

testimony to the difficulty which members of social groups with lower social standing – in this case, many of them working class, and many of minority ethnicity – encounter in having their narratives accepted – indeed, even listened to – in criminal justice settings. In effect, these defendants' agency was effaced through the criminal justice authorities' grant of epistemic preference to an IT programme.[21]

Closely related to epistemic injustice – but also, arguably, underpinning the difficulty in motivating political action to tackle material injustice – are what we might call injustices of standing, or of concern and respect. To fully participate in a political community marked by reciprocity, individuals and groups have to be accorded a certain level of standing and respect: indeed, this standing is arguably a precondition of political membership or inclusion: of being a subject of justice. This basic form of standing or status is not, of course, the same as being approved of, admired or liked; indeed in the case of serious offenders, those things are inevitably compromised. But within any broadly liberal schema, basic political standing needs to survive criminal conviction, and indeed underpins standards of due process in the administration of criminal justice. And arguably, the development in some jurisdictions of penal mechanisms such as continuing (or even perpetual) civic disqualifications following a conviction[22] both violates and represents an underlying failure of this basic precept of just standing. One might regard injustices of standing as a broad category of which epistemic injustice is one distinctive upshot.

The philosophical debates, therefore, have provided us with three distinct but intersecting conceptions of injustice, which pose difficult questions for criminal justice, potentially undermining the state's authority to enforce the criminal law – and in practice, producing forms of injustice which are all too often mutually reinforcing. These forms of injustice provide critical tools for an analysis of all aspects of criminal justice – the scope and extent of criminal law; the practices of policing and prosecution; sentencing and the execution of punishment. Indeed, some philosophers have gone so far as to claim that such injustices can

21 Lackey (n 19). This case, moreover, illustrates both the intuitive plausibility, and the limits, of Jennifer Lackey's concept of agential testimonial injustice, which she argues explains as cases of genuine injustice the excessive credibility accorded to testimony such as confessions, even absent the social biases emphasised in Fricker's definition of epistemic injustice. The criminal justice officials in this case clearly gave excessive credibility to the IT system, but of course without doing that system – unlike the victims of a naively credited false confession – an injustice.
22 James B Jacobs, *The Eternal Criminal Record* (Harvard University Press 2015).

be sufficient entirely to undermine the state's very standing to 'blame' or call offenders to account.[23]

Note, moreover, two further features of even this parsimonious analysis of philosophical theories of justice and their upshot for criminal justice. First, each of these forms of injustice potentially affects the criminal justice system's construction and treatment of not only offenders but also victims. Just as a society's material injustices condition the scope and fairness of the opportunities that differently situated groups have to conform their behaviour to the law, the way in which their behaviour and testimony will be received and interpreted, and the standing which they enjoy, they also condition their likelihood of becoming a victim; particularly of certain forms of crime. Furthermore, the injustices have an impact on the likelihood of having their complaint about criminal victimisation dealt with, attended to and believed; and the respect and consideration with which they are likely to be treated by legal and criminal justice agents. Perhaps the most obvious example here would be the longstanding disbelief and deficits of respect encountered by victims (particularly female, and probably yet more so, racially or class-marginalised female victims) of domestic abuse and sexual assault.[24] But much the same applies to, for example, residents of poor areas who do not benefit from adequate policing; or young black men who find themselves presumptively criminalised when they are in fact victims or witnesses – a spectacular example being that of Dwayne Brooks following the racist murder of his friend Stephen Lawrence, documented in a subsequent inquiry.[25]

---

23 Duff (n 4); R A Duff, 'Moral and Criminal Responsibility: Answering and Refusing to Answer' in D Justin Coates and Neal A Tognazzini (eds), *Oxford Studies in Agency and Responsibility*, vol 5 (Oxford University Press 2019); James Edwards, 'Standing to Hold Responsible' (2019) 16 Journal of Moral Philosophy 437; Victor Tadros, 'Poverty and Criminal Responsibility' (2009) 43 Journal of Value Inquiry 391; Gary Watson, 'Standing in Judgment' in D Justin Coates and Neal A Tognazzini (eds), *Blame: Its Nature and Norms* (Oxford University Press 2012); Gary Watson, 'A Moral Predicament in the Criminal Law' (2015) 58 Inquiry 168. For critical discussion, see Nicola Lacey and Hanna Pickard, 'Why Standing to Blame May Be Lost but Authority to Hold Accountable Retained: Criminal Law as a Regulative Public Institution' (2021) 104 The Monist 265; Jules Holroyd and Federico Picinali, 'Excluding Evidence for Integrity's Sake' in Christian Dahlman, Alex Stein and Giovanni Tuzet (eds), *Philosophical Foundations of Law* (Oxford University Press 2021).

24 Hanna Pickard, 'Responsibility and Explanations of Rape' in Iviola Solanke (ed), *On Crime, Society and Responsibility in the Work of Nicola Lacey* (Oxford University Press 2021); James Chalmers, Fiona Leverick and Vanessa E Munro, 'Why the Jury Is, and Should Still Be, out on Rape Deliberation' (2021) 9 Criminal Law Review 753; James Chalmers, Fiona Leverick and Vanessa Munro, 'The Provenance of What Is Proven: Exploring (Mock) Jury Deliberation in Scottish Rape Trials' (2021) 48 Journal of Law and Society 226.

25 William MacPherson, 'The Stephen Lawrence Inquiry' (1999) Cm 4262-I <https://assets.publishing.service.gov.uk/government/uploads/system/uploads/attachment_data/file/277111/4262.pdf>.

Second, the normative resources provided by philosophical conceptions of justice and of the upshot of social injustice for criminal justice include – if less obviously – resources for the critical analysis of what we might see as the opposite end of the criminal justice spectrum to the 'dark ghetto': crimes of the powerful. A litmus test of the justice of a criminal justice system is its treatment of all on equal terms. A failure to attend to the crimes of those who benefit from material advantages, as well as the advantages of credibility and of status, unjustified by the precepts of justice, pose just as sharp a challenge to the authority and legitimacy of criminal justice as do material, epistemic and standing injustices in relation to the disadvantaged or disrespected. In particular, these injustices of unfair advantage, as we might call them, also pose a subtle but real threat to the overall legitimacy of the system. We know from extensive empirical research[26] that perceptions of procedural justice are important to trust in institutions – and hence, potentially, to their stability and potential efficacy. Unjust advantages in this terrain, particularly where so extensive that they may be regarded as creating a sphere of criminal justice impunity for the elite, are hence potentially toxic to perceived legitimacy. But they are also, crucially, corrosive of the state's normative claim to legitimate authority. And as we shall see in the second section of this chapter, recent political-economic developments in the rich democracies have created fertile conditions for just such a crisis of authority.

Criminal law's framing of social injustice

Criminal law, it goes without saying, operates with its own, internal conception of justice: doing (legal)/criminal justice is, definitionally, what criminal law aspires to do. But what it means to do criminal justice in legal terms is, first, foremost and – for some legal theorists and lawyers – exclusively defined by the law itself. This entails complying with core precepts of due process and procedural fairness such as the right to trial before an impartial tribunal, the presumption of innocence and the right to have the case against one proven to a distinctively high

26 Tom R Tyler, 'Procedural Justice, Legitimacy, and the Effective Rule of Law' (2003) 30 Crime & Justice 283; Tom R Tyler, 'Psychological Perspectives on Legitimacy' (2006) 57 Annual Review of Psychology 375; Justice Tankebe and Alison Liebling (eds), *Legitimacy and Criminal Justice: An International Exploration* (Oxford University Press 2013). See more generally the ongoing work of the Yale Justice Collaboratory Yale Law School, 'Procedural Justice – Yale Law School' <https://law.yale.edu/justice-collaboratory/procedural-justice> accessed 27 February 2023.

standard: features which are now strongly associated with the perhaps somewhat broader-than-strictly-legal figure of 'human rights'. But it also means, quite simply, having the existing criminal law (including, where applicable, sentencing norms) applied to each defendant accurately, even-handedly and fairly. From the legal point of view, the proposition that background social injustice can generally be brought into the courtroom to argue for the defendant's exoneration would be regarded as threatening to both the law's authority and its core focus on individual responsibility, founded in the notion of agency consisting in adequately engaged cognitive and volitional capacities at the time of the crime.[27] The requirement of proof of responsibility or *mens rea* itself is of course relevant to distributive justice: underpinning Hart's conception of responsibility as engaged cognitive and volitional capacities is the thought that this is what is necessary to provide a 'fair opportunity' to comply with the law. In this sense, the responsibility requirement arguably also reduces the chances of the criminogenic conditions of background injustice entrapping offenders into norm infractions to as great an extent as would a system of stricter liability. But the idea that criminal law's standards might be regarded as not applying, or not applying with their full force, to defendants simply because of their experience of injustice would be regarded as straightforwardly counter to the functions and distinctive *modus operandi* of criminal law,[28] and this marks limits – albeit fluid and contested – to criminal law's potential accommodation of questions of background injustice. And while, as we shall see below, criminal law and procedure has indeed found ways in which to mitigate the degree to which it reflects and compounds background injustice, criminal law's orientation to binary decision-making – guilty or not guilty – limits its flexibility, at least in relation to decisions about liability.

Of course, this normative insulation of legal discourse is not beyond critique: both critical and socio-legal traditions in criminal law scholarship have done much to expose the ideological assumptions and power relations underlying, the practical upshot of, and the contradictions

27 H L A Hart, *Punishment and Responsibility* (Clarendon Press 1968).

28 Nicola Lacey, *State Punishment: Political Principles and Community Values* (Routledge 1988); Nicola Lacey, 'Community Culture and Criminalisation' in Rowan Cruft, Matthew H Kramer and Mark R Reiff (eds), *Crime, Punishment and Responsibility: The Jurisprudence of Antony Duff* (Oxford University Press 2011); Nicola Lacey, *In Search of Criminal Responsibility: Ideas, Interests and Institutions* (Oxford University Press 2016).

implicit in this form of supposed legal autonomy.[29] In particular, the recent 'preventive turn' in criminal law, alongside the emergence of hybrid risk/character-based practices of responsibility attribution in areas as diverse as terrorism, low-level public disorder and joint enterprise killings are testimony to just such porosity between law and power.[30] As Carvalho has argued, the cultural task of criminal law in upholding the hegemonic hold of civil order is a complex one, given the many gaps between criminal law's claim to be doing justice and the social realities of criminalisation, which must be glossed over:

> The apparent unity and coherence of civil order, the sense of civic identity and belonging it fosters, are largely the product of the dominant ideological apparatus preserved by the state, by its effort to maintain its hold on common sense.[31]

There are limits, accordingly, to the extent to which criminal law can put its coding logic in question without compromising its own authority.

These limitations, however, do not entail that the content, interpretation and enforcement of criminal law is entirely insulated from broader concerns about justice. For example, in many systems featuring a jury as the trier of fact in some criminal cases, the possibility of 'jury nullification' operates as a safety valve: a jury can simply refuse to convict in circumstances where it regards conviction as unjust.[32] Apart from such 'perverse' jury verdicts, systems of criminal law such as that of England and Wales have three main ways of making adjustments or framing their approach so as to respond to issues of injustice, and to mitigate, resolve or even pre-empt their impact on criminalisation. These accommodations can happen at various stages of the process. First, they may be accounted for during the legislative process, either in framing the law or in deciding whether or not to criminalise an activity in the first place. The framing of statutory criminal defences – for example, the recent introduction of the partial 'loss of control' defence to murder in English criminal law; or

29 Nicola Lacey, Celia Wells and Oliver Quick, *Reconstructing Criminal Law* (3rd edn, Butterworths 1998); Alan Norrie, *Crime, Reason and History* (3rd edn, Cambridge University Press 2014).
30 Andrew Ashworth and Lucia Zedner, *Preventive Justice* (Oxford University Press 2014); Henrique Carvalho, *The Preventive Turn in Criminal Law* (University Press 2017); Lacey, *In Search of Criminal Responsibility: Ideas, Interests and Institutions* (n 28).
31 Henrique Carvalho, 'Dangerous Patterns: Joint Enterprise and the Culture of Criminal Law' [2022] Social & Legal Studies 1, 6.
32 This jury discretion is of course itself vulnerable to the impact of, for example, epistemic injustice. See Chalmers, Leverick and Munro, 'Why the Jury Is, and Should Still Be, out on Rape Deliberation' (n 24); Chalmers, Leverick and Munro, 'The Provenance of What Is Proven' (n 24).

indeed of new or amended forms of criminalisation – illustrates the ways which concerns about the upshot of social injustice for criminal justice can filter into the law-making process. Another good example would be the opposition to legislation that would require citizens or residents to carry identity cards on the basis that criminalisation of the failure to carry a card would almost certainly lead to unevenness in enforcement which would reflect background social injustices.[33] In addition, recent reforms of criminal procedure might also be seen as geared to enhance epistemic justice in the criminal process, including special provision for vulnerable witnesses, protocols governing cross-examination and other such legislative and policy initiatives.[34]

The second mechanism by which English criminal law fine-tunes its rules in ways that speak directly or indirectly to background injustice is the realm of common law defences.[35] Defences such as self-defence or duress recognise that some defendants encounter special barriers to conformity to an extent which either justifies their commission of an act otherwise defined as criminal or (more often) attenuates the link between act and offender, undermining or mitigating individual responsibility by reason of cognitive or volitional deficits, some of them arising from social context. The preference for defences that speak to deficits of responsibility rather than justifications of actions reflects the importance attached to not diluting the force of criminal law's prohibition. In comparison, recognising justificatory defences might be seen as effectively allowing the offender to redraw the boundaries of criminal law. The case of necessity – tellingly reframed by English courts in terms of the concept of 'duress of circumstances', hence narrowing the law's view of the defence's grounding to those situations which can be analogised to human-imposed duress – is a case in point. Courts across many jurisdictions have exhibited concern that a capacious justificatory defence of necessity would, in effect, invite defendants to redefine the scope of criminal law as it applies to them.[36] A yet more complex case is that of so-called 'cultural defences': claims that the defendant's distinctive life experience and values might shape their perceptions or capacities in

33 See, for example, the pressure group Liberty's evidence to the Home Affairs Committee on the Government's proposal to introduce national identity cards in 2003: <https://www.dematerialisedid.com/PDFs/id-card-evidence-to-home-affairs-committee-dec.pdf> accessed 23 August 2023.

34 I am grateful to Federico Picinali for alerting me to this point.

35 John Gardner, *Offences and Defences* (Oxford University Press 2018); Jeremy Horder, *Excusing Crime* (Oxford University Press 2003).

36 Norrie (n 29) Part IV; Lacey, Wells and Quick (n 28) 49–53, 313–36.

such a way as to undermine their capacity or opportunity to conform to the law. (Note, of course, the resonance here with philosophical debates about the normative upshot of implicit bias).[37]

The criminal law finds itself in a bind here. Should, for example, a young man brought up in a highly sexist, macho environment in which women are represented as likely to lie about their desire for sex be for this reason held to a different standard in his assessment of a sexual partner's consent to sex?[38] Equally controversially – and speaking rather to issues of material injustice – given what we know about the association between background injustice and patterns of criminal behaviour, should criminal law entertain a defence of 'rotten social background', acknowledging that systemic injustice materially affects the fairness of a defendant's opportunity to conform to the law?[39] To advocates of such a defence, its enactment would be an apt and common-sensical recognition of the fact that systemic injustices affect the scope of opportunity to remain law-abiding and the scale of temptations and pressure to offend: a necessary corrective to structurally produced inequality before the law.[40] To its critics, it is a mechanism that fundamentally undermines criminal law's integrity and universality; fails, in the light of the fact that many highly disadvantaged people do not commit offences, to establish adequate causal linkages between 'rotten' background and a particular criminal offence; and disrespects the agency of the disadvantaged.[41]

Before leaving the terrain of the defences, it is important to note that the boundaries between acceptance and refusal to see background injustices as relevant to criminal liability are more blurred than the

37 See above, discussion following n 15.

38 Lacey, 'Community Culture and Criminalisation' (n 27); Pickard (n 23).

39 David Bazelon, 'The Morality of the Criminal Law' (1976) 49 S. California Law Rev 385; Delgado (n 2); Nicola Lacey, 'Socializing the Subject of Criminal Law? Criminal Responsibility and the Purposes of Criminalization' (2016) 99 Marquette Law Review 541.

40 Erin I Kelly, *The Limits of Blame: Rethinking Punishment and Responsibility* (Harvard University Press 2018). See more generally Thomas Andrew Green, *Freedom and Criminal Responsibility in American Legal Thought* (Cambridge University Press 2014).

41 Michael S Moore, 'Causation and the Excuses' (1985) 73 California Law Review 1091; Moore (n 9); Stephen J Morse, 'The Twilight of Welfare Criminology' (1979) 49 S. California Law Rev 1247; Stephen J Morse, 'Deprivation and Desert' in William C Heffernan and John Kleinig (eds), *From Social Justice to Criminal Justice: Poverty in the Administration of Criminal Law* (Oxford University Press 2000); Stephen J Morse, 'Severe Environmental Deprivation (Aka RSB): A Tragedy, Not a Defense' (2011) 2 Alabama Civil Rights & Civil Liberties Law Review 147; Paul H Robinson, 'Are We Responsible for Who We Are – The Challenge for Criminal Law Theory in the Defenses of Coercive Indoctrination and Rotten Social Background' (2011) 2 Alabama Civil Rights & Civil Liberties Law Review 53. One might even argue that a statutory defence encompassing the upshot of structural injustices which the state could have tackled is a contradiction: the state in a sense acknowledging its own lack of authority. I am grateful to Valeria Ruiz Perez for discussion on this point.

previous discussion has implied. In a number of areas, the judicial and statutory development of defences in recent years has made efforts to accommodate, within certain limits, questions of background material injustice, epistemic injustice and injustice of standing. One example serves to illustrate all three considerations. In various jurisdictions, the boundaries around defences have come under pressure as a result of the growing recognition that the experience of long-term violence and abuse, often within the family or a sexual relationship, can affect defendants' capacities of self-control and even their perceptions. Given that the opportunity to avoid being subjected to these pressures or threats is itself undermined by material injustice such as poverty or lack of access to alternative housing; and that victims' voices need to be given standing, this has generated a great deal of criticism, and in several jurisdictions, has led to important (though still insufficient)[42] changes in the scope of defences such as self-defence and the partial defence of 'provocation' – since replaced in England and Wales. In both cases, the requirement of immediacy of reaction has been modified in the light of a greater sensitivity to the situation of the long-term victim of abuse; and 'provocation' has been replaced with a more capaciously defined 'loss of control' defence with a particular aspiration to render the defence more gender-neutral in its application. It is also the case that psychological and psychiatric understandings of the way in which early experiences of deprivation or abuse can shape development has fed increasingly into expert testimony in mental incapacity defences. But it remains true that criminal law operates – and sees itself as having to operate – with a robust presumption of sanity, and a parsimonious accommodation in particular of volitional defects.[43]

Thirdly, criminal law, broadly defined, may make its most direct accommodation of background injustices at the pre-conviction and post-conviction stages – perhaps most obviously in sentencing decisions. At this stage, pre-sentence reports detailing relevant social and psychological background serve in many jurisdictions more fully to contextualise the offence against the offender's psychological and

42 Aileen McColgan, 'In Defence of Battered Women Who Kill' (1993) 13 Oxford Journal of Legal Studies 508; Kit Kinports, 'So Much Activity, so Little Change: A Reply to the Critics of Battered Women's Self-Defense' (2004) 23 Saint Louis University Public Law Review 155; Sophie Kate Howes, Katy Swaine Williams and Harriet Wistrich, 'Women Who Kill: Why Self-Defence Rarely Works for Women Who Kill Their Abuser' (2021) Criminal Law Review 945; Rachel McPherson and others, 'Women and Self-Defence: An Empirical and Doctrinal Analysis' (2022) 18 International Journal of Law in Context 461.
43 Norrie (n 29) 237–273.

material conditions and opportunities. It is accepted that the severity of the sentence, usually within a more or less strictly defined range, should be adjusted according to broad mitigating (and perhaps, aggravating) conditions. The scope for background injustices to shape criteria of mitigation or aggravation are, however, defined to a greater or lesser extent in different legal systems, and are defined moreover in relation to varying sentencing principles.[44] Where desert is regarded as the primary distributive sentencing principle, the argument rehearsed above – does 'rotten social background' truly undermine individual desert? – may simply be reiterated; while consequence-oriented sentencing principles such as reform or deterrence may afford a different scope for injustice-based adjustment. Note that this sort of adjustment is also open to police officers and prosecutors, who usually work within very broad parameters of discretion in how they carry out their enforcement, recording and prosecution decisions. To take a particular example, the public interest criterion for prosecutions in England and Wales could certainly be interpreted so as to afford scope for a social injustice-sensitive policy, particularly in relation to less serious offences; while the 'reasonable prospect of conviction' test might be regarded as risking exacerbating background injustices, particularly of the epistemic kind. Unfortunately, notwithstanding these possibilities for adjustment, it seems that background epistemic injustices and injustices of standing often serve to intensify unjust patterns of discretionary criminal enforcement.

44 For a recent example of judicial efforts to address this issue, see the Italian Constitutional Court's decision in Judgment 251/2012, which addressed the Constitutional legitimacy of article 69(4) of the penal code, as modified by the *ex-Cirielli*, where it 'prohibited the prevalence of the mitigating factors in article 73(5)' of Italian Drugs law (d.P.R 309/1990); and *R v Morris* (2021) ONCA 68A, in which the Ontario Court of Appeals considered in some detail the relevance of anti-black racism to sentencing mitigation. Another recent focus of judicial concern, in New Zealand, for example, has been the upshot for sentencing of systemic deprivation and intergenerational trauma caused by colonial history: Joseph Williams, 'Build a Bridge and Get over It: The Role of Colonial Dispossession in Contemporary Indigenous Offending and What We Should Do about It' (2020) 18 New Zealand Journal of Public and International Law 3. I am grateful to Zelia Gallo, Richard Martin and Nicole Roughan for these references. In recent research, Marie Manikis has also argued for an expanded focus at the sentencing stage beyond the individual's circumstances towards a recognition of state responsibility in shaping them: Marie Manikis, 'Recognising State Blame in Sentencing: A Communicative and Relational Framework' (2022) 81 The Cambridge Law Journal 294, while Christopher Lewis has argued that previous convictions entailing ongoing exclusions and disadvantages should be regarded as mitigation in sentencing: Christopher Lewis, 'The Paradox of Recidivism' (2021) 70 Emory Law Journal 1209. A somewhat different example would be where evidence that an offence has been motivated by the desire to protest a background injustice, such as the impact of climate change, is treated as mitigation.

Criminological conceptions of social injustice

Criminology, broadly understood as the effort to produce systematic accounts of the nature, causes and implications of crime, has its origins in the classical theories of Beccaria[45] among others. With the development of proto-medical and psychiatric sciences in the nineteenth century, a supposedly scientific 'positivist' school of criminology emerged in the work of Lombroso and others.[46] In their earliest forms, neither classicism nor positivism showed much interest in the broad environment in which crimes occurred. For the classicists, crime was simply the product of rational choices under prevailing social conditions, with the penal project the establishment of deterrent sanctions apt to shape incentives and to optimise the balance of outcomes.[47] For the positivist, crime was the product of criminal character or atavism.[48] But even at this early stage, Lombroso himself acknowledged that in the case of the less serious offenders, social causes might intersect with criminal propensity to produce crime. And through the twentieth and into the twenty-first centuries, virtually every criminological paradigm – not only the dominant, sociological theories of crime, but even the refined versions of positivism and of rational choice theory which continue to feature in this increasingly diverse discipline – recognise the key importance of social, cultural and spatial context in constraining choice, shaping cognitive and emotional development, and influencing life opportunities at every level.[49] Modern day socio-biological, neurophysiological and other forms of positivism largely acknowledge and explore the interaction between social and personal/psychological characteristics, while sociological criminologists remain convinced that the primary explanation of crime lies in the shape of the social world.[50] Increasingly, criminologists acknowledge that the diversity of their subject matter – ranging as it potentially does from violent offences through property offences, drug offences, street crime to highly planned cybercrime and fraud – is unlikely to be susceptible of a unitary explanation; rather, each of the

---

45 Cesare Beccaria, *On Crimes and Punishments and Other Writings* (ed Aaron Thomas), University of Toronto Press 2008 (fp 1764).
46 Cesare Lombroso, *L'uomo Delinquente* (Fratelli Bocca 1878).
47 Newburn (n 3) 123–129.
48 ibid 130–140.
49 ibid 181–261.
50 ibid 143–180; Travis C Pratt, Michael G Turner and Alex R Piquero, 'Parental Socialization and Community Context: A Longitudinal Analysis of the Structural Sources of Low Self-Control' (2004) 41 The Journal of Research in Crime and Delinquency 219.

main paradigms in the history of the discipline is accepted as having some contribution to make to our understanding of the phenomenon, or perhaps phenomena, of crime.

The predominance of entirely or partially sociological theories of crime from the early twentieth century on has created a disciplinary context highly open to the analysis of the impact of structural and systemic injustice on the incidence of crime, and indeed one that aspires to embed criminological theory within the broad range of explanatory social sciences.[51] The early Chicago 'Social Ecology' School[52] focused on the spatial concentration of crime in Chicago's 'zone of transition': an area of the city marked by high levels of mobility, with successive waves of migrants moving in and sometimes, on; by poor housing; by poor infrastructure; and by social disorganisation. Robert K. Merton's 'strain theory'[53] explained crime as a reaction to the frustrations of life for many in a society in which they share the approved goals of material success, yet are unable to reach those goals by approved means. Resituating Emile Durkheim's influential conception of 'anomie',[54] Merton mapped the different possible reactions to these strains. In a world in which legitimate goals cannot be reached by certain groups by legitimate means, one might say it is only rational for those groups to find creative strategies to avoid the force of social norms about means, and indeed to find ways of rationalising their behaviour within alternative networks and frames of meaning.[55] Edwin Sutherland's theory of 'differential association'[56] explored the impact of networks and peer groups in shaping social behaviour and attachment to norms, in a hugely influential precursor to the burgeoning criminological studies of delinquency, the formation of criminal or alternative subcultures, and the social conditions conducing to their development. Life cycle research, including that using the rich databases accumulated in Chicago from the early twentieth century on, has shed light on the links between crime and the life course; and urban sociology has been influential in exploring the links between the urban context, deprivation, social disorganisation, migration, racism and

---

51 John Braithwaite, *Macrocriminology and Freedom* (Australian National University Press 2022).
52 Newburn (n 3) 202–208.
53 Robert K Merton, 'Social Structure and Anomie' (1938) 3 American Sociological Review 672.
54 Emile Durkheim, *The Division of Labour in Society* (Steven Lukes ed, Palgrave Macmillan 2013).
55 David Matza and Gresham M Sykes, 'Juvenile Delinquency and Subterranean Values' (1961) 26 American Sociological Review 712.
56 Edwin Hardin Sutherland, *Principles of Criminology* (3rd edn, JB Lippincott Company 1939).

deindustrialisation from the 1970s on.[57] Cultural and phenomenological criminologies have explored the ways in which cultural attachments and the experience of crime underpin its production, and criminologists have also explored the cultural influence of media constructions of crime.[58]

Each of these paradigms is, evidently, apt to produce interpretations which invite analysis of how far social injustice is involved in shaping patterns of crime. But, with very few exceptions until the 1970s,[59] criminologists did not tend to ponder the political or normative questions arising from their analyses. For example, Merton's strain theory might well be thought to invite a critique of American capitalism and consumerism as criminogenic,[60] while the social ecology school and its successors, alongside urban sociology, invite a critical analysis of the emergence of urban poverty, race and class prejudices, and lack of opportunity. One partial exception to the criminological tendency to restrict itself to explanatory terrain was 'labelling theory': the proposition that deviance, understood as the (inevitably selective) social application of a label, is amplified by a process of primary, secondary, tertiary ... labelling. In other words, anyone labelled, or associated with those labelled as deviant, is thereby more likely to attract further labelling: a case of 'give a dog a bad name…'.[61] The upshot was the troubling thought that society's response to crime – 'criminal justice' – is itself criminogenic. Labelling theory encouraged and informed the 'sociology of deviance' and 'critical criminologies' of the 1970s.[62] The latter were also influenced by a more general revival of interest in Marxist thought, symbolised in the criminal justice sphere by the reissuing of Rusche and Kircheimer's 1930s classic, *Punishment and Social Structure*, in 1969.[63]

In the view of these critical criminologies, it was not enough to expose and explore the social causes of crime. Where the relevant

57 Sampson and Wilson (n 6); William Julius Wilson, *The Truly Disadvantaged: The Inner City, the Underclass, and Public Policy* (Chicago University Press 1987); William Julius Wilson, *When Work Disappears: The World of the New Urban Poor* (Knopf 1996); Robert J Sampson, 'Urban Black Violence: The Effect of Male Joblessness and Family Disruption' (1987) 93 American Journal of Sociology 348; Robert J Sampson, 'The Place of Context' (2013) 51 Criminology 1.

58 Stanley Cohen, *Folk Devils and Moral Panics: The Creation of the Mods and Rockers* (Routledge 1972); Stuart Hall and others, *Policing the Crisis: Mugging, the State and Law and Order* (Bloomsbury Publishing Plc 1978).

59 Willem Adriaan Bonger, *Criminality and Economic Conditions* (Little, Brown, and Company 1916) <http://link.library.utoronto.ca/eir/EIRdetail.cfm?Resources__ID=506216&T=F> accessed 27 February 2023.

60 Steven F Messner and Richard Rosenfeld, *Crime and the American Dream* (Wadsworth Cengage Learning 2001).

61 Howard S Becker, *Outsiders: Studies in the Sociology of Deviance* (Macmillan 1963).

62 Newburn (n 3) 263–291.

63 Georg Rusche and Otto Kirchheimer, *Punishment and Social Structure* (Russell Sage 1969).

explanation was grounded in part or in whole in social phenomena such as poverty, inequality, racism, economic or cultural exclusion – or conversely, impunity for crimes of the powerful – it was the job of the criminologist to expose, criticise and if possible, counter these injustices. In short: if the social causes of crime include key elements of social injustice, criminology could not be neutral; it should be morally and politically engaged. These critical criminologies in turn invited a partial reaction in the form of so-called 'Left Realist' criminologies, which drew attention to the fact that the impact of crime was itself marked by patterns of material disadvantage – a development which, with important consequences, established victims of crime as a central concern of the discipline and its policy upshot.[64]

Both critical and primarily explanatory criminologies, as well as a burgeoning tradition of scholarship engaging specifically with the social origins, role and upshot of penality, epitomised by the journal *Punishment and Society* established under David Garland's editorship in 1999, flourish today. How do they assess the impact or explain the origins of the different forms of social injustice delineated in the philosophical debates? Probably the most obvious way in which they do so has to do with the very clear correlation between being subject to unjust material deprivation and an increased probability of committing/being labelled as committing crime. Across the world, statistical analysis, surveys and qualitative research show that crime clusters among the less advantaged social groups: those enduring poor housing, subject to various forms of prejudice, lacking educational or employment opportunities, in disorganised urban and family contexts. Conversely, criminal justice responses tend to single out these groups, and the forms of crime stereotypically associated with them – drug use, street crime, burglary, robbery – for particular control and penal attention.[65] In addition, we now know that the experience of childhood deprivation, abuse or malnourishment affects psychological development, including the inculcation of the power of self-control, with decisive implications for life chances and the capacity to avoid crime.[66] To the extent that we see material inequalities as unjust, most criminologists would conclude, notwithstanding the fact that many 'truly disadvantaged'[67] individuals manage to avoid it, that social injustice is a key cause of crime; and moreover that the impact of labelling and

---

64 Kinsey, Lea and Young (n 7); Newburn (n 3) 281–296.

65 Reiman (n 2).

66 Sampson, 'The Place of Context' (n 57).

67 Wilson, *The Truly Disadvantaged: The Inner City, the Underclass, and Public Policy* (n 57).

punishment serves to entrench and exacerbate that injustice. For some radical criminologists this implies that the only way forward is abolition in one of its various guises;[68] or that crime should be regarded as a form of resistance; or that the exposure of injustice is criminology's core task, while the questions of how to tackle and of how to analyse it more deeply are for the politician, social policy scholar or moral/political philosopher. And while there is a long tradition of so-called 'administrative criminology', which sees its core task as shaping social policy,[69] its engagement with broad questions of structural or social aetiology have been relatively few, with a focus instead on producing effective forms of crime control or prevention.

Epistemic injustices, too, have often been exposed by criminological research and featured in explanations of crime, and in particular of the actions and reactions of law enforcement officials (as well as members of the public in reporting crime) which do much to shape the conception and image of crime. It is a challenge, of course, to research the ways in which epistemic injustices such as implicit biases, stereotypes and other filters shape the social construction of crime. But, both ethnographic research[70] and statistical patterns of practices such as stop and search[71] suggest that prejudices about the veracity and credibility of certain groups – notably, young black urban men and other racialised minorities – are decisive in shaping policing practices. Conversely, epistemic injustices shape the reception of victim testimony, from the police station to the courtroom and beyond. The example of sexual offences, where survivors have often told researchers about the experience of being silenced (indeed further assaulted) in court, shows this all too clearly. It seems inevitable that these factors also affect jury decision-making;[72] and while in many countries there is now an effort to educate judicial decision-makers about implicit bias, it would be optimistic to think that these have

68 Thomas Mathiesen, *The Politics of Abolition* (Martin Robertson 1974); Thomas Mathiesen, *The Politics of Abolition Revisited* (Routledge 2014); Nicolas Carrier and Justin Piché, 'The State of Abolitionism' (2015) XII Champ pénal/Penal field <https://journals.openedition.org/champpenal/9164> accessed 27 February 2023.

69 Lucia Zedner and Andrew Ashworth, *The Criminological Foundations of Penal Policy: Essays in Honour of Roger Hood* (Oxford University Press 2003).

70 For example, Didier Fassin, *Death of A Traveller: A Counter-Investigation* (Polity Press 2021).

71 David Lammy, 'The Lammy Review: Final Report' (2017) <https://www.gov.uk/government/publications/lammy-review-final-report>.

72 Cheryl Thomas, 'The 21st Century Jury: Contempt, Bias and the Impact of Jury Service' (2020) Criminal Law Review 987; Fiona Leverick, 'What Do We Know about Rape Myths and Juror Decision Making?' (2020) 24 The International Journal of Evidence & Proof 255. On evidence from Scotland, see Chalmers, Leverick and Munro, 'Why the Jury Is, and Should Still Be, out on Rape Deliberation' (n 24); Chalmers, Leverick and Munro, 'The Provenance of What Is Proven' (n 24).

been successful, even where they have been substantial. More broadly, the experience of being on the receiving end of racism, sexism or other forms of prejudice over the life course seem highly likely to shape not only attitudes and psychological/emotional development but also life chances. To take just one example, recent autobiographical accounts in the wake of the 'Black Lives Matter' movement have testified to the sense of exclusion felt by racialised minorities as children in an education system in which forms of knowledge of particular relevance to their lives – black, Global South or working class history, for example – have been marginalised in the curriculum, and where any effort to voice a distinctive experience or to question the parameters of accredited knowledge is either ignored or met with hostility.[73]

Perhaps yet more obvious from the findings of sociological criminology over the decades is, however, the impact of injustices of standing, status and respect. This is not only a matter of the disrespect involved in criminal justice enforcement practices shaped by prejudice or implicit bias. It is also a factor in how those who are labelled as criminal are treated, and even of how we think of the very concept of crime. If certain groups are, de facto or even, as in the case of long-lasting post-sentence disqualifications, formally marginalised within the political system or excluded from the franchise,[74] can we say that the conditions of reciprocity underlying a just social order are truly met? And can we believe that, for example, prison conditions in this country or the United States would be as they are if a greater proportion of those sent to prison were of high social status?[75] Prison research over the decades evidences widespread (albeit varying across systems) disrespect reaching well beyond the specific disapproval of crime.[76] Conversely, ethnographic and other qualitative research on marginalised communities in which crime is frequent show how important the search for respect remains for those involved in offending.[77] Indeed, within differential association and subcultural theory it is precisely this search for a meaningful

---

73 See, for example, Akala, *Natives: Race and Class in the Ruins of Empire* (Two Roads 2018).

74 Amy E Lerman and Vesla M Weaver, *Arresting Citizenship: The Democratic Consequences of American Crime Control* (University of Chicago Press 2014); Bruce Western, *Punishment and Inequality in America* (Russell Sage Foundation 2006).

75 James Q Whitman, *Harsh Justice: Criminal Punishment and the Widening Divide between America and Europe* (Oxford University Press 2003).

76 Pat Carlen, *Women's Imprisonment: A Study in Social Control* (Routledge and Kegan Paul 1983); Alison Liebling and Helen Arnold, *Prisons and Their Moral Performance: A Study of Values, Quality, and Prison Life* (Oxford University Press 2004).

77 Philippe Bourgois, *In Search of Respect: Selling Crack in El Barrio*, vol 10 (Cambridge University Press 2002); Gary Watson, *Criminal Justice and Respect* (Oxford University Press 2020).

peer group and mutual respect which underpins certain forms of offending. Criminology and urban sociology, are capable, in short, of illuminating the role of all three forms of injustice at an empirical level through a range of quantitative and qualitative methodologies. However, criminologists take different positions on whether it is part of their scholarly role to engage in the explicit identification or critique of those injustices.

The evolving political economy of criminal justice and social injustice

To understand the implications of structural injustice for criminal justice, it is also important to look at broad political-economic and associated cultural developments over time. Many forms of sociological criminology are sympathetic to this proposition, and changing cultural norms in particular have attracted a great deal of attention. But, other than in Marxist criminological approaches[78] and with a few honourable exceptions,[79] the impact of macro-economic change and of the institutional structure of the political economy on crime has featured relatively little in criminological analysis. This is an important lacuna, not least because there is strong reason to think that some decisive changes in the political economy of many countries, including but not only the wealthiest democracies who claim to espouse liberal principles of justice, have been of great importance to both the social phenomena of crime and attitudes towards it.[80] A comprehensive survey, which would require rigorous comparative treatment, is well beyond the scope of this chapter, but two key aspects require mention.

Changes in the economy and labour market: Economic exclusion and increasing inequalities

The economic changes which swept the industrial world in the 1970s are well documented and widely known. The oil crisis of that decade provided one significant economic shock. Increasing globalisation

---

78 Bonger (n 59); Rusche and Kirchheimer (n 63); Richard Quinney, *The Social Reality of Crime* (Little Brown 1970).

79 Steven Box, *Recession, Crime and Punishment* (Macmillan 1987); Jock Young, *The Exclusive Society: Social Exclusion, Crime and Difference in Late Modernity* (Sage 1999); David Garland, *The Culture of Control* (Oxford University Press 2001).

80 Nicola Lacey and Hanna Pickard, 'To Blame or to Forgive? Reconciling Punishment and Forgiveness in Criminal Justice' (2015) 35 Oxford Journal of Legal Studies 665.

undercut the economic basis for industrial production in the richer countries. The upshot was the disappearance, over a remarkably short period of time, of secure, often unionised, and reasonably well-paid jobs for those with basic but not advanced levels of education underpinning what are recognised in the labour market as 'skills'. The impact of these changes was exacerbated, in many countries, and perhaps most spectacularly the United States, by the impact of the accumulating effects of long-term racism as well as by class-based disrespect – the latter fatefully reflected in Hillary Clinton's infamous 'deplorables' comment during the 2016 election campaign. There is good reason to think that these structural changes in the labour market produced criminogenic conditions. We know that the economic insecurity occasioned for many brought distress, loss of self-esteem and respect among those whose place in the economy, and their social status with it, disappeared within just a few years.[81] These conditions of economic precarity, social marginalisation, bleak housing conditions, poor quality education, and inadequate public infrastructure of the urban centres hollowed out by deindustrialisation are precisely those that criminological theories have associated with an elevated incidence of crime. And indeed, crime rates – including violent crime rates – soared in the United States in the wake of deindustrialisation, and rose significantly in many other western societies until the common, decisive downturn in crime in the mid 1990s, adding to the conditions fostering social disorganisation, counter-cultural attachments and incentives to flout criminal law's constraints or to retreat into illegal drug (or more recently, opioid) addiction.[82]

Political economists, like primarily empirical criminologists, focus on the explanatory power of social, political and economic factors; some of them, like deindustrialisation, hard for governments to avoid; others, like the erosion of welfare benefits, otherwise. But they do not tend to dwell on whether these changes should be accounted structural social injustices. But there has been an increasing focus in sociology

81 Wilson, *The Truly Disadvantaged: The Inner City, the Underclass, and Public Policy* (n 57); Wilson, *When Work Disappears: The World of the New Urban Poor* (n 57); William Julius Wilson, *More than Just Race* (WW Norton 2009).

82 Marie Gottschalk, *Caught: The Prison State and the Lockdown of American Politics* (University of Chicago Press 2015); Robert Reiner, *Law and Order: An Honest Citizen's Guide to Crime and Control* (Polity Press 2007); Zelia Gallo, Nicola Lacey and David Soskice, 'Comparing Serious Violent Crime in the United States and England and Wales: Why It Matters, and How It Can Be Done' in Kevin R Reitz (ed), *American Exceptionalism in Crime and Punishment* (Oxford University Press 2018); Lisa L Miller, *The Myth of Mob Rule: Violent Crime and Democratic Politics* (Oxford University Press 2016).

and to some extent, political science on the normative upshot of these broad changes. One particular focus has been a marked emphasis on the links between inequality and crime. Increasing inequality between the middle classes and those in the 'precariat'[83] has been prompted both by the diminishing opportunities of the portion of the population with fewest skills, social capital and employment options. There are stubborn barriers to escaping their situation given that the new, often service sector or professional jobs emerging out of the gradual transition to a 'knowledge economy' generally require a much higher level of formal qualifications than did old industrial jobs, which for many are replaced by insecure forms of employment such as 'zero hours contracts'. The resulting economic and psychological precarity arguably has the further consequence of engendering resentment which has decisive impacts on levels of participation and trust in political systems, with further ramifications in terms of those systems' capacity to build consensus for penal reform or moderation. On the other hand, and particularly in the most recent iterations of financialised capitalism, we have the emergence of a super-rich 0.1 per cent. Those who commit financially and otherwise exploitative crime but can buy, or may lead them to think they can buy, political or other influence appear to have some impunity from usual social constraints, including criminalisation. Perhaps yet more important, there is a risk that perceptions of such impunity, along with diminishing levels of trust in politicians and criminal justice institutions, threaten the perceived legitimacy of criminal justice – as well as, from a normative point of view, undermining that legitimacy.

There has, accordingly, developed an extensive literature which tries to assess the links between (putatively unjust) inequalities and both crime and criminal justice responses to crime.[84] Precise causal links – as opposed to correlations – are difficult to pin down;[85] but historical,[86]

83 Mike Savage, *Social Class in the 21st Century* (Penguin Books 2015); Savage (n 8).
84 Hagan and Peterson (n 5); Muller and Wildeman (n 4); Nicola Lacey and others, *Tracing the Relationship between Inequality, Crime and Punishment: Space, Time and Politics* (n 5); Muller and Wildeman (n 5).
85 Lacey and Soskice (n 5).
86 David Garland, *Punishment and Welfare: A History of Penal Strategies* (Gower Publishing 1985); David Garland, *Punishment and Modern Society* (Oxford University Press 1990); Garland, *The Culture of Control* (n 79); Lacey, *In Search of Criminal Responsibility: Ideas, Interests and Institutions* (n 28).

comparative[87] and life course research[88] gives us some purchase on the broad macro-conditions at issue here. To take a recent and compelling example, Robert Sampson and Ash Smith have identified,[89] on the basis of the extensive Chicago life course study,[90] a spectacular difference in the chances of committing crime and of avoiding criminality as between the research cohort growing up in the 1970s and that growing up just 15 or so years later. The scale of the change is perhaps most tellingly evoked by the fact that the *most* criminally active of the second cohort was involved in crime at about the same level as the *least* criminally involved of the first cohort – reflecting what Sampson and Smith call a 'birth lottery'. Sampson is still working on various hypotheses about the range of macro and micro changes that underpin this remarkable finding; but one factor stands out. The first cohort went through their education, training and search for employment at the height of the economic, social and psychological disruptions of deindustrialisation and urban decline; while the second cohort did so during a period of renewed growth and the beginnings of urban revival in Chicago, at a time when the upswing in crime was giving way to the extended crime decline seen from the mid-1990s.

Changes in attitudes to crime and in the conditions under which criminal justice policy is formed in the political sphere

In addition to the large macro-economic and accompanying social developments of the 1970s, this period saw, in many countries, but most carefully documented in the United States, changing attitudes to crime.[91] On the one hand, particularly in individualistic liberal market economies[92] in which states' perceived capacity to control the economy was in decline, criminal justice policy became a tempting focus for

87 Nicola Lacey, *The Prisoners' Dilemma: Political Economy and Punishment in Contemporary Democracies* (Cambridge University Press 2008); Lacey and Soskice (n 5); Mick Cavadino and James Dignan, *Penal Systems: A Comparative Approach* (Sage 2006); John R Sutton, 'The Political Economy of Imprisonment in Affluent Western Democracies, 1960—1990' (2004) 69 American Sociological Review 472; Liora Lazarus, *Contrasting Prisoners' Rights* (Oxford University Press 2004).

88 Sampson, 'Urban Black Violence' (n 57); Sampson, 'The Place of Context' (n 57).

89 Robert J Sampson and L Ash Smith, 'Rethinking Criminal Propensity and Character: Cohort Inequalities and the Power of Social Change' (2021) 50 Crime and Justice 13.

90 The data in this study allows for analysis over a substantial period, controlling for a wide range of differences including education and employment status, capacity for self-control, family background, mental and physical health.

91 Peter K Enns, *Incarceration Nation: How the United States Became the Most Punitive Democracy in the World* (Cambridge University Press 2016); McPherson and others (n 42).

92 Peter A Hall and David Soskice (eds), *Varieties of Capitalism: The Institutional Foundations of Comparative Advantage* (Oxford University Press 2013); Lacey, *The Prisoners' Dilemma: Political Economy and Punishment in Contemporary Democracies* (n 87).

electoral competition. There is a lively debate about how far this had to do with changing social attitudes attendant on rising crime[93] and how this reflected manipulations by politicians of crime policy as a facially neutral but racially coded response, particularly in countries such as the United States with a history of racist associations of crime with African Americans.[94] It has also been argued that the widespread sense of lived injustice paradoxically contributed to increasingly punitive attitudes and an orientation to the 'pleasure' of punishment, in a psychological dynamic in which offenders become the object of an ostensibly satisfying hostility which seems to offer relief from suffering.[95] What is incontrovertible is that the competitive, first-past-the-post political systems featured in most liberal market countries tended to produce an 'arms race' between the two main political parties as to which could prove itself 'tougher' on crime; while the coordinated market economies of the Nordic region and of northern Europe managed better, through their consensus and compromise-oriented political systems, to sustain the stability and moderation of their crime policy even amid rising crime, as well as the relative generosity of their welfare provision.[96] The liberal market economies, which feature higher levels of inequality as measured by the Gini coefficient, higher rates of illiteracy and child poverty, and higher levels of residential segregation, conversely struggle to moderate the temper of criminal policy.[97] While this would be hard to establish comparatively, it seems likely that these sorts of socio-economic conditions are also conducive to higher levels of epistemic injustice.[98]

Intractable inequalities at both ends of the distribution, alongside the lifeworlds these inequalities produce, have become a key focus across

---

93 Nicola Lacey and David Soskice, 'Crime, Punishment and Segregation in the United States: The Paradox of Local Democracy' (2015) 17 Punishment & Society 454; Lacey and Soskice (n 5); Gallo, Lacey and Soskice (n 82); Enns (n 91).

94 Katherine Beckett, *Making Crime Pay: Law and Order in Contemporary American Politics* (Oxford University Press 1997).

95 Anastasia Chamberlen and Henrique Carvalho, 'Feeling the Absence of Justice: Notes on Our Pathological Reliance on Punitive Justice' (2022) 61 Howard Journal of Crime and Justice 87.

96 Though even in these jurisdictions, recent developments have begun to put pressure on the longstanding consensus, and made clearer the exclusionary dynamics which can afflict highly coordinated political economies: Vanessa Barker, *Nordic Nationalism and Penal Order: Walling the Welfare State* (Routledge 2019).

97 Lacey, *The Prisoners' Dilemma: Political Economy and Punishment in Contemporary Democracies* (n 87); Lacey and Soskice (n 93).

98 While my argument here is restricted to the so-called advanced capitalist democracies, the links between polarisation, inequality and the quality of criminal justice almost certainly characterise a wider range of countries, including, for example, those of Latin America: see Massimo Sozzo, *Prisons, Inmates and Governance in Latin America* (Palgrave Macmillan 2022).

the social sciences, including economics,[99] politics,[100] anthropology[101] and sociology.[102] Not all of these literatures assume inequality to imply structural injustice; nor do they necessarily prescribe solutions.[103] But their very interest in inequality is premised on its salience, and a sense that at a minimum, we need to understand its origins as a precursor to debating what, if anything, can be done about it. And in some iterations, this social science literature implies a radical critique of criminal justice as it exists, within structurally unjust societies, today,[104] both in its upshot for the disadvantaged, and in the opportunities it affords for elite impunity.

Social injustice and the legitimacy of criminal justice today

So far, this chapter has set out a conceptual framework within which to explore the links between social and criminal justice; mapped the place and upshot of those links within a number of disciplines; and considered some recent developments in political economy and society which might be thought to pose new or exacerbated challenges to the project of pursuing criminal justice in increasingly unequal democracies. But, of course, the interest and significance of these links does not lie in intellectual or analytic reasons alone. Rather, such scholarship is generally motivated by a range of other concerns. These include the upshot of the analysis for public policy and the potential for change and reform, implying the need for a clear understanding of the conditions of existence of both the links themselves and any prospect of weakening or breaking

---

99 Piketty, *Capital in the Twenty-First Century* (n 8); Piketty, *Capital and Ideology* (n 8); Branko Milanovic, *Global Inequality: A New Approach for the Age of Globalization* (Harvard University Press 2018); Joseph E Stiglitz, *The Price of Inequality. How Today's Divided Society Endangers Our Future* (Penguin 2013); Anne Case and Angus Deaton, 'America's Killer Capitalism' (*Project Syndicate*) <https://www.project-syndicate.org/magazine/american-capitalism-no-excuses-for-deaths-of-despair-by-anne-case-and-angus-deaton-2021-12> accessed 27 February 2023. We should also mention the ongoing IFS Deaton Review on Inequalities in the 21st Century: Robert Joyce and Xiaowei Xu, 'Inequalities in the Twenty-First Century: Introducing the IFS Deaton Review' (The IFS 2019) <http://default/publications/inequalities-twenty-first-century-introducing-ifs-deaton-review> accessed 22 August 2022.
100 Jonathan Hopkin, 'The Politics of Piketty: What Political Science Can Learn from, and Contribute to, the Debate on Capital in the 21st Century' (2014) 65 The British Journal of Sociology 678; Anne Phillips, *Unconditional Equals* (Princeton University Press 2021); Carsten Jensen and Kees van Kersbergen, *The Politics of Inequality* (Palgrave Macmillan 2016).
101 Insa Lee Koch, *Personalizing the State: An Anthropology of Law, Politics, and Welfare in Austerity Britain* (Oxford University Press 2018); Bourgois (n 77); Alice Goffman, *On The Run* (University of Chicago Press 2014).
102 Savage (n 83); Savage (n 8); Richard Sennett, *Respect in a World of Inequality* (WW Norton 2003).
103 For an example of one that does, see Atkinson 2015, (n 8).
104 Didier Fassin, *The Will to Punish* (Oxford University Press 2018); Fassin (n 70).

them; its upshot for the stability, effectiveness and perceived legitimacy of criminal justice; and its upshot for the political or even moral legitimacy of the exercise of the state's criminal justice power. In my discussion so far, I have moved between the second and third of these considerations, without addressing them directly. In this section, mainly leaving aside the question of the potential for reform, which would require a much more textured discussion relative to particular systems, I will conclude by considering the second and third considerations: how far does social injustice affect the stability and efficacy of criminal justice? And to what extent, if at all, does it undermine the state's authority to punish?

As far as the stability and efficacy of criminal justice is concerned, the overwhelming evidence is that criminal justice systems can maintain a remarkable degree of stability even where a significant number of the populace believe that they are scarred in substance and/or enforcement by background social injustice. This is notwithstanding considerable evidence about the importance of perceptions of procedural fairness to the perceived legitimacy of criminal justice,[105] as well as of the impact of perceptions of social injustice and of the impunity of the powerful in underpinning acts of disobedience or protest.[106] Of course, such situations produce resistance, some of it violent: in recent UK history, think of the case of the miners' strike of the 1980s or the various urban riots over the last 30 years; widespread criticism of racial disproportionalities across the criminal justice system, most spectacularly in the exercise of police powers of stop and search;[107] protests at the policing of demonstrations protesting racism, climate change or gendered violence; and instances of apparent jury nullification in the attempted enforcement of public order charges in such cases. Across the Atlantic, the brutal murder of George Floyd by a police officer and the ensuing Black Lives Matters protests across the country and indeed beyond, came close to undermining the viability of the Minneapolis police department and called forth, in a significant emerging form of modified abolitionism, the call to 'defund the police' and to reallocate the funds dedicated to policing to other forms of local service more likely to produce safety and respect across social groups. Moreover, the question of what obligation those who are not unduly affected by the upshot of social injustice for criminalisation

105 Tyler, 'Procedural Justice, Legitimacy, and the Effective Rule of Law' (n 26); Tyler, 'Psychological Perspectives on Legitimacy' (n 26).
106 Paul Lewis and others, 'Reading the Riots: Investigating England's Summer of Disorder' (*The London School of Economics and Political Science and The Guardian*, 2011) <http://eprints.lse.ac.uk/46297/> accessed 23 August 2023.
107 Lammy (n 71).

bear in terms of protest, resistance or efforts at reform is undoubtedly an important and urgent one.[108] But notwithstanding the value of abolitionist thought in sharpening our ethical sensibility and expanding our sense of the boundaries of the possible,[109] a call for full blown abolition remains marginal; and even this egregious instance, which promised the institutionalisation of a more moderate abolitionism, seems to have lost some momentum. Meanwhile the entry of social media onto the scene of public debate has both provided new resources for broadcasting evidence of egregious forms of substantive and epistemic injustice in the exercise of criminal justice power, while also providing a new platform for the diffusion of forms of hate and prejudice which underpin those very injustices and the toleration they have been accorded. The ensuing dynamics are still working themselves out in our increasingly polarised societies.

At the other end of the inequality spectrum, the occasional prosecution of elite offenders like Bernie Madoff, Jeffrey Epstein and Jonathan Aitken perhaps keep the lid on perceptions, potentially corrosive to the perceived legitimacy of criminal justice, that the rich are above the law. At the level of *realpolitik*, we would have to conclude that criminal justice systems within relatively affluent and stable democracies have a remarkable ability to legitimate themselves with an adequate portion of the population to sustain their stability, even in the face of widespread acknowledgement that their enforcement bears the marks of the whole panoply of background injustices. Most people seem to think, in other words, that the justice of conviction and punishment is insulated from that of the background conditions: conditions which mean that the opportunities of avoiding offending are radically unequal; and that those on the receiving ends of various kinds of prejudice or marginalisation are more likely to be prosecuted, less likely to be believed when they speak in their own defence, and more likely to be on the receiving end of the most intrusive and degrading aspects of punishment. Even in an unjust society, it seems, many believe that it still makes sense to 'do criminal justice'.

This belief may stem from strictly retributivist views underpinned by a narrow conception of factors that affect moral desert. Recent decades have seen an intensified public moralism itself facilitated by social media. It has also perhaps been exacerbated by not just polarisation

---

108 Ekow N Yankah, 'Whose Burden to Bear? Privilege, Lawbreaking and Race' (2022) 16 Criminal Law and Philosophy 13.

109 Tommie Shelby, *The Idea of Prison Abolition* (Princeton University Press 2022); Dorothy Roberts, 'Abolition Constitutionalism' (2019) 133 Harvard Law Review 122.

but also resentment of the relative progress of certain groups – women, minorities – who until recently constituted reassuring comparators for the groups who lost out most radically in the wake of deindustrialisation.[110] If one regards criminal law in moral terms, and punishment as the just response to blameworthy wrongdoing – as western penal discourse and indeed theory have increasingly invited us to do over the last 50 years – it is intuitively plausible to think that even if offenders have themselves suffered unfair treatment, this does not undermine their guilt in committing offences.[111] Whether because a persisting faith in the formal justice of the legal system or because of a substantive attachment to the core norms of the criminal law, criminal justice – or perhaps we should say, criminal law and punishment – remains largely taken for granted as a core and legitimate state institution. And the resilience of the criminal justice systems of a wide range of societies over a long period in which the public and popular philosophy of punishment has changed markedly suggests that many believe they would be worse off living under a system without criminal justice. We find it hard to contemplate living in a world in which there exists no police force, or at least publicly funded institution, to call on in the event of, say, burglary or an assault; or where serious offences such as violent crimes are not met with any decisive state response. The supposed overall effects of criminal justice are largely seen to be, on balance, positive. Or, perhaps, the least-worst solution available.

But this is not, of course, a zero-sum matter. Social movements for the reform of criminal justice to mitigate the upshot of what are understood to be material, epistemic and status injustices, are frequent and sometimes successful – as in the case of the long struggle for the repeal of laws criminalising homosexuality in many western countries from the 1950s on. Nor is it to say that there is no point at which the perceived illegitimacy of the criminal justice system would be such as to prompt such widespread resistance that the system is undermined or destroyed. But this seems unlikely to happen other than in the context of a radical collapse in perceptions of the state's legitimacy and authority overall.[112] And that sort of collapse/withdrawal of civic consent, likewise, seems likely to be inhibited by people's pragmatic assessment of the balance of advantage. To misquote Hilaire Belloc, it is a case of

110 Arlie Russell Hochschild, *Strangers in Their Own Land: Anger and Mourning on the American Right* (The New Press 2016).
111 Moore (n 41).
112 Matt Matravers, '"Who's Still Standing?" A Comment on Antony Duff's Preconditions of Criminal Liability' (2006) 3 Journal of Moral Philosophy 320.

keeping hold of states for fear of yet a grimmer fate. But this should not be a recipe for complacency: we have enough evidence of the upshot of a corrosion of trust among a substantial minority of the populace to know that efforts at mitigating the upshot of social injustice for criminal justice are urgently required, and that a failure to attend to these gaps between criminal justice's avowed aspiration and the realities of criminalisation may undermine political trust and participation in ways which threaten the capacity of political systems to deliver reform.

If this analysis of the upshot of perceived injustice for the stability and viability of criminal justice leads to an unsatisfyingly muddy conclusion, perhaps we can say something more decisive at the normative level. For on anything approaching Shelby's Rawlsian approach[113] – and as widely acknowledged by philosophers and criminal law theorists[114] – even many countries proud of their liberal democratic conventions exhibit and on one view, are complicit in (through their failure to address) not only those injustices but their bearing on the fairness of criminalisation and punishment. But does any injustice undermine the normative legitimacy of the system, as a whole or in relation to particular groups such as the poor or victims of racism and other forms of exclusion, as Shelby suggests?

This question of course relates to the broader issue of what the justification for 'criminal law as punishment' is.[115] And at the risk of leading us towards another unsatisfyingly muddy conclusion, I would suggest that any normative theory of criminal justice which contains – as the vast majority do – some element of consequence-sensitivity – in other words, which sees the normative test of criminal justice as resting in whole or in part in its contribution to human welfare and the protection of autonomy or dominion,[116] will have to accept the need to make a balancing assessment and one without a very clear normative threshold. If we concede that background injustice is inevitably felt in and even magnified by the enforcement of criminal law, the question arises whether we regard the consequences of injustice for offenders to be such as to

113 Shelby, 'Justice, Deviance, and the Dark Ghetto' (n 12); Shelby, *Dark Ghettos* (n 152); Shelby, *The Idea of Prison Abolition* (n 109).
114 Duff (n 4); Tadros (n 23); Watson, 'A Moral Predicament in the Criminal Law' (n 23); Lacey, *State Punishment: Political Principles and Community Values* (n 28).
115 Vincent Chiao, 'What Is the Criminal Law For?' (2016) 35 Law and Philosophy 137; Vincent Chiao, *Criminal Law in the Age of the Administrative State* (Oxford University Press 2019); Lacey and Pickard, 'Why Standing to Blame May Be Lost but Authority to Hold Accountable Retained' (n 223).
116 John Braithwaite and Philip Pettit, *Not Just Deserts: A Republican Theory of Criminal Justice* (Oxford University Press 1990); Lacey, *State Punishment: Political Principles and Community Values* (n 28).

outweigh the other social costs, including to victims who are frequently themselves subject to background injustice, which would proceed from a judgement that the state lacks authority to punish. There is a tension, in other words, between a collective good and individual injustices. Shelby argues, persuasively, that while the state has lost its authority to hold those in the ghetto accountable for their offences, they have nonetheless a moral duty to their fellow residents, to whom they are doing wrong. But this says nothing about how those victims should go about enforcing those duties in the absence of a legitimate state mechanism geared to doing so. For even the mildest and most qualified consequentialist, then, the normative question about the legitimacy yields no clearer an answer than the positive questions explored above.

Yet, this is to pose the issue in unduly stark terms. It presents a binary between legitimacy and illegitimacy. One part of the solution here, as suggested by Chamberlen and Carvalho, is to discard the idea of justice as an absolute goal to be reached, and rather to conceive it as an 'ongoing practice ... [and] ... a collective, intersubjective endeavour'.[117] Like legitimation itself,[118] it is always a work in progress, and one to which a range of abolitionist endeavours and reformist programmes – therapeutic and restorative justice, alternative mechanisms of dispute resolution based in communities, restraint or protest on the part of the advantaged among many others – can contribute something of value. If we think about the different ways in which social injustice echoes through the practice of criminal 'justice', as the analysis I have offered aspires to help us do, we can correspondingly think of the criminal process in more disaggregated terms as a set of arrangements, protocols and institutions, each of which may be subject to incremental reform. Again responding to the consequence-sensitive normative intuition, this implies that our political responsibility here is to work constantly towards reducing criminal injustices, thereby strengthening the state's claim to authority, rather than to bemoan the impossibility of perfect justice.[119] In this sense, the diversification of the broad category of abolitionist thought is a welcome development.

If we regard the criminal law in moral terms as a system of ascribing not only responsibility but blame, the argument that the state loses its

117 Chamberlen and Carvalho (n 95) 97.

118 David Beetham, *The Legitimation of Power* (2nd edn, Palgrave Macmillan 2013).

119 Rocio Lorca has suggested that in cases such as those of extreme poverty, state authority to punish is indeed absent, though a weaker form of political justification grounded in necessity may be present: Rocio Lorca, 'Punishing the Poor and the Limits of Legality' (2022) 18 Law, Culture and The Humanities 424.

standing to call to account where its own actions amount to complicity or hypocrisy is persuasive.[120] But if we regard criminal law, as Hanna Pickard and I have argued we should, in political terms, as a regulatory system geared to certain valued social ends, or as a system that underpins the authority of public institutions,[121] it follows that our assessment of its overall legitimacy must take into account not merely the legitimacy of state authority but also the overall balance of likely outcomes for human welfare under different reform scenarios, as well as the overarching question of social justice in relation to each discrete aspect of the institutions of criminal justice. In a system of criminal law and punishment oriented not to moral blame but to a holding to account oriented to forgiveness,[122] it also follows that the harms caused by the inevitable reflection of social injustices in the enforcement of criminal law would be mitigated. In a criminal process structured so as to avoid the stigmatising dynamics of censure and affective blame, and oriented instead to institutional counterparts of forgiveness, to rehabilitation, and to reintegration – as well, ideally, as providing a separate institutional framework providing support and compensation to victims of crime[123] – the inevitable degree to which the pursuit of criminal justice reflects and reproduces social injustices would at least be balanced by significant public goods and constructive policies benefitting not only victims but also offenders affected by background injustice. This approach would also, arguably, militate towards a reluctance to criminalise protest against social injustice.[124]

Is this a counsel for despair or for a woolly relativism? In my view, not at all. Exposing the upshot of social injustices for criminal (in)justice is a hugely important contribution to political discourse – as indeed social movements such as Black Lives Matter show very clearly. Ideally, it invites not merely criminal justice reform but also a reassessment of the scope

---

120 Yet it is worth noting that even authors like Duff and Watson, who make a powerful case for the state's complicity in criminal injustice, in effect, embrace the 'muddy' conclusion rather than seeing this injustice as undermining the state's overall authority to criminalise and punish or making the case for abolition, they envisage modifying the degree of injustice through concessions at the sentencing stage and other institutional modifications aimed at longer term change. Duff (n 23); Edwards (n 23); Watson, 'Standing in Judgment' (n 23).

121 Lindsay Farmer, *Making the Modern Criminal Law: Criminalization and Civil Order* (Oxford University Press 2016); Chiao, 'What Is the Criminal Law For?' (n 115); Chiao, *Criminal Law in the Age of the Administrative State* (n 115); Lacey and Pickard, 'Why Standing to Blame May Be Lost but Authority to Hold Accountable Retained' (n 23).

122 Lacey and Pickard, 'To Blame or to Forgive?' (n 80).

123 Nicola Lacey and Hanna Pickard, 'A Dual-Process Approach to Criminal Law: Victims and the Clinical Model of Responsibility without Blame' (2019) 27 The Journal of Political Philosophy 229.

124 Gustavo A Beade, 'Who Can Blame Whom? Moral Standing to Blame and Punish Deprived Citizens' (2019) 13 Criminal Law and Philosophy 271.

of criminal law's regulatory reach and the potential for finding resources for preventing and responding to crime through a wide range of non-criminal justice means: in the organisation of the economy, of the welfare system, of social provision, and of access to the sort of education which gives real opportunities under prevailing economic conditions.[125] The larger challenge here is, of course, to tackle the background injustices that inevitably echo through criminal justice, and build up the social institutions – public services and community infrastructures providing education, health care, welfare – which can mitigate social injustice. But none of these valuable things can come about other than through political action and persuasion – as well, particularly in the case of epistemic injustice and injustices of standing and respect, as engaging each other and those with whom we associate in discussion, and reflecting honestly and critically on our own implicit biases and prejudices. In the final analysis, then, the recent decline in political participation[126] in many countries – itself shaped by the perceptions of elite impunity and state illegitimacy – is probably the greatest contemporary threat to the important project of combatting social injustice and in doing so, attenuating the links between social and criminal injustice. The effort to rebuild the cultural and institutional bases for effective democratic participation in our fragmented societies presents itself, accordingly, as one of the most important contemporary challenges facing the pursuit of not only social but also criminal justice.

125 Braithwaite (n 51); Frederick Wilmot-Smith, *Equal Justice: Fair Legal Systems in an Unfair World* (Harvard University Press 2019).
126 Alan Siaroff, 'The Decline of Political Participation: An Empirical Overview of Voter Turnout and Party Membership' in Joan DeBardeleben and Jon H Pammett (eds), *Activating the Citizen: Dilemmas of Participation in Europe and Canada* (Palgrave Macmillan UK 2009).

8
Interrogating responsibility, agency and (in)justice in domestic abuse suicides

Vanessa E. Munro[1]

Introduction

Though the precise scale of domestic abuse-related suicide in England and Wales has been acknowledged as a significant 'known unknown' by academics, third sector experts and policymakers alike, it has been widely accepted to be substantial; potentially accounting for many more deaths per annum than occur as a result of domestic homicide. Despite this, until recently at least, there had been little dedicated research in the UK to explore the links between domestic abuse and suicidality, to understand what factors mediate and moderate risk, and to inform more effective mechanisms for identification, intervention and prevention by services. In 2022, the Government's Domestic Abuse Plan acknowledged the 'concern'[2] that advocates had been raising about this issue for some time, noting that 'in too many cases' the harms perpetrated by abusers

1 This chapter draws on research that has been undertaken across a series of projects, including activity funded by the ESRC and Home Office, in respect of which I have benefitted from collaboration with colleagues at REFUGE and AAFDA, as well as involvement of a number of academic co-researchers, as referenced throughout the discussion. I am much indebted to all of those partnerships for enabling, supporting and improving the underpinning research. I am also grateful to the professionals and family members who have participated as interviewees, and to the victims of domestic abuse whose case files (in life and death) have formed part of the underlying dataset.

2 Home Office, 'Tackling Domestic Abuse Plan' (Command Paper 639) (2022), 7 <https://www.gov.uk/government/publications/tackling-domestic-abuse-plan/tackling-domestic-abuse-plan-command-paper-639-accessible-version> accessed 23 August 2023.

'can result in a victim taking their own life'.[3] This concern is clearly merited, but expressing it in this way also raises difficult questions about how best to respond since this is a context in which the actions of a perpetrator of abuse are indeed pivotal in precipitating suicidality, but more structural and systemic failings to identify, intervene and protect against the risk of suicide among victims of domestic abuse are also rife, with perpetrators often orchestrating or deploying the predictability of those failings to further cement their control. This raises complicated questions about cause and consequence, freedom and constraint, and about how to recognise – without hierarchy – vectors of individual and collective responsibility.

In this chapter, I explore these complexities through the lens of Iris Marion Young's analysis of the causes, dynamics and consequences of structural injustice, and reflect on the potential – and potential pitfalls – of her adoption of a forward-looking focus on task responsibility in this context. To do so, I rely on analyses that I have developed over time with various colleagues, inspired initially by the case of *R v Dhaliwal* in 2006, in which the Crown Prosecution Service in England and Wales brought unsuccessful manslaughter charges against an abusive husband who subjected his wife to sustained psychological abuse prior to her suicide.[4] Among other things, the advent of that case highlighted the dearth of knowledge in the UK regarding the scale and dynamics of suicidality among victims of domestic abuse, which undermined the potential to develop a robust foundation for establishing a perpetrator's liability for death.[5] Across three subsequent projects, I have, therefore, worked with academic and policy colleagues to uncover the scale and dynamics of suicidality among those who experience domestic abuse;[6] evaluate the content of, and processes in relation to, Domestic Homicide Reviews (DHRs)

3 ibid, 11.

4 *R v Dhaliwal* [2006] EWCA Crim 1139.

5 Vanessa E Munro and Sangeeta Shah, 'R v Dhaliwal: Reconstructing Manslaughter in Cases of Domestic Violence Suicide' in Clare McGlynn, Rosemary Hunter and Erika Rackley (eds), *Feminist Judgments: From Theory to Practice* (Hart Publishing 2010).

6 Ruth Aitken and Vanessa E Munro, 'Domestic Abuse and Suicide: Exploring the Links with Refuge's Client Base and Work Force' (*REFUGE* 2018) <http://wrap.warwick.ac.uk/103609/> accessed 23 August 2023.

in cases of domestic abuse suicide;[7] and explore criminal justice and third sector professionals' understandings of the links between domestic abuse and suicide, and their assessments as to where the appropriate boundaries of responsibility for victims' deaths lie.[8]

Together, as detailed below, this body of work sketches a complicated picture in which there is little doubt that experiencing domestic abuse causes substantial harm and trauma to victims, can reduce or obliterate their self-confidence and sense of agency, isolate them from sources of support and create conditions in which taking their own lives can come to feel like their only escape. This *is* a consequence of the actions of perpetrators; and yet responsibility for suicide in the context of domestic abuse is also a multi-layered phenomenon, with causative factors shifting in and out of view over time and context, and intersectional vulnerabilities (for example, in relation to mental ill-health, alcohol/substance misuse, or financial, housing or immigration status precarity) variously predating, arising from or being amplified by the effects of abuse. In addition, victims' engagement with services frequently cements their experiences of invisibility and lack of import, bolstering their perception of the futility of alternative routes to escape or safety, in ways that perpetrators often directly rely upon to extend their control.

It is this, I will argue, that makes the issue of domestic abuse-related suicide a fruitful – but also challenging – testing ground for Young's approach. In the first part of the chapter, I will briefly explore the existing situation in England and Wales, in relation to holding perpetrators of domestic abuse criminally liable for the suicide of their victims: an issue on which the doctrinal authorities regarding tests of

---

7 Sarah Dangar, Vanessa E Munro and Lotte Young Andrade, 'Learning Legacies: An Analysis of Domestic Homicide Reviews in Cases of Domestic Abuse Suicide: Project Report' (2023) <http://wrap.warwick.ac.uk/174206/1/WRAP-learning-legacies-analysis-domestic-homicide-reviews-cases-domestic-abuse-suicide-2023.pdf> accessed 23 August 2023. See also Sarah Dangar, Vanessa E Munro and Lotte Young Andrade, 'Learning Legacies: Better Understanding the Dynamics of Domestic Abuse Suicidality Through Domestic Homicide Reviews' (2024) *Journal of Gender Based Violence* <https://doi.org/10.1332/23986808Y2024D000000037>; and Sarah Dangar, Vanessa E Munro and Lotte Young Andrade, 'Unchartered Territory: Navigating Voice, Accountability and Prevention in Suicide-Related Domestic Homicide Reviews in England and Wales' (forthcoming).

8 Vanessa E Munro, Vanessa Bettinson and Mandy Burton, 'Coercion, Control and Criminal Responsibility: Exploring Professional Responses to Offending and Suicidality in the Context of Domestically Abusive Relationships', *Social and Legal Studies*, available at <https://journals.sagepub.com/doi/10.1177/09646639231198342>. See also Vanessa Bettinson, Mandy Burton and Vanessa E Munro, 'An Offence We Could All Do With Learning More About: Identifying and Responding to Coercion in Intimate Partner Relationships: Project Report', available at <https://wrap.warwick.ac.uk%2F179870%2F1%2FWRAP-identifying-responding-coercion-intimate-partner-relationships-key-findings-23.pdf>.

causation remain unclear. Highlighting the extent to which building a case for such liability relies on clear evidence of the scale and dynamics of domestic abuse suicide, I will turn in the second part to discuss the current knowledge in this area. As a necessary part of that discussion, I will also use empirical data and case studies to highlight the complex interweaving of personal, relational and structural strands of injustice experienced by victims, which complicates any singular narrative of causal responsibility. In that context, I will suggest that Young's work can provide a valuable lens through which to understand victims' multiple layers of oppression and the challenges that they encounter in engaging with services purportedly designed to assist them. At the same time, however, I will also caution that this ought not to eclipse the ways in which perpetrators operate in this multi-layered context, often orchestrating and benefitting from victims' structural disempowerment and disappointing engagement with support services in order to compound the effects of abuse.

The importance, but difficulty, of holding these vectors of responsibility together is also highlighted in the third and final part of the chapter where, having situated victims' experiences of suicidality within the frames of structural injustice, I turn to explore the response envisaged and actioned through the medium of Domestic Homicide Reviews (DHRs) in particular. In many respects, DHRs provide an interesting application of Young's approach, reflecting her aspiration for a forward-looking and collective responsibility that learns lessons to break cycles of abuse and injustice. Considering the strengths and weaknesses of DHRs in suicide cases, I highlight the tensions that can arise regarding the competing interests at stake, engagement in blame-shifting, and divergent aspirations for their outcomes. More specifically, I suggest that a key challenge to realising Young's goal here lies in the failure to expose and disrupt the power dynamics that infuse and inform the very possibility of engaging in discussions about responsibility and (in)justice within the DHR space – whether between perpetrators and victims, victims and service providers, professionals and bereaved families, or between agencies. Suspicion of the lingering presence of blaming logics among participants in suicide DHRs also highlights the difficulties of achieving a forward-looking and transparent learning process, and underscores the extent to which interrogating responsibility effectively requires engagement with reason and emotion, silencing and co-option, and expediency and legacy.

Domestic abuse and perpetrators' liability for suicide

Setting the scene for this discussion of domestic abuse, suicidality and structural injustice requires going back – at least – to the decision of the Court of Appeal in the 2006 case of *R v Dhaliwal* in which, as noted above, a failed attempt was made by the Crown Prosecution Service (CPS) in England and Wales to bring manslaughter charges against an abusive husband who subjected his wife to sustained psychological abuse prior to her suicide.[9] That prosecution failed because, to ground liability for unlawful act manslaughter, there had to be a triggering 'unlawful and dangerous' act committed by the accused that caused the death. Though there were incidents of physical violence within the relationship that might have been relied upon, the CPS had grounded the manslaughter charge exclusively on the accused's infliction of emotional and psychological abuse upon the victim over the course of their relationship, including in the time immediately preceding her suicide. Since the court concluded that psychological harm (in contrast to psychiatric harm) was not recognised as bodily harm for the purposes of the Offences Against the Person Act 1861, and the expert witnesses in the case could not agree as to whether the injury sustained by the deceased prior to her death reached the diagnostic threshold for psychiatric labelling, there was no foundational criminal act committed; and as such, no possibility of clearing the first hurdle of the manslaughter test.

In its aftermath, several commentators subjected the approach taken in *Dhaliwal* to criticism. Stannard insisted, for example, that 'it is an affront to justice that the criminal law is unable to cope with' such situations, and highlighted the absurdity of the outcome that 'if I give someone a slight push and it unexpectedly kills them, it is manslaughter, but if I hound them to their death by a sustained course of psychological and emotional abuse it is not'.[10] Likewise, in our feminist reconstruction and reimagining of the decision in *Dhaliwal*, Sangeeta Shah and I cast doubt on the appropriateness of focusing on the type rather than severity of harm caused, and questioned the certainty that courts often purport to accredit to psychiatric diagnoses, given their fundamental reliance on shifting and frequently contested criteria.[11] Our resultant call to open up definitions of bodily harm to a more expansive interpretation, at least in

9 *R v Dhaliwal* [2006] EWCA Crim 1139.

10 John Stannard, 'Sticks, Stones and Words: Emotional Harm and the English Criminal Law' (2010) 74(6) Journal of Criminal Law 533, 534.

11 Vanessa E Munro and Sangeeta Shah, above n 5.

this context, has been somewhat superseded, however, by two key events since *Dhaliwal*. First, the expansion of complex post-traumatic stress disorder within the International Classification of Diseases to include many of the adverse psychological consequences observed in domestically abused victims, thereby providing increased scope for recognition of infliction of psychiatric injury. Secondly, the establishment under the Serious Crime Act 2015 of an offence of coercive and controlling behaviour, which includes within its remit a range of positive acts that produce psychological harms. Where established, the offence will now provide the foundational criminal act required to meet the first stage of the manslaughter test in cases where victims have taken their own lives.

But passing this first hurdle does not, of course, conclude the question of perpetrators' liability for death in domestic abuse suicide cases. There is the further question of causation. Obiter remarks in *Dhaliwal* indicated some openness to finding causality, particularly where the victim was of a 'fragile and vulnerable personality', but the application and limits of that approach were not tested. Since *Dhaliwal*, though there has been one successful prosecution for manslaughter in England, in a 2017 case involving domestic abuse suicide, that conviction was as a consequence of the defendant's guilty plea ahead of trial and so the issue of causation was again not tested.[12] Thus, especially given that the courts have been clear that 'causation is not a single unvarying concept to be mechanically applied without regard to the context in which the question arises',[13] the precise outcome of that analysis in the context of domestic abuse suicide remains uncertain;[14] and while some commentators have pointed to the more recent decision in *Wallace*, where an accused was convicted of manslaughter in relation to the voluntary euthanasia of a victim whom she had subjected to a dramatic and disfiguring acid attack, the circumstances of that case (and of the victim) can be differentiated in a number of potentially significant ways that might impact determinations of causal responsibility.[15]

One thing that is clear, though, is that the test to be applied here in relation to causation is not a factual 'but for' one that requires the perpetrator's conduct to be the *only* cause; instead, it suffices that their conduct was a 'substantial and operative' cause, potentially among others.

---

12 <https://www.bbc.co.uk/news/uk-england-stoke-staffordshire-48091219> accessed 23 April 2024.

13 *R v Kennedy (No 2)* [2008] 1 AC 269 at para [15].

14 Vanessa E Munro and Ruth Aitken, 'Adding Insult to Injury? The Criminal Law's Response to Domestic Abuse-Related Suicide in England and Wales' (2018) 9 Criminal Law Review 732.

15 *R v Wallace* [2018] EWCA Crim 690.

Applying that standard to establish liability for death in our feminist reimagining of *Dhaliwal*, Sangeeta Shah and I emphasised that:

> ... the abuser does not pull the trigger or provide the rope. The victim may even see the act of suicide as a form of liberation or a final expression of rebellion or subversion against a partner's control. But this does not mean that the abuser is not a significant cause of death, and nor does it mean that the act of taking life is a reflection of voluntary agency.[16]

It is this more situated and nuanced understanding of the effects upon victims of experiencing domestic abuse that enables connections of responsibility to be charted to perpetrators' conduct – sometimes in a fairly linear way, sometimes more circuitously. But such charting itself requires an evidence base that addresses the extent and ways in which domestic abuse increases risks of suicidality – collectively and individually – and explores the impact of intersecting vulnerabilities, injustices and interventions in navigating those risks.

As discussed in the next section, in England and Wales, this evidence base has been relatively slow to develop, and is still evolving. However, there is now a body of work that documents the significantly heightened prevalence of suicidality among victims of domestic abuse, and the ways in which that suicidality can be linked to specific mediators and moderators of risk, which extend not only to the type and duration of abuse experienced but to the availability of alternative support and safety strategies for victims, and their pre- or co-existing vulnerabilities.

Domestic abuse, suicidality and structural injustice

Prior to the decision in *Dhaliwal*, evidence regarding the links between domestic abuse and suicide, in the English and Welsh context, was extremely limited. In 2001, a report was published which estimated that as many as half of all women in Asian communities who had attempted suicide or self-harmed may have suffered domestic abuse, but this was based on a small and localised sample.[17] Meanwhile, in 2004, Walby had extrapolated from wider data sources to suggest that more than one-third

16 Vanessa E Munro and Sangeeta Shah, above n 5, at p. 270.
17 Khatidja Chantler, Erica Burman, Janet Batsleer and Colsom Bashir, 'Attempted Suicide and Self-Harm (South Asian Women): Project Report' (Manchester, Salford and Trafford Health Action Zone, 2001), available at <https://core.ac.uk/download/pdf/161885447.pdf>.

of all female suicides in England and Wales *may* have been caused by women being subjected to domestic abuse.[18] But in the wake of *Dhaliwal*, there has been a more dedicated focus on exposing the extent and nature of these connections. In 2010, Southall Black Sisters produced their 'Safe and Sane' report which documented that across 409 domestically abused women that the organisation had worked with, 44 per cent had contemplated suicide or self-harm and a further 18 per cent had made attempts to do so.[19] In addition, in the eight-year period covered in the research, a further eight women had ended their lives by suicide.

Following on from this, in 2017, I worked with REFUGE (a major national domestic abuse charity in England) to analyse the case files of clients who had interacted with the service between April 2015 and March 2017. Within this, we identified a core sample of 3,519 clients who were (i) aged over 18, (ii) had completed all questions on a CORE-10 assessment designed to measure psychological distress, and (iii) had provided a history of abuse to their caseworkers, which often also involved completion of a risk assessment tool (the 'DASH') that is widely utilised by agencies in the domestic abuse context to assist with client safety planning. Though likely to be an underestimate given significant barriers to disclosing, our analysis revealed that 24 per cent of clients in that sample had responded positively to one or more measures of suicidality, with 18.9 per cent feeling suicidal currently or recently, and 18.3 per cent having made plans to end their lives, with 3.1 per cent declaring that they had made at least one suicide attempt.[20]

This reflects a level of suicidality that is substantially higher than that observed in the general population, confirming findings internationally that had previously indicated that women who experienced physical or sexual violence were nearly four times more likely to attempt suicide than non-victimised counterparts.[21] Such prevalence has subsequently been

18 Sylvia Walby, 'The Cost of Domestic Violence' (Women and Equality Unit, Department of Trade and Industry, 2004), available at <https://eprints.lancs.ac.uk/id/eprint/55255/1/cost_of_dv_report_sept04.pdf>.

19 Hannana Siddiqui and Meena Patel, 'Safe and Sane: A Model of Intervention on Domestic Violence and Mental Health, Suicide and Self-Harm Among Black and Minority Ethnic Women' (Southall Black Sisters, 2010), available at <https://southallblacksisters.org.uk/product/safe-and-sane-report/>.

20 Ruth Aitken and Vanessa E Munro, above n 6.

21 Karen Devries, Charlotte Watts, Mieko Yoshihama, Ligia Kiss, Lilia Blima Schraiber, Negussie Deyessa, Lori Heise, Julia Durand, Jessie Mbwambo, Henrica Jansen, Yemane Berhane, Mary Ellsberg, Claudia Garcia-Moreno, 'Violence Against Women is Strongly Associated with Suicide Attempts: Evidence from the WHO Multi-Country Study on Women's Health and Domestic Violence Against Women' (2011) 73(1) Social Science and Medicine 79, available at <https://pubmed.ncbi.nlm.nih.gov/21676510/>.

further supported at the domestic level, moreover, by analysis of the 2014 Adult Psychiatric Morbidity Survey in England, which found that – after adjusting for other variables – past year suicide attempts were almost three times more common in victims of intimate partner abuse, and almost four times more common among those who had been victimised in the past year.[22]

Importantly, suicidality was represented in the REFUGE sample across a diverse range of types of abuse experienced. However, the correlation was heightened where the abuse was cumulative, sustained over a longer period of time, or perpetrated by more than one person. Perhaps unsurprisingly, those who expressed suicidality scored significantly higher than their non-suicidal peers in the Core-10 psychological distress questionnaire, with measures tied to feeling despairing and hopeless, or depressed and isolated, being particularly prominent; and often intersecting in complicated ways with increased prevalence of issues in relation to the misuse of drugs or alcohol.[23] These connections between suicidality, isolation, and substance misuse as a coping mechanism in the context of abuse have also been identified more recently by other scholars,[24] and there is a growing literature exploring connections to feelings of hopelessness as a precipitator of suicide, both in general[25] and in the domestic abuse context.[26]

Our findings in these regards were also supported in the REFUGE study by interviews with caseworkers who reported acute concerns regarding the adequacy of support provided to clients at risk of, or experiencing suicidality. Staff spoke of feeling a responsibility to plug gaps in provision of services, particularly in relation to mental health and counselling support. They also spoke about the lack of professional

---

22 Sally McManus, Sylvia Walby, Estela Capelas Barbosa, Louis Appleby, Traolach Brugha and Paul Bebbington, 'Intimate Partner Violence, Suicidality, and Self-Harm: A Probability Sample Survey of the General Population in England' (2022) 9(7) The Lancet Psychiatry 574, available at <https://www.thelancet.com/journals/lanpsy/article/PIIS2215-0366(22)00151-1/fulltext>.

23 Vanessa E Munro and Ruth Aitken, 'From Hoping to Help: Identifying and Responding to Suicidality Amongst Victims of Domestic Abuse' (2020) 26(1) International Review of Victimology 29, available at <https://journals.sagepub.com/doi/10.1177/0269758018824160>.

24 Jane Monckton-Smith, Hannana Siddiqui, Sue Haile and Alexandra Sandham, 'Building a Temporal Sequence for Developing Prevention Strategies, Risk Assessment and Perpetrator Interventions in Domestic Abuse Related Suicide, Honour Killing, and Intimate Partner Homicide: Project Report' (2022) University of Gloucestershire, available at <https://eprints.glos.ac.uk/10579/>.

25 Rory O'Connor, 'Suicidal Behaviour as a Cry of Pain: Test of a Psychological Model' 7(4) Archives of Suicide Research 297, available at <https://www.tandfonline.com/doi/abs/10.1080/713848941>.

26 Christine Christie, James Rockey, Caroline Bradbury-Jones, Siddharta Bandyopadhyay and Heather Flowe, 'Domestic Abuse Links to Suicide: Rapid Review, Fieldwork and Quantitative Analysis Report' (University of Birmingham 2023), available at <osf.io/4t9ab>.

curiosity among those with whom victims most often interacted, including – in particular – GPs, hospital A&E departments, police, housing and social services. This meant that opportunities were often missed; not only to identify and offer support in relation to domestic abuse, but to consider the risks that victims might pose to themselves, alongside any risks identified as posed to them, or their children, by perpetrators.

Thus, without abdicating or absolving the role and responsibility of perpetrators, this emerging evidence brings a more complex picture to the fore. In particular, it highlights how linear attributions of cause and responsibility can be complicated by intersecting structural and systemic factors that not only compound the harmful effects of abuse, but present barriers to disclosure, protection or rescue, intensifying the experience of hopelessness often identified within narratives of suicidality. It draws attention, in other words, to interlocking layers of personal, situational and systemic vulnerability, and casts light on the ways in which they constrain victims' capacities and resources for self-development and self-determination; effects which are core to Young's understanding of the modes and consequences of oppression.

The implications of this were also clear in the accounts of victims' lives and deaths contained in the Domestic Homicide Reviews ('DHRs') that colleagues and I recently analysed as part of a Home Office-funded study.[27] Those reviews were replete with examples of this intricate and encompassing web of injustice. Indeed, it was clear that, while domestic abuse is often conceptualised as the paradigm form of private violence, many victims among this cohort were struggling for safety in plain sight. For example, just over half had engaged with specialist domestic abuse services, and almost two-thirds had engaged with mental health and/or counselling services, with similar proportions having attended hospital or A&E departments with injuries connected to their abuse. Three-quarters were known to have been in regular contact with their GPs, with many cases evidencing concerns or disclosures about abuse during those consultations. In addition, over 90 per cent had some history of contact with the police, often as a consequence of domestic abuse reports in relation to current or previous partners; and more than half had prior or ongoing contact with housing services, often due to their being in a precarious housing situation that was making it more difficult to leave an abusive partner. There was evidence that the victim had difficulties with drugs or alcohol in approximately half of cases, though less than 30 per

---

27 Sarah Dangar, Vanessa E Munro and Lotte Young Andrade (2023), above n 7.

cent had accessed specialist addiction support. Sixty-three per cent had dependent children, and in half of those cases, the children were still living in the same household at the time of death. But in over one-third of DHRs, concerns about the custody of children and/or the threat or actuality of social services intervention was documented in the victim's case files.

These findings further align with those of Bates et al in relation to 39 domestic abuse-related suicides referred to them by police in the year 2020–2021 as part of a wider Domestic Homicide Project. Not only did that study conclude that perpetrators in those suicide cases were three times more likely to have engaged in coercive and controlling behaviour (often alongside physical or sexual violence) than those identified as perpetrators in other intimate partner homicides,[28] but that victims in suicide cases had particularly high levels of agency involvement prior to death. Thus, it concluded that: 'the relatively high number of suspected victim suicide cases already known to mental health and/or domestic abuse services suggests that for some of these victims there were, or could have been, opportunities to offer support'.[29]

Despite this, and echoing concerns raised by Independent Domestic Violence Advisors within the REFUGE project, across the DHRs that my colleagues and I reviewed, there were recurring themes in relation to a lack of confidence and curiosity among the professionals with whom these victims interacted, whether in regard to asking questions about domestic abuse, about suicide, or about any link between the two. Concerns were often also raised about the suitability of current risk assessment tools for identifying the harmful effects of coercive and controlling behaviour, and recognising in particular the ways in which perpetrators' sustained attacks on a victim's self-worth and networks of social support generate barriers to engagement and a sense of hopelessness. The inadequacy of resourcing and training in this context, and the failure of agencies to respond holistically rather than adopting a siloed focus were also highlighted, compounded in many cases by poor protocols and practices in relation to information sharing.[30]

---

28 Lis Bates, Katharine Hoeger, Melanie-Jane Stoneman and Angela Whitaker, 'Domestic Homicides and Suspected Victim Suicides During the Covid-19 Pandemic 2020-21' (Vulnerability Knowledge and Practice Programme, Home Office 2021), 58. Available at <https://assets.publishing.service.gov.uk/government/uploads/system/uploads/attachment_data/file/1013128/Domestic_homicides_and_suspected_victim_suicides_during_the_Covid-19_Pandemic_2020-2021.pdf>.

29 ibid, at 68.

30 For further discussion, see also Sarah Dangar, Vanessa E Munro and Lotte Young Andrade, 'Learning Legacies: Understanding the Dynamics of Domestic Abuse Suicidality Through Domestic Homicide Reviews'(forthcoming), above n 7.

In DHR 16, for example, the victim experienced prior trauma as a result of which she had physical disabilities. After the breakdown of a 30-year marriage, she became involved in a relationship with a new partner who had an established history of serious violence, and who – over the course of the 11 months prior to her death – subjected her to sustained physical and psychological abuse. In the two months after she married the perpetrator (a marriage that she suggested subsequently she had not wanted to enter into), the victim lost five stone in weight. The GP with whom she was in contact during this time was aware of her abuse within the previous marriage and also in her current relationship. He noted on her records that there had been recent call-outs from police and victim support, and that she was in 'acute distress' during an appointment. Nonetheless, rather than probing further, he noted that she 'was a large lady' and so her dramatic weight loss was to be welcomed. Meanwhile, following her decision to support the perpetrator's prosecution for violence and abuse against her, the police failed to properly refer the victim's case to a multi-agency risk assessment conference, and she was informed in error that the perpetrator had been released on bail when in fact he was remanded in custody. Fearful of retaliation, she responded to this news by telling her support worker that 'it was as though the magistrates had signed her death warrant'. She took her life two days later.

This underscores the importance of so-called 'professional curiosity' to identify and properly assess abuse-related risks, but it also highlights the profoundly negative effects associated with being let down, or responded to unsympathetically by those services that victims might look to for support, safety or justice. Across the DHRs, there were many victims who reported to the police multiple times, but were told – either by police or prosecutors – that there was insufficient evidence to prosecute; as well as victims denied additional security measures by local authority housing teams because of their ongoing contact with perpetrators, or victims threatened with removal from specialist refuges because they lacked the financial resources to pay their rent. So too, there were examples of agencies closing files on clients only recently marked and referred to them as 'high risk' because, in the midst of navigating often complex and chaotic lives, including struggling with addiction issues or restricted freedoms, they had not returned calls or attended meetings.

In several of the cases that we looked at, or learned about through family member interviews, children were removed, or at risk of removal, from the custody of victims because of agencies' concerns about their ongoing involvement with perpetrators or about their mental (in)stability as a result of the domestic abuse. Of course, the harms to children of being exposed to or witnessing domestic abuse cannot be underestimated, but irrespective of the merits or demerits of the decision in terms of child protection, it was often clear that this removal had a profound effect on victims and that it was not always managed in a suitably trauma-informed manner. One family member we interviewed commented, 'they [social services] seem to think anybody who's suicidal, they just have to put the kids on child protection and not actually support the parent to get the help they need'.[31] Meanwhile another recounted that, a couple of months prior to her suicide, her daughter had been told by her social worker, during a special Mothers' Day visit that had been arranged at a local community centre as part of supervised contact arrangements, that her children were to be removed permanently: 'the children were sat in the next room waiting for their mum with flowers and chocolates and cards, … and she was broken'.[32] For these family members, there was no question that this loss of their children – of 'their anchor'[33] – was a key factor in compounding their loved one's feelings of hopelessness.

Many such experiences and findings within the suicide DHRs map onto themes identified across other domestic homicide reviews.[34] They are all important. But what a structural injustice lens might allow us to bring more clearly to the fore are the ways in which they are not isolated examples of poor engagement, easily remedied with extra training or additional resource. Instead, they reflect how domestic abuse is conceptualised and responded to socially and institutionally, the extent to which mental health and suicidality remain taboo or at least difficult subjects, and the ways in which personal and situational precarity in one context infuses interactions with services in another, affirming narratives

---

31 Family Member 5 – Sarah Dangar, Vanessa E Munro and Lotte Young Andrade (2023), above n 7, at 42.

32 Family Member 8 – Sarah Dangar, Vanessa E Munro and Lotte Young Andrade (2023), above n 7, at 43.

33 Family Member 5 – Sarah Dangar, Vanessa E Munro and Lotte Young Andrade (2023), above n 7, at 54.

34 See, for example, Nicola Sharp-Jeffs and Liz Kelly, 'DHR Case Analysis: Report for Standing Together' (2016), available at <https://coercivecontrol.ripfa.org.uk/wp-content/uploads/Standing_together_dom_homicide_review_analysis.pdf>; Bear Monique, 'London Domestic Homicide Review Case Analysis and Review of Local Authorities DHR Processes' (Standing Together 2019), available at <https://static1.squarespace.com/static/5ee0be2588f1e349401c832c/t/5f633ee1e0e0be6ec5b858a1/1600339696014/Standing+Together+London+DHR+Review+Report.pdf>; Richard Potter, 'Key Findings From Analysis of Domestic Homicide Reviews: October 2019 to September 2020' (Home Office 2022), available at <https://www.gov.uk/government/publications/key-findings-from-analysis-of-domestic-homicide-reviews/key-findings-from-analysis-of-domestic-homicide-reviews>. For further discussion, see Sarah Dangar, Vanessa E Munro and Lotte Young Andrade (2023), above n 7.

of victims as 'hard to engage' in their safety-planning or unreasonably reluctant to disclose and seek support from agencies, including those who wield power over them and have been felt to let them down previously.

Young observes that 'structural injustice occurs as a consequence of many individuals and institutions acting to pursue their particular goals and interests, for the most part within the limits of accepted rules and norms'.[35] Agencies' engagement with domestic abuse victims is indeed often conducted within the parameters of their own commissioning model or expertise (be that addiction counselling, mental health, or children's services). In many respects, this is desirable and appropriate, but the experiences of suicidal victims of domestic abuse demonstrate powerfully the ways in which this can also frustrate the potential to recognise and respond holistically to an intersection of injustices. And at the root of this, as Young reminds us, is the reality that these structures and systems are not empty processes. They are living mechanisms populated by the actions, interactions and one might add *inactions* of people within them. None of this is to diminish the role of the perpetrator in causing harm, and ultimately death, to the victim, but it is to observe that the actions of professionals in the service of operational and systemic goals can compound that harm, isolation and sense of hopelessness.

In her work, Young speaks to the ways in which social structures constrain 'indirectly and cumulatively' by 'blocking possibilities', and draws on the analogy by Marilyn Frye of the birdcage, apt since 'looked at one by one, no wire is capable of preventing a bird from flying. It is the joint relationship of the wires that prevents flight.'[36] The conduct of an individual perpetrator of abuse *can* no doubt prevent a victim from finding freedom, but the additional effects of intersecting vulnerabilities and/or underwhelming agency engagement can make efforts at escape feel all the more futile, precisely because they are. At the same time, though, it is also important to bear in mind the involvement in and orchestration of those structural dynamics *by* the perpetrator as part of the abuse. Coercive control perpetrators consciously manipulate and capitalise upon the reliability of systemic failures to cement the dynamics of domination and oppression in abusive relationships and to render victims' hopelessness a self-fulfilling prophecy. Concerns about immigration or housing precarity, financial insecurity, removal of children, or the risk of not being believed or positioned as an aggressor by police, are – for

35 Iris Marion Young, *Responsibility for Justice* (Oxford University Press 2011), 52.
36 ibid, 55.

example – routinely relied upon by perpetrators to augment their control over victims. These strategies are not developed in a vacuum and thus the dynamics at play between these structural and interpersonal forms of injustice are complex and often mutually reaffirming.

In the next section, I explore one mechanism and institutional process for responding to domestic abuse suicides, namely the Domestic Homicide Review (DHR). I suggest that this may offer potential to better open up the reflective space for identifying, understanding and challenging the complex intersection of these multiple vectors of vulnerability and disempowerment.

Domestic homicide reviews: a responsible response?

First implemented in England and Wales in 2011, DHRs are designed to be distinct from a criminal justice investigation (whether in respect of offences committed against the victim while they were alive or in respect of offences related to their death), which focuses primarily on retrospective attribution of blame and where appropriate, imposition of punishment on perpetrators. Instead, DHRs are intended to provide a contextual exploration of the broad circumstances in which the death occurred, with a view to facilitating constructive accountability and learning lessons that can ensure improved safeguarding, service provision and interventions. As Home Office guidance puts it: 'reviews should illuminate the past to make the future safer'.[37] For family members of the deceased, their participation within reviews can also perform an additional, and equally crucial, function by affording the opportunity to articulate and gain some recognition from agencies of the experiences of their loved ones, and potentially provide some 'closure' in respect of their death.

The paradigm case in mind when the DHR regime was first designed and implemented was clearly where the perpetrator had directly inflicted fatal violence upon a victim, and such scenarios have continued to dominate the work of DHR panels since. But, in 2016, recognising the emerging concern regarding the links between domestic abuse and suicidality, which have become increasingly pronounced, the Home Office took steps to extend the remit of DHRs, creating a statutory duty

37 Home Office, 'Multi-Agency Statutory Guidance for the Conduct of Domestic Homicide Reviews' (2016, Home Office), at 6. Available at <https://assets.publishing.service.gov.uk/government/uploads/system/uploads/attachment_data/file/575273/DHR-Statutory-Guidance-161206.pdf>.

for all Community Safety Partnerships to commission them in relation to any death that 'has or appears to have' resulted from domestic abuse.[38] The guidance now stipulates that:

> … where a victim took their own life (suicide) and the circumstances give rise to concern, for example, it emerges that there was coercive controlling behaviour in the relationship, a review should be undertaken, even if a suspect is not charged with any offence or they are tried and acquitted.[39]

There is much that is left open to interpretation here regarding what level and types of evidence will suffice to 'give rise to concern' sufficient to merit the commissioning of a DHR in suicide cases,[40] but the expansion of the regime to such cases does provide an important opportunity for engagement and shared reflection regarding the factors that contributed to the victim's death, and what might have been done to have prevented it.

In this sense, the DHR – with its focus on resolution beyond recrimination – can provide an instructive example of Iris Marion Young's ambition to overcome injustice through collective responsibility-taking rather than backward-looking attribution of liability. As the discussion above indicates, without displacing the centrality of the perpetrator, there is often a complex interaction of various relational, personal, situational, social and structural factors that influence the ways in which domestic abuse is perpetrated, experienced and responded to, as well as its links to suicidality. A DHR can provide a space and process through which to bring these to light. However, this holding – in tension and in dialogue – of backward- and forward-looking responsibility is a demanding task, and potentially all the more so in the domestic homicide context due to the profound loss that each death represents and the legacies it leaves.

Moreover, as my colleagues and I have argued elsewhere, the process goals envisaged in this context are likely to be even harder to achieve in suicide cases than in the domestic *homicide* cases for which DHRs were initially conceived.[41] In those latter instances, the death occurs as a result of fatal infliction of direct violence, which is then typically prosecuted and established to be the result (at least to some degree) of a blameworthy

38 Home Office, above n 39, at p. 5.
39 Home Office, above n 39, at p. 6.
40 See further, Sarah Dangar, Vanessa E Munro and Lotte Young Andrade, 'Unchartered Territory: Navigating Voice, Accountability and Prevention in Suicide-Related Domestic Homicide Reviews in England and Wales' (forthcoming), above n 7.
41 Sarah Dangar, Vanessa E Munro and Lotte Young Andrade (2023), above n 7.

act by the perpetrator. With that attribution in place, the DHR process is 'freed up' to learn lessons about agency engagement that will better protect future victims in the face of similar risk, without directly troubling the causal responsibility for death that has been attributed. By contrast, in suicide cases, matters may be considerably more complicated; and this is alluded to even in the Home Office guidance through its reference to the potential lack of criminal charging or responsibility of perpetrators. As I discuss further below, this means that there may be different motivations at play among participants in suicide DHRs, a more cautious calculus as to the risks and benefits of candour, and an operation of the process 'in the shadows' of more retrospective criminal justice logics.

In her discussion of agency learning, Young rightly identifies the ways in which 'a blame language can be inappropriate and unproductive'[42] because, among other things, it tends to oversimplify the causes of injustice, underplays the contributory role of structures and 'produces defensiveness and unproductive blame-switching' between institutions or agencies.[43] Though DHRs are intended to transcend such limitations, exploration of the content, conducting and outcomes of reviews in suicide cases suggest substantial difficulties in creating and maintaining, for this purpose, a space that both is, and is felt to be, safe by the various agencies involved. Among the key strategies deployed to avoid responsibility, Young identifies reification through which the 'system' is positioned as having a momentum and logic of its own that makes it impossible for agencies or individuals within the system to do anything differently; strategies of distancing that indicate there are other agencies or individuals who are more acutely engaged and bear a greater responsibility for action or inaction; and strategies of denial that narrowly delineate agency or individual roles to indicate that it was never within their remit to behave differently or that it was beyond the scope of their permissible actions to do so in the absence of cooperation from others, including, in the case of domestic abuse, the victim who is thus positioned as 'unresponsive'. All of these strategies were evident to some degree across the suicide DHRs we analysed, and their effects emerged as a recurrent theme in interviews with professionals and bereaved family members.[44]

---

42 Young, above n 35, at 116.

43 ibid, at 117.

44 See further, Sarah Dangar, Vanessa E Munro and Lotte Young Andrade, 'Unchartered Territory: Navigating Voice, Accountability and Prevention in Suicide-Related Domestic Homicide Reviews in England and Wales' (forthcoming), above n 7.

In DHR 11, for example, a 27-year-old woman had been in a succession of abusive relationships, several of which were known about by police and other agencies. She also had a history of drug and alcohol dependency alongside intermittent periods of rough sleeping and sex work. Despite her repeatedly raising concerns about suffering from psychosis and engaging in numerous acts of severe self-harm, she was denied a proper mental health assessment because agencies were either unable to engage her sufficiently for appointments or her use of drugs made full assessment and diagnosis difficult. Relevant information was not effectively shared across hospital, mental health, GP, addiction and domestic abuse services. Indeed, the DHR Chair noted that 'the issue of substance use became the focus along with the view that services needed to wait for the adult to be ready to engage'. Though in many respects a damning indictment of the ways in which siloed agency involvement prevented a proper risk and needs assessment in this case, the DHR's ultimate proposals for learning and reform were limited: 'professionals may need to think more laterally when undertaking assessments' while noting that 'these interventions are complex and would have required cooperation' from her.

Meanwhile, in DHR 19, a 20-year-old woman took her life within one month of being advised by police that her allegations of rape against an ex-partner were not to be pursued, at least in part because of evidence that she had ongoing contact with him. Despite her prior engagement with both domestic abuse and sexual violence services, previous suicide attempts as a result of which she was on a waiting list for counselling, and the fact that it was on record that – after giving her police interview about the rapes – she had told the officer in charge that she could no longer cope, had no support from family or friends and had made an attempt on her life the previous evening, the deceased was offered no additional support in relation to, or in the aftermath of, this 'no further action' decision. Though critical of this lack of consideration in relation to the emotional impact of discontinuance, which it described as 'particularly concerning', the DHR focused more broadly on the lack of a victim strategy within the police force and the need for professionals to confirm engagement with other services before discharging their care. These are important considerations, but they disperse responsibility to a level of abstraction, while distracting from systemic issues about why rape complaints are dropped and how this is communicated, sidelining the impact of resource shortages on waiting lists for counselling which pose barriers to victim care, and doing little to interrogate the ways in which victims are often responsibilised but rarely empowered within agency engagements.

These strategies of reification, distancing and denial are evident, moreover, not only in relation to agency involvement during the life of the victim, but in their responses in the aftermath of death. During our DHR study, professionals and bereaved family members alike raised concerns about the adequacy of investigations conducted by police at the initial suicide scene, even in cases where there were substantial records of domestic abuse. As one DHR Chair put it, 'it's almost like once they've decided that it's not a murder, then it's just over to the coroner and they don't really look into it'.[45] This is undoubtedly an issue about resource and training, but interviewees suggested that it also reflected a failure to understand domestic abuse and its links to suicidality. This was well-illustrated, moreover, in a separate study exploring criminal justice professionals' perspectives on domestic abuse suicidality, within which one Magistrate that we interviewed remarked, for example, that 'a police officer would find it hard that anybody would take their own life because they've got an awkward husband'.[46] Bereaved family members in the DHR research also spoke of the ways in which they felt that their concerns about the role of abuse in causing death were dismissed by agencies, with professionals often automatically positioning them as 'too emotional' to be heard both despite and because of their familiarity with the experiences, needs and vulnerabilities of the victim.[47]

For those family members who ultimately did contribute to a suicide DHR, there were also mixed experiences. Though Home Office guidance is clear that family members should be seen as key stakeholders, with unique and important insights to offer in respect of victims' experiences, hierarchies of knowledge were often still at play in this process, with family members sometimes reporting that they felt their consultation and inclusion could be tokenistic or partial. This, in turn, mapped onto wider dynamics of power that some family members felt infused the DHR process. As one put it, 'I felt my Chair was a perpetrator in his own right … I've just seen my daughter go through all this bullying with the perpetrator but yet you're trying to control and bully … and that's how I felt he was bullying me and controlling me. And I thought that's just literally what she's experienced and yet you're trying to do this to me.'[48]

45 DHR Chair 3 – See further, Sarah Dangar, Vanessa E. Munro and Lotte Young Andrade (2023), above n 7.

46 Mag 6 – Vanessa E. Munro, Vanessa Bettinson and Mandy Burton, above n 8.

47 See further, 'Unchartered Territory: Navigating Voice, Accountability and Prevention in Suicide-Related Domestic Homicide Reviews in England and Wales' (2024), above n 7.

48 Family Member Focus Group – Sarah Dangar, Vanessa E Munro and Lotte Young Andrade (2023), above n 7, at 81.

Meanwhile, for other family members, more acute difficulties lay not in how *they* were dealt with through the DHR process, but in how they felt agencies were scrutinised and held to account. There was often disappointment tied to the recommendations that emerged, which they felt lacked ambition, precision or urgency. As one put it:

> ... it's all the same recommendations, all the same learning outcomes, isn't it, working together, sharing information, you know, it's all the same old, same old, same old. But do things change ... nobody stuck their neck out. Nobody. Nobody chose to go the extra mile or be professionally curious ... until we start doing this, things aren't going to change, women are never going to be safe.[49]

Another described the DHR as 'lacklustre with no ability to challenge any agencies involved ... I was disappointed it was not robust or probing, I felt as if the Chair was sitting on the fence ... We understand the report isn't meant to point the finger, it is to learn lessons, but I don't feel this was achieved.'[50]

Though professionals sometimes attributed this to family members' unrealistic aspirations for what the DHR process could achieve, family members located it in their sense that agencies protected themselves or each other from thorough-going critique, notwithstanding the purportedly safe and self-critical learning ethos of the DHR.

To the extent that this is true, it highlights the ways in which conducting DHRs in suicide cases may pose distinctive and heightened challenges. Among other things, there is a one-sidedness to the evidence available, both in the sense that the victim is deceased and that there may be no confirmed perpetrator, which means that data about agencies' interactions with a partner often cannot be included. So too, there may be safety risks for professional and family contributors as a result of the alleged perpetrator still being at liberty, which can impact the process and its outcomes.[51] At the same time, however, these concerns about the practical impact of DHRs also map onto a wider concern that critics

49 Family Member 4 – Sarah Dangar, Vanessa E Munro and Lotte Young Andrade (2023), above n 7, at 82.

50 Family Member 2 – Sarah Dangar, Vanessa E Munro and Lotte Young Andrade (2023), above n 7, at 83.

51 See further, Sarah Dangar, Vanessa E Munro and Lotte Young Andrade, 'Unchartered Territory: Navigating Voice, Accountability and Prevention in Suicide-Related Domestic Homicide Reviews in England and Wales' (forthcoming), above n 7.

have raised about the ability in Young's social responsibility approach to enact sufficiently concrete and tangible outcomes. As Goodin and Barry have put it:

> ... insofar as these claims concerning backward-looking allocation of liability are correct, the effects of the interacting contributions that would be required from so many people to overcome structural injustice will be likewise extraordinarily difficult to assemble into an individual-level plan-of-future-action.[52]

In that sense, the modest, localised and often more mundane focus within suicide DHR recommendations, on improved information sharing, more professional curiosity, or better record-keeping, for example, might be understood to reflect something of a paralysis in the face of the wider interaction of issues of attitude, aptitude and resource that, in relation to domestic abuse, fundamentally requires a whole society response.

In addition, the different motivations with which parties might enter into suicide DHRs may also be pertinent, albeit that the form those motivations take can be complex and shifting. While agencies might – formally at least – embark on DHRs, when commissioned, in the spirit of future learning, for family members, their desire to protect future victims from the fate of their loved one often sits alongside a hope that the DHR will provide some vindication of their account of the death, and specifically of the abuser's role within it. Though family members may not seek to 'blame' agencies, they may be seeking a sense of justice and closure from past wrongs, and in some cases, may harbour hope that, through the DHR, scope for further criminal investigations might be re-opened. As one put it, 'for us the damage is done. No-one can fix it. Even at this stage, if we were to get to the point where they did find a bit of evidence and could go forward with the prosecution, it would be amazing for us as a family, it would give us some closure',[53] while another commented in terms of what they want from the process: 'learnings, yes, but ... what I want to be able to do is to use it to go to the police and the coroners and say, you need to relook, you need to reopen the investigation, or you need to give us an apology'.[54]

52 Robert E Goodin and Christian Barry, 'Responsibility for Structural Injustice: A Third Thought' (2021) 20(4) Politics, Philosophy and Economics 339, 343.
53 Family Member 9 – Sarah Dangar, Vanessa E Munro and Lotte Young Andrade, above n 7, at 83.
54 Family Member 3 – Sarah Dangar, Vanessa E Munro and Lotte Young Andrade, above n 7, at 83.

Young is clear on the theory that 'the liability model of responsibility … is inappropriate for assigning responsibility in relation to structural injustice'[55] and that the logics at play are distinctive in each context and that they ought not to be intertwined. And yet, in the suicide DHR context, we can see how this can be particularly challenging. Unlike in other DHRs, there has often been no moment for that retrospective liability attribution, no moment of formal condemnation of the perpetrator's behaviour, and so also no platform for the kind of acknowledgment that comes from agencies when the existence of abuse and its role in a loved one's death is formally and fully recognised. In this context, it may be far more difficult to neatly delineate backward- and forward-looking dimensions. It may also be difficult to meet the desire, articulated by one family member, not to attribute blame to a perpetrator but to 'take blame away from the victim' and to say that 'this person isn't to blame for their death'.[56] Indeed, as one Chair put it, their focus on future learning notwithstanding, suicide DHRs can take place in 'a room full of blame', with the deceased 'at the epicentre':[57] blame, for example, of the perpetrator for the abuse, of agencies and/or families for failing to protect, of the police for failing to adequately investigate the circumstances of the death, and even of the victim for her failure to leave the relationship.

Conclusion

It is clear that what one professional described as perpetrators' 'asset-stripping'[58] of victims in domestically abusive relationships extends beyond their individual and material attributes to their social networks and cultural capital. These are not parallel dimensions of abuse that dovetail at the destination of disadvantage, but interlocking trajectories that require strategic disruptions, and which can only be properly accounted for if we preserve a focus on power dynamics. Attending to this is vital if we are to understand the circumstances in which deaths by suicide occur in this context, and the factors that might mediate or moderate suicidality, thereby creating opportunities for more effective prevention and intervention. In a context in which the requirement to

55 Young, above n 35, at 98.
56 Family Member 7 – Sarah Dangar, Vanessa E Munro and Lotte Young Andrade, above n 7, at 83.
57 DHR Chair 7 – See, further, Sarah Dangar, Vanessa E Munro and Lotte Young Andrade (2023), above n 7.
58 DHR Chair 3 – See, further, Sarah Dangar, Vanessa E Munro and Lotte Young Andrade (2023), above n 7.

establish perpetrators' liability for death does not demand a singularity of cause, there is – in theory at least – no reason to shy away from this more complex and nuanced analysis. And yet, while there appears to be a growing appreciation among professionals of the severity of psychological harm in domestic abuse settings and the extent to which taking one's life 'must feel like the only way out on some occasions',[59] anxiety remains that this can be overwhelmed by the 'noise' invited into analysis by other vulnerabilities that may be targeted by abusers, or caused or worsened by abuse.[60] The space that DHRs allow for scrutiny of the life of the victim and their service engagements may further amplify that noise, but doing so is also vital to truly understand the hopelessness and isolation that surrounds victims' suicidality. Without this, it is not possible to develop risk assessment tools, support provision and prevention strategies, both within and across agencies, that are capable of improving victims' prospects for equality and safety. Iris Marion Young's optimism regarding the potential to acknowledge, hold and navigate these tensions between different vectors of injustice, and thereby generate a richer and more enriching account of social responsibility, is welcome, despite its challenges. So too, the ambition to take perpetrators' responsibility for death seriously, without constructing a zero-sum game that absolves social and institutional structures of their sustaining and supporting roles in the context of domestic abuse suicide, ought not to be abandoned; despite the difficulties that, as have been discussed in this chapter, the ambition currently poses to both criminal courts and DHR processes alike.

59 Police 4 – Vanessa E Munro, Vanessa Bettinson and Mandy Burton, above n 8.
60 PSCOT 1 – Vanessa E Munro, Vanessa Bettinson and Mandy Burton, above n 8.

9

Structural injustice and human rights: the case of begging

Virginia Mantouvalou[1]

Introduction

What is the role of the law in relation to structural injustice? Can we identify problematic legal rules with an appearance of legitimacy that increases and perpetuates the disadvantage of the worst off? How can these legal rules be challenged? In this chapter, I consider these questions by using the example of begging.[2]

In the first part, I explain what begging is and place its criminalisation against the background of a pattern of states' punitive attitudes towards poverty.[3] People beg because they are excluded from society and resort to begging in public spaces in order to survive.[4] Some also view begging as work.[5] However, the act of begging is a criminal offence in many legal orders. The criminalisation of begging is said to be justified on several grounds, including the interests of those who beg, the protection of public order or the interests of businesses that

---

1 I am grateful to Hugh Collins, Beth Watts-Cobbe and Jo Wolff for constructive comments on a draft, and to all participants of the workshop on *Structural Injustice and the Law*, hosted at UCL Faculty of Laws.

2 In my book *Structural Injustice and Workers' Rights* (Oxford University Press 2023), I examine these questions in relation to precarious work.

3 For a detailed discussion of these patterns in the USA, see Loic Wacquant, *Punishing the Poor – The Neoliberal Government of Social Insecurity* (Duke University Press 2009).

4 See, for instance, the discussion in Catherine Kennedy and Suzanne Fitzpatrick, 'Begging, Rough Sleeping and Social Exclusion' (2001) 38 Urban Studies 2001.

5 Alexander Kwesi Kassah, 'Begging as Work: A Study of People with Mobility Difficulties in Accra, Ghana' (2008) 23 Disability and Society 163; Stephen E Lankenau, 'Stronger than Dirt – Public Humiliation and Status Enhancement among Panhandlers' (1999) 28 Journal of Contemporary Ethnography 288; Johannes Lenhard, 'The Hopeful Labour of Begging – Homeless People's Struggles for a Better Life in Paris' (2021) 39 Society and Space 792.

are disrupted by the practice.[6] Through criminal enforcement, people who beg are removed from the streets while those who find them disruptive benefit from their removal from public spaces. However, the reasons that are put forward as justifications for the criminalisation of begging should be scrutinised closely. This criminalisation reinforces structures of injustice that affect some of the most disadvantaged people in society, while many benefit from this situation, as I explain building on the work of Iris Marion Young.[7] The criminalisation of begging contributes to the clustering of disadvantage[8] and creates what I have described elsewhere as 'state-mediated structural injustice',[9] namely situations where the state, through legal rules with an appearance of legitimacy, perpetuates structural injustice.

In the second part of the chapter, I turn to human rights law and consider its role in allocating state responsibility for the criminalisation of begging. Two regional human rights courts, the European Court of Human Rights (ECtHR) and the African Court of Human and Peoples' Rights (AfCtHPR), found that the criminalisation of begging was incompatible with states' human rights obligations, including the rights to private life, freedom of expression and freedom of movement that are protected in many legal documents.[10] People who beg are socially excluded and disadvantaged for many reasons.[11] Human rights law cannot, of course, address all instances of structural injustice faced by them, for the reasons why individuals end up begging are multiple and complex, and much needs to be done for their needs to be met. In addition, it is important to emphasise that the requirement to decriminalise begging on the basis of human rights law does not

6 For an overview of justifications, see Sarah Johnsen, Beth Watts and Suzanne Fitzpatrick, 'Rebalancing the Rhetoric: A Normative Analysis of Enforcement in Street Homelessness Policy' (2021) 58 Urban Studies 355. For an overview of the history of the laws, see Christopher Roberts, 'Discretion and the Rule of Law: The Significance and Endurance of Vagrancy and Vagrancy-Type Laws in England, the British Empire and the British Colonial World', (2023) 33 Duke Journal of Comparative & International Law 181.

7 Iris Marion Young, *Responsibility for Justice* (Oxford University Press 2011).

8 The concept of clustering of disadvantage was coined and analysed in Jonathan Wolff and Avner de-Shalit, *Disadvantage* (Oxford University Press 2007).

9 I develop this framework and apply it to the rights of precarious workers in Mantouvalou (n 2), Chapter 2.

10 European Court of Human Rights, *Lacatus v Switzerland*, App No 14065/15, Judgment of 19 January 2021 (in French only), hereafter cited as *Lacatus*; African Court of Human and People's Rights, Advisory Opinion on the Compatibility of Vagrancy Laws with the African Charter of Human and Peoples' Rights and Other Human Rights Instruments Applicable in Africa, Advisory Opinion 1 of 2018, 4 December 2020.

11 Suzanne Fitzpatrick, Sarah Johnsen and Michael White, 'Multiple Exclusion Homelessness in the UK: Key Patterns and Intersections' (2011) 10 Social Policy and Society 501.

exhaust states' duties of justice towards people who are destitute, homeless and who beg. These people should have access to support and assistance to stop begging and sleeping rough, and to live flourishing lives, access work and accommodation. However, human rights law can serve as a diagnostic tool, help advance a strong moral argument in public debates at least in relation to certain serious forms of injustice, raise awareness, provide support to civil society organisations that focus on poverty, challenge existing law structures, impose on states an urgent requirement for legal change, and possibly contribute towards cultural and broader social change. In short, the discussion of the criminalisation of begging exemplifies how human rights law can be used to destabilise some structures that perpetuate grave injustice towards the most disadvantaged.

Punishing the poor and structural injustice

What is begging?

People who beg ask passers-by for money in a public space. Those who beg are often rough sleepers, which means that they sleep in the open air or in spaces that are not designed for habitation (such as car parks). The extent of the overlap between those who beg and those who sleep rough is not straightforward and data on begging is limited.[12] What is clear is that these two, often overlapping, categories comprise some of the most disadvantaged groups in society.[13] Empirical research in the UK has shown that many people who beg are homeless before starting to beg, and further examined how homelessness occurs in the first place.[14]

Fitzpatrick and Kennedy conducted an empirical study in Edinburgh and Glasgow and explained that homeless people came from disadvantaged and poor backgrounds, while also having experienced trauma early in their lives.[15] According to their study, many developed addiction to alcohol or drugs as a result of their trauma. When people in the study started sleeping rough, their addiction increased. According

12 See Suzanne Fitzpatrick and Catherine Kennedy, 'The Links between Begging and Rough Sleeping: A Question of Legitimacy' (2001) 16 Housing Studies 549; Public Health England (PHE), 'Evidence Review: Adults with complex needs (with a particular focus on street begging and street sleeping)' (PHE Publications 2018) 28–29.
13 ibid PHE at 29.
14 See Suzanne Fitzpatrick, Glen Bramley and Sarah Johnsen, 'Pathways into Multiple Exclusion Homelessness in Seven UK Cities' (2012) 50 Urban Studies 148.
15 Fitzpatrick and Kennedy (n 12).

to the same study, the participants had limited work opportunities, and these were mainly casual work. A combination of factors was identified as interrelated routes into homelessness, including relationship breakdowns, leaving residential care or prison, experiencing eviction and losing their jobs. Many had lost access to welfare benefits because of reasons such as relationship breakdowns or moving city.[16] One interviewee with a criminal record explained that he had to choose between criminal activity and begging, and he decided to beg in order to stay out of prison.[17]

Other research has highlighted that homeless people have experienced a number of traumatic incidents early on in life, and emphasised that they experience 'multiple exclusion homelessness', whereby a number of forms of deep social exclusion interact and overlap.[18] In relation to the experience of begging itself, empirical research has explained that it is very challenging, and that people are driven to it by desperation and as a means of survival.[19] Moreover, begging has stigma attached to it. People who beg may experience abuse by passers-by and may have been victims of crime, including rape.

Even though those who beg are often viewed as passive recipients of support, there is no sharp division between begging and work. A line of literature explores begging as work,[20] while categories of people who may be prosecuted as beggars may be street vendors or sex workers. International Labour Organisation (ILO) research defined begging as 'a range of activities whereby an individual asks a stranger for money on the basis of being poor or needing charitable donations for health or religious reasons. Beggars may also sell small items, such as dusters or flowers, in return for money that may have little to do with the value of the item for sale'.[21] The ILO definition suggests that the boundary between begging and work is not always clear. Conduct, such as the activity of street vendors, may be classified as begging but can also be viewed as work.[22] Other street-life categories that may bear similarities to begging include

16 ibid 559.
17 ibid 560.
18 Suzanne Fitzpatrick, Sarah Johnsen and Michael White, 'Multiple Exclusion Homelessness in the UK: Key Patterns and Intersections' (2011) 10 Social Policy and Society 501.
19 See, for instance, Fitzpatrick, Bramley and Johnsen (n 14).
20 See the literature above (n 5).
21 ILO, 'A Rapid Assessment of Bonded Labour in Domestic Work and Begging in Pakistan' (2004) 22.
22 On challenges faced by street vendors, see ILO, 'The Regulatory Framework and the Informal Economy' (no date) <https://www.ilo.org/wcmsp5/groups/public/@ed_emp/@emp_policy/documents/publication/wcms_210451.pdf> accessed 12 October 2023.

charity collections, busking, and selling publications such as the *Big Issue* in the UK.[23]

Ethnographic studies report that, indeed, people who beg often describe their activity as work. Kassah explained that, when viewed as work, begging took on positive meaning and value. The framing of begging as work empowered his interviewees, who were people with disabilities.[24] Lenhard argued that begging should be understood as 'labour of hope';[25] providing structure, purpose and connections in people's lives, while also serving as a way to create opportunities for their future. He suggested that people who beg put in significant labour, both physically and emotionally; for instance, by choosing the best spot, developing relationships and networks with people, overcoming shame, standing or walking, and creating narratives to share with passers-by from whom they ask money.[26]

It is important not to normalise begging, of course. People who beg are poor, destitute and homeless. They live deprived lives to which society should respond by supporting them to obtain housing and 'mainstream' work, by which I mean here work other than begging. However, the above literature on begging as work brings out the expressive function of begging to which we will return later on. People who beg often use their interactions with strangers to convey their plight, explain why they are poor, homeless, needy and worthy of support. The expressive value of begging is important both for the person who begs but also for the recipient of the message.[27]

Criminalisation

Begging is increasingly criminalised in many legal orders. Criminalisation is supposed to address conduct constituting a distinctive kind of moral wrong, with criminal law having a 'distinctively moral voice'.[28] However, in recent years it has been observed that we are faced with a 'crisis of overcriminalisation' that exposes too many people to prosecution and conviction, even for conduct that does not merit such

---

23 The *Big Issue* is a magazine sold by homeless people in the UK. On all these categories, see Joe Hermer, *Begging, Law and Power in Public Spaces* (Hart 2019) Chapter 3.
24 Kassah (n 5) 168 ff.
25 Lenhard (n 5) 803 ff.
26 ibid 805.
27 Arthur Schafer, 'The Expressive Liberty of Beggars: Why it Matters to Them and to Us' (Canadian Centre for Policy Alternatives, September 2007).
28 AP Simester and Andrew von Hirsch, *Crimes, Harms, and Wrongs* (Hart 2014), 4.

state response.[29] The criminalisation of begging has to be examined against this background. Analysis of the law in 38 Member States of the Council of Europe showed that only nine of them do not criminalise begging as such.[30] Eighteen Member States criminalise begging at the national level,[31] while in other Member States, it is criminalised at local level.[32] From states criminalising it at national level, six criminalise only intrusive or aggressive forms of begging.[33] Begging is also criminalised in the majority of African countries,[34] where the criminal offence is viewed as a relic from colonialism,[35] and in many other legal orders.[36]

In England and Wales, begging is a criminal offence under the Vagrancy Act 1824, which has been influential in many countries. Section 3 of the Vagrancy Act states that:

> every person wandering abroad, or placing himself or herself in any public place, street, highway, court, or passage, to beg or gather alms, or causing or procuring or encouraging any child or children so to do; shall be deemed an idle and disorderly person within the true intent and meaning of this Act.

Historically, the first vagrancy laws targeted those who were viewed as idle and refusing to work, and were designed to force people to accept work at a low wage in order to supply low-paid workers to landowners.[37] These laws were developed on the assumption that there is a duty to work.[38] Other functions of vagrancy laws over the

---

29 See, for instance, the discussion in Anthony Duff, *The Realm of Criminal Law* (Oxford University Press 2018), Introduction.

30 Albania, Andorra, Finland, Georgia, Greece, Moldova, Portugal, Slovakia and Ukraine.

31 Azerbaijan, Cyprus, Croatia, Estonia, France, Hungary, Ireland, Italy, Liechtenstein, Luxembourg, Montenegro, Poland, Romania, UK, San Marino, Serbia, Slovenia and Turkey.

32 See *Lacatus*, paras 19–26.

33 Estonia, France, Ireland, Italy, Serbia and Slovenia.

34 Algeria, Burundi, Burkina Faso, Cameroon, Chad, Comoros, Republic of Congo, Cote d'Ivoire, Gabon, Guinea, Madagascar, Mauritania, Mali, Morocco, Niger, Sahrawi Arab Democratic Republic, Senegal, Togo, Botswana, Gambia, Malawi, Nigeria, Seychelles, Uganda, Zambia, Mauritius, Namibia and Sierra Leone.

35 See Samuel Okiror, 'Poverty: African Vagrancy Laws Continue to Discriminate, Despite Court Victories' (International Bar Association 31 May 2023).

36 See Roberts (n 6) 190 ff who also explains why these laws have not been challenged effectively, 238–239.

37 William J Chambliss, 'A Sociological Analysis of the Law of Vagrancy' (1964) 12 Social Problems 67, 69.

38 A L Beier, 'A New Serfdom: Labor Laws, Vagrancy Statutes, and Labor Discipline in England, 1350–1800', in A L Beier and Paul Ocobock (eds), *Cast Out – Vagrancy and Homelessness in Global and Historical Perspective* (Ohio University Press 2011), 35.

years have included targeting activities that are viewed as immoral and preventing crime.[39]

Studies on the implementation of the Vagrancy Act in recent years, particularly in relation to arrests and prosecutions for begging, show that it has been used by the authorities to punish the poor, and not in a way that was sensitive to their social welfare.[40] In data of the Crown Prosecution Service in 2016 it was indicated that there were 2,365 arrests under Section 3 of the Vagrancy Act in England in 2015–2016,[41] while a significant increase is noticeable since 2006–2007. The Vagrancy Act is in the process of being repealed,[42] but thousands of arrests are still being made in recent years under the archaic legislation, and there are concerns that it will be replaced with similar criminal rules.[43] In addition to the Vagrancy Act, Section 35 of the Anti-Social Behaviour, Crime and Policing Act 2014 gives police officers the power to disperse individuals or groups from public spaces or private land used by the public, if they are likely to engage in anti-social behaviour. As a result, Public Spaces Protection Orders under Chapter 2 of the Act are used to prohibit homeless people from being in specific places and to stop them from begging.[44]

In the book *No Fixed Abode*, the journalist Maeve McClenaghan discussed how people end up homeless, and explained their interactions with state authorities. In this context, she described how some homeless people are fined and even imprisoned for begging. For instance, a man in Gloucester, UK was sent to prison because he broke the order that banned him from begging in the centre of the city. The judge hearing the case said that 'it is a persistent disobedience of court orders but I will be sending a man to prison for asking for food when he was hungry'.[45] Another person was fined £150 for begging, which was taken out of his welfare benefits. This made him poorer and pushed him closer to continuing to beg.[46] It is also important to highlight that empirical research has shown that when there is enforcement of criminal law

39 Roberts (n 6) 185.
40 See the thorough analysis of Joe Hermer, *Begging, Law and Power in Public Spaces* (Hart 2019), Chapter 4.
41 Available at <https://www.whatdotheyknow.com/request/being_an_incorrigible_rogue> accessed 12 October 2023.
42 Police, Crime, Sentencing and Courts Act 2022, section 81.
43 See Tom Wall, 'Thousands of People Arrested Under Archaic Vagrancy Act' (The Observer 2 April 2023).
44 Kevin J Brown, 'The Hyper Regulation of Public Space: The Use and Abuse of Public Spaces Protection Orders in England and Wales' (2017) 37 Legal Studies 543.
45 See Maeve McClenaghan, *No Fixed Abode – Life and Death Among the UK's Forgotten Homeless* (Picador 2020), 158.
46 ibid 159.

on begging, there is evidence that this leads to 'activity displacement', which means that people who cannot beg anymore turn to other activities that are criminalised, such as shoplifting, or sex work.[47]

Begging is associated with some of the most extreme forms of poverty but is often presented as a matter of personal choice. A standard narrative in popular press and political discourse is that people who beg engage in the activity because it is lucrative or because they are idle and prefer not to work.[48] The key reason put forward nowadays to justify the criminalisation of begging, in turn, is the protection of public order. People who beg may obstruct access to places and the authorities purport to stop this. Pedestrians may also find it uncomfortable to be faced by people who are homeless, because they may feel guilty, or may find their interactions upsetting or frustrating. Moreover, shop-owners may be concerned about the effects of homeless people on their business interests who may beg outside their shops. Finally, it may also be said that those who beg pose threats to communities by engaging in disorderly or other criminal behaviour. It is very questionable whether these allegations are supported by evidence or whether they are merely based on prejudice. Evidence suggests that sometimes people are fined simply for being offered money by passers-by.[49] However, the state's response to this social problem that is connected to poverty and disadvantage is the criminalisation of the poor and disadvantaged for the sole reason that they are in public space or because they may express their plight publicly and ask for money.

What we saw above is that people who beg are poor and homeless, and that begging is, for them, a means for survival; not a lifestyle choice. Begging is criminalised, and the authorities put forward several justifications for its criminalisation, involving the interests of people who beg, the interests of pedestrians, and the interests of shop-owners. Closer scrutiny, though, suggests that the disadvantage of people who beg is compounded by criminalising begging, while many others benefit from removing people who beg from the streets.

47 Suzanne Fitzpatrick and Sarah Johnsen, 'The Use of Enforcement to Combat "Street Culture" in England: An Ethical Approach?', (2009) 3 Ethics and Social Welfare 284, 295. See further Fitzpatrick and Johnsen, 'The Impact of Enforcement on Street Users in England' (Joseph Rowntree Foundation 2007).

48 See, for instance, 'Beggars on Streets are not Homeless, they are Fraudsters, Say Police', (Telegraph 25 February 2018).

49 McClenaghan (n 45), 158.

Punishing the poor

The justification for criminalising begging should be scrutinised closely. The criminalisation of begging can also be examined against a broader background of punitive attitudes towards people who are poor, which have also become prevalent in recent years in the context of welfare conditionality.[50] There are parallels to draw between the criminalisation of begging and the punitiveness of welfare conditionality schemes.

Welfare conditionality schemes make welfare benefits conditional upon an obligation to apply for and accept work, for otherwise, welfare claimants are punished by losing social support. Welfare conditionality schemes have become especially punitive in recent years.[51] The underlying justification for the increased punitiveness is captured in the work of scholars like Lawrence Mead, one of the main advocates of welfare conditionality in the USA and the UK, who argued that:

> [t]he poverty of today's underclass differs appreciably from poverty in the past: underclass poverty stems less from the absence of opportunity than from the inability or reluctance to take advantage of opportunity. The plight of the underclass suggests that the competence of many of the poor–their capacity to look after and take care of themselves–can no longer be taken for granted as it could in the past.[52]

On Mead's view, the problem of some people living in poverty is that they are idle and do not therefore pursue existing work opportunities, which as we saw earlier, has also been used as a justification for the criminalisation of begging. The purpose of welfare conditionality and one of the purposes of the ban on begging is to get people into work.

Against this background, in recent years, strict welfare conditionality schemes have been developed and become more punitive than in the past. Analyses of sanction reforms in several countries show that schemes

---

50 Virginia Mantouvalou, 'Welfare-to-Work, Structural Injustice and Human Rights' (2020) 83 Modern Law Review 929.

51 For a historical overview that traces the origins of welfare-to-work programmes in English Poor Laws of the seventeenth century, see Amir Paz-Fuchs, *Welfare to Work* (Oxford University Press 2008), Chapter 2, and Frances Fox Piven and Richard A Cloward, *Regulating the Poor – The Functions of Public Welfare* (2nd edn, Vintage 1993). See also Simon Deakin and Frank Wilkinson, *The Law of the Labour Market* (Oxford University Press 2005), Chapter 3. For detailed analysis of the evolution of social security and welfare conditionality in the twentieth and twenty-first century, see Michael Adler, *Cruel, Inhuman or Degrading Treatment? Benefit Sanctions in the UK* (Palgrave Macmillan 2018), Chapter 2.

52 Lawrence Mead, 'The New Politics of the New Poverty' (1991) 103 Public Interest 3, 3.

have become more coercive than they used to be.[53] Reform patterns of activation policies across Europe show that benefits are less generous, access to these has been restricted, the suitability of jobs that claimants are required to accept has been revised, the monitoring of claimants has intensified, and the obligation to accept jobs has been strengthened.[54] At the same time, people on benefits started being regularly presented in the press, policy and political discourse as 'benefit cheats'; a concept that also drove the welfare reform agenda.[55]

Such is the cruelty of the sanctions that the UK Universal Credit system has been likened to the penal system by Adler because the fines imposed at times exceed fines imposed by criminal courts, as he showed, arguing persuasively that they are deeply problematic for disciplining and managing the poor.[56] Wright, Fletcher and Stewart explained that sanctioning of welfare benefits claimants leads to their suffering.[57] They argued that suffering encompasses not only material deprivation but also the experience of domination and repression, as well as feelings of humiliation, anger and so on. Empirical research has further highlighted that sanctioned individuals tend to be disadvantaged and often homeless.[58] It has been shown that welfare conditionality schemes with harsh sanctions force people into non-standard, precarious work that they do not want to do.[59] In addition, it was shown that people are punished, not for refusing to take these jobs, 'but for being unable to do so because of poverty, homelessness and ill health'.[60] The parallels with the criminalisation of begging are obvious: the main underlying idea of the

---

53 Australia, Austria, Belgium, Canada, Denmark, Finland, France, Germany, Greece, Ireland, Italy, Japan, the Netherlands, New Zealand, Norway, Portugal, Spain, South Korea, Sweden, Switzerland, and the United Kingdom. See Carlo Knotz, 'Why Countries "Get Tough on the Work Shy": The Role of Adverse Economic Conditions' (2019) 48 Journal of Social Policy 615.

54 Daniel Seikel and Dorothee Spannagel, 'Activation and In-Work Poverty', in Henning Lohmann and Ive Marx (eds), *Handbook on In-Work Poverty* (Edward Elgar 2018) 245, 249. See also Anja Eleveld, 'The European Pillar of Social Rights and the Instrumentalization of the Right to Adequate Minimum Income Benefits' in Tania Bazzani and Reinhard Singer (eds), *Dealing with Unemployment: Labour Market Policy Trends* (Humboldt-Universität zu Berlin 2018), 95.

55 See Simon Duffy and Jonathan Wolff, 'No More Benefit Cheats' (2022) 91 Royal Institute of Philosophy Supplement 103.

56 Michael Adler, 'A New Leviathan: Benefit Sanctions in the Twenty-first Century' (2016) 43 Journal of Law and Society 195.

57 Sharon Wright, Del Roy Fletcher and Alasdair B R Stewart, 'Punitive Benefit Sanctions, Welfare Conditionality, and the Social Abuse of Unemployed People in Britain: Transforming Claimants into Offenders?' (2020) 54 Social Policy and Administration 278.

58 Kesia Reeve, 'Welfare Conditionality, Benefit Sanctions and Homelessness in the UK: Ending the "Something for Nothing Culture" or Punishing the Poor?' (2017) 25 Journal of Poverty and Social Justice 65.

59 Seikel and Spannagel (n 54); Mantouvalou (n 50).

60 Reeve (n 58) 75.

punitiveness is that people who are poor are idle, that their situation is a matter of personal choice, and that the state should punish them if they do not pursue work opportunities.

Structural injustice

Building on recent scholarship on structural injustice, in what follows I suggest that we can sharpen the diagnosis of the problem, and assess the role of the law in these situations. It was earlier said that the criminalisation of begging has at times been justified on the basis of individual responsibility. The argument is that people who beg choose this way of living because they do not want to work. However, we also observed that legal rules that purport to get people into work often compound their disadvantage, and that in fact, people who are poor find themselves in this situation because of unjust structures. Writing about responsibility for structural injustice, Iris Marion Young explained that it differs from injustice perpetuated by individuals and injustice perpetuated by the state or other powerful institutions.[61] In a much-cited passage from her influential book *Responsibility for Justice*, Young said that structural injustice:

> exists when social processes put large groups of persons under systematic threat of domination or deprivation of the means to develop and exercise their capacities, at the same time that these processes enable others to dominate or to have a wide range of opportunities for developing and exercising capacities available to them. Structural injustice is a kind of moral wrong distinct from the wrongful action of an individual agent or the repressive policies of a state. Structural injustice occurs as a consequence of many individuals and institutions acting to pursue their particular goals and interests, for the most part within the limits of accepted rules and norms.[62]

Having presented the story of Sandy, a single mother who found herself on the verge of homelessness with no identifiable agent to blame for this situation, Young explained that in instances of structural injustice, we cannot identify backward-looking responsibility. If Sandy herself or other people with whom she interacted are not responsible for her situation, could it be said that the state is responsible? Young says that the state cannot be

61 Young (n 7)45.
62 ibid 52.

blamed for the wrong that Sandy suffered, because there is no concrete law or policy in the situation she describes that directly harmed her. To support the point, Young refers to state action where there is responsibility for harm and explains that Sandy's story was different to the victims of Zimbabwe's former president, Robert Mugabe, who were evicted when he razed the shantytowns where they lived, or black and Jewish people who were forbidden from buying or renting property in the United States.[63] In examples such as these, states cause injustice to individuals and groups through direct action with intention to harm through their laws and policies. In comparison, the situation of Sandy exemplified structural injustice.

There is no question that some laws and policies cause direct harm to people. But, in the case of Sandy and in Young's view, no such laws are involved. Young acknowledged that '[s]ome laws, such as municipal zoning laws, and some policies, such as private investment policies, contribute to the structural processes that cause Sandy's plight, but none can be singled out as the major cause'.[64] On the one hand, then, she refers to laws that cause harm directly, while on the other hand, she refers to laws that might have contributed to harm, but which are not the major cause. Young does not explore the role of the law further in the case of Sandy, as this is not her focus.

Other scholars who have analysed the concept of structural injustice, though, focused on the role of powerful actors in creating or perpetuating injustice, and have paid closer attention to the role of the law. Haslanger examined structural oppression, referred specifically to laws, institutions and practices that can be oppressive,[65] and explained that policymakers sometimes intentionally adopt oppressive policies. I explained that sometimes structural injustice is state-mediated, because we can identify legislative schemes that promote aims with an appearance of legitimacy, which compound disadvantage of large numbers of people, while many benefit from this situation.[66] McKeown identified three different types of structural injustice: pure, avoidable and deliberate structural injustice. She developed her thesis to emphasise that the role of powerful agents should be central in the analyses of responsibility for structural injustice.[67] For her, pure structural injustice exists when we cannot identify a perpetrator, as this is the result of actions of many actors who

63 ibid 47.
64 ibid.
65 Sally Haslanger, *Resisting Reality* (Oxford University Press 2012), Chapter 11.
66 Mantouvalou (n 2).
67 Maeve McKeown, 'Structural Injustice' (2021) 16 Philosophy Compass 1, 4–5.

are not blameworthy and which can only be addressed through collective action. Avoidable structural injustice exists when there are powerful agents that fail to change unjust structures, even though they are able to do so. McKeown argued that homelessness, for instance, is an example of avoidable structural injustice, while Young presents it as an instance of pure structural injustice. Deliberate structural injustice is defined as a situation whereby agents are deliberately perpetuating conditions of background injustice for their benefit, while again they have power to change them. Watts-Cobbe and McMordie analysed legislation on homelessness particularly, and explained the specific role of institutions and actors for the injustice that homeless people face.[68]

The criminalisation of begging can be described as an instantiation of avoidable structural injustice. When considering the role of legal rules such as the ones that I discuss here, it is difficult to identify whether the authorities deliberately perpetuate injustice. As mentioned earlier, the authorities put forward justifications for the criminalisation of begging that have an appearance of legitimacy on a number of grounds.[69] It is an example of criminal laws that have an appearance of legitimacy but which, in reality, compound the disadvantage of some of the most excluded members in society.

In examining begging alongside other punitive attitudes towards the poor, we see that punitiveness is not an isolated instance but part of a pattern of states' responses towards those in poverty in a manner that compounds their disadvantage, while many benefit from this situation. It is well established that the machinery of criminal law is often used against people who are poor who are in this way trapped in cycles of disadvantage:[70] from poverty, to encounters with criminal justice and imprisonment, and then back into poverty, crime and precarious work. In her work, because of the way that she analysed and developed the concept of structural injustice, Young explained that there is no backward-looking responsibility to address the injustice, but that everyone with a connection to the injustice has forward-looking, political responsibility to do this.[71] However, when we identify instances where identifiable legal rules compound and perpetuate disadvantage, the state has political responsibility to change

68 Watts-Cobbe and McMordie, this volume.
69 For analysis of different justifications of the criminalisation of homelessness and begging, see Johnsen, Watts and Fitzpatrick (n 6).
70 See, for example, Jeffrey Reiman, *The Rich Get Richer and the Poor Get Prison – Ideology, Class and Criminal Justice* (John Wiley & Sons 1979); Loic Wacquant, *Punishing the Poor* (Duke University Press 2009).
71 Young describes this as the social connection model of responsibility. See Young (n 7), Chapter 4.

these legal rules. This is both forward-looking political responsibility, but also backward-looking: it is due to the role that legal rules have played in creating and perpetuating structural injustice. In what follows, I argue that state authorities may also have legal responsibility to change some of these rules when they are in breach of human rights law.

Human rights

In recent years, two regional human rights monitoring bodies, the ECtHR and the AfCtHPR, examined the compatibility of the criminalisation of begging with human rights law and raised serious questions. Can human rights law be employed to challenge some of the unjust rules and destabilise the structures that are my focus here? Before turning to this question in relation to the criminalisation of begging in particular, a few introductory remarks are due to explain the role of human rights law in this context.

Many human rights instruments at national and supranational level were not traditionally adopted to address structural oppression, exploitation and other such wrongs. Their primary purpose was to protect civil and political rights, such as the right to life and freedom of expression, following the atrocities of the Second World War. The protection of these rights was often monitored by courts and other bodies through individual petitions. Social and economic rights, such as the right to housing and the right to work, were included in separate treaties that were monitored through non-judicial mechanisms. Yet over the years, the division between civil and social rights became less watertight at supranational level and in several national legal orders. Human rights courts protected people's social and labour rights through civil and political rights documents,[72] while poverty started to be viewed as a possible ground of prohibited discrimination.[73]

72 Virginia Mantouvalou, 'Labour Rights in the European Convention on Human Rights: An Intellectual Justification for an Integrated Approach to Interpretation' (2013) 13 Human Rights Law Review 529; Keith Ewing and John Hendy, 'The Dramatic Implications of *Demir and Baykara*' (2010) 39 Industrial Law Journal 2; Tzehainesh Teklè, 'The Contribution of the ILO's International Labour Standards System to the European Court of Human Rights' Jurisprudence in the Field of Non-Discrimination' (2020) 49 Industrial Law Journal 86.

73 For examples from several jurisdictions, see Olivier de Schutter, 'A Human Rights-Based Approach to Measuring Poverty', in *Research Handbook on Human Rights and Poverty*, M F Davis, M Kjaerum and A Lyons (eds), Edward Elgar 2021, p 2 at 5 ff; Sarah Ganty, 'Poverty as Misrecognition – What Role for Antidiscrimination Law in Europe' (2021) 21 Human Rights Law Review 962; Shreya Atrey, 'The Intersectional Case of Poverty in Discrimination Law' (2018) 18 Human Rights Law Review 411; Sandra Fredman, 'Redistribution and Recognition: Reconciling Inequalities', (2007) 23 South African Journal on Human Rights 214.

Turning to the European Convention on Human Rights (ECHR) system, first, addressing issues of poverty that are my focus in this piece was not the primary purpose of the Convention when originally adopted. However, the case-law of the Court evolved over the years and addressed the responsibility of the state in relation to poverty and destitution. This occurred, for instance, in the context of Article 3 that prohibits inhuman and degrading treatment. The Court examined the question whether destitution may in certain conditions violate the provision. In *Larioshina v Russia*, it said that 'a complaint about a wholly insufficient amount of pension and other social benefits may, in principle, raise an issue under Article 3 of the Convention which prohibits inhuman and degrading treatment'.[74] In *MSS v Belgium and Greece*,[75] the Grand Chamber of the Court ruled that leaving asylum seekers in conditions of destitution and homelessness constituted a violation of Article 3, while the UK House of Lords reached a similar conclusion in *Limbuela, Tesema and Adam*.[76] According to *Limbuela*, there has to be deliberate state action that denies the satisfaction of basic needs, such as shelter or food, and this has to be of such severity as to have seriously detrimental effects or cause serious suffering.[77]

In the context of the African Union (AU), the African Charter of Human and People's Rights (ACHPR or Charter) was adopted in 1981 with one of its stated values being to eliminate colonialism.[78] It contains both rights that have typically been classified as civil and political (and hence traditionally justiciable) and economic and social (and hence traditionally non-justiciable).[79] Even though it does not contain a right to

74 *Larioshina v Russia*, App No 56869/00, Judgment of 23 April 2002.

75 *MSS v Belgium and Greece*, App No 30696/09, Grand Chamber Judgment of 21 January 2011.

76 *Regina v Secretary of State for the Home Department (Appellant), ex parte Adam (FC) (Respondent); Regina v Secretary of State for the Home Department (Appellant), ex parte Limbuela (FC) (Respondent); Regina v Secretary of State for the Home Department (Appellant), ex parte Tesema (FC) (Respondent) (Conjoined Appeals)* [2006] 1 AC 396.

77 ibid paras 7–8, per Lord Bingham.

78 See the Preamble of the Charter and Article 20(2) that provides as follows: 'Colonized or oppressed peoples shall have the right to free themselves from the bonds of domination by resorting to any means recognized by the international community.' The Charter of the African Union also has the eradication of colonialism as one of its primary purposes: Article II, 1(d). For early analyses of the Charter, see A Bolaji Akinyemi, 'The African Charter of Human and Peoples' Rights: An Overview' (1985) 46 Indian Journal of Political Science 207; B Obinna Okere, 'The Protection of Human Rights in Africa and the African Charter on Human and Peoples' Rights: A Comparative Analysis with the European and American Systems' (1984) Human Rights Quarterly 141.

79 For an overview of social rights in the African Charter, see Mashood A Baderin, 'The African Commission on Human and Peoples' Rights and the Implementation of Economic, Social, and Cultural Rights in Africa', in Mashood Baderin and Robert McCorquodale (eds), *Economic, Social and Cultural Rights in Action* (Oxford University Press 2007) 139; Manisuli Ssenyonjo, 'The Protection of Economic, Social and Cultural Rights under the African Charter', in Danwood Mzikenge Chirwa and Lilian Chenwi (eds), *The Protection of Economic, Social and Cultural Rights in Africa* (Cambridge University Press 2016), 91.

food or a right to housing, the African Commission on Human and Peoples' Rights, which was established by the Charter, has extended the Charter's scope to protect the right to food and the right to housing as components of the right to life, the right to property and the right to family life.[80] The Charter is also monitored by the AfCtHPR, the principal judicial body of the AU,[81] that provides authoritative and advisory opinions. The African human rights system contains several other human rights instruments that are well-suited to address questions of poverty.[82]

Are these mechanisms suitable to address structural problems of the kind that I discuss in this chapter? It is of course very challenging to make general empirical assessments about whether human rights law is effective in practice as this involves a variety of factors (such as different actors of the state, non-state actors, differences from one field of activity to another, as well as differences between countries and regions of the world).[83] The answer to this question will vary from one legal order to another but some general remarks can be made. First of all, human rights can serve as a diagnostic tool for injustices. Further, in relation to the ECHR in particular, which is a very influential and effective document, when there is a ruling of the ECtHR that finds a violation, respondent states do not only comply by offering an individual remedy. The effects of judgments can be broader and may include changes in laws that were at stake in the judgment and changes in state policy and practice. In any legal order, strategic litigation can have a particularly important role to play when individuals and organisations collaborate to challenge laws that impact many.[84]

Civil society organisations are 'allies of international courts' in this context, pressing for change in response to international human

80 *Social and Economic Rights Action Centre (SERAC) & Another v Nigeria* (2001) AHRLR 60 (ACHPR 2001) (SERAC).

81 The AfCtHPR was set up by virtue of Article 1 of the Protocol to the African Charter on Human and Peoples' Rights in 1998, and entered into force in 2004. See the discussion in Maria A Sanchez, 'The African Court on Human and Peoples' Rights: Forging a Jurisdictional Frontier in Post-colonial Human Rights' (2023) 19 International Journal of Law in Context 352.

82 For an overview of this regional human rights system in relation to poverty, see Bright Nkrumah, 'The Potential of the African Human Rights System in Addressing Poverty', in Ebenezer Durojaye and Gladys Mirugi-Mukundi (eds), *Exploring the Link Between Poverty and Human Rights in Africa* (Pretoria University Law Press 2020), 217.

83 See, for instance, the following books: Kathryn Sikkink, *Evidence for Hope – Making Human Rights Work in the 21st Century* (Princeton University Press 2018); Grainne de Burca, *Reframing Human Rights in a Turbulent Era* (Oxford University Press 2021).

84 On the effects of strategic human rights litigation, see Helen Duffy, *Strategic Human Rights Litigation – Understanding and Maximising Impact* (Hart 2018), Chapter 4.

rights law rulings.[85] This observation has also been made in relation to the African human rights system; particularly in relation to the role of NGOs that have an 'observer' status and can lobby for reform.[86] Legal reform can be an important step towards structural change. In addition to removing legal barriers inhibiting access to rights, findings of courts and other monitoring bodies can also inspire and influence public debate, raise awareness and motivate other actors to engage with problems that lie in the roots of the injustice.[87] Decisions or reports of non-judicial bodies may not lead to immediate legal change, and levels of compliance may be low. However, they are often used by civil society organisations campaigning for legal change, by national human rights institutions or by courts interpreting legal documents. They can therefore feed into reform processes in these and many other ways. Finally, there is of course a real concern that decisions of monitoring bodies may not go far enough in protecting people against inequality, exclusion and disadvantage. Even then, these rulings raise awareness and generate debates in academic, civil society, policy and other circles.

Criminalisation of begging as a violation of human rights law

The criminalisation of begging has concerned human rights institutions during the last few years both at supranational and at national level. It has been discussed in Reports of the UN Special Rapporteur on Extreme Poverty and Human Rights, for instance, whose role is to examine and report on the rights of those living in extreme poverty. The Special Rapporteur analysed measures that control, punish and stigmatise people living in poverty and viewed the criminalisation of begging as a violation of the principle of equality and non-discrimination.[88] The Special Rapporteur said:

> Bans on begging and vagrancy represent serious violations of the principles of equality and non-discrimination. Such measures give law enforcement officials wide discretion in their application and

85 See Filiz Kahraman, 'Activists as Allies of International Courts: Assessing the Impact of Legal Mobilization at International Courts', in Steven A Boutcher, Corey S Shdaimah and Michael W Yarbrough (eds), *Research Handbook on Law, Movements and Social Change* (Edward Elgar 2023), 211.
86 Nkrumah (n 82), 235–236.
87 See the discussion in Sally Haslanger, 'Culture and Critique' (2017) 91 Aristotelian Society Supplementary Volume 149.
88 UN Human Rights Council, *Report of the UN Special Rapporteur on Extreme Poverty and Human Rights*, Magdalena Sepúlveda Carmona, UN Doc A/66/265 (2011), paras 30–33.

increase the vulnerability of persons living in poverty to harassment and violence. They serve only to contribute to the perpetuation of discriminatory societal attitudes towards the poorest and most vulnerable.[89]

The Lacatus case

Significantly, the criminalisation of begging was examined under the European Convention on Human Rights in the important judgment *Lacatus v Switzerland.*[90] The Applicant was a Romanian national and a member of the Roma community. She was illiterate and unemployed, and did not receive welfare benefits. She begged in Geneva in order to have an income to meet her survival needs. Over a period of three years, she was fined by the police repeatedly because begging in public spaces was prohibited under Swiss criminal legislation. The fines imposed on her were of 100 CHF each time. She appealed against the fines but was unsuccessful and was required to pay 500 CHF or face five days in prison. In domestic courts, she claimed unsuccessfully that her treatment amounted to discrimination and that it violated her freedom of expression.

Before the ECtHR, *Lacatus* claimed that her treatment by the Swiss authorities violated her right to private life (Article 8 of the ECHR), her freedom of expression (Article 10 of the ECHR), and the prohibition of discrimination (Article 14 of the ECHR). The Respondent Government raised several of the usual justifications of the criminalisation of begging, including the interests of shop owners, consumers, and tourists.[91] It also argued that people who beg are often victims of human trafficking, which was presented as an additional reason why criminalisation of begging is justified.[92]

The ECtHR only examined the complaint under Article 8 of the Convention that protects the right to private life.[93] The provision has been interpreted broadly over the years, covering a number of issues,

---

89 ibid para 32.

90 *Lacatus* (n 10). For critical analysis, see Sarah Ganty, 'The Double-Edged ECtHR *Lăcătuş* Judgment on Criminalisation of Begging: *Da Mihi Elimo Sinam Propter Amorem Dei*' (2022) 3 *European Convention on Human Rights Law Review* 393.

91 ibid paras 77–79.

92 ibid para 79.

93 Article 8 provides as follows: '1. Everyone has the right to respect for his private and family life, his home and his correspondence. 2. There shall be no interference by a public authority with the exercise of this right except such as is in accordance with the law and is necessary in a democratic society in the interests of national security, public safety or the economic well-being of the country, for the prevention of disorder or crime, for the protection of health or morals, or for the protection of the rights and freedoms of others.'

including activities in public space.[94] Lacatus claimed that the prohibition of begging in public spaces, which was her only source of income since she received no welfare support, was illiterate, extremely poor and a victim of discrimination as a member of the Roma community, violated the Convention.

The ECtHR explained that Article 8 protects a broad range of activities, including activities that take place in public space. It also noted the importance of the claim as an issue of human dignity because having no means necessary for survival is an issue of dignity, and begging was the only way in which the Applicant could overcome inhuman and precarious living conditions.[95] Begging was therefore regarded as falling within the scope of Article 8(1) of the ECHR. With respect to the second paragraph of the provision that permits limitations, the ECtHR accepted that the restriction of the right to private life was prescribed by law in this instance, and was open to the argument that the prohibition of certain aspects of begging (specifically aggressive begging) may have a legitimate aim (the protection of public order and the rights of others). Having recognised that there is no consensus at European level on the matter, as Member States of the Council of Europe approach differently the issue of begging, the ECtHR pointed particularly to the fact that a number of Member States do not criminalise begging. It took into account the precarious position of the Applicant, and explained that the deprivation of her liberty would only increase her vulnerability and disadvantage.[96] The ECtHR also rejected the argument that the criminalisation of begging is justified because people who beg are victims of human trafficking. It explained that the criminalisation of victims of human trafficking is not an effective response to the problem, pointing in particular to the findings of the Group of Experts on Action against Trafficking in Human Beings, the Council of Europe specialist body on human trafficking, which had highlighted that criminalisation can only increase the precarity of people who are victims of exploitation.[97] The ECtHR further explained that making poverty less visible and attracting investment is not a legitimate aim that can be pursued through the

94 *Von Hannover v Germany* (No 2) [95]. Other examples that illustrate the broad coverage of article 8 include *Niemietz v Germany*, App No 13710/88, judgment of 16 December 1992; *Sidabras and Dziautas v Lithuania*, App Nos 55480/00 and 59330/00, judgment of 27 July 2004.
95 *Lacatus* para 56.
96 ibid para 109.
97 ibid para 112.

criminalisation of begging[98] and concluded that the blanket ban violated the Applicant's right to private life.

It was said earlier in this piece that the boundary between work and begging is not always clear. The act of begging could be conceptualised and experienced as work, according to some literature.[99] The Court did not examine the criminalisation of begging as a violation of the right to work in *Lacatus*, which would have also brought the claim within the material scope of the right to private life.[100] If aspects of street life, such as vending magazines, sex work or other such activities, are prosecuted by the authorities under laws that criminalise begging, the criminalisation of this conduct would constitute an instance of criminalising work. The Court has in the past protected access to work as an element of the right to private life in the case of *Niemietz*, where it ruled that:

> [r]espect for private life must ... comprise to a certain degree the right to establish and develop relationships with other human beings. There appears, furthermore, to be no reason of principle why this understanding of the notion of 'private life' should be taken to exclude activities of a professional or business nature since it is, after all, in the course of their working lives that the majority of people have a significant, if not the greatest, opportunity of developing relationships with the outside world.[101]

The ban on begging raises similar issues for people who, through begging, gain an income and build relationships with others. Given that begging itself can be viewed as work, and that people who beg often build and develop relationships with others when begging, the criminalisation and particularly the blanket ban could be viewed as problematic under Article 8 of the ECHR, and a disproportionate interference with the right to private life for people who have no other income or welfare support.

The Court also missed the opportunity to examine the ban on begging under the protection of freedom of expression in Article 10 of the ECHR, even though the European Roma Rights Centre intervened precisely to support this point. Given the novelty of the issue for this

98 ibid para 113.

99 See literature cited above (n 5).

100 The right to work is not explicitly protected in the ECHR, but has been read into Article 8. See Virginia Mantouvalou, 'Work and Private Life: *Sidabras and Dziautas v Lithuania*' (2005) 30 European Law Review 573.

101 *Niemietz*, above (n 94) para 29.

Court, it is unfortunate that the opportunity was not pursued.[102] Had it been used, it is hard to see how this would not be found to constitute a violation of freedom of expression. The ECtHR protects speech strongly; including speech that shocks, offends or disturbs. Statements by people who beg may be about their personal story (explaining the reasons why they are poor and homeless), but they may also be political statements, highlighting how the system has failed them. Political speech enjoys particularly strong protection in the ECHR because of its value for democracy.[103]

Bans on begging in the United States have often been ruled by courts to violate the First Amendment that protects freedom of speech, and academic scholarship has argued that free speech is affected both in relation to those who beg and in relation to the recipients of the message.[104] A federal judge who struck down a ban said insightfully:

> The First Amendment does not permit a city to cater to the preference of one group, in this case tourists or downtown shoppers, to avoid the expressive acts of others, in this case panhandlers, simply on the basis that the privileged group does not like what is being expressed.[105]

In addition, the ECtHR missed the opportunity in *Lacatus* to examine the complaint as a matter of discrimination. The rights of Roma have often been examined under the Convention, and the Court has frequently ruled that they are victims of discrimination.[106] It is well-established that the criminalisation of begging has a disproportionate negative impact on Roma and Travellers, and particularly Roma women and children.[107] The *Lacatus* case provided an opportunity to assess both the question of discrimination on the ground of poverty, and as a matter of intersectional

102 As was highlighted also in the dissenting opinions in the judgment. See also Ganty, above (n 90) 412 ff.

103 For an overview, see Council of Europe Information Document SG/Inf (2022)36, 'Freedom of Political Speech: An Imperative for Democracy' (6 October 2022).

104 For an overview of US vagrancy laws and constitutional challenges, see Risa L Goluboff and Adam Sorensen, 'United States Vagrancy Laws' (Oxford Research Encyclopedia of American History 20 December 2018). On free speech particularly, see Helen Hershkoff and Adam S Cohen, 'Begging to Differ: The First Amendment and the Right to Beg' (1991) 104 Harvard Law Review 896.

105 *McLaughlin v City of Lowell*, 140 F. Supp.3d 177 (D. Mass. 2015).

106 See the landmark *DH v the Czech Republic*, App No 57325/00, Grand Chamber Judgment of 13 November 2007.

107 Thematic report of the Committee of Experts on Roma and Traveller Issues (ADI-ROM) on legislation and policies related to begging, with special focus on children, CM(2022)194-add2-final, 1 February 2023, section 1.1.

discrimination on grounds of gender, social status and race.[108] However, the Court did not examine these issues here.[109]

Despite this, there is no question that *Lacatus* is a landmark judgment, and one that has the potential to disrupt legal rules that perpetuate injustice towards the most disadvantaged. Following *Lacatus*, Switzerland suspended the law that criminalised begging.[110] On the basis of this judgment, a further case has been brought to Strasbourg against Denmark by a Romanian national who was convicted of begging and sentenced to 20 days imprisonment.[111] Similar steps may be considered in other Council of Europe Member States – at least those that impose a blanket ban on begging. Finally, the principles of *Lacatus* should also be extended to other punitive attitudes towards the poor to which I referred earlier, and particularly to welfare sanctions that leave welfare benefit claimants destitute. Imposing harsh sanctions on people for the sole reason that they are poor and claim welfare support raises pressing questions under human rights law, as the section that follows further explains.

Vagrancy laws under the African human rights system

The criminalisation of begging was addressed by the AfCtHPR in the Advisory Opinion on the Compatibility of Vagrancy Laws with the ACHPR and other Human Rights Instruments Applicable in Africa.[112] The submission to the Court was made on behalf of a large coalition of civil society organisations that were represented by the Pan African Lawyers Union (PALU). They challenged the compatibility of vagrancy laws and by-laws that criminalise begging, homelessness and unemployment in many African countries with the ACHPR (also known as Banjul Charter), the African Charter on the Rights and Welfare of the Child, and the Protocol

---

108 Another ground that can be invoked in relation to the criminalisation of begging is disability, when a claimant is a person with a disability.

109 For an example where a Court considered intersectional discrimination, see *Mahlangu and Another v Minister of Labour and Others* (CCT306/19) [2020] ZACC 24. See the analysis in Shreya Atrey, 'Beyond Discrimination: Mahlangu and the Use of Intersectionality as a General Theory of Constitutional Interpretation' (2021) International Journal of Discrimination and the Law 168; see also Virginia Mantouvalou and Natalie Sedacca, 'The Human Rights of Domestic Workers: *Mahlangu v Ministry of Labour* and the Transformative Nature of the South African Constitution' (UK Labour Law Blog 11 December 2020).

110 See the discussion by Corina Heri, 'Beg Your Pardon!: Criminalisation of Poverty and the Human Right to Beg in *Lacatus v Switzerland*' (Strasbourg Observers 10 February 2021) available at <https://strasbourgobservers.com/2021/02/10/beg-your-pardon-criminalisation-of-poverty-and-the-human-right-to-beg-in-lacatus-v-switzerland/> accessed 12 October 2023.

111 *Dian v Denmark*, App No 44002/22, communicated on 16 January 2023.

112 Advisory Opinion, above n 10.

on the Rights of Women in Africa. The main problem with these laws, according to PALU, is that they are too vague and lead to discriminatory treatment of vulnerable individuals, that they do not criminalise conduct but people's status as 'poor', that they lead to overcrowding of prisons, and that their enforcement is contrary to principles of the rule of law, such as the presumption of innocence.

In its Advisory Opinion, the AfCtHPR found that by criminalising vagrancy, these laws punish the most underprivileged and marginalised people in society, and violate the prohibition of discrimination and the right to equality before the law,[113] the right to dignity,[114] the right to liberty,[115] the right to a fair trial,[116] freedom of movement,[117] and the protection of the family.[118]

Several aspects of the Opinion are noteworthy, but I would particularly like to highlight two points: first, the AfCtHPR accepted that the criminalisation of vagrancy is equivalent to criminalisation of *status*.[119] It was earlier said that, at times, people are arrested, fined and possibly even imprisoned for the sole reason that they sit in the streets and may be given coins, or because they beg for money in order to meet their survival needs. The Court noted that the laws in question are incompatible with the prohibition of discrimination because they criminalise individuals because of their status as vagrants, 'often defined as "any person who does not have a fixed abode nor means of subsistence, and who does not practice a trade or profession," a "suspected person or reputed thief who has no visible means of subsistence and cannot give a good account of him or herself" or "someone who loiters or is idle and who does not have a visible means of subsistence and cannot give a good account of him or herself"'.[120]

113 Articles 2 and 3 of the African Charter of Human and Peoples' Rights.
114 Article 5.
115 Article 6.
116 Article 7.
117 Article 12.
118 Article 18.
119 This aspect of the criminalisation of vagrancy has also been discussed in decisions of US courts and the relevant academic literature. See, for instance, the dissent by Justices Black and Douglas in *Edelman v California*, 344 U.S. 357 (1953); for discussion, see Forrest Lacey, 'Vagrancy and Other Crimes of Personal Condition' (1953) 66 Harvard Law Review 1203.
120 Advisory Opinion, para 69.

As a result, these laws:

> effectively, punish the poor and underprivileged, including but not limited to the homeless, the disabled, the gender-nonconforming, sex workers, hawkers, street vendors, and individuals who otherwise use public spaces to earn a living. Notably, however, individuals under such difficult circumstances are already challenged in enjoying their other rights including more specifically their socio-economic rights. Vagrancy laws, therefore, serve to exacerbate their situation by further depriving them of their right to be treated equally before the law.[121]

It is their status as poor that is criminalised, in other words, rather than conduct that is aggressive. On this matter, the Court explained that a person's status is a prohibited ground of discrimination under the Charter. It went on to say that '[i]n relation to the application of vagrancy laws, no reasonable justification exists for the distinction that the law imposes between those classified as vagrants and the rest of the population except their economic status'.[122] It explained that those categorised as vagrant often have not committed any other crime so their arrest does not contribute towards crime reduction.

A second point to highlight from the Opinion is the fact that the AfCtHPR questioned not only the implementation of the laws, but their proposed justification too. It said that:

> even if vagrancy laws contribute to the prevention of crimes in some cases, other less-restrictive measures such as offering vocational training for the unemployed and providing shelter for the homeless adults and children are readily available for dealing with the situation of persons caught by vagrancy laws.[123]

The AfCtHPR therefore posited that criminalisation is the wrong measure to address poverty and marginalisation, and emphasised that what is needed in reality is unemployment support and housing for the homeless. This statement reflects awareness that structural measures ought to be taken to support people in destitution, rather than individual measures that criminalise them. This argument has oftentimes been

121 Advisory Opinion, para 70.
122 Advisory Opinion, para 72.
123 Advisory Opinion, para 101.

made in countries that resort to criminalisation instead of adopting legal responses that support people who are in a precarious position,[124] and this recognition is important to highlight.

The Advisory Opinion was described as a major advancement of human rights in Africa, which needs to be followed up by legislative change in national legal orders.[125] It was commented that '[i]t is now incumbent upon State actors, human rights organisations, and other relevant stakeholders to push decisively for legislative, policy and administrative reforms to give effect to the Court's ruling'. This is an important point. Courts and other monitoring bodies alone cannot bring about legal and structural change. An advisory opinion particularly is not legally binding in any case, so state authorities do not have a legal duty to comply. Even when the laws are repealed, their legacy may persist, as Roberts observed in relation to other legal challenges of vagrancy laws.[126] Yet, with the support of civil society and other actors, human rights rulings can provide an important mechanism that can destabilise unjust legal structures.

Conclusion

The criminalisation of begging is an instance of state-mediated structural injustice: legal rules with an appearance of legitimacy in reality compound disadvantage and perpetuate structures of injustice. State authorities that have enacted and enforce the legislation are responsible for this situation. The state has political responsibility to change the unjust rules. It also has legal responsibility to do so on the basis of human rights law; including the right to private life, the prohibition of discrimination and freedom of expression. Decriminalising begging will not remove all structures that oppress those who are destitute, homeless and socially excluded. The reasons why individuals find themselves in this position involve a variety of factors, including their race and poverty, while many other legal rules also contribute to this situation. In addition, crucially,

124 See Virginia Mantouvalou, 'The UK Modern Slavery Act Three Years On' (2018) 81 Modern Law Review 1017.
125 Open Society Initiative for Southern Africa, 'Vagrancy laws must fall! A landmark decision by the African Court on Human and Peoples' Rights' (9 December 2020) <https://osisa.org/vagrancy-laws-must-fall-a-landmark-decision-by-the-african-court-on-human-and-peoples-rights/> accessed 12 October 2023; International Justice Resource Center, 'African Court Issues Landmark Advisory Opinion Rejecting Vagrancy Laws' (9 December 2020) <https://ijrcenter.org/2020/12/09/african-rights-court-issues-landmark-advisory-opinion-rejecting-vagrancy-laws/> accessed 12 October 2023. See also Roberts (n 6) 245–246.
126 Roberts (n 6) 227 ff.

the decriminalisation of begging does not exhaust the duties of justice that societies owe to people who are destitute, and who need meaningful welfare and other state support to live both dignified and flourishing lives. Decriminalising begging, though, can be a significant step that will remove some of the most unjust and oppressive structures.

10
Structural injustice, homelessness and the law

Beth Watts-Cobbe and Lynne McMordie

Introduction

In *Responsibility for Justice*,[1] Iris Marion Young presents homelessness as an archetypal structural injustice. In this chapter, we focus on homelessness in Great Britain (GB), its drivers and policy responses to it, to interrogate and critique Young's thinking. We begin in the next section by outlining Young's account of structural injustice, and her use of the hypothetical case of Sandy to exemplify it. Here we also place our discussion in the context of definitional debates about what circumstances count as homelessness. This sets the groundwork for our subsequent discussion of whether homelessness can reasonably be counted as a structural injustice in Young's terms. We argue that homelessness lacks three of the key features that characterise such injustices for Young, relating to the complexity of its causal drivers, the role of wrongful actions or policies in generating it, and whether it is an unintended and regretted outcome for key actors. We show that key drivers of homelessness can be isolated and identified, and that it can be understood as the foreseeable and predictable consequence (in part) of wrongful actions or policies.

This position has important consequences for Young's arguments regarding responsibility for this injustice – in backward 'blame' and forward 'task' looking senses. Reflecting the key features of structural injustices, Young sees the law as having a limited role in resolving them, endorsing a forward-looking and diffuse 'social connectedness' model of responsibility. In the final substantive section of the chapter, we show

1 Iris Marion Young, *Responsibility for Justice* (Oxford University Press 2013).

that homelessness policy in Great Britain mounts a direct challenge to this restrictive view of the law, by placing forward-looking and legally enforceable responsibility on local authorities to prevent, relieve or resolve homelessness in individual cases. Furthermore, Young's emphasis on diffusing responsibility for injustices like homelessness to society at large fails to recognise the disproportionate power that specific institutions or actors have, and ignores the risks of such a diffuse model of responsibility.

Structural injustice and homelessness

According to Young, a structural injustice is a 'particular kind of moral wrong'[2] distinct from other forms of harm or wrong that come about because of 'the wrongful action of an individual agent or the repressive policies of a state'.[3] A structural injustice exists, by contrast:

> ... when social processes put large groups of persons under systematic threat of domination or deprivation of the means to develop and exercise their capacities... Structural injustice occurs as a consequence of many individuals acting to pursue their particular goals and interests, for the most part within the limits of accepted rules and norms.[4]

A 'restrictive approach to law' follows from this account of the nature of structural injustices.[5] For Young, the fact that structural injustice arises from 'the combination of actions and interactions of a large number of public and private individuals and institutional actors'[6] means that the law has only a very limited role to play both as a generator of structural injustice, and as a resolution or effective response to it.

In making these arguments, Young ultimately seeks to argue for a particular view of who is responsible for injustice. Specifically, she seeks to depart from standard frameworks of moral and legal responsibility that assign it to particular agents based primarily on whether they can be said to be liable or at fault for causing the harm in question (the 'liability model of responsibility'). For Young, this will not do in

2 ibid 44.
3 ibid 52.
4 ibid 52.
5 Letsas, this volume.
6 Young (n 1) 52.

cases of structural injustice, as no one actor, set of actors, institution or policy can be held culpable for the injustice in question. Young instead advocates for what she calls the social connection model of responsibility, according to which:

> … all those who contribute by their actions to structural processes with some unjust outcomes share responsibility for the injustice. This responsibility is not primarily backward-looking, as the attribution of guilt or fault is, but rather primarily forward-looking. Being responsible in relation to structural injustice means that one has an obligation to join with others who share that responsibility in order to transform the structural processes to make their outcomes less unjust.[7]

Young's social connection model is in essence a call to collective action, and an attempt to motivate her audience to take shared responsibility for and engage together in resolving major social issues.

Young uses homelessness, as experienced by hypothetical Sandy, a lone mother residing in an unspecified city, as a key example in developing the idea of structural injustice. Sandy is the lone parent of two children, living in a poorly maintained apartment building which has been bought by a developer for conversion. Sandy faces eviction and begins the search for alternative accommodation. She cannot find options that she can afford within commuting distance of her work and in a neighbourhood that she feels is safe for her children. Sandy applies for a housing subsidy programme, but faces a two-year wait for financial assistance via this route. In the end, Sandy settles on a one-bedroom apartment. She intends to sleep on the sofa and her children will share the bedroom. She plans to make do with the lack of a washing machine or dryer in the flat or building and the commute that will require her to buy and run a car out of her limited income. But it is not to be: Sandy cannot fund the deposit required for the flat (her most affordable option) and so faces imminent eviction and imminent homelessness after all.

Young was writing in an American context, and in reflecting on Sandy's circumstances draws on facts about the USA (its socio-economic, regulatory and policy context, etc.), but the arguments put forward clearly seek to contribute to debates about injustice more generally. Exploring Young's ideas through the lens of other national contexts offers a fruitful

---

7 ibid 96.

means to test and critically interrogate her theory of social justice. GB is a particularly apt context within which to explore Young's ideas for two reasons. First, substantial empirical evidence is available regarding the incidence and causes of homelessness, providing a real-world counterpoint to Young's hypothetical account of Sandy's circumstances, and the conclusions she draws from it regarding responsibility for injustice. Second, it offers a policy and legal context for homelessness that is quite distinct from the USA, in particular with regard to the legal rights-based approaches to homelessness pursued across GB's devolved nations, England, Scotland and Wales.[8] It therefore offers an especially interesting context in which to consider Young's restrictive view of the law in relation to injustice.

While in the public mind, homelessness is most often associated with sleeping on the street, in this chapter, we use the term to refer to a broader set of circumstances of acute housing need in line with legal, policy and academic usage in the UK and internationally.[9] On such a view, people in a range of distinct housing circumstances are considered homeless, including those without any accommodation at all (sleeping in the streets, but also in public buildings like bus and train stations, or in cars), people living in temporary or crisis accommodation (like night shelters, hostels or refuges), and people living in severely inadequate and/or insecure accommodation (for example, people sharing with friends or family informally and with no security, living under threat of violence, squatting, or in extremely overcrowded conditions).[10] Legal responses to homeless in GB are a particular focus in this chapter, and it is therefore worth noting that the statutory definitions of homelessness in England, Wales and Scotland are also broad, counting as legally homeless those who have no accommodation available to them that it is 'reasonable' to expect them to live in together with their family.[11] Note that on such accounts, Sandy would be considered homeless *prior* to

8 While we do not consider the case of Northern Ireland here, homelessness law in Northern Ireland shares its historic routes and much of its current general form with the other UK countries. Those interested can read more here: Suzanne Fitzpatrick, Hal Pawson, Glen Bramely, Jenny Wood, Mark Stephens, Joe Frey and Lynne McMordie, 'The Homelessness Monitor: Northern Ireland 2020' (Crisis 2020).

9 Jenn Nichols, Andre Volmert, Daniel Busso, Marisa Gerstein Pineau, Moira O'Neil and Nat Kendall-Taylor, 'Reframing Homelessness in the United Kingdom' (Frameworks Institute 2018).

10 Volker Busch-Geertsema, Dennis Culhane and Suzanne Fitzpatrick 'Developing a global framework for conceptualising and measuring homelessness' (2016) 55 Habitat International 124 <https://doi.org/10.1016/j.habitatint.2016.03.004>.

11 Housing Act 1996, ss 175–176 (England); Housing (Wales) Act 2014, ss 55–56; Housing (Scotland) Act 1987, s 24.

her anticipated eviction, and indeed potentially had she accessed the one-bedroom flat she sought given the overcrowding and lack of basic facilities available.

Is homelessness a structural injustice?

Three characteristics of Sandy's situation are important for Young in counting it as an example of structural injustice:

1) that its drivers are complex and multi-faceted
2) that it is not the result of wrong or unlawful action
3) that it is not the intended outcome of any actor or set of actors.

In this section, we deploy evidence on the drivers of homelessness in the UK to critically engage with Young's claim that homelessness has these features. In doing so, we acknowledge that homelessness *is* a structural phenomenon, *in the sense that* many of the drivers of homelessness are 'structural', and that homelessness is an egregious 'injustice'. Our critique centres on whether homelessness can helpfully be considered a 'Youngian' structural injustice.

Complex and multifaceted causation

In Young's construction, Sandy's situation 'arises from the combination of actions and interactions of a large number of public and private individual and institutional actors'.[12] In other words, the drivers of Sandy's situation are complex and multi-faceted. Such an emphasis on the complexity of the causes of homelessness is common in the media and among politicians, and the charge of complexity is of course true of all real-world social phenomena outside of a controlled laboratory environment.[13] Drawing on an explanatory framework of critical realism, Bramley and Fitzpatrick argue that the idea that the causes of social phenomena are complex does not mean that they are unfathomable, with this very much the case with regards to the causal mechanisms of homelessness. Recognition of the complexity of homelessness causation should mark 'not the end but the beginning of the analytical journey', they argue, with intellectual efforts expended not on lamenting its complexity

12 Young (n 1) 52.
13 Glen Bramley and Suzanne Fitzpatrick 'Homelessness in the UK: Who is Most at Risk?' (2018). 33 Housing Studies 96.

but on understanding 'the nature of these interactions, including the relevant direction(s) of causation, and the relative dominance of different generative mechanisms'.[14]

Bramley and Fitzpatrick use representative household survey data to postulate and test the key 'generative mechanisms' driving homelessness in the UK. They demonstrate that (childhood) poverty is a powerful predictor of (adult) homelessness, and that while health and support needs and behavioural issues (like addiction) contribute to homelessness risk, such components have less explanatory power than experience of poverty. They identify social support networks (having a partner or living in a multi-adult household) as key protective components in relation to homelessness risk, though note that this protective impact is not strong enough to counter the effects of material poverty. They also find that wider contextual factors, specifically local labour and housing market contexts, impact homelessness risk, albeit that these 'area effects' are weaker than the impacts of individual and household-level variables. The authors' finding that housing market pressures have a more direct effect on homelessness than labour market conditions[15] reflects that the link between the labour market and housing status is substantially weakened in the UK by state provision of benefits, particularly housing allowances covering or contributing to the rent of low income households (albeit that the capacity of these social protections to prevent homelessness has been significantly undermined since 2010).[16]

Administrative data collected by local authorities across the UK provide further insights on the causes of homelessness. Local authorities who are obliged (see below) to assist households experiencing or at risk of homelessness ask those they assist about the immediate reasons for their situation. This data indicates the immediate triggers of people's housing crisis and how the balance of such triggers has changed over time. In England and Scotland, the most important triggers in recent years are being asked to leave current accommodation, disputes within the household, and the ending of a tenancy.[17] In England, the importance

14 ibid 98.

15 Over the longer term, labour market conditions will impact poverty levels in a locality and thus homelessness.

16 Chris O'Leary and Tom Simcock, 'Policy Failure or F***up: Homelessness and Welfare Reform in England' (2020) 37 Housing Studies 1379.

17 Beth Watts, Glen Bramley, Suzanne Fitzpatrick, Hal Pawson and Gillian Young, 'The Homelessness Monitor: Scotland 2021' (Crisis 2021); Beth Watts, Glen Bramley, Hal Pawson, Gillian Young, Suzanne Fitzpatrick and Lynne McMordie, 'The Homelessness Monitor: England 2022' (Crisis 2022).

of the ending of private rental tenancies as a trigger of homelessness has radically increased over the last decade or so,[18] reflecting the displacement of low-income tenants away from pressured housing market areas, especially in the context of less generous housing benefit levels.[19]

International evidence supports the view that poverty is a major driver of homelessness, including in the USA where Young's analysis focuses.[20] Available research indicates that countries like the USA and the UK with more challenging structural contexts (problematic housing and labour market contexts, weaker welfare safety nets) tend to see a higher prevalence of homelessness than countries with (relatively) well-functioning housing and labour markets and stronger social protections.[21] These differences in prevalence relate to differences in the profile of homeless households, with those in the former set of countries seeing a lower prevalence of complex personal problems (relating to addiction, criminality, etc) among their proportionately larger homeless population, and the latter seeing a higher proportion of complex needs among the proportionately smaller group experiencing homelessness.[22]

These sources of evidence on homelessness causation in the UK and beyond are consistent with Young's emphasis on the 'trivial truth' that its causes are complex and multi-faceted. But they also make clear that, despite this complexity, available data allows us to single out and isolate drivers of homelessness. A focus on complexity alone obscures this and leads to unwarranted pessimism regarding our ability to identify actors, sets of actors, institutional rules, norms, policies and laws that generate homelessness risk in particular contexts for particular people. By extension, to emphasise only the diffuse and shared nature

18 Suzanne Fitzpatrick, Hal Pawson, Glen Bramley, Jenny Wood, Beth Watts, Mark Stephens and Janice Blenkinsopp, 'The Homelessness Monitor: England 2019' (Crisis 2019).

19 Suzanne Fitzpatrick, Hal Pawson, Glen Bramley, Steve Wilcox, Beth Watts and Jenny Wood, 'The Homelessness Monitor: England 2018' (Crisis 2018).

20 Brendan O'Flaherty, 'Wrong Person and Wrong Place: For Homelessness, the Conjunction is What Matters' (2004) 13 Journal of Housing Economics 1 <https://doi.org/10.1016/j.jhe.2003.12.001>.

21 Mark Stephens and Suzanne Fitzpatrick, 'Welfare Regimes, Housing Systems and Homelessness: How are They Linked?' (2007) 1 *European Journal of Homelessness* 201.

22 Marybeth Shinn, 'International Homelessness: Policy, Socio-cultural, and Individual Perspectives' (2007) 63 Journal of Social Issues 657 <https://spssi.onlinelibrary.wiley.com/doi/abs/10.1111/j.1540-4560.2007.00529.x>; Paul A Toro, Carolyn J Tompsett, Sylvie Lombardo, Piere Philippot, Hilde Nachtergael, Benoit Galand, Natascha Schlienz, Nadine Stammel, Yanelia Yabar, Marc Blume, Linda MacKay and Kate Harbey, 'Homelessness in Europe and the United States: A Comparison of Prevalence and Public Opinion' (2007) 63 Journal of Social Issues 505 <https://psycnet.apa.org/record/2007-12598-003>; Lars Benjaminsen and Stefan Andrade, 'Testing a Typology of Homelessness across Welfare Regimes: Shelter use in Denmark and the USA' (2015) 30(6) Housing Studies 858; Lars Benjaminsen, 'Homelessness in a Scandinavian Welfare State: The Risk of Shelter use in the Danish Adult Population' (2016) 53 Urban Studies 2041.

of responsibility for homelessness is to leave some of the most powerful tools for addressing it packed in the policy toolbox out of arm's reach. Using the data and evidence described above, it is possible to identify both actors and policies with (partial) backward-looking responsibility for homelessness; to take action to minimise their capacity to generate homelessness in the future; *and* to identify actors, institutions, policies, and norms that have particular power to prevent, relieve or resolve homelessness in a forward-looking sense.[23] We provide specific examples in the following sections.

Not the result of wrongful action or policies

According to Young, Sandy's predicament is not the result of wrong or unlawful action, and this feature is central to her conception of structural injustices. Young explains that in Sandy's case, while some of the actors involved 'do things that are individually wrong, such as break the law, or deceive, or behave in ruthless ways toward others, many others try to be law-abiding and decent even as they try to pursue their own interests'.[24] This is problematic in the case of homelessness in two ways.

First, Young's account appears to take the current shape of policy and law as a largely fixed and exogenous component in the generation of homelessness, neither subject to change nor ethical scrutiny. This is very surprising, given that the law is patently a changing and mutable set of rules and institutions. One clear and relevant example concerns regulation of the private rented housing sector, in particular regarding security of tenure. As noted above, the ending of such tenancies is a major driver of homelessness, particularly in England, and one whose importance increased dramatically over the 2010s, reflecting an increasingly pressured housing market context and rising rents in high-demand areas, combined with the reduced generosity of welfare payments.[25] The introduction of eviction moratoria[26] during the Covid-19 pandemic years radically curtailed the ending of private rental tenancies as a generative mechanism of homelessness across Great Britain. On one key measure,[27] homelessness caused in this

23 For a similar line of argument focusing on a different example, sweatshop labour, see McKeown, this volume.
24 Young (n 1) 52.
25 Fitzpatrick (n 18).
26 Coronavirus Act 2020 (England); Coronavirus (Scotland) Act 2020 asp 7.
27 The number of applicants owed prevention or relief duties.

way reduced by 37 per cent in 2020–2021 compared to the previous year in England,[28] with radical declines in similar measures also seen in Scotland.[29] Scotland also introduced restrictions on evictions in response to the 2023 cost of living crisis.[30]

Beyond these crisis contexts, private rented sector regulation has been subject to ongoing reform across the GB nations, with many policy levers available to enhance the security of tenants and reduce their risk of eviction and homelessness.[31] These include restrictions to the grounds on which tenants can be evicted, extensions to notice periods, pre-possession action requirements on landlords, and minimum tenancy lengths.[32] Scotland and Wales have been faster to adopt reforms seeking to better protect tenants, but at the time of writing, the UK Government have just introduced the Renters (Reform) Bill to parliament, which seeks to end 'no fault' evictions in England alongside a range of other measures.[33] This example highlights that Young's idea that homelessness can be considered a structural injustice because its causes are 'lawful' fails to account for the contingent nature of the law, its different shape and contours in different jurisdictions, and shifts in relevant legal frameworks over time.

The second reason why Young's emphasis on Sandy's predicament not being the result of wrongful or unlawful action is problematic, is that it elides the distinction between legality and moral rightness/wrongness. In relation to homelessness in the UK, there are numerous examples of legal structures that are generally considered to be ethically problematic, and actions that while lawful might justifiably be considered morally questionable. Building on the private rented sector regulation example above, it is at least a matter of debate whether a landlord who decides to evict a tenant who is paying their rent and taking appropriate care of the property purely to relet it at a higher rent level is acting ethically. 'Revenge evictions', where landlords evict tenants to avoid carrying out requested repair work on the property, were, until 2015, perfectly legal in England, but it is hard to imagine

28 Watts 2022 (n 17).
29 Watts 2021 (n 17).
30 Cost of Living (Tenant Protection) (Scotland) Act. SP 2022 asp 10.
31 Tom Moore, 'The Convergence, Divergence and Changing Geography of Regulation in the UK's Private Rented Sector' (2017) 17 International Journal of Housing Policy 444.
32 Watts 2022 (n 17); Wendy Wilson, Cassie Barton and Hannah Cromarty, 'The End of "No Fault" Section 21 Evictions (England)' (Number 08658, House of Commons Library 2023).
33 The Renters (Reform) Bill 2023. HC Bill 308 2022–2023; Wilson (n 30).

an argument that could defend them as ethically permissible.[34] Other examples abound of legal structures relevant to homelessness that are widely considered to be ethically problematic, including the exclusion of most single person ('non priority') households[35] and some households deemed to have become homeless 'intentionally'[36] from the main rehousing duties imposed by homelessness law in England and Wales.

While we do not here take up the gambit of establishing the moral rightness or wrongness of these policies, we hope to have established at least that it is an open question whether they are morally permissible or justified. It is therefore far from clear to us that Sandy's hypothetical circumstances, or those of a similar household in the GB context, are not the result of wrongful actions or policies. Scrutinising and reforming laws and policies that structure Sandy's circumstances, the options available to her and the legally permitted courses of action allowed on the part of her landlord, ought to be a key focus in seeking to better address homelessness. Young's emphasis on shared forward-looking responsibility, however, risks shifting the focus away from such reform and towards more micro-individual or local-level interventions which by their very nature will impact at a smaller scale than nationwide legal reform, and may even be counterproductive or generative of additional harms (see below).

Unintended and regretted

The final feature of Sandy's homelessness important to its characterisation by Young as a structural injustice is that it is not the intended outcome of any actor(s) or policy(ies), and is moreover likely to be a source of regret to relevant stakeholders and institutions:

> Sandy's plight points to a fact that applies to many cities around the world. Too many people must pay half their income for cramped and poorly maintained housing, and too many people lack private housing altogether. *Presumably, in none of the cities is the situation the intended outcome of the actions of any persons or policies of any institution. Presumably, this is a situation that most people regret,* and some of them even take action to mitigate it, such as setting

34 Anna Clarke, Charlotte Hamilton, Michael Jones and Kathryn Muir, 'Poverty, Evictions and Forced Moves' (Joseph Rowntree Foundation 2017).
35 Housing Act 1996, s191.
36 Housing Act 1996, s191; HWA 2014 s.75(2).

> up homeless shelters or donating to them. Vulnerability to housing deprivation for large numbers of people is nevertheless a normal outcome of contemporary housing markets (emphasis added).[37]

This passage is problematic for a number of reasons. First, Young's emphasis on the city-level neglects that in most countries some, if not many or most, of the policy and legal decisions taken that influence the level and distribution of homelessness risk occur at the national level, for instance, those related to national welfare programmes and housing supply targets and funding regimes. Indeed, in the UK, the national Housing Benefit system, large (by international standards) social housing sector and statutory homelessness system (see below) are seen to be important pillars of a more protective structural context for homelessness than in, say, the USA.[38]

Second, it seems to us indisputable that in some national and city contexts, particular agents, institutions or policies do indeed intend, and not regret, housing deprivation, including homelessness, as an outcome. Landlords who choose not to maintain and complete repairs on their rented properties, and organisations that defend their right to do so, are an obvious example.[39] Perhaps a less obvious example are evictions policies and frontline staff decisions within hostels and shelters, which see people experiencing homelessness evicted or excluded with no other immediate options for shelter available.[40] While such decisions may sometimes be deemed necessary in the face of anti-social behaviour, violence or other serious rule-breaking, the homelessness that results cannot accurately be conceived of as unintended, and of course eviction and exclusion to street homelessness often occur for more minor infringements, where an argument of necessity holds limited, if any, weight.[41]

Third, where actors and institutions really do not intend homelessness and housing deprivation as an outcome, this does not mean they have done what might reasonably have been expected to prevent it. If we understand the generative mechanisms driving homelessness *and*

37 Young (n 1) 64.

38 Suzanne Fitzpatrick, Hal Pawson, Glen Bramley and Steve Wilcox, 'The Homelessness Monitor: England 2011' (Crisis 2011).

39 Clarke (n 34).

40 Lynne McMordie, 'Avoidance Strategies: Stress, Appraisal and Coping in Hostel Accommodation' (2021) 36 Housing Studies 380; Beth Watts, Lynne McMordie, Melisa Espinoza, Dora Welker and Sarah Johnsen, 'Greater Manchester's A Bed Every Night Programme: An Independent Evaluation' (Full Report, Heriot-Watt University 2021).

41 McMordie (n 40).

the components that work to prevent its actualisation, then its occurrence can be understood and foreseen, perhaps not always in each individual case but certainly in terms of the level of homelessness risk faced by particular groups.[42] One clear UK example of policy that is demonstrably linked to homelessness, yet continuously pursued by Westminster governments since 2010, relates to Local Housing Allowance (LHA) rates – the mechanism for calculating the maximum housing benefit entitlement for low-income households who are renting privately. Since 2011, stringent caps on the levels of LHA that can be claimed[43] and the freezing of LHA rates[44] despite rising market rent levels have led to increasing gaps between the rent tenants on Housing Benefit must pay and the levels of benefit to which they are entitled.[45] Restoring LHA levels to cover actual rents has been put forward as a key policy move to help prevent homelessness but one that has not been pursued. Indeed, LHA levels were refrozen from Autumn 2022 despite the serious cost of living crisis. At best, we can understand the position of political leaders and policymakers here as one of wilful ignorance or thoughtlessness. Young's emphasis on intention neglects this dynamic of key actors failing to seek out or turning a blind eye to clear evidence that certain policy decisions and/or the failure to invest in demonstrably effective interventions to prevent it are likely to lead to increases in homelessness. Housing deprivation and homelessness as a result of these policies may not have been explicitly intended, but was foreseeable and preventable. Whether or not this outcome is regretted is, in our view, irrelevant to the moral equation in the context of clear responsibility for its occurrence.

Responsibility for structural injustice

In the previous sections we have shown that homelessness as experienced in the UK does not fit particularly well with the characteristics Young sees as central to structural injustices. While the drivers of homelessness are indeed complex, this complexity does not prevent the specification of distinct generative mechanisms and the actors implicated in them. Nor can we straightforwardly reject the idea that homelessness is the outcome of policies, laws and actions that cannot be considered 'wrong' or 'bad'. We have seen that some specific aspects of law can be identified that are

42 Bramley (n 13).
43 Housing Benefit and Council Tax Benefit Circular S1/2011.
44 For four years from 2016, and then again in 2023–2024.
45 Jasmine Basran, 'Restoring Local Housing Allowance Rates to Prevent Homelessness' (Crisis 2019).

profoundly ethically problematic and operate as generative mechanisms that reliably actualise homelessness in particular contexts. It is also far from clear that homelessness is the 'unintended outcome' of policies or actions, or rather it is not clear that it being an unintended outcome gets key actors 'off the hook' morally speaking. Our perspective diverges from Young's not only in seeing aspects of the law as implicated in generating homelessness, but also in preventing and resolving it.

In this section, we challenge Young's restrictive view of the role of law in resolving homelessness, by positing homelessness legislation across the GB nations as playing a central role in addressing it. We also consider where legal responsibility for homelessness might best be placed. Having rehabilitated the law as playing a central role in responding to homelessness, we close this section by highlighting the risks of relying on diffuse social responsibility for key injustices, as Young encourages us to.

Homelessness legislation in GB

The foundations of current homelessness law in England, Scotland and Wales lie in the Housing (Homeless Persons) Act, 1977, which imposed enforceable duties on local authorities across GB to provide advice and substantive help, including accommodation, to people facing homelessness. Its provisions were subsequently incorporated into separate legislation in England, Wales[46] and Scotland,[47] and the devolution of housing and homelessness-related powers to these jurisdictions means that the specific shape and nature of homelessness law and local authorities' duties now diverges significantly between them. This being said, the legal frameworks hold in common some key features pertinent to our exploration of Young's ideas on structural injustice.

First, the legal duties placed upon local authorities by the 1977 Act and subsequent legislation are specific and clear enough to give individuals to whom those duties are owed legal recourse where authorities fail to meet them.[48] In other words, these duties create legally enforceable 'rights' on the part of people experiencing homelessness. Such black letter rights to assistance for people facing homelessness

46 Part 7 of the Housing Act 1996.

47 Housing (Scotland) Act 1987.

48 Suzanne Fitzpatrick and Liz Davies, 'The "Ideal" Homelessness Law: Balancing "Rights Centred" and "Professional-centred" Social Policy' (2021) 43 Journal of Social Welfare and Family Law 175.

are highly unusual internationally, where charitable, faith-based and discretionary approaches predominate.[49]

Second, as discussed above, these legal frameworks provide definitions of 'homelessness' that are extremely wide, extending far beyond narrow or minimalist definitions covering only street homelessness to include people living in accommodation that it is not 'reasonable' to expect them to live in, for example, due to overcrowding or experiencing domestic abuse within the home. The group owed assistance under this legislation is also broad in the sense that those at clear and imminent *risk* of homelessness are entitled to help, as well as those already actually experiencing it.[50]

Third, the main rehousing entitlement under homelessness legislation in England, Scotland and Wales is to *settled* accommodation (and suitable temporary accommodation while it is secured). In a few European states and New York City, there is a right to *emergency* shelter, but in the GB context, the entitlement for households qualifying for the main rehousing duty is to settled accommodation, usually in the form of a secure social housing tenancy.

Fourth and finally, entitlements to accommodation under homelessness legislation have historically been conditional on specific criteria, these being whether the household is in 'priority need',[51] meaning whether it includes children or individuals who pass a very strict 'vulnerability' test, and whether they are deemed to have become homeless 'intentionally',[52] i.e. are culpable for their own homelessness. Only households deemed to be in priority need and unintentionally homeless were traditionally entitled to the main rehousing duty, and these filtering devices meant that thousands of single person (or couple) households were excluded from the entitlements originally introduced by the homelessness legislation. However, over the last two decades, legal reforms have reduced – sometimes incrementally and sometimes dramatically – the reach of these rationing criteria and extended substantive entitlements

---

49 Suzanne Fitzpatrick, Volker Busch-Geertsema, Beth Watts, Jenny Wood, Marie-Therese Haj Ahmad and Jill McIntyre, 'Ending Street Homelessness in Vanguard Cities Across the Globe: An International Comparative Study' (Heriot-Watt University 2022); Suzanne Fitzpatrick and Mark Stephens, 'Homelessness, Need and Desert in the Allocation of Council Housing' (1999) 14 Housing Studies 413.

50 Fitzpatrick (n 48).

51 Housing Act 1996, s189(1) and Homelessness (Priority Need for Accommodation) (England) Order 2002, SI 2002/2051; Housing (Wales) Act 2014, s70; Housing (Scotland) Act 1987, s25, now repealed.

52 Housing Act 1996, s191; Housing (Wales) Act 2014, s77; Housing (Scotland) Act 1987, s26.

to accommodation to much wider groups.[53] Indeed, as it stands, virtually all homeless households in England, Scotland and Wales have substantial entitlements to help from local authorities in preventing, relieving and/or resolving their homelessness. In Scotland, this mainly reflects the abolition of the 'priority need' criterion from 2012,[54] whereas in England and Wales, it reflects the introduction of priority need and intentionality blind 'prevention and relief' duties.[55]

So what is the relevance of GB homelessness law to Young's arguments regarding structural injustices and who is responsible for them? The duties placed upon local authorities across GB in responding to homelessness highlight an option for who might be deemed responsible for injustices, one that we would argue is not given the space it deserves by Young. The placing of these legal duties on local authorities accords with the Youngian (and others)[56] view that we should be willing to separate backward-looking (or 'blame') responsibility from forward-looking (or 'task') responsibility. In the vast majority of cases, local authority housing departments are not responsible for causing the homelessness they are tasked to prevent, relieve or resolve.[57] But unlinking these forms of responsibility does not mean we have to embrace a diffuse, shared 'social connection' model of responsibility as Young would like us to. Instead, the public policy choice can be to make an institution responsible for homelessness that it is not directly culpable for, but is well placed – and can be resourced – to prevent, resolve or ameliorate it. How and in what circumstances the relevant institution must respond can be, and *is* in the GB case, clearly laid out in law, monitored via administrative statistics, and subject to ongoing review, evaluation and legal reform. The impact of the law in addressing the injustice of homelessness can be changed, quite

53 The key acts being: Housing (Scotland) Act 2001; the Homelessness Etc. (Scotland) Act 2003; the Housing (Wales) Act 2014; and Homelessness Reduction Act 2017 (England).

54 Via the Homelessness Etc. (Scotland) Act 2003.

55 Via the Housing (Wales) Act 2014; and Homelessness Reduction Act 2017 (England); Beth Watts, Glen Bramley, Suzanne Fitzpatrick, Lynne McMordie, Hal Pawson and Gillian Young, 'The Homelessness Monitor: Great Britain 2022' (Crisis 2022).

56 Robert E Goodin and Christian Barry, 'Responsibility for Structural Injustice: A Third Thought' (2021) 20/4 Politics, Philosophy and Economics 339; Peter King, 'What do we Mean by Responsibility? The Case of UK Housing Benefit Reform' (2006) 21(2) Journal of Housing and the Built Environment 111.

57 This might be the case in specific circumstances where someone in council housing is evicted, and then owed the rehousing duty by the same authority that initiated eviction proceedings against them. Intentional homelessness provisions might break the link between the local authority's responsibility for the household's homelessness and their responsibility to resolve it, on the basis that the household themselves are responsible for behaving in a way that brought about their eviction; for example, by engaging in anti-social behaviour or not paying their rent when it is deemed they could have done.

transparently and purposefully, by amending, for example, the definition of homelessness that is employed, the nature of the entitlements afforded, and the qualifying criteria that deter those entitlements.

Administrative homelessness statistics show the scale of impacts of these legal frameworks in practice. In England, for example, in 2020–2021, just over 21,000 homeless households accepted a tenancy offer made to them because they were owed the 'main rehousing duty' by their local authority, with a further 69,000 households having accommodation secured for them under local authority 'prevention duties' and 66,000 under local authority 'relief' duties.[58] Similarly, in Scotland and Wales, tens of thousands of households every year are assisted into accommodation (or to maintain existing accommodation that was at risk) by virtue of their entitlements under homelessness law. Tens of thousands more households across GB are temporarily accommodated by local authorities while awaiting a settled housing offer. Evaluations of these legal frameworks demonstrate their positive impacts, while not shying away from their limitations and scope for further improvements. A 2012 article reporting findings from a survey of 2,500 respondents who had been assisted under English homelessness law concluded that:

> ... there appeared to be significant net improvements in the quality of life of homeless families after they had received assistance ... Given their overall social and economic disadvantage, this can be viewed as contributing to an important welfare gain. While the largest net improvement was reported by those families who had moved into settled housing, even those still in temporary accommodation (most of it self-contained) tended to report a higher quality of life than when they were living in their 'last settled accommodation'. The explanation seems to be the statutory system's capacity to not only protect low-income families from 'literal homelessness', but also to move them from stressful personal and accommodation circumstances into more appropriate housing environments.[59]

Research examining legal reforms that have extended and strengthened the original 1977 Act has also drawn positive conclusions, in particular regarding the shift towards efforts to prevent homelessness occurring in the first place and moves to enfranchise single people to benefit from

58 Watts 2022 (n 17).

59 Suzanne Fitzpatrick and Nicholas Pleace, 'The Statutory Homelessness System in England: A Fair and Effective Rights-based Model?' (2012) 27 Housing Studies 232, 247.

rehousing duties as well as families.[60] For those awaiting settled rehousing and with no alternative, temporary accommodation can offer safe harbour and stability, particularly when of decent quality and self-contained, the most common form of temporary accommodation provided in Scotland.[61] More generally, providing housing assistance as of right, rather than on a discretionary basis, has been shown to benefit those effected by empowering them as 'rights holders' rather than supplicating them as grateful beneficiaries of state or charitable largesse.[62]

Statutory homelessness legislation across GB thus offers substantial substantive help to hundreds of thousands of households every year, help that cannot lawfully be refused due to lack of funds, the political inclinations of incumbent local officials, the vagaries of the housing market, or the interests and motives of volunteers or churches, as we see in other countries' responses to homelessness.[63] To be sure, the statutory homeless frameworks in operation across GB have their weaknesses and limitations. The Homelessness Reduction Act (2017), which prescribes the duties of English local authorities to homeless households, radically extended the assistance owed to single homeless households, who largely missed out on substantive assistance to find or access accommodation before it came into force. But gaps in the legal framework mean that in 2020–2021, over 22,000 homeless households were deemed not to be in priority need or to be homeless intentionally and thus not owed the main rehousing duty. In addition, the poor quality and unsuitability of some temporary accommodation placements; especially in higher demand areas like London,[64] and the negative impacts of stays in temporary

60 A Ahmed, M Wilding, A Gibbons, K Jones and I Madoc-Jones, 'Post-implementation Evaluation of Part 2 of the Housing Act (Wales) 2014: Final Report' (GSR report number 46/2018, Welsh Government, 2018); Peter Mackie, Tim Gray, Caroline Hughes, Iolo Madoc-Jones, Victoria Mousteri, Hal Pawson, Nick Spyropoulos, Tamsin Stirling, Helen Taylor and Beth Watts, 'Review of Priority Need in Wales' (GSR report number 70/2020, Welsh Government 2019); ICF with Kantar Public and Heriot-Watt University, 'Evaluation of the Implementation of the Homelessness Reduction Act: Final Report (Ministry of Housing, Communities and Local Government 2020).

61 Beth Watts, Mandy Littlewood, Janice Blenkinsopp and Fiona Jackson, 'Temporary Accommodation in Scotland: Final Report' (Social Bite 2018); Beth Watts and Janice Blenkinsopp, 'Valuing Control over One's Immediate Living Environment: How Homelessness Responses Corrode Capabilities' (2022) 39 Housing, Theory and Society 98.

62 Beth Watts, 'Homelessness, Empowerment and Self-reliance in Scotland and Ireland: The Impact of Legal Rights to Housing for Homeless People' (2014) 43 Journal of Social Policy 793.

63 Fitzpatrick (n 48).

64 Human Rights Watch, '"I Want Us to Live Like Humans Again" Families in Temporary Accommodation in London' (Human Rights Watch 2022); Paul Hackett and Maura Farrelly, 'Temporary Accommodation at Crisis Point: Frontline Perspectives from London and Greater Manchester' (The Smith Institute 2022).

accommodation are well-documented.[65] Finally, despite the uniquely generous and enforceable legal rights owed to homeless households across GB, and further improvements to responses during the Covid-19 pandemic, some individuals continue to experience the most extreme form of homelessness, i.e. rough sleeping. This is even the case in Scotland, where protections for single people experiencing homelessness are (arguably) strongest,[66] though levels of rough sleeping reached historic lows, approaching zero in major cities, during the pandemic.[67]

Acknowledging these weaknesses and limitations in many cases simply underlines the broad thrust of our argument that the law is a fundamentally important component in preventing and resolving homelessness, as many (though not all) of these issues can and in some jurisdictions are being addressed via further legal reform. The policy and legal innovation and 'leap-frogging' seen across the GB nations since the devolution of housing and homelessness powers to Wales and Scotland over the last quarter century show the potential for ongoing reforms that further strengthen these legal entitlements, improve associated outcomes, and minimise their unintended consequences. In Wales, gaps in support to households considered non priority-need are now to be addressed by the phasing out of the priority need criterion.[68] In Scotland, reforms are in progress to strengthen the prevention of homelessness.[69] At a more theoretical level, Fitzpatrick and Davies have analysed homelessness law across GB in order to sketch what they see as 'the 'ideal' homelessness law', with a key focus on strengthening the aspects of current law that seek to prevent, rather than respond to homelessness.[70]

Locating responsibility for homelessness

The previous section made the point that GB homelessness law tasks local authorities with addressing homelessness, even though they are not directly culpable for it in the vast majority of cases, thus breaking the link between liability and responsibility, as Young argues is necessary. This raises the question of whether local authority housing departments are

65 Watts 2018 (n 61); Suzanne Fitzpatrick, Glen Bramley, Lynne McMordie, Hal Pawson, Beth Watts-Cobbe and Gillian Young, 'The Homelessness Monitor: England 2023' (Crisis 2023).
66 Beth Watts, Glen Bramley, Suzanne Fitzpatrick, Lynne McMordie, Hal Pawson and Gillian Young, 'The Homelessness Monitor: Great Britain 2022' (Crisis 2022).
67 Watts 2021 (n 17).
68 Watts (n 66).
69 Watts 2021 (n 17).
70 Fitzpatrick (n 48).

the most efficacious place to locate this responsibility, and whether there might be alternative or additional loci of such responsibility.

Research on homelessness and severe and multiple deprivation has made clear that far from being 'hard to reach', people experiencing homelessness interact with the state and institutions on multiple and repeated occasions over the life course, in the run up to an episode of homelessness and while experiencing it.[71] It is increasingly recognised that these 'touch points' are intervention opportunities that have, to date, been insufficiently recognised in efforts to prevent and respond to homelessness. Analysis of health and homelessness-related administrative data in Scotland has clearly shown that health service utilisation increases preceding an episode of homelessness.[72] Health and social care professionals may therefore be well placed to pick up on homelessness risk, particularly where social care or social services staff provide support within a person's home, but those working outside the home – such as GPs – may also be able to identify homelessness risk where patients present with symptoms linked to housing distress or increased risk of homelessness. So, too, teachers and other educational professionals may pick up on young people's housing insecurity,[73] while local authority council tax departments or even private utility companies may be able to signal homelessness risk when households fall into arrears on their bills.[74] In light of this, some have argued that local authority housing departments are unfairly left singularly 'carrying the can' for homelessness, when responsibility should actually be extended more widely across public bodies.[75]

These kinds of insights have driven legal reforms in GB. In England, various public bodies are now under a duty to refer households they consider at risk of homelessness to their local authority, and in Wales these duties go further, to require cooperation on the part of some public authorities in responding to homelessness.[76]

---

71 Glen Bramley, Suzanne Fitzpatrick, Jenny Wood, Filio Sosenko, Janice Blenkinsopp, Mandy Littlewood, Claire Frew, Toriqul Bashar, Jill McIntyre and Sarah Johnsen, 'Hard Edges Scotland' (Lankelly Chase 2019); Andrew Waugh, Auren Clarke, Josie Knowles and David Rowley, 'Health and Homelessness in Scotland' (Scottish Government Social Research 2018).

72 Waugh (n 71).

73 Beth Watts, Sarah Johnsen and Filip Sosenko, 'Youth Homelessness in the UK: A Review for The OVO Foundation' (Heriot-Watt University 2015).

74 Beth Watts, Glen Bramley, Janice Blenkinsopp and Jill McIntyre, 'Homelessness Prevention in Newcastle: Examining the Role of the "Local State" in the Context of Austerity and Welfare Reforms' (Heriot-Watt University 2019).

75 Bramley (n 71).

76 Fitzpatrick (n 48).

In Scotland, legal reforms currently in train will go furthest in sharing responsibility for identifying homelessness risk, preventing it from occurring, and addressing it when it does.[77] The relevance of these developments to Young's arguments regarding structural injustice, is to underline the wide range of policy options available in terms of assigning forward-looking 'task' responsibility for homelessness, and the ways such responsibility can be *strategically* expanded to precise institutions and actors, linked to their capacity to effectively address homelessness in particular ways. These developments also show that far from the law playing only a limited role in addressing the injustice of homelessness, in the British context, legal developments can drive forward the opening of new fronts in society's ability to effectively respond to homelessness.

The risks of diffuse responsibility

We have argued that Young's emphasis on diffused, forward-looking responsibility for the social injustice of homelessness may be unhelpful to understanding and addressing its causes. But an emphasis on diffuse responsibility that calls everyone to take responsibility for tackling homelessness has wider and more insidious weaknesses. Evidence shows that public understanding of homelessness is often limited, with individualism and personal responsibility tending to dominate in thinking around its causes, and rough sleeping often taken as its only legitimate form.[78] While many feel that they have a personal responsibility to respond to homelessness, understandings that frame the phenomenon as both inevitable and intractable remain strong,[79] and thus the public's sense of what works, and for whom can tend toward ameliorative responses and subsistence provisions that are not only ineffective, but sometimes actively generative of harm.[80] All manner

77 Crisis, 'Preventing Homelessness in Scotland: Recommendations for Legal Duties to Prevent Homelessness: A Report from the Prevention Review Group' (Crisis 2021).
78 Crisis, 'Framing Homelessness Project: Public Attitudes Tracking Wave Three Debrief' (Crisis 2022); Nichols (n 7); Moira O'Neil, Marisa Gerstein Pineau, Nat Kendall-Taylor, Andrew Volmert and Allison Stevens, 'Finding a Better Frame: How to Create More Effective Messages on Homelessness in the United Kingdom' (Frameworks Institute 2017).
79 Crisis (n 78).
80 Ciara Keenan, Sarah Miller, Jennifer Hanratty, Terri Pigott, Jayne Hamilton, Christopher Coughlan, Peter Mackie, Suzanne Fitzpatrick and John Cowman, 'Accommodation-based Interventions for Individuals Experiencing, or at Risk of Experiencing, Homelessness: A Network Meta-analysis' (The Campbell Collaboration 2021).

of novel interventions, from crisp-packet sleeping bags[81] to mobile bathing facilities[82] and even wheelie bin sleeping pods,[83] can draw attention and funding away from more effective, evidence-driven and housing-led responses that work to prevent homelessness and resolve it where it occurs, while doing little to support much-needed shifts in public attitudes toward homelessness. It is also extremely challenging to hold individual volunteers, charitable organisations and faith-groups to account for their ineffective or harmful responses. Weaknesses in national statutory homelessness laws, by contrast, can be subject to rigorous measurement, evaluation, review and challenge through local and national democratic processes, as well as via legal challenge through the courts.

Conclusion

Young's account of the causation of homelessness and housing deprivation not only denies the possibility of clearly identifying the generative mechanisms of this social injustice, but also obscures the actors and institutions best placed and resourced to prevent the activation of these mechanisms, and thus their actualisation in experiences of homelessness and housing crisis. Instead, Young insists that the causes of homelessness are so complex as to be unfathomable and responsibility best arbitrarily diffused across an indeterminate collective. This approach lends itself to a muddle of well-meaning but often weak and sometimes counterproductive actions of a plethora of actors, the vast majority of whom do not have the power to manage and transform the generative mechanisms of social phenomena in the way that powerful actors – and crucially legislators and incumbent governments – do. In neglecting the vital role that the law can – and in the case of England, Scotland and Wales *does* – play in moulding the generative mechanisms of homelessness, Young's approach to the injustice of homelessness is decidedly anti-preventative, and problematically oriented towards amelioration. The GB case shows how the law can be moulded and reformed to both mitigate homelessness risk in the first place, and also to respond effectively to it when it does

81 'If you have Nothing, This is Something' (*Crisp Packet Project*) <https://crisppacketproject.com/> accessed 10 January 2023.
82 Cameron Parsell and Beth Watts, 'Charity and Justice: A Reflection on New Forms of Homelessness Provision in Australia' (2017) 11 European Journal of Homelessness 65.
83 Alex Spencer, 'Entrepreneur Peter Dawe Creates "Sleeping bin" for the Homeless' (*Cambridge Independent*, 29 January 2020) <https://www.cambridgeindependent.co.uk/news/entrepreneur-peter-dawe-creates-sleeping-bin-for-the-homeless-9097878/> accessed 25 August 2023.

occur, and thus reveals it as a powerful, evolving and accountable tool in tackling structural injustice.

It is beyond the scope of our argument to critique Young's account of structural injustice in its entirety, or its application to other empirical phenomenon beyond that of homelessness. We agree wholeheartedly with Young that people's lives are profoundly affected by the social structures in which they live, through no fault of their own, and that remedying these injustices is a moral imperative and a marker of a just society. Our problematisation of Young's argument in the light of the reality of homelessness in England, Scotland and Wales nevertheless suggests that her characterisation of the key features of such injustice needs further refinement by those taking forward her legacy. Our analysis also suggests an important ongoing agenda for scholars interested in the intersection of social science and political philosophy, this being to ensure that the development of concepts and theories within political philosophy make appropriate use of relevant empirical evidence on the nature and drivers of the social injustices under the spotlight, and existing legal and public policy responses to them, in a diversity of international contexts.

11

Structural injustice and the regulatory public body landscape

Jude Browne

Introduction

Legal wrongdoing is not, in and of itself, a cause of structural injustice according to Iris Marion Young, whose work first popularised the concept of structural injustice.[1] However, law and governmental policy, as central features of how societies and states are shaped and operate, are inevitably entrenched in the background conditions of structural injustice which, as I shall explain, is where we might have the greatest impact in effecting structural change. As a method for addressing structural injustice, Young was sceptical of the state's capabilities. However, the following account is my interpretation of how her scholarship, in conversation with the work of others, helps us to think through that very problem nevertheless.

Structural injustice

We tend to think of injustice as grounded in blame, culpability, guilt and fault.[2] Such 'fault-based injustices' are either legal wrongs or the sort of moral wrong that transgresses the acceptable norms of a given context or society. While fault-based injustices can be direct, indirect, intentional or unintentional forms of liability, there is always an identifiable agent whose

1 Iris Marion Young, *Responsibility for Justice* (Oxford University Press 2011).

2 My interpretation of Young's account of structural injustice focuses on a particular feature that I suggest is mostly overlooked in the literature – that of the untraceability of structural injustice. I suggest that this is a defining feature of structural injustice in Young's work with important political implications (for a detailed discussion, see Jude Browne, *Political Responsibility and Tech Governance* (Cambridge University Press 2024).

actions can be readily traced to a particular injustice. However, fault-based injustice is not the appropriate way of understanding structural injustice.[3] Rather than by traceable acts of wrongdoing (whether legal or moral), structural injustice is generated by a vast array of structural processes that emanate from the accumulated, multitudinous 'everyday' actions of individuals, groups and institutions operating 'within given institutional rules and accepted norms'.[4] These processes are so convoluted that they are not meaningfully traceable to any particular agent or agents but nevertheless act as the background conditions to structural injustice. They are generated by masses of relations of social position that accumulatively shape the opportunities and life prospects, including both material and social resources, of everyone in those positions and are inherently intersectional.[5] Critics of Young's work worry that to define structural injustice as 'beyond blame' is to let 'off the hook' of responsibility for structural injustices, those who merely stand back from injustice, or those who are protected by ignorance or privilege (not least through the law).[6] However, I see Young's argument as attempting to deliver quite the opposite – the requirement to take up responsibility for a much broader set of injustices than those only readily traceable to individual, group or institutional liability.

At the centre of Young's account, is what she calls 'political responsibility' for addressing structural injustice. This form of responsibility is distinct from individuals, groups or institutions abiding by laws or aligning with moral norms in a given context.[7] Rather, political responsibility requires collective public engagement in macro-level reform aimed at changing the background conditions of structural injustice. This requires taking up a structural point of view which:

> ... not only understand[s] the social constraints and opportunities people confront as objective facts. It also means taking a broad macro point of view on the society that identifies its major social

3 Young (n 1).
4 ibid 53.
5 Young acknowledges the work of many others such as Jean-Paul Sartre, *Critique of Dialectical Reason* (tr Alan Sheridan-Smith, New Left Books 1976); Pierre Bourdieu, *Distinction: A Social Critique of the Judgement of Taste* (tr Richard Nice, Harvard University Press 1984); Christopher Kutz, *Complicity: Ethics and Law for a Collective Age* (Cambridge University Press 2000); William H Sewell, *Logics of History: Social Theory and Social Transformations* (University of Chicago Press 2005).
6 Martha Nusbaum, 'Foreword' in Young (n 1); Michael Goodhart, *Injustice: Political Theory for the Real World* (Oxford University Press 2018).
7 Young (n 1) 98.

positions – general categories that define these constraints and opportunities – and how these positions relate to one another systematically.[8]

We might assume that membership of a particular political community would render individuals, groups and institutions responsible for any sort of injustice that operates within their particular community. However, Young argues that what motivates political responsibility (in fact, as with guilt-based responsibility) is *action*; 'it is a mystification to say that people bear responsibility simply because they are members of a political community, and not because of anything at all that they have done or not done'.[9] On Young's view, everyone who is connected in virtue of their *contributions* to the background conditions of structural injustice is responsible, not by having traceably caused or intended injustice, but because they have acted in ways that have accumulatively contributed to the macro-level processes that enable structural injustice through their participation in the seemingly neutral activities of everyday life. Young calls her approach 'the social connection model of responsibility' and sees it as an alternative to the liability-based model of responsibility grounded in the legal and moral duties motivated by traceable fault-based injustice.[10] To be clear, Young sees these two different forms of injustice and their respectively corresponding forms of responsibility as closely co-existing and equally important.

At play within the background conditions of any structurally unjust outcome are the macro effects of general economic, cultural, political and social dynamics layered through with billions of individual, group and institutional actions, habits and expressed beliefs. I have suggested elsewhere that it is helpful to understand structural injustice as the consequence of 'structural actions' that are to be found among legally and morally accepted pursuits of private interest in a given context (i.e. those which cannot be identified as liability-based).[11] This clarification helps us to draw the distinction between, on the one hand, actions that render individuals and institutions liable for direct or indirect wrongdoing (either legal or moral fault) and on the other hand, those 'legitimate' pursuits of private interest (acceptable habits, expressed beliefs, actions) which, in a convoluted, untraceable way, contribute to the conditions that serve as the

8 ibid 56.
9 ibid 80.
10 ibid 110.
11 Browne (n 2). This account inevitably relies on some degree of relativity across different societies and different individuals who will judge liability and structural injustices differently according to their legal and moral norms.

background conditions of structurally harmful outcomes. Inevitably, both structural and liability-based injustices will be closely imbricated and often very difficult to disentangle. However, drawing a distinction is important in order to acknowledge a much greater set of injustices than those grounded in liability and also to ensure that political responses to injustice are not limited to tracing liability. To take one recent example, we could say that Amazon's infamous recruitment algorithm that was found to discriminate against women was morally wrong even though it was trained on big data that merely reflected human bias. This is a question of liability (although not necessarily a straightforward one).[12] However, the bigger structural question is why are so many of us increasingly dependent on artificial intelligence to make decisions for us that we do not, and in many cases never will, understand?

Young does not see the responsibility to address structural injustice as a duty because such a relationship requires a direct traceable link between an agent and a particular injustice (as with the duty not to break the law nor be negligent, for example).[13] Rather, she views the responsibility to address the background conditions of structural injustice as a discretionary responsibility. On the basis that we are all invariably connected to vast amounts of background conditions to structural injustice, I find the idea of an 'imperfect responsibility' whereby individuals *do whatever they can,* rather than attempting to trace a defined set of duties, is a compelling and practicable way of thinking about the responsibility to act against structural injustice.[14]

Young's social connection model of responsibility sought to explain the counterintuitive question of why responsibility lay with those who were not readily traceable to a given structural injustice.[15] This is a difficult political challenge, not least because the state's legal systems

12 Amazon abandoned its algorithm for recruitment after failing to find a way to amend its bias against women. Like any other algorithm, it was trained to observe patterns in large data sets as a way of predicting outcomes. As Jeffrey Dastin explains, 'In Amazon's case, its algorithm used all CVs submitted to the company over a ten-year period to learn how to spot the best candidates. Given the low proportion of women working in the company, as in most technology companies, the algorithm quickly spotted male dominance and thought it was a factor in success. In effect, Amazon's system taught itself that male candidates were preferable. It penalized resumes that included the word "women's", as in "women's chess club captain"'; Jeffrey Dastin, 'Amazon Scraps Secret AI Recruiting Tool that Showed Bias against Women' (2018) <http://www.reuters.com/article/us-amazon-com-jobs-automation-insight/amazon-scraps-secret-ai-recruiting-tool-that-showed-bias-against-women-idUSKCN1MK08G> accessed 12 January 2023.

13 Young (n 1), 143.

14 See Browne (n 2) and also Robin Zheng's account of 'moral aspiration' in 'Moral Criticism and Structural Injustice' (2021) 130 *Mind* 503 for more detailed discussion.

15 Young (n 1), 110.

that we tend to rely on to secure justice are very firmly grounded in the liability-based model of responsibility. Indeed, the implication of Young's argument is that to attempt to ground responses to structural injustice in liability would be a great waste of political resources. Instead of trying to trace the untraceable, we ought to instead focus our political energies on the general background conditions of structural injustices such as increasing economic precarity (while continuing to direct fault-based solutions to fault-based injustices).

Young suspected that the state was not capable of addressing structural injustice due to its capture by private interests:

> We cannot turn to the state or international institutions as arbiters in a struggle between the interests that produce structural processes with unjust outcomes and interests in changing those processes. The policies and programs that states and international organisations enact themselves tend more to reflect the outcome of those struggles than to balance between them or adjudicate them.[16]

Instead, Young thought that through 'vocal criticism, organised contestations, a measure of indignation, and concerted public pressure' individuals, groups and institutions could take up collective political responsibility through social movements to bring people together to focus on structural injustice.[17] This approach has been shared with many structural injustice scholars.[18] As part of civil society campaigns, there will of course be elements of fault-based injustice as well as a structural focus on broader macro-level economic, cultural, political and social power dynamics.[19] Certainly, much positive change to the way governments and industry respond to public calls of injustice come through civil society social movements. Recent examples of successful social movements include climate activism and Black Lives Matter. These sorts of approaches remain a vitally important mechanism of change but they are not sufficient: social movements tend to rely on methods of

16 ibid 151.

17 ibid.

18 See for example, Sally Haslanger, 'What Is a (Social) Structural Explanation?' (2016) 179 Philosophical Studies 113; Clarissa Hayward, 'Responsibility and Ignorance: On Dismantling Structural Injustice' (2017) 79 The Journal of Politics 396.

19 See Browne (n 2) for a more detailed discussion on the potential for transition from structural to liability-based solutions as a result of new epistemologies. I suggest there that Young's account tends to be static with limited attention to how structural change affects the way injustices are responded to and that political responsibility has much broader scope than structural injustice.

protest, or semi-legal methods of occupation and obstruction, which can be very effective but are often challenging to fund and sustain over long periods of time with directed effect. These methods also tend to be driven by a small number of committed activists who must galvanise larger numbers around 'big messages' but tend to struggle to bring those numbers into complex operative discussion on how to get governments to help their objectives. Famously, when asked what action should be taken to combat climate degradation, Greta Thunberg, perhaps the most famous climate change activist in the world, replied 'it is nothing to do with me'.[20] This is, of course, not a statement about lack of knowledge, imagination or care but rather a reminder that our political and institutional leaders are the ones with the power to coordinate larger-scale change.

What is more, there are serious limits to public engagement with policy-making despite best intentions. As Christopher Achen and Larry Bartels argue:

> Human beings are busy with their lives. Most have school or a job consuming many hours of the day. They also have meals to prepare, homes to clean, and bills to pay. They may have children to raise or elderly parents to care for. They may also be coping with unemployment, business reverses, illness, addictions, divorce, or other personal and family troubles. For most, leisure time is at a premium. Sorting out … policy … is not a high priority for them. Without shirking more immediate and more important obligations, people cannot engage in much well-informed, thoughtful political deliberation …[21]

They go on to argue that even for those who attempt to engage with the details of political debate before making a considered decision, most are only able to scratch the surface with little grasp of the wider context or future implications. This is what Anthony Downs called 'rational ignorance'.[22] What tends to grow into the spaces created by rational ignorance is simplified binary politics – in or out, with us or against us, group versus group. These sorts of binary politics invariably lead us to

---

20 BBC, 'Greta Thunberg: Who Is the Climate Campaigner and What Are Her Aims?' (5 November 2021) <http://www.bbc.co.uk/news/world-europe-49918719> accessed 12 January 2023.

21 Christopher Achen and Larry Bartels, *Democracy for Realists: Why Elections Do Not Produce Responsive Government* (Princeton University Press 2017) 9.

22 Anthony Downs, 'An Economic Theory of Political Action in a Democracy' (1957) 65 Journal of Political Economy 135, 139.

new and renewed forms of division and segregation and present a serious challenge to designing effective public policy with a macrostructural focus. As Roberto Foa and Yascha Mounk observe, there is an 'active embrace of illiberal movements hostile to pluralistic institutions'.[23] Populist politics is on the rise and often includes narratives of '"pure people" versus the "corrupt elite"'[24] or 'harness disaffection and amplify otherwise legitimate concerns in ways that manipulate public will'.[25] James Fishkin crystallises the problem of political response: 'listen to the people and get the angry voices of populism or rely on widely distrusted elites and get policies that seem out of touch with the public's concerns. Populism or technocracy?'[26] Neither populism or technocracy is a good context for designing policy to address the background conditions of structural injustice. Indeed, the common narrative that technocrats are out of touch with the people and populists distort the 'public interest' for their own ends, has encouraged policy-making institutions to combine their efforts with more direct citizen engagement through public polling, focus groups or public consultation.

Public opinion

UK governments tend to be very fond of nationwide polls as a means of testing public opinion. Indeed, since it was used extensively for the Vote Leave Campaign in 2016,[27] which led to Brexit, public polling is something of an obsession in Downing Street, as voiced here by an unnamed government official:

> The internal polling [in Downing Street] is pretty extensive every day ... We get an overnight breakdown of surveys of 2,000 adults. We get stats on how worried people are, people's perceptions of risk, whether they feel they're being served by government information,

23 Roberto Foa and Yascha Mounk, 'Youth and the Populist Wave' (2019) 45 (9–10) Philosophy and Social Criticism 1013. Also see Simon Niemeyer and Julia Jennstål, 'Scaling Up Deliberative Effects – Applying Lessons of Mini-Publics' in André Bächtiger and others (eds), *The Oxford Handbook of Deliberative Democracy* (Oxford University Press 2018).
24 Anna Grzymala-Busse, Didi Kuo, Francis Fukuyama and Michael McFaul, *Global Populisms and their Challenges*. Stanford University White Paper (Stanford University 2020) 1 <https://stanford.app.box.com/s/0afiu4963qjy4gicahz2ji5x27tednaf> accessed 30 August 2022.
25 Niemeyer and Jennstål (n 23), 329.
26 James Fishkin, *Democracy When The People Are Thinking* (Oxford University Press 2018) 3.
27 The UK's withdrawal from the European Union on 31 January 2020 based on a national referendum held in the UK on 23 June 2016, in which 52 per cent of the voting population voted to leave.

whether we've got the balance right between the economy and healthcare, polling on people's finances, thoughts on the NHS.[28]

The way this sort of approach works is that a respected polling company, such as YouGov, will have about a million UK citizens on its books at any one time. These will have been reached through targeted advertising and if accepted, individuals are paid a fee every time they fill in a survey on request. For each survey a smaller number, such as 2,000, are chosen according to, at the very least, some basic social characteristics such as age, gender, socio-economic status, education, and depending on the question, more will be added such as place of birth, voting behaviour, education level, etc. Once the polling data is collected, it is weighted against the national profile of adults (using the same sorts of criteria) in large-scale data sets such as Census data, Labour Force Survey, General Election data and ONS data. There is no doubt public polling is a highly valuable exercise and certainly helps to access much more of the public's plurality when designing policy in its name. However, these sorts of data give us an account of what we *already* think. There is little room for engagement with alternative experiences, debate or what Young called 'self-transcendence'[29] – the development of a willingness to be open to a different way of conceiving of and solving collective problems altogether. If the focus is what people only share already then 'each finds in the other only a mirror for him or herself'.[30] For those filling in the polling surveys, there is no encouragement to step back and look at the 'choice architecture'[31] of the options from which to choose nor indeed that of the life decisions they make. Rather, what is registered is multiple choice selection on a simplified version of politics – in or out, X versus Y.

The foremost UK polling company, YouGov, has as its advertising slogan 'Share your opinion, Earn money, Shape the news'. While this is an accurate description of an important service to contemporary politics, it reveals an absence of speculation about one's structural relations to others and the opportunity to consider evidence from alternative views or listen to stories of others who experienced unjust structural outcomes. In

28 'Boris Johnson Turns to Polling and "Common Sense"' (*Politico*, 13 May 2020) <http://www.politico.eu/article/boris-johnsons-coronavirus-fudge/> accessed 12 January 2023.
29 Iris Marion Young, *Intersecting Voices: Dilemmas of Gender, Political Philosophy and Policy* (Princeton University Press 1997) 66.
30 ibid. See also Achen and Bartels (n 21) who argue that bias is enhanced by democracy whereby voters merely seek out politicians whose views are most closely aligned with theirs.
31 This is a phrase that I borrow here from Haslanger (n 18) 15, which refers to the conditions in which people make decisions.

my account of structural injustice, I see the active development of a habit of 'structural speculation' – thinking openly about which of our beliefs and behaviour may be structural actions – is a necessary precursor to developing a collective structural perspective and acting to effect change as part of political responsibility.[32]

Focus groups and public consultation processes are also limited methods. Focus groups, while providing some opportunity for discussion, are not furnished with the opportunity to debate with a range of experts and competing evidence. Moreover, those invited to take part are not recorded for the general public to follow but tend rather to be small and private gatherings focused on a narrow set of policy ideas.

Public consultation, on the other hand, does tend to be public in that it usually comes in the form of written material submitted by the public over several weeks in relation to a new policy being considered by the Government and the materials are then published on a related government website for anyone interested to see. However, this opportunity only comes to those who are specifically looking for a particular consultation process on government websites (and even then, they are quite hard to find!). Such consultation processes tend to be organised around an information document about which the public can write to the relevant committee through an online portal. Not surprisingly, these processes tend to be dominated by private interest groups and industry, and receive very little engagement from the general public.

However, while important, it is not sufficient to hope that citizens will invest enough time and commitment in speculating on the details of injustice through civil society. This sort of problem is what Achen and Bartels call the '"folk theory of democracy" whereby citizens are assumed to make coherent and intelligible policy decisions, on which governments then act'.[33] Nor is it enough to conduct political responsibility by public poll, which reflects back what we already assume, much like the echo chambers of Twitter, nor the limited procedures of focus groups and public consultation as discussed. Particularly because of the convoluted nature of structural actions and their relationship to structural injustice, a great deal of thought and effort is required to begin to form a coherent picture (a structural perspective) of the macro-scale challenges. Here, I find the work by Jugov and Ypi illuminating. Their focus is on the ways in which those on the sharp end of a particular structural injustice might become

32 It is worth noting, that in the legal context, speculation is a negative alternative to 'hard evidence' when attempting to ascertain liability.
33 Achen and Bartels (n 21) 1.

aware that some of their actions are in fact structural actions that play a part in perpetuating the background conditions of a structural injustice that oppresses them. As they argue, 'different political responsibilities might correspond to different degrees of epistemic awareness depending on agents' perception of and ability to reflect on the injustice they suffer within a structure'.[34] Even though the convoluted and complex elements of structural injustice are too obtuse to map onto individuals, groups or institutions in a meaningful way that could be traced to liability, the effects of structural injustice have a systematic or stable quality that serve to constrain certain individuals, groups or institutions. Young's view was that because structural injustices operate beyond the usual legal and moral frameworks for thinking about injustice, they are all too often disregarded as misfortune or bad luck. These are serious challenges to a thorny political problem.

Young was fully aware that laws or policies could easily result in an injustice that could be argued to fall within the liability model of responsibility. We might think of some immigration laws that render vulnerable people much *more* vulnerable, for example.[35] However, the much harder task is to think of the more complex, convoluted relationship between laws and policies imbricated with structural actions that contribute to the background conditions of structural injustice. Despite the problem of untraceability, I suggest that a fundamental shift in addressing structural injustice can be attempted nevertheless by providing a greater opportunity for ordinary people to adjust the weight of private interest in the design process of the laws and policies that shape their societies. In so doing, state functions could better facilitate opportunities to speculate on the structural actions that occur as a consequence of laws and policies (or the lack thereof) that potentially lie in the background conditions of structural injustice. This would go some way to countering Young's concerns about the power dynamics that characterise the capture of the state's functions by private interest in the context of structural injustice. As Beardsworth explains '[f]or Young, a state has too many interests in these structures to be politically responsible'.[36]

34 Tamara Jugov and Lea Ypi, 'Structural Injustice, Epistemic Opacity, and the Responsibilities of the Oppressed' (2019) 50 Journal of Social Philosophy 7, 12.
35 Ellen Fotheringham and Caitlin Boswell, '"Unequal Impacts": How UK Immigration Law and Policy Affected Migrants' Experiences of the Covid-19 Pandemic' (Public Interest Law Centre, May 2022) <http://www.jcwi.org.uk/Handlers/Download.ashx?IDMF=6b9ce180-ef73-4d33-970f-88fa300feffd> accessed 12 January 2023.
36 Richard Beardsworth, 'From Moral to Political Responsibility in a Globalized Age' (2015) 29 Ethics & International Affairs 71.

I suggest a lay-centric approach be built into the mechanisms of governance. This is likely to have a much more fruitful impact on structural injustice than limiting approaches to tracing fault, risk and rights abuses grounded in liability. Rather, the emphasis would be on a speculative exercise in thinking about how everyday occurrences bolstered by our laws and public policy contribute to the background conditions of structural injustice.

Here I draw on some inspiration from an experimental form of political deliberation, the mini-public, which creates the opportunity for the public to speculate and give policymakers a much richer sense of what the plurality of experiences connected to structural injustices might be. There has of course been a great deal of scholarship on mini-publics[37] in different formats but none has been focused on the regulatory public body landscape in the way I shall come on to sketch.

Mini-publics

The attraction of the mini-public model lies in its simple but uncommon deliberative features.[38] While there are varying models of the mini-public, common features are as follows: the selection of members is made randomly through, for example, the electoral register by an independent polling company according to gender, age, location and social class.

None are politicians. Administration and running costs are met by the state. No member is paid (although expenses such as travel and childcare are met). Members are exposed to competing expert evidence and submissions by other interested parties such as individual members of the public, social movements, industry experts, NGOs, charities and the state, etc. There is a facilitated discussion and debate that is streamed live to the general public, and an anonymous private vote on various elements of the proceedings at the end.

The potential of mini-publics lies not in duty, nor office, nor liability, nor representation of particular interest groups (beyond a minimal selection process of a range of representative social characteristics), but rather in the dynamic of ordinary people being exposed to a plurality of situated knowledge and considering competing evidence and the stories of others while operating in conditions practically conducive to a functional mini-public. That is to say, that a new sort of political habit is

37 See for example, André Bächtiger, John S. Dryzek, Jane Mansbridge, Mark E. Warren (eds), *The Oxford Handbook of Deliberative Democracy* (Oxford University Press 2018); Cristina Lafont, *Democracy Without Shortcuts* (Oxford University Press 2019); Fishkin (n 26).
38 Fishkin (n 26).

choreographed. Key also is the opportunity for the wider public to view the mini-public's journey of speculation and contemplate the various aspects of deliberation. I am not arguing, however, that a lay-centric element will bring particular knowledge to a particular, and perhaps complex, technical problem. Rather, I am arguing that such an element rebalances the interests at play in policy-making beyond (often market-enhancing) considerations of liability. Because so many policy decisions are encased in specialist and private interest, very little of the ordinary person's lived experience and their potential for structural speculation, are a feature of policy-making decisions. That said, the mini-public model is not without limitations.

The limits of mini-publics

While I am convinced that a well-functioning mini-public produces something that reaches well beyond the sum of its parts, it is an extremely complicated and expensive model of governance.[39] Mini-publics tend to take a long time to reach a conclusion (often a year or more) and without sufficient numbers of highly trained facilitators, it is easy to imagine how they might develop some of the chaotic elements of the infamous UK Handforth Parish Council.[40] All deliberative theorists require that participants commit to mutually respectful behaviour and consider each other political equals in order for the deliberative process to be successful. Ian Shapiro, however, argues that mini-publics serve to distract from the real power dynamics of politics.[41] His argument is that the powerful political actors are not interested or motivated to enter into respectful and equally weighted political dialogue but instead will operate through other channels such as regulatory capture which I discuss elsewhere.[42] Mini-publics are not usually given the power to make policy decisions and are primarily situated outside of governance or policy-making mechanisms with no substantive links to state level policy decision-making. This

39 For example, the costs of the Irish Citizens' Assembly (*Tionól Saoránach*) in July 2016 were met by Government set at €2 million. See Taoiseach, 'Department of An Taoiseach: Citizens Assembly' (Dáil debates, 4 October 2016 <https://www.kildarestreet.com/wrans/?id=2019-03-26a.175> accessed 23 August 2023.

40 BBC, Handforth Parish Council: Jackie Weaver 'did not have the authority' (29 March 2022) <https://www.bbc.co.uk/news/uk-england-manchester-60913569> accessed 23 August 2023.

41 Ian Shapiro, *Politics Against Domination* (Harvard University Press 2016).

42 See Browne (n 2).

is perhaps the most important limitation as much of our democratic governance mechanisms are linked to market or other private interests.[43]

Certainly, there is vociferous criticism of the idea that mini-publics function well as decision-making entities. Simone Chambers and Cristina Lafont, for example, argue that to do so would be to detach the mini-public from the wider public – 'rule by the minority'.[44] Bearing in mind these criticisms, I suggest attempting to extract several positive elements of the mini-public for addressing structural injustice into a different approach to policy-making and regulation in order to avoid some of the shortcomings of this model.

In what follows, I look to the regulatory public body. While its current reputation suffers from its association with undemocratic technocrats discussed above, I see potential for reform into a new kind of public body landscape that offers the opportunity for ordinary people to speculate on some of the power dynamics that form a part of the background conditions to structural injustices operating at the macro level. Before discussing the possibility of reform, however, first it is important to understand what a public body currently is and how it functions. I focus on the UK context by way of example.[45]

The public body model

Within a democracy, the normative purpose of a regulatory public body is the protection of the public interest on the grounds that constraint on private, especially business, interests can be a positive practice that benefits society.[46] Public bodies operating at arms-length from ministers,

---

43 Danielle S Allen, 'Toward a Connected Society' in E Lewis and N Cantor (eds), *Our Compelling Interests: The Value of Diversity for Democracy and a Prosperous Society* (Princeton University Press 2016); Patricia Hill Collins, 'The Difference That Power Makes: Intersectionality and Participatory Democracy' (2017) 8 Investigaciones Feministas 19; Wendy Brown, *In the Ruins of Neoliberalism: The Rise of Anti-Democratic Politics in the West* (Columbia University Press 2019).

44 Simone Chambers, 'Rhetoric and the Public Sphere: Has Deliberative Democracy Abandoned Mass Democracy?' (2009) 37(3) Political Theory 323; Cristina Lafont, 'Deliberation, Participation and Democratic Legitimacy: Should Deliberative Mini-Publics Shape Public Policy?' (2015) 23 Journal of Political Philosophy 40.

45 Similar bodies, in some sense, exist in all governments around the world and are referred to, for example, as 'regulators', 'agencies', 'authorities, 'committees' or 'quangos'.

46 Shane O'Neill, *Recognition, Equality and Democracy* (Routledge 2008); Tom Christensen and Per Laegreid, 'Complexity and hybrid public administration' (2010) 11 Public Organization Review 407.

come in different forms,[47] contributing to the processes of governance, devising and delivering on a range of public services and broadly speaking, working within a strategic framework set by government. In the UK, there are currently 295 such bodies employing over 300,000 staff and with government funding of more than £220 billion. These range from NHS England and the Secret Intelligence Service (MI6) to St John Soanes Museum in London.[48] I am particularly interested in public bodies that are not part of a government department but are nonetheless under some form of political oversight (Non-Departmental Public Bodies – NDPBs). These sorts of public bodies are required to deliberate and advise government on how best to serve the public interest in what are sometimes very technical and complex fields such as financial regulation, medical research or technological innovation.[49] Many public bodies have direct regulatory powers.

Public bodies tend to be heavily populated by experts and industry representatives and are therefore subject to much criticism due to the power and public resources they hold beyond the direct control of elected politicians.[50] Levi-Faur describes public bodies as a 'necessary evil' for translating the complex and demanding nature of the bodies' remit to career politicians.[51] Indeed, the more specialised and technical the object of regulation is, the less likely it is that elected politicians are sufficiently knowledgeable to make informed decisions in the interests of the public.[52] Public bodies, often nicknamed 'quangos,' are an essential part of the governance mechanisms of the British state. Dommett and others describe how regulatory public bodies are much

47 Central government arm's-length bodies (ALBs) consist of executive agencies (EAs), non-departmental public bodies (NDPBs) and non-ministerial departments (NMDs). EAs are business units within departments responsible for undertaking executive functions: see Cabinet Office, 'Classification Of Public Bodies: Guidance For Departments' (2016)<https://assets.publishing.service.gov.uk/government/uploads/system/uploads/attachment_data/file/519571/Classification-of-Public_Bodies-Guidance-for-Departments.pdf> accessed 23 August 2023.

48 UK Cabinet Office, 'Guidance on the Undertaking of Reviews of Public Bodies' (Press Release, HMG, 2022) <http://www.gov.uk/government/publications/public-bodies-review-programme/guidance-on-the-undertaking-of-reviews-of-public-bodies > accessed 12 January 2023. See the following link for more detailed information on various shapes and sizes of public bodies in the UK: <http://www.gov.uk/guidance/public-bodies-reform#public-bodies-reform-programme-2020-to-2025> accessed 1 May 2023.

49 See for example <http://www.gov.uk/government/organisation> accessed 23 August 2023.

50 David Runciman, *How Democracy Ends* (Profile Books 2018).

51 David Levi-Faur (ed), 'Regulation and Regulatory Governance' in *Handbook on the Politics of Regulation* (Edward Elgar Publishing 2011), 15.

52 Barry M Mitnick 'Capturing "Capture": Definition and Mechanisms' in *Handbook on the Politics of Regulation* (Edward Elgar Publishing 2011), 34–49.

'maligned' as 'unaccountable, profligate and bureaucratic'.[53] Bickerton and Accetti 'observe a growing concentration of power in the hands of a set of unelected "regulatory bodies", drawing their legitimacy primarily from their technical competence and administrative expertise', creating 'a depoliticised form of "technocracy", where what is at stake is the preservation of the possibility of politics itself'.[54] Although democratic politics are meant to orientate the exercise of power towards the public interest, the expert elites who command large government resources, regulatory powers and make policies that seem out of touch with the public's concerns are increasingly seen as creating a democratic deficit.[55]

This sort of negative narrative about public bodies heavily dominates the fields of public policy, law and regulation studies and has been central to the dramatic reduction in the number of public bodies across the international regulatory landscape.[56] Indeed, in recent years, 290 public bodies have been abolished in the UK, a further 165 public bodies were merged into fewer than 70, and the functions of over 50 further public bodies were moved out of the public sector, into the private sector. In total, more than 600 public bodies have been dismantled in the past decade.

For those public bodies that survived, they have been subjected to a slew of new reforms that often required them to extract the majority of their running budgets from the very sector they were created to regulate and more explicitly, they are required to actively facilitate private enterprise growth.[57] Although the normative function of a public body is to protect the public interest, I suggest that increasingly the 'public interest' has been reduced to a notion of hazard and risk grounded in liability that excludes crucial structural considerations. Here the public body's role in the mitigation of market failure looms large and the public interest all too often manifests as merely checks and balances on potential wrongdoing such as unsafe practices, corrupt practitioners, false advertising, substandard products and discriminatory behaviours. The management of these is of course important as well as necessary to

---

53 Katharine Dommett, Matthew Flinders, Chris Skelcher and Katherine Toukiss, 'Did They "Read Before Burning"? The Coalition and Quangos' (2014) 85 The Political Quarterly 133, 134.
54 Christopher Bickerton and Carlo Invernizzi Accetti, 'Populism and Technocracy: Opposites or Complements?' (2017) 20 Critical Review of International Social and Political Philosophy 193.
55 Levi-Faur (n 51).
56 See for example, Daniel Carpenter and David Moss (eds), *Preventing Regulatory Capture: Special Interest Influence and How to Limit It* (Cambridge University Press 2013); Jude Browne, 'The Regulatory Gift: Politics, Regulation and Governance' (2020) 14 Regulation and Governance 165.
57 UK Cabinet Office (n 48).

maintain market confidence, but I argue, achieves too little else in the public interest. I suggest that there is a failure to address the more complex structural harms emanating from the accumulated, unintended and uncoordinated outcomes of the structural actions of individuals, groups and institutions.[58] Given that those who are economically vulnerable or socially marginalised tend to suffer structural injustice rather than elites or corporations, surely these structural dynamics are of the utmost public interest too and should be reflected as such in the functions of the public body. As Runciman argues, many people feel ignored by legal and policy-making processes largely dependent on technocratic thinking, that seem no longer to be designed to benefit an increasingly unequal and diverse population.[59]

Why then might we consider the public body as helpful for addressing the background conditions of structural injustice?

Lay-centric reform of the public body

While the public body landscape has become somewhat unpopular in the public imaginary as a form of 'Technocracy', and for politicians, an association with burdensome regulation, the status quo need not be the default. I argue we need to think again.

The primary features of the new model of public body aimed at including a structural focus would continue to include several current public body features. It would remain a government-funded recommendatory body, operating at arm's-length so as to be independent of political steering with subsequent regulatory powers on settled specified remits. Central to the function of a public body would be a range of expertise emanating from specialists with differing perspectives and the ability to explain and interpret the underlying technicalities of any particular question or concern.

Interestingly, if we look to what was once widely considered as the 'gold standard' design for public bodies, the Warnock Report, which led to the world-leading Human Fertilisation and Embryology Authority in

58 Elsewhere, I have discussed the difficult task of conceptually distinguishing indirect discrimination from structural injustice (Jude Browne, 'The Political Implication of the "Untraceability" of Structural Injustice', (2023) *Contemporary Political Theory*. Early View: <https://link.springer.com/article/10.1057/s41296-023-00634-4>. Nevertheless, I find Ó Cinnéide's account of legal innovations beyond liability (in this volume), particularly illuminating on the shift in law's operative lexicon to include positive obligations 'to ensure individuals were able to effectively enjoy their rights'. See also my discussion of 'imperfect responsibilities' to address structural injustice in 'The Political Implication of the "Untraceability" of Structural Injustice'.
59 Runciman (n 50).

the UK,[60] we can see that an important recommendation back then was that such bodies ought to be led by a lay-person – someone chosen for their 'ordinariness as a member of the public' rather than their expertise or special insight to the technology in question. This feature of the public body did not manifest in any substantial way and if we look to the chairs of public bodies, although there are many impressive figures, they tend to be institutional leaders, more often than not corporate leaders.[61] In the new public body model, I suggest lay members ought to be selected, much like jury service, based on a range of demographic census data (age, ethnicity, gender, geography, socio-economic status, etc) and given a basic introduction to a format designed to encourage innovative thinking and openness to new, sometimes complex and technical ideas. Much like the mini-public, the lay members would be exposed to different technical opinions and recommendations, their discussions would be publicly recorded and their vote (where relevant), along with other specialist members of the public body, would be anonymous.

The inclusion of a permanent but rotating panel of lay members of course does not provide perfect representation of the plurality of experience in policy-making, but it is the most practical link to a more diverse set of public concerns and interests that, if built into the deliberations of law and policy-making, will ensure at least that the public interest is more likely to override that of private or industry interest and rebalance some of the background conditions of structural injustice. Because structural injustice is not traceable to agents of fault, as such, I have suggested that the most effective way of addressing structural

---

60 The Warnock Committee had been set up in response to the growing public anxiety around the emergence of new reproductive technologies culminating in the first ever child, Louise Brown, born in 1978, using in vitro fertilisation (IVF), a reproductive technology developed by Edwards and Steptoe in Cambridgeshire in the UK. One of the HFEA's primary functions is to license, monitor, and regulate provision of all fertility treatments (such as IVF, gamete and embryo freezing, and pre-implantation genetic diagnosis) and any research involving the use of human gametes and embryos in the UK. For example, the HFEA prohibits the implantation of nonhuman embryos or gametes or admixed embryos (part human, part non-human embryos) in humans and also prohibits human cloning as well as techniques such as embryo sex selection. As set out in the Warnock Report, the call for such a public body rested on the understanding that 'public concern about the techniques …[involving gametes and embryos] needs to be reflected in public policy'; Dame M Warnock, *Department of Health and Social Security: Report of the Committee of Inquiry into Human Fertilisation and Embryology* (HMSO, 1984) 75–79 <http://www.bioeticacs.org/iceb/documentos/Warnock_Report_of_the_Committee_of_Inquiry_into_Human_Fertilisation_and_Embryology_1984.pdf> accessed 18 January 2023.

61 Interestingly, Ireland, which has one of the world's only standing Citizen Assemblies, provided an alternative solution and uses non-partisan members of the Irish Judiciary whose responsibility is to professionally and impartially coordinate proceedings much like a court of law while the members of the assembly are entirely lay. See details of Irish Citizen's Assembly: <http://www.citizensassembly.ie/en/> accessed 23 August 2023.

injustice is to consider its background conditions where we see dynamics such as gaping inequality and increasing precarity. In simple terms, creating fora within our governance systems that, with elements of the mini-public model, enable the possibility of lay members, together with specialists, to speculate on the nature of structural actions, is a great deal more promising than the current policy-making practices, which predominantly tend to be grounded in liability. It is a simple idea but to bring a range of lay voices directly into the mix of discussions on, for example, the governance of financial institutions, the environment, or technological innovations is a productive exercise in speculating on how best to rebalance the background conditions of structural injustice.[62]

As I have suggested, almost by design, state consultation processes with the public do not attract the views of those most disconnected from complex technical policy-making circles and those most likely to suffer from structural injustice. It is not that the lay-centric public body can provide a simple solution to each structural injustice, but it does ensure engagement with a plurality of situated knowledge where members of the public are able to bring their concerns, experiences and views and try to make sense of their relational connections to the background conditions of structural injustice, directly within the governance process.

Conclusion

Young's work on structural injustice leads us to an uncomfortable political realisation. The usual tools deployed for addressing injustice – the tracing of liability in contextual moral or legal terms – are not useful for structural injustice which is much more complex and amorphous in shape. Even though no simple solution is apparent, I have argued that one useful approach is to focus specifically on the question of whose interests are at play in the construction of the state's laws and regulation, which are deeply imbricated in the background conditions of structural injustice. I have argued that reshaping the regulatory public body landscape to incorporate a lay-centric element can only be an improvement in addressing structural injustice. Contra Young's suspicions, there is possibility for state machinery to become more directly and purposefully attuned to such a task.

---

62 See Browne (n 2) for fuller discussion.

12

Free or unfree? Depicting structural injustice in courtrooms and in film

Guy Mundlak

Introduction

In Ken Loach's film (2007) *It's a Free World*, Angie gets sacked from a dead-end job and establishes a recruitment agency that brings migrant workers to the UK, gradually slipping into the shady domains of undocumented migration. The title is ironic. Angie's decisions hardly amount to a conceivable image of freedom, pointing instead at the conditions set by harshly constituted markets, cruel politics and gender-racial hierarchies. Throughout most of his films, Ken Loach, the master of docudrama in the fields of labour, work and the social sphere more generally, depicts narratives that point at the political and social responsibility for the unfortunate fate of individuals. These are individuals who engage in lawful and unlawful practices of survival and resistance, attempting to find their way despite a highly constrained range of choices.

If the legal system were to meet Loach's protagonists – Angie who takes part in a value chain that engages in wage theft, Daniel who draws graffiti on the walls of the welfare offices, or Sam who violates landlords' property rights – in all likelihood they would be defendants in criminal proceedings. As defendants, they would probably have to plea to the court for mercy. They might also appear as proactive plaintiffs who present their misfortune in the limited terminology accorded by the legal process – such as 'lack of due process'. If they come before the court, the protagonists will realise that courts crop *the structure* and focus on a particular moment of time, a discrete interaction, which is captured on the assumption that the judicial process does not seek to change the world. Broad questions regarding the morality of the socio-economic structure are often considered immaterial. By contrast, a film can stretch the protagonists' narrative and reveal a life story, conflicts, rational and humanly irrational behaviours, documenting the lack of alternatives, particularly for people in poverty, dependence and subordination.

This article seeks to juxtapose the judicial process with a line-up of Ken Loach's films, which represent the docudrama genre. Putting the two side by side may be regarded as a category mistake. To state the case in caricature, courts decide real life disputes, and are committed to rules of procedure and evidence, constitutional and organisational constraints; films enjoy infinite degrees of freedom, with an eye to artistic perfection, funding opportunities and popular patronage. Courts are a public institution; films are a private creation. Courts claim to be apolitical while films take part in the making of politics. However, placing the two on the same plane has a dual purpose. First, the storytelling capacity of film highlights the limitations of the judicial process. Second, both film and judicial cases are intended to shape and constitute individuals' acceptance or rejection of the 'structure'; they take part in legitimising and rebelling against it. The discussion is not a prescription for change, and films are not an alternative to law, nor do they tell how the legal system should change. Unlike other studies of law and film, the films that are studied here are not about the legal system and therefore their impact on its reform are indirect. The purpose of this discussion is first and foremost reflective and is intended, on the one hand to draw attention to the limits of the judicial process and its absence from experiences of social insecurity, and on the other hand, on the power of judicial reasoning in taking part, with other forms of expression, in leading change.

The first section introduces the idea of structural injustice and fits it within Loach's docudrama genre. The second section surveys seven films, offering a qualitative reading of the cinematic text and extracting insights on structure, injustice, and the subjects' choices within and outside the domains of what is legally permissible. The third section juxtaposes the cinematic narrative with the judicial one. At first, the study seeks to put them side by side, illuminating the blind spots of the judicial process. This contrast is apt for reflecting on the notion of liability, and resonates with a focus on backward justice, which seeks to identify the culprits and the appropriate means to address their wrongs. In the second stage, the study compares the cinematic narrative with the judicial one, where their objectives are similar. Comparing the two makes it possible to identify the political and educational role of films and courts in depicting social positions. This comparison is focused on forward-looking responsibility because it calls for action towards the root causes of injustice.[1]

Structural injustice in Loach's docudrama

The work of Ken Loach is a prime example of the docudrama genre, with a focus on class, work (labour) and welfare. I find it particularly useful to teach and explain what Iris Marion Young designates as structural injustice.[2] Her work follows and develops threads of structure developed by Marx, weaving in contemporary class and identity theories of structural power.[3] For my purpose of juxtaposing law and film, her work serves as an apt anchor, even when it is noted that some aspects of this account are contested.[4] I then turn to placing Loach's cinematography in the context of the genre, and conclude by tying the two together with a demonstration of how the concept of structural injustice is highly influential in his work and can be studied from his films.

Structural injustice

The focus of 'structural injustice' is on social-economic aspects of lifehood. *Structure* refers to a broad set of political institutions, social interactions and market outcomes. Sangiovanni details these components, including among them 'rules, concepts, beliefs, assumptions, conventions, recipes, scenarios, principles of action and habits of speech'.[5] Various components interact to produce the structure, which is then experienced by individuals, consciously or unconsciously, as debilitating. *Injustice* refers to an ongoing situation of insecurity in the social-economic sphere (for example, in food and in housing), and a lack of social insurance to cushion against social risks. These forms of injustice deny individuals their autonomy, control over one's life story and dignity.

---

1 For the difference between backward- and forward-looking justice, see the discussion in the first section 'Structural injustice in Loach's docudrama'.

2 Young's theory of structural injustice was incrementally developed and fully captured in Iris Marion Young, *Responsibility for Justice* (Oxford University Press 2011).

3 Maeve McKeown, 'Structural Injustice' (2021) 16(7) Philosophy Compass e12757.

4 This critique is based on some common grounds that are taken from: Andrea Sangiovanni, 'Structural injustice and individual responsibility' (2018) 49 Journal of Social Philosophy 461; Martha Nussbaum, 'Foreword', in Iris Marion Young, *Responsibility for Justice* (Oxford University Press 2011), ix–xxv; Robert E. Goodin and Christian Barry, 'Responsibility for Structural Injustice: A Third Thought' (2021) 20(4) Politics, Philosophy & Economics 339; McKeown, ibid, surveys the critique and alternative approaches, while maintaining Young's theory centre-stage.

5 ibid, Sangiovanni.

Structural injustice denotes a moral wrong that is distinct from harm caused by discrete private interactions, and from that which is attributable to discrete actions and policies of the state (or other powerful institutions). In stylised fashion, the concept of structural injustice turns our attention away from identifying blame for past action to seeking responsibility for future transformation of the structure. This shift is explained by the limited range of choices individuals have within the given structure. The structure assigns and locks individuals into social roles – both those who are victims of misfortune, and those who are seemingly perpetrators but simply obediently complying with the scripts of an unjust structure. When considering that choices and acts of individuals are embedded in the structure, common day interactions can be viewed differently. For example, in the daily interaction in welfare offices, where welfare recipients must prove they are sufficiently poor and morally eligible for state aid, there is a meeting between the public agent's disbelief and the private recipient's humiliation. The decisions of welfare officers may appear to be harsh and unjust, but they are reasoned by the rule of law, the need for consistency and coherence among many decisions, the need to divide a limited budget in a fair fashion and the like.[6] At the same time, welfare recipients include those who are clearly in poverty, some who seek to cheat the system, and many who conceal informal work because the welfare allowance cannot adequately cover high interest loans or other financial needs. Circumstances bring together in the same room the welfare officers and welfare recipients in poverty, placing them on opposite sides of the desk, where the nature of conditional benefits dictates an inevitable script.

It is claimed that traditional considerations of blame and liability, designated as 'backward-looking', are immaterial for moral and instrumental reasons. Morally, the fact that individual choices and agency are constrained by the structure affects our perception of moral wrong. Instrumentally, Young lists several reasons for abstaining from assigning blame and guilt. These include the concern with a focus on immaterial past occurrences that cannot affect the future, on agents who are only the messengers of bad practices but not those who devised them, and on 'normal social structures' that are practised without it being asked why they are essential. Due to these factors, a focus on blame may lead to subjects' defensive behaviour, rather than their embrace of change.

6 See Lea Ypi, 'On Dominated Dominators' in this volume. The structure dictates the actions and possibilities for all the agents involved.

Instead, Young argues that structural injustice requires a different kind of response, one that is forward-looking and seeks to amend the structure itself. Responsibility means to take action to change the future, rather than assign blame for past actions within the structural domain. With the change of structure there will also be a change in individuals' behaviour. The switch to forward-looking change places responsibility on the community – often state-wide, but it can also be a local community, a transnational one, or communities of traits and identities. Future-looking responsibility can only be facilitated by encouraging collective action.

A recurring critique of Young's framework concerns the sharp dichotomies between backward and forward, between blame and responsibility, between individuals and community. In different ways, authors ask: why are individuals required to take part in collective action for future transformation of the structure, while individuals' compliance with the structure in the past and present is an exempted moral category.[7]

Docudrama

Quantitative studies, highlighting macro-social processes, can direct our gaze away from individuals to the structure and its aggregate outcomes. Alternatively, structural injustice is aptly depicted in narratives. Even Young resorts to storytelling in her presentation of the concept.[8] Qualitative studies can depict how the debilitating effect of the structure builds up. This requires the observation of multiple encounters with the institutions, practices, attitudes and scripts composing the structure. To convey how unforgiving these encounters are, cinematic storytelling can be particularly helpful.

Ken Loach's work is situated along the continuum of docudrama, bridging the fiction form at one end and the documentary at the other. The framing of the genre as being on a continuum admits of different forms, such as Loach's depiction of social reality through fiction, or the dramatisation of real-life events (*Pride*), including significant political moments (*Made in Dagenham*) and biographies (*Norma Rae*), re-enactment of real-life stories (*Chronicle of a Summer*), and the director's dramatisation of his filmmaking efforts (Michael Moore's *Roger and Me*). The differences between these categories are not clear-cut. They can be portrayed as leaning on different weights of the documentary and fiction, or qualitatively different uses of each.

---

7 See McKeown (n 3).
8 Young (n 2), Chapter 2.

While some situate the docudrama on a continuum, others underscore that many films are hybrid forms that simultaneously integrate both components. Documentary films are not merely an accidental gaze of reality. They encapsulate decisions on forms of representation (interviews, documentation and explanation, on-site and real-time filming), the time span, whose point of view is favoured and more.[9] At the same time, reality is constantly at the background of fiction and drama. The docudrama is aptly described by stating that it is 'not a programme category, it is a debate'.[10] Docudramas therefore require an ethical clarity that instructs the viewers' understanding of what they are watching. The film should be honest in distancing itself from the pretence of the documentary genre, and at the same time, clear in the ways it still documents reality.

Loach is not alone in his docudrama mission.[11] He is clearly *a* leading director in the genre of social realism, which carries a focus on 'naturalistic stories of working-class characters and function as critiques of entrenched economic and social structures'.[12] There are several reasons for the focus on the works of Ken Loach. Although his work is based on fiction, his texts, often written together with Paul Laverty (a lawyer and activist), incline toward the documentary. Their scripts lean heavily on fiction, but with the explicit aim of depicting harsh realities – often related to the spheres of work, labour, welfare and class. The characters are composite prototypes of social position – a woman on welfare, an hourly paid construction worker, or a migrant cleaning worker.[13] Dramatisation affords a personified view of the character, making it possible to relate to the person as unique, rather than a prototype. The composite nature of the character and her story facilitates more didactic filmmaking, advancing an ideological, political or instructional purpose.

---

9 'There's nothing inherently objective about documentaries. Every time someone chooses a particular section of an interview and juxtaposes it with a particular piece of music, they are steering the audience': Jason Deans, 'Kosminsky defends docudrama', *The Guardian* (UK, 17 October 2005); Bill Nichols, *Representing Reality: Issues and Concepts in Documentary* (Bloomington: Indiana University Press 1991).

10 Andrew Goodwin and Paul Kerr, *Drama-documentary, Dossier 19* (British Film Institute, 1984), 1.

11 Philip Mosely, *The Cinema of the Dardenne Brothers* (Wallflower Press 2013); Alice Bardan, 'The New European Cinema of Precarity: a Transnational Perspective', in Ewa Mazierska (ed), *Work in Cinema: Labor and the Human Condition* (Palgrave Macmillan New York 2013), 69.

12 Andrew Lapin, 'Who Needs Social Realism?' (*Jewish Currents* 12 August 2019). Also see Lester D Friedman, *Fires were Started: British Cinema and Thatcherism* (Wallflower Press 2006), 261.

13 On the normative importance of social positions to the theory of structural injustice, see George Letsas, 'Structural Injustice and the Law: A Philosophical Framework', in this volume.

Title	*Year*	*Main theme*[14]
Riff Raff	1991	A construction worker squats in an abandoned estate, struggles to improve working conditions and is involved with his colleagues in acts of resistance against the employer.
Raining Stones	1993	A family that is coping and maintaining dignity at times of economic depression, depicting strategies such as resistance and theft, dealing with unpaid debts, informal work, violence and charity.
Bread and Roses	2000	An undocumented female migrant from Mexico lands a cleaning job in Los Angeles, while getting involved in the SEIU's Justice for Janitors' organising campaign.
The Navigators	2001	Railway workers are transferred to a private employer at a time of privatising British Rail. They learn that, while their jobs remained, the rules and norms have changed considerably.
It's a Free World	2007	A single parent who lost her job in a recruitment agency opens one of her own, only to realise that becoming an independent entrepreneur does not change the economic circumstances underlying the labour market.
I, Daniel Blake	2016	The accidental meeting of two welfare recipients leads to a depiction of the struggle they endure in their interaction with the public system that is intended to help them.
Sorry We Missed You	2019	Resorting to working in a deliveries company, a family man learns the precarious implications for his whole family's economic and psychological wellbeing.

Table 12.1: Loach's films discussed in this study

The documenting dimension is highlighted by reference to actual events, such as the 'Justice for Janitors' organising campaign of the Service Employees International Union (SEIU), or the privatisation of British Rail. Furthermore, the films are made on location in the hidden backyards of British society, and the actors are mostly amateurs and acting novices,

14 For more detail about the plot, see Loach's listing in IMDb (https://www.imdb.com/name/nm0516360/), or in the Sixteen Films productions website (https://www.sixteenfilms.co.uk/) accessed 23 August 2023.

featuring local cultures and accents. Loach insists on displaying common and mundane rituals. But side by side, he also provides extraordinary dramatic elements that catch attention, with tear-jerking moments, (arguably) extreme forms of coping with social injustice, as well as acts of resistance that I will explore in the following section. The dramatic elements invite empathy and tolerance, an objective no less important than the documentary's informational function.[15]

Towards a reading of Loach's cinematography

The examples used here are taken from films that directly address labour market issues, from three decades of Loach's cinematic work: earlier works are not included here.

The seven films are thematically connected by their critique of class relations, social inequality and the root causes of poverty.[16] There is progress and change along the timeline of the selected films.[17] Earlier films demonstrated the struggle of the unemployed and low-waged workers at times when unemployment surged (1990–1993) and the Conservative government maintained Thatcher's neoliberal policies. In later years, there has been more of a focus on specific themes – privatisation, trade unions' organising, temporary work and (recruitment) agencies, welfare-to-work programmes and the gig economy.

Structural injustice in Loach's cinematography

The structure

> What choice do they have?
>
> One or two may slip through the net, but for the rest of them it's mapped out – no work, no hope, it's just despair.
>
> All they got is crime, booze, families are breaking up. (*Raining Stones*)

The depiction of the 'structure' begins in the earlier films (*Riff Raff* and *Raining Stones*) with a general portrayal of unemployment and the cutback of the welfare state. Later films illuminate particular aspects

15 Tony Brown, 'Using Film in Teaching and Learning about Changing Societies' (2011) 30(2) International Journal of Lifelong Education 233.

16 Harvey Kaye, *British Marxist Historians* (Zero Books 2022).

17 Clive James Nwonka, '"You're What's Wrong with Me": Fish Tank, The Selfish Giant and the Language of Contemporary British Social Realism' (2014) 12(3) New Cinemas: Journal of Contemporary Film 205.

of the structure. For example, *The Navigators* depicts the outcomes of privatisation. Privatisation designates a general set of political ideas, beliefs, assumptions and practices that assign virtue to ruthless market competition. The importance of structure is conveyed by the idea that the same workers attend the same workplace, performing the same job and adhering to familiar routines. The director continues to film at the same sites, but all that is familiar undergoes significant change. The new competition is explained by stating that 'from now – just doing the job is not enough'. Collective agreements are terminated and companies seek to out-compete one another, leading to poor management practices and compromising workers' sense of security and rights. In the new economy 'the customer is the focus'. The workers' lot is irrelevant. 'They put us in an algorithm that we have no choice [but to comply or resign – GM].'

Another target of critique are the welfare-to-work programmes and other modes of targeted social welfare assistance schemes.[18] There is nothing intrinsically wrong with conditional benefits. They allegedly aid in channelling benefits to those who are most in need and eliminate opportunistic reliance on public funding. At the same time, they are not sensitive to the great variations in the causes of poverty or need and their many faces. *I, Daniel Blake* portrays the lack of respect for individual need and dignity. The storyline demonstrates the problems associated with welfare conditionality, and the way the interplay between rules and discretion works against the recipients of conditional benefits. While the film aptly demonstrates the structural problem associated with strict rules, it does not explore the alternatives. The literature on welfare regimes holds that discretion is necessary in a strict rules-based conditional grant, enabling the humane aspect of welfare administration.[19] A different direction of structural change suggests that where universal entitlements are in place, such as child or old age benefits for all and not just for the poor, there is lesser need for rules-based conditional granting to begin with.[20]

By contrast to the active policy-making involved in privatisation and conditional welfare schemes, the gig economy is nurtured by the state's withdrawal from labour market regulation. In *Sorry we Missed You,* the gig economy is described as the outcome of consumer capitalism,

---

18 Virginia Mantouvalou, 'Welfare-to-work, Structural Injustice and Human Rights' (2020) 83 (5) The Modern Law Review 929; Amir Paz Fuchs, *Welfare-to-Work: Conditional Rights in Social Policy* (Oxford University Press 2008).

19 Richard M. Titmuss, 'Welfare "Rights", Law and Discretion' (1971), 42 (2) The Political Quarterly 113.

20 Gosta Esping-Andersen, *The Three Worlds of Welfare Capitalism* (Princeton University Press 1990).

whereby consumers are guaranteed price and service that can only be delivered by compromising the workers' share and rights. This process is complemented by cutthroat competition that dictates the agents' choices. As the manager of a deliveries service explains to the 'franchisee' driver:

> I am not a nasty bastard.
>
> I create a protective shield around this depo.
>
> All they [consumers – GM] care about is price and delivery.
>
> This box [points at the barcode scanner – GM] is in competition with all the black boxes around the country, and that decides who lives and who dies.
>
> I want the Apples, Amazons and Zaras for *my drivers*.

The impact of consumer-driven value chain capitalism and the fragmentation of the employment relationship ('fissuring')[21] are an important part of the structure. As property owners in high-rise office buildings claim, 'I don't pay the cleaning workers, talk to their employer' (*Bread and Roses*).[22] Value chains blur a sense of responsibility for workers, and therefore the traditional forms of collective bargaining against a well-defined employer are increasingly losing ground. The actual power that contractors, who are the direct contractual employers, wield to respond to their workers' needs is very limited, as they must cater to the whims of the property owners. Tough competition among contractors – cleaning, security, transportation and other services – further fuels their efforts to fight workers' organising drives.

Another problem that is highlighted in *Bread and Roses* and then carried over into *It's a Free World* is the difficulty of building communities of solidarity and action from *within* the workers' bench.[23] Documenting conflicts between workers, especially those who are situated on the lower rungs of the structure, reveals workers who must cope with a triple disadvantage vis-à-vis the state, their employer and their peers. There are several examples of class fragmentation.

---

21 David Weil, *The Fissured Workplace* (Harvard University Press 2017).

22 On the 'Justice for Janitors' campaign that is depicted in the film, see Roger Waldinger, Chris Erickson, Ruth Milkman, Daniel J B Mitchell, Abel Valenzuela, Kent Wong and Maurice Zeitlin, 'Helots No More: A Case Study of the Justice for Janitors Campaign in Los Angeles', in Kate Bronfenbrenner , Sheldon Friedman, Richard W Hurd, Rudolph A Oswald and Ronald L Seeber (eds), *Organizing to Win* (ULR Press 1997).

23 Claus Offe and Helmut Wiesenthal, 'Two Logics of Collective Action' (1980) 1(1) Political Power and Social Theory 67.

First, both films highlight structural aspects of migration, where migrants move from areas of unemployment and poor living conditions to countries offering greater opportunities – real or imagined. But migration is a moral trap and a challenge to liberal theory. *It's a Free World* demonstrates how low-waged work and precarious options become the focal point for migrants' choice of employment. Employers want them, particularly the undocumented, because their immigration status drains their power resources. The recruitment agency wants them because they are willing to pay high transaction fees, encouraging circular migration instead of long-term residence that is discouraged by the state. In this triad of interests, the option of paying wages on par with those of domestic British workers may undermine the whole migration structure, leaving migrants in their home countries, where there are pockets of high unemployment or political threat. In both films, migrant workers, documented and undocumented alike, are portrayed as struggling in a system that is highly restrictive. Success in climbing from the worst situation (absolute lack of housing, health care, food) to just poor situations (insecurity in housing, health and food) is dependent on silent compliance with regressive and abusive labour market practices. The state's migration law does not help and even worsens the options they do have. Community building among migrants becomes particularly daunting as their individual survival is constantly at risk if they take part in collective action (*Bread and Roses*) and may not even appear as an option (*It's a Free World*).

Second, the films depict market-driven cutthroat competition among workers. Community building in the 'Justice for Janitors' organising drive must overcome hostility between identity groups – African Americans, Hispanic Americans, migrants from Eastern Europe and migrants from central America. Language, mentality and culture create invisible borders that organisers must undo. At the same time, for the cleaning contractors, they serve as useful divisive strategies to fragment the occupational community and class-based solidarity along identity lines. In (the imaginary) *Free World*, the film depicts the gender aspect, where women who have been downplayed, harassed and devalued, seek empowerment by turning the gender hierarchy upside down, relying on sexual charm to recruit an all-male clientele, and the male migrants are even sexually objectified by the women. Individuals' survival, just as much as group-based oppression of women, racial minorities and migrants, is shown to be to the detriment of community building rather than a source of power.

A third structural aspect emphasises the flourishing practice of precarious employment. Angie complains that 'she changed 30 jobs – from one shitty job to another', even though she was in recruitment – HR – and not in blue-collar work that characterises the workers depicted in the other films. She draws on her previous experience to her advantage, leading to recruitment and mediated employment of day jobs – the epitome of precarity. The film shows how precarity has become the norm in the labour market, but is still condemned by others, whether Angie's 'old school' father who is disturbed by her entrepreneurship, or the public school authorities who are morally disturbed by the fact that Angie is in the business of recruitment for precarious employment. It is a form of structural hypocrisy.

To conclude, the two films' narratives point at the way structure limits choice. In *It's a Free World,* Angie tells her business partner Rose, who suffers from guilt over the recruitment company's practice, that she can pay the workers for the money lost from her own share of the profits – 'It's a free world', she tells her. At the same time, the film demonstrates how Rose is trapped in the unfair business, where powerful collectors withhold the workers' wages, forcing her to face the workers who are left without a penny. Hardly a free world. This irony is repeated in *Sorry We Missed You,* where the driver is offered two unattractive options – to buy a van of his own and shoulder the risk or use the company's vans and pay huge amounts for the privilege of certainty. As the boss tells him, 'it's your business … and like everything else around here – it's your choice'. Of course, in the driver's position as an independent contractor, which is forced upon him, there is perhaps no other choice but between two evils. No character in any of the seven films experiences a significant sense of freedom or meaningful choice.

Limited choices are not only 'unfree', they are subtly a form of structural violence practised by state and market agents alike. Officers in the welfare office or public service and managers in private companies are well dressed, sometimes rough ('boys will be boys') and sometimes formally polite and aloof. They are tall, they block the way, they have the last word, they show concern, but they will not take no for an answer. Both plot and visualisation indicate that they hold the power in its different forms – to directly affect the choices that protagonists make, to limit the range of options they have, and to influence consciousness as to what is proper or not.[24]

---

24 Steven Lukes, *Three Dimensions of Power* (2nd edn, Palgrave Macmillan 2005); Hannah Arendt, *On Violence* (Harcourt Brace 1969).

Injustice

What does injustice look like? The earlier films, *Riff Raff* and *Raining Stones*, focus on a detailed view of life in the informal economy. On the income side, the focus is on informal work, ultra-micro entrepreneurship for survival and theft. On the side of expenses, alternatives to lawful expenditures, such as squatting, are a means of addressing homelessness.

Normative options are painted in grim colours. Lawful work is only available based on temp work, on-demand work, agency work, lack of protection from dismissals, poor health and safety conditions, time squeeze, sexual harassment and abuse. Throughout the three decades of Loach's narrative (notably starting with *Riff Raff* and *The Navigators*), it is possible to follow the development of the practice of rolling all employment-related expenses, such as courses, training, uniforms, travel time and sick days, to the workers themselves, which reaches perfection in the gig economy of *Sorry We Missed You*. Similarly, on-demand work arrangements take no consideration of any dependable schedule that accommodates personhood. The timeline of the films makes it possible to posit the hype about the current gig economy as a natural extension of common practices that were well established in the past.

Reliance on charity can be classified as part of the structure or its outcomes. The films demonstrate an ambivalence towards charity, associating it with the loss of pride and dignity. On the one hand, *Raining Stones* depicts a stubborn refusal to receive help from the church in buying a communion dress for a girl.[25] On the other hand, the food charity in *I, Daniel Blake* is also a space in which the perils of dependency and dire need can lead to the release of restraints and social inhibitions.

Without institutional welfare support and with the ambivalence towards charity options, injustice is associated with insecurity that leads to poor economic judgement and strategies. It is known that people in poverty pay more for lack of capacity to plan.[26] For example, a woman in the community housing centre explains that 'the faucet leaked for two years and then I had to replace all the carpets (and got into debt)' (*Raining Stones*). Economic reserves or formal support would have made an easy fix of the faucet a more economically sensible option.

---

25 Such seemingly irrational pride was also described in legal literature – Lucie E White, 'Subordination, Rhetorical Survival Skills, and Sunday Shoes: Notes on the Hearing of Mrs. G.' in Katharine T Bartlett and Rosanne Kennedy (eds), *Feminist Legal Theory* (Routledge 1991).

26 Ronald U Mendoza, 'Why do the Poor Pay More? Exploring the Poverty Penalty Concept' (2011) 23 (1) Journal of International Development 1.

The films further tie the dire situation of people in precarious positions to the lack of access to health care, particularly in the United States where at the time *Bread and Roses* was made, the state offered meagre public assurance for those not holding private health care plans. Similarly, the films underscore the precarity of housing options. Homelessness is a continuum, ranging from absolute deprivation (*Riff Raff*) to publicly administered relocation that augments economic insecurity rather than resolving it (*I, Daniel Blake*).

Economic insecurity spirals into the breakdown of family structure: a father risks his family to buy a communion dress, a sister works in sex work to support her family, lack of time flexibility makes it necessary to choose between risking a job or attending to children, a van for the father is purchased at the cost of the wife spending much time in public transportation. The economics of household management reveal a dissonance between economic rationality and a sense of non-commodified commitment: 'I am doing this for my sister who's been working 16 hours a day ... and for [a worker] who looks like our mother' (*Bread and Roses*).

Together, these features amount to injustice, described by Abby in *Sorry We Missed You*: 'I dream I am sinking in quicksand and the children are trying to pull us out'. While injustice is surveyed here through examples that are easier to summarise in writing, the sense of 'sinking' and suffocation is best conveyed by such measures as a close-up on the character's face, or a shift in the gaze from the storyteller's (the director, or alternatively, the viewer) point of view to the character's point of view.

Choices people make against the backdrop of the structure – victims, perpetrators and blame

Those who suffer injustice against the backdrop of the existing structure are rarely portrayed as using the structure itself to remedy their deficient situation. Daniel Blake starts his journey in the welfare offices but learns that the structure of the welfare system will not accommodate his needs. Particularly illustrative is his statement about the system's 'digital by default' policy, claiming he is a 'pencil by default'. People are expected to serve the structure, rather than to lean on a structure that accommodates them.[27] Similarly, the construction workers (*Riff Raff*) and railroad maintenance workers (*The Navigators*) learn that complaining

27 Guy Davidov and Guy Mundlak, 'Accommodating All?' (or: 'Ask Not What You Can Do for the Labour Market; Ask What the Labour Market Can Do for You') in Roger Blanpain and Frank Hendrickx (eds), (Wolters Kluwer 2016).

about safety issues is likely to end in immediate termination. The delivery worker learns that pleading for time-off to secure mental wellbeing and adequate sleep will carry harsh economic consequences (*Sorry We Missed You*).

With an eye to being structure-compliant, the films not only describe but almost laud the virtues of education as a way of enabling mobilisation away from the structural disadvantage. Sometimes the protagonists are already on track (*Bread and Roses*) or actively encourage their children, even when they remain reluctant (*Sorry We Missed You*), and sometimes education serves as an aspiration that maybe will never be achieved (*I, Daniel Blake*).

The alternative to drawing on the structure for change is to ignore it altogether, illustrated by the squatters in *Riff Raff* – some of whom are Marxist ideologists, but most of whom have simply grown to be apathetic. Those who suffer injustice are shown to adjust and adapt, often working their way around the law, the prevailing norms and moral benchmarks. Survival tactics include illegal connections to electricity and gas (*Riff Raff*), theft (*Raining Stones*), or concealing an accident (*The Navigators*). Somewhat similar, but nonetheless distinct in motivation, are actions of resistance. These range from mockery, such as pushing all the buttons on the elevator in a high-rise tower (*Bread and Roses*), through protest – graffiti on the welfare office's wall (*I, Daniel Blake*) – to intentional damage such as setting a fire (*Riff Raff*). The only constructive action displayed throughout the films is the trade union's organising drive at the centre of *Bread and Roses*. But even this strategy is caught in the grey area between fulfilling the legal right to associate and the need to deploy unlawful strategies, such as illegal entry into private property. By contrast, strictly sticking to the legal rules is not an option.

All seven films tell a story of compassion for those who cannot make ends meet within the structure. The framing of the personal story explains the motivation for resistance, the alternatives or lack thereof, and dilemmas that individuals face. At the same time, although Young warns against assigning blame to those who act as the civil servants of the structure, Loach aligns with her critics and differentiates between them. He distinguishes between the 'good' and 'bad' frontline managers (or welfare officials) almost in caricature form. The 'good guys' include the manager of a community centre (*Raining Stones*), a frontline manager who tries to soften the harsh effects of privatisation (*The Navigators*), and a caring welfare officer (*I, Daniel Blake*). And then there are 'the bad guys' who don't care about human life (*Riff Raff*), bust the union and its supporters (*Bread and Roses*), and don't seem to care about welfare recipients or workers as human beings (*I, Daniel Blake*, *Sorry We Missed You*). Nothing in their portrayal suggests they should be excused from blame. With much nuance, victims who have become perpetrators (*Bread and Roses*, *It's a Free World*) are left to the audience to judge, with what seems to be the hope that the audience will remain uncomfortable, rather than quickly arrive at a verdict.

Loach doesn't fully contradict Young's claim regarding blame. Even the manager of the gig delivery operation explains that harsh management is the only way to ensure the business succeeds in an environment of fierce competition. Hence, while the story castigates heartless behaviour it also offers the structural account. This view is juxtaposed with the question of blame in interpersonal relations, whereby Abby says to her partner, clearly bringing the voice of mature wisdom to the plot: 'I am not blaming you ... It's not about right or wrong' (*Sorry We Missed You*). The political and personal are strongly linked, mirroring one another.[28]

While *Bread and Roses* illustrates the union campaign as trajectory for a collective responsibility to change, trade unions appear in other films as powerless, irrelevant, or even part of the problem (*The Navigators*). In all the other films the source of power lies in interpersonal bonds, within the family or community, or even among former strangers (*I, Daniel Blake*).[29] As the father-in-law in *Raining Stones* says, 'We never invented the system, son, but it is up for us to change'. However, such statements of recognition remain for the most part an ideal for someone to act upon, but with no candidates for the task. Redemption exists but is rare and its effects are limited.

The legal system

For the purpose of this article, it is also important to mention the role of law generally, and of the courts in particular. The role of courts is easy to survey. It is mentioned in passing in *Bread and Roses*, where a judicial order to refrain from placing obstacles to the workers' right to organise is noted. But it is made clear that the boss does not understand it and it therefore has no real impact. There is also mention of an unfulfilled right to a hearing in an administrative appeal process (*I, Daniel Blake*), demonstrating all the possible structural obstacles to a fair day before

28 Margaret Frye, 'The Myth of Agency and the Misattribution of Blame in Collective Imaginaries of the Future' (2019) 70(3) The British Journal of Sociology 721.

29 On the importance of bringing strangers together as a form of collective action, see the account of the Dardenne Brothers' films in Lauren Berlant, *Cruel Optimism* (Duke University Press Books 2011), 161.

the law. These are aligned with the sociological analysis of barriers to the legal process: the difficulty of naming the wrong a subject experienced, to assign the blame to a responsible agent, and to manage the costs associated with claiming rights in court.[30] One must be a dedicated viewer to trace scant references to the legal process in these films.

By contrast, the legal system is constantly personified through policemen, public education authorities or private security guards. The message is clear – 'stay away from the police …' (*Raining Stones*); police and security guards harass workers (*Bread and Roses*); and educational staff blame parents for neglecting their children (*It's a Free World* and *Sorry We Missed You*). There are exceptional moments, as when the police officer candidly wants to help a child losing the right path, but even then – help is still conditioned on the child's cooperation with the social dictates of the structure (*Sorry We Missed You*).

Juxtaposing film and legal process

Following the reading of structural injustice in Loach's films, it is possible to turn to the meeting of law and art. Should law and art, in this case film, be put together on the same playing field?[31] Are cinematic portrayals of structural injustice relevant for those who are asking about injustice in law?

There is a twofold answer that affirms such a project. The first part focuses on what Young designates as the 'backward' perspective. Here I argue that the legal response to events that have taken place and reached the court suffers from a structural flaw of its own. The judicial process does not deal well with critically exposing the structure and its unjust effects. The abovementioned films contribute to highlighting this weakness. The second part focuses on Young's 'forward' perspective. Law and art take part in social processes of transformation. In this they can compete or cooperate, but they are engaged in a similar mission. This of course depends on the point of view of a particular judge or filmmaker, but the major claim is that the two *can* be viewed as players on the same field.

30 William L F Felstiner, Richard L Abel and Austin Sarat, 'The Emergence and Transformation of Disputes: Naming, Blaming, Claiming…' (1980) 15 Law and Society Review 631.
31 Compare Orit Kamir, *Framed: Women in Law and Film* (Duke University Press Books 2006). Kamir offers a threefold typology of the relationship between law and film. Of particular importance in her classification are the jurisprudential views that films provide when documenting the legal process. This category is latent here because, as demonstrated, the absence of the legal process in the films' narration is striking.

The focus in the following sections is not on 'law' generally, but on the judicial process. The first part can be easily adapted to administrative tribunals and even decisions by frontline bureaucrats, such as officials of the educational system who can administer sanctions against children and their families. I will refer to all of these in shorthand as 'judicial processes'. The second part of this section is more focused on courts and case-law proper, whose visibility is greater than that of quasi-judicial institutions. Unlike the detailed analysis of Loach's films, the discussion here remains at the level of general observations on the adjudicative process. They are not driven from any one legal system, and are claimed to be representative of the adjudicative logic.

'Backward-looking' – compensating for the blind spots of the judicial process

As demonstrated in the analysis of the films, the judicial process plays a minor role and remains in the background, never reaching the stage of making a difference to the subjects in a state of structural injustice. The protagonists' stance towards the law, designating the formalities of the 'structure,' is therefore along two axes. First, they are trying to cope, adjust, choose between the lesser evils, and 'get by' within the domain permitted by the law. The films depict low-waged and dead-end jobs as the price of acceptance and indicate how little promise they carry. The alternative is resistance, which designates confrontation with the law, either formal through appeal, or informal through action. Resistance can be a matter of individual choice, from within a limited set of options. It can be morally defensible even when held uncooperative or even unlawful.[32] It can take the form of a collective voice.[33]

Resistance therefore brings subjects to court as plaintiffs when they seek to act within the structure, or as defendants when they act to contest it. In both instances, the socio-economic structure is viewed through the prisms of legal categories, narratives and rhetoric.[34] Narratives in court must conform to the structure of the legal process, including rules regarding the presentation of evidence, burden of proof and relevance. That is, the narrative that the subject presents must conform with a

---

32 Tommie Shelby, *Dark Ghettos: Injustice, Dissent and Reform* (Harvard University Press 2017), 252–274.

33 Patricia Ewick and Susan Silbey, 'Narrating Social Structure: Stories of Resistance to Legal Authority' (2003) 108(6) American Journal of Sociology 1328; Shiri Regev-Messalem, 'Claiming Citizenship: The Political Dimension of Welfare Fraud' (2013) 38(4) Law & Social Inquiry 993.

34 Jerome Bruner and Anthony Amsterdam, *Minding the Law* (Harvard University Press 2009), 2.

sole focus on the individual who attends the court, with attention to a constrained notion of time and place, and with insistence on the relevance to the legal cause of action.

Well documented are the social barriers to entering the legal process, at least as a plaintiff who initiates it, for all the general reasons associated with structural injustice to begin with. These include the lack of financial resources that are needed to obtain counsel, the asymmetry between the parties, the fear of people in poverty from public institutions, or their sense of awe. Further limitations are found in substantive law, and these change from one legal regime to another. Critical scrutiny reveals that even staple elements of social law have been found to extend short-term help, while at the same time solidifying and legitimising a highly limiting structure.[35] There are, however, a host of legal norms – formal and informal – governing the process of adjudication, which further disadvantage parties who seek to challenge the structure.

Formally, a plaintiff or a defendant facing the structure encounters presumptions that favour the status quo. This is most evident when the administrative state is a side to the legal process, but also when the overarching managerial prerogative is concerned. Moreover, individuals who want to demonstrate that the structure works against them must abstract and generalise from the particular incidence that brought them to court. Rules on discovery, use of statistics to display systemic bias, and witnesses who can help overcome restrictions on hearsay can serve as a solution to the intrinsic individuation of the adjudicative process. However, each of these must overcome many procedural hurdles, and together they impose hefty costs.

The statute of limitations requires narrowing the timeline of events leading to the act that is presented in court. Those who are in a state of structural injustice are more likely to confront limitations than those who are in a state of power. Less hermetic but equally effective are barriers such as the 'doctrine of laches', which acts against a side who could have made a claim in real time or shortly thereafter but waited. The timeline is not only restricted when looking back, but also deficient in terms of allowing a forward-looking perspective. Judges do not know the consequences of their decisions, unless these have high media visibility, which is not usually the case. There is no feedback loop for systemic learning of the impact that legal agents have.

35 Zoe Adams, 'A Structural Approach to Labour Law' (2022) 46(3) Cambridge Journal of Economics 447.

Finally, the legal process is focused on a discrete cause of action and does not embrace people telling their life story or explaining their distrust of the law, or more generally of the system and structure. The legal process further requires a focus on the substantive legal building blocks that must be proved in court, but these are not necessarily indicative of what really bothers the deprived party.

While formal rules already curtail the ability of individuals to make their legal claim, the legal culture layers further obstacles. The practical and mundane constraints that characterise the legal process (for example, judges' severe time constraints), together with doctrines that have evolved from the separation of powers, resonate with judges' reluctance to address philosophical or broad policy questions, therefore masking the impact of structure on the choices that individuals make. Judges themselves become agents whose actions are dictated, or at least channelled by the structure.[36] Sometimes a judge will state that a certain outcome may seem unjust but that she is bound by the law's dictates. Such a statement may express an authentic dissonance the judge is experiencing, but it may also be a way to cover up her sympathy for the structure, while paying lip service to some imagined public sympathy for the victim.

I am not arguing this in essentialist terms. There are judges who succeed in identifying and exposing deficiencies in the prevailing structure. However, corresponding with Young's view of transformation, an individual judge may find it difficult to induce change. A judge may give affirmation to resistance informally, finding a way to dismiss a case or otherwise resolve it in favour of the subject in a state of injustice. This is a quick fix that does not amend the structure itself. By contrast, a judge may want to make a public statement to spark or accelerate a process of transformation, as will be discussed in the next section, only to draw rebuke from the appellate court. However, the rightful search for coherence in the common law judicial system places obstacles of all kinds in the way of judges seeking to induce structural change in a system that is geared to preserving the status quo.

All of these barriers to the legal process and its limitations *are themselves part of the structure leading to injustice*. They all have a logic that judges ascertain, such as securing formal equality among plaintiffs or defendants, obtaining reliable evidence, and institutional efficiency.

---

36 Duncan Kennedy, 'Freedom and Constraint in Adjudication: A Critical Phenomenology' (1986) 36 The Journal of Legal Education 518.

This is where film can offer perspectives that are not bound by the same judicial concerns, revealing the underlying causes of resistance and considering how to affect its social meaning. First, Loach's use of the composite narrative is especially instructive as it is individual and collective at the same time. It draws empathy towards the individual, with the understanding that the individual is not unique and therefore the resistance of one may reflect the experiences of many. Where a judge may be wholly disheartened by a statement that 'everyone does that', or that 'it's not me but the system is fundamentally flawed', the film accommodates and invites such a perspective.

Second, the filmmaker can choose the framing of time and place for the story. He can start the film at the end and then flashback, or start with early childhood memories. For example, in *Sorry We Missed You*, browsing through old photographs is used to insert the story about a mortgage foreclosed during some financial mishap, accentuating the current sense of insecurity. The filmmaker can choose the venues to display where structure produces injustice – home, neighbourhood, or politics. He can involve multiple agents and is not constrained by legal structures of responsibility. The filmmaker is a 'know it all' who does not need to prove reality, and instead can write it.[37]

Finally, unlike the judge who tries to present the judicial account as neutral, the director chooses a gaze. He can display the protagonist's point of view or a bystander's point of view. The liberty of the gaze is in direct contrast to the allegedly neutral judicial gaze. The ethics of film merely requires being explicit in extending this invitation, while the ethics of the judicial process requires displaying neutrality as the single acceptable choice.

'Forward-looking' – mobilising change through film and law

The role of film as an instrument to reveal the blind spots of adjudication is based on the differentiated functions that film and case-law perform. At the same time, with the switch from the backward-looking to the forward-looking perspective, case-law and film also have shared functions:

> Both law and film are dominant players in the construction of concepts such as subject, community, personal and collective identity, memory, gender roles, justice, and truth; they each offer

37 Jean-Louis Baudry, 'Ideological Effects and Basic Cinematographic Apparatus', in Philip Rosen (ed), *Narrative, Apparatus, Ideology A Film Theory Reader* (Columbia University Press 1986); Bill Nichols, *Representing Reality: Issues and Concepts in Documentary* (Indiana University Press 1991).

major sociocultural arenas in which collective hopes, dreams, beliefs, anxieties, and frustrations are publicly portrayed, evaluated, and enacted.[38]

For example, both law and film may seek intentionally to narrow the gender wage gap. A judge can do that through strictly legal measures, such as imposing pecuniary costs on employers who discriminate against women. A judge may also address the prescriptive aspect of the case by citing studies that demonstrate the economic harm caused to society by the gender wage gap, or studies that focus on the infringement of dignity that women experience at work. In the same vein, films seek to draw sympathy, but can also be aimed at encouraging action. Some filmmakers claim they have no intention of doing that. They entertain, even if touching on hurtful issues. Others produce websites with educational materials and calls for action.[39]

Whether intentional or not, the docudrama text is out there for viewers to learn and use. *I, Daniel Blake* was screened to judges and to frontline officials in welfare offices for instructional purposes. Trade union organisers in Europe have reported that they took out the video of *Bread and Roses* and developed an organising culture around group viewing of the film.[40] Films are useful for instructional purposes in educational settings.[41] Films can actually make a political difference by raising awareness that carries electoral implications. A prime example is the Belgian 'Rosetta Law', in which the Dardenne Brothers' film title (*Rosetta*) was associated with the proposed law securing minimum wage for youth. The film depicted despairing attempts of a young teen to keep a job and reach a tenable future for herself and her alcoholic mother. The plot personified the proposed political instrument, drawing public support that could not be gained from the mere presentation of legal technicalities and jargon.[42]

Films and cases partially overlap in their objectives, but they each have their comparative strengths and weaknesses. While a film with an indirect political impact can be found, it is clearly easier to find a legal case that attracted political attention and induced change. But it would take greater imagination to see how cases could draw sympathy for the

38 Kamir (n 31), 2.

39 Lapin (n 12).

40 Guy Mundlak, *Organizing Matters: Two Logics of Trade Union Representation* (Elgar and ILO 2020), 2.

41 Tom Zaniello, *Working Stiffs, Union Maids, Reds and Riffraff: Organized Guide to Films About Labor* (ILR Press 1996); Bardan, (n 11).

42 Berlant, (n 29) 165; also see the interview with the Directors – Xan Brooks, 'We're the Same: One Person, Four Eyes', *The Guardian*, (London, 9 February 2006).

parties in the way a film can for its subjects. Consider this comparison in the following paragraphs regarding the seemingly factual accounts, the normative and ideological functions, emotional triggers, the capacity to motivate action and the presentation of alternative futures.

Films, even when fully documentary, and clearly when they intertwine with drama, make no pretence of conveying a totally neutral account of 'real life,' but rather the director's subjective selection of artefacts to display. While legal rhetoric may convey a stronger sense of realism, particularly after it has been filtered through the safety measures of the rules of procedure and evidence, it is also a subjective instrument. The judges author stories in which they select what to present and how, thereby constituting the readers' understanding of the world, its practices and even their own position within the general structure.[43] The story that judges tell is aimed simultaneously at the parties, at the legal community, including other judges and lawyers, and is sometimes conveyed through the media to the general audience.

The judicial narrative becomes naturalised over time. Judges create categories of right and wrong, explain ideas by the logic of their own discipline, and seek to persuade their readers by careful linguistic choices that favour some viewpoints and reject others. Legal ideas can be forged in leading cases of the Supreme Court, but also in daily routine litigation. The public also adopts legal categories, narratives and rhetoric, incorporating legal terms into daily conversation and identifying them as signifying distinct moral truths. The law and public discourses intermesh. But 'familiarity insulates habitual ways of thinking from inspections that might find them senseless, needless and unserviceable'.[44] In this cyclical process of stabilising social norms that compose the structure, it is important to provide different lenses which offer different categories, narratives and rhetoric. Films can extend the prism of the unexpected, hone the lens of doubt and enhance social critique.

Films and case-law are not neutral signifiers of the past and the present, and they are certainly not neutral predictors of future behaviour. The difference between cinematic and legal narratives may point at the difference between normative and ideological teachings. The normative theory will be based on careful reading of past judgments, ensuring coherence and continuity, or on transformative ideas drawn from jurisprudence and political theory. By contrast, as film scholars note,

---

43 James Boyd White, *The Legal Imagination* (abridged edn, University of Chicago Press 1985).
44 Bruner and Amsterdam (n 34), 2.

Loach's work advances highly ideological and political claims.[45] However, the contrast between the legal-normative and the cinematic-ideological should not be overstated. Critical reading of adjudication reveals the strong ideological thrust animating the text: 'judicial law making has been the vehicle of ideological projects'.[46] While legal theorists seek to demarcate clear boundaries between law and politics, the two fields should be recognised as being constantly in dialogue.

While the normative and the ideological messages are intertwined, films are clearly different from case-law where it comes to triggering emotional response.[47] Good films are those that help viewers approach a topic from an emotional and not just rational and analytic viewpoint. To engage viewers, the film must have a point, a story or a moral that provides a different way of understanding situations.[48] Arguably stirring emotions is not an end in itself, but an instrumental strategy towards other ends (for example, prompting viewers to act, fight, or change). It is therefore important to observe what kind of emotions the film arouses. A critique of *Sorry We Missed You* questioned its stirring up guilt among consumers.[49] Others may think that capturing consumers' attention and directing it to structural injustice is necessary to reimagine the way consumer capitalism has been naturalised and is being taken for granted as a necessary social outcome.

Well-argued legal claims, ideological statements and emotional traps can all bring about change. Over time there has been a shift in documentary practice from an accidental gaze to more reflexive, experimental and personal approaches. These are being used by women, racial minorities, and LGBTQ groups to change social norms.[50] In this, films teach viewers how to be 'courageous, inventive, steadfast and so forth'.[51] Compared to case-law, films can often reach a broader audience.

Finally, impact is important when there is a notion of how the structure must change. Reimagining the future requires moving beyond the exposition of the structure, offering clear alternative narratives.[52]

---

45 Baudry (n 37).

46 Duncan Kennedy, *A Critique of Adjudication* (Harvard University Press 1997).

47 Hugo Mauerhofer, 'Psychology of Film Experience' (1949) 8 Penguin Film Review 103.

48 Brown (n 15); Marshall Ganz, 'Why Stories Matter: The Art and Craft of Social Change' (2018) <https://commonslibrary.org/why-stories-matter-the-art-and-craft-of-social-change/> accessed 23 August 2023.

49 Lapin (n 12).

50 Bill Nichols, *Blurred Boundaries: Questions of Meaning in Contemporary Culture* (Indiana University Press 1995) 92–106.

51 Brown, (n 15) 236.

52 Michèle Lamont, 'From "Having" to "Being": Self-worth and the Current Crisis of American Society' (2019), 70(3) The British Journal of Sociology 660.

Case-law can point at very concrete recommendations for change or general guidelines (for example, proportionality). But as regards alternative futures, fiction has a greater potential to outline a more just future(s). It can be used to outline the challenges ahead and open the readers' (or viewers') imagination.[53] However, Loach's films, which stick to describing present failures, do not outline any alternative. They tend to end on a grim note of unforgiving despair, or at most, bittersweet success. This may be an uncompromising Loachian trademark – forcing the viewers to fully sense the dark present, while avoiding the catharsis of utopian optimism. One must turn to other films, but with a much smaller audience, that are more explicit in their call for action and in marking the paths forward.[54]

Conclusion

Based on the proposed comparison, the differences between law and film do not seem as striking as they appear at first. Nevertheless, the fundamental difference remains, as case-law addresses real-life incidences in which real people's liberty and dignity are at stake. A film is not the operation of the sovereign, it is not an act of state, and it is accorded the privilege of free speech to satisfy and advance the marketplace of ideas. Which of the two is more effective? This of course begs the question regarding what the purpose is.

To summarise the juxtaposition of film and case-law, it is possible to draw again on Kennedy, who claims that his goal is to:

> … reveal the large role played by the legal system; to delegitimate the outcomes, achieved through the legal system by exposing them as political when they masquerade as neutral; to show that they are in some sense unjust and that their injustice contributes to the larger injustice of the society as a whole; to be, thereby, a radicalizing force on those who read and accept the analysis; and to suggest ways that a radicalizing force on those who read and accept the analysis; and to suggest ways that a radicalizing project should approach the task of making the system less unjust through political action.[55]

53 Olivia Bina, Sandra Mateus, Lavinia Pereira and Annalisa Caffa, 'The Future Imagined: Exploring Fiction as a Means of Reflecting on Today's Grand Societal Challenges and Tomorrow's Options' (2017) 86 Futures 166.
54 See Bardan (n 11).
55 Kennedy, *A Critique of Adjudication* (n 46) 280.

The viewing of film is supportive of such goals. It exposes the contribution of adjudication to the foundations of an unjust structure and at the same time, it complements the legal process in raising awareness of injustice and sympathy for its victims. For the legal community, the comparison suggests that films (and fiction, prose or arts) are essential to highlight the deficiencies and limitations of the legal process itself. Teaching structure to lawyers should extend beyond the traditional analysis of statutes and cases. The distinct framing, ideological bluntness, emotional identification and freeform possibilities of drawing alternative futures, even if underutilised, can supplement the legal form.

When law students become judges or lawyers, the relevance of art and film is further accentuated. It aids in reflecting on one's role within the structure. Once the structure is depicted, it requires a more humble view of the law but also, somewhat paradoxically, a growing legal consciousness that structure can and should be challenged. The former requires judges, as well as the representatives of the state and powerful corporations, to adopt, even if momentarily, the unique point of view a film offers and the voice it grants to those who are structurally disempowered. This can aid in decentring the courtroom and viewing it instead as part of an assembly of confrontations individuals have with the 'structure'. The latter calls for considering strategic litigation that attempts at using law to change the structure, rather than continuously work within it.

Index

www.ingramcontent.com/pod-product-compliance
Lightning Source LLC
LaVergne TN
LVHW021043100926
847340LV00003B/8
* 9 7 8 1 8 0 0 0 8 7 3 4 7 *